THE
CHRISTIAN
IN
COMPLETE
ARMOUR

THE
CHRISTIAN
IN
COMPLETE
ARMOUR

Daily Readings in Spiritual Warfare

WILLIAM GURNALL

MOODY PUBLISLERS
CHICAGO

First published in three volumes in 1655, 1658, and 1662

Revised and reprinted in 1864 by Blackie & Son, Glasgow, Scotland

The 1864 edition (unabridged) republished by the Banner of Truth Trust, Edinburgh, Scotland, in 1964, 1974, and 1979

Material in the 1994 edition from the 1864 edition (Volume 1) revised and abridged, published by World Challenge, Inc., David Wilkerson Crusades, Lindale, Texas, U.S.A., in association with the Banner of Truth Trust, 1986

© WORLD CHALLENGE, INC., 1986
Volume 2 © WORLD CHALLENGE, INC., 1988
Volume 3 © WORLD CHALLENGE, INC., 1989

Moody Publishers Edition
© 1994 by
JAMES S. BELL JR.

All Scripture quotations, unless indicated, are taken from the King James Version.

ISBN-10: 0-8024-1177-0
ISBN-13: 978-0-8024-1177-8

7 9 10 8 6

Printed in the United States of America

To my sister Cathy
Put on this solid armor for the battles you fight
and look to the Lord of Hosts
who causes you to triumph in all things

William Gurnall (1616–1679) was a graduate of Emmanuel College, Cambridge, England, a university under strong Puritan influence. His life's work was as pastor of the Church of Christ, in Suffolk.

James Stuart Bell Jr., is the owner of Whitestone Communications, a literary development agency. He was formerly the executive editor at Moody Publishers. He has cover or inside credit as author, compiler, or editor on over 100 titles. A graduate of College of the Holy Cross, he continued his education at University College, Dublin, where he received his M.A.

INTRODUCTION

C. S. Lewis stated that Satan's strategy is best served by either personal disbelief in his existence or an exaggerated reverence for his power. Either extreme serves his purpose of deceiving and dominating the human race. And both extremes are quite prevalent in contemporary culture. Secular humanism has postulated a material universe, devoid of spirit. On the other hand multiple branches of the New Age movement serve Satan in his various manifestations. Even the church today is guilty of this polarity. Many "rational" Christians downplay demonic activity in their spiritual walk while others find a demon behind every bush.

One thing is certain—today Christians find spiritual growth an uphill battle. We know it's not just our own weaknesses or the culture's anti-Christian bias, but also a powerful personal Enemy who seeks to defeat us every step of the way. Thus, there is an upsurge of interest in spiritual warfare material. Most of us haven't experienced demonic deliverances, but we know what it is like to be buffeted by Satan when our "armor" is not securely fastened and in use. True, Ephesians 6 explains the spiritual armor and its purposes. Yet we still desire to better understand the wiles and tactics of Satan and the practical implications of each piece of armor to resist him. In other words we don't wish to be guilty of the extremes mentioned above but to knowledgeably deal with our Adversary who is under the power of God.

Some books have touched on various aspects of the subject, but only one down through the ages is all encompassing. *The Christian in Complete Armour* by William Gurnall is a masterpiece, providing you with the tools for spiritual victory over an Enemy we finally comprehend. Gurnall provides practical insight into the sword, shield, helmet, breastplate, belt, and shoes.

William Gurnall (1616–79) was a graduate of Emmanuel College, Cambridge, England, a university under strong Puritan influence. His life's work was as pastor of the Church of Christ,

Lavenham, in Suffolk. Lavenham today is a tourist center, and I have personally enjoyed its fine medieval and Tudor buildings, some of which date before Gurnall himself. As a shepherd of souls, Gurnall's knowledge is extraordinary, yet his style is practical and to the point. He combines the sweet encouragement of the love and mercy of Christ with the vicious opposition of Satan and the impending judgment of God. One is always removed from mundane temporal distractions to the ultimate concerns of eternity—fought out in the here and now. Gurnall has a unique way of motivating us into God's service, daily redeeming the time because of the presence of evil, and the need to press in with "violence" to apprehend the Kingdom of God. The author does not mince words. He states near the beginning:

"Cowards never won heaven. Do not claim that you are begotten of God and have His royal blood running in your veins unless you can prove your lineage by this heroic spirit; to dare to be holy in spite of men and devils."

J. C. Ryle, a great nineteenth-century saint wondered how Gurnall could put some great truth, so concisely and fully, into so few words. In this devotional volume, I have attempted this in a similar vein—to take many great truths, concisely stated, and reduce them to 365 daily readings. It is my sincere hope that if read each morning, the reader will venture forth in the complete armor of God, victorious over the principalities in heavenly places which war against our souls.

The reader who finds this volume useful may also wish to consult *Memos to God,* a prayer journal based on selected readings from the works of E. M. Bounds and the prayers of Henry Thornton (Chicago: Moody, 1994).

ACKNOWLEDGMENTS

T hough I have never met them, I owe a great debt to Ruthanne Garlock, Kay King, Karen Sloan and Candy Coan of World Challenge, Inc. As editors, they produced a clear, readable modern abridgment of the original editions begun in the 1650's. This work was published in three paperback volumes by the Banner of Truth Trust in 1986. A reprint of the 1864 edition of the original work (unabridged) is also available from Banner of Truth. They are worth obtaining for a fuller treatment of the author's material.

THE CHRISTIAN'S CALL TO COURAGE

*Who among us has not learned from his own experience
that it requires another spirit than the world can
give to follow Christ fully?*

There are so many who profess Christ and so few who are in fact Christians; so many who go into the field against Satan, and so few who come out conquerors. All may have a desire to be successful soldiers, but few have the courage and determination to grapple with the difficulties that accost them on the way to victory. All Israel followed Moses joyfully out of Egypt. But when their stomachs were a little pinched with hunger, and their immediate desires deferred, they were ready at once to retreat. They preferred the bondage of Pharaoh to the promised blessings of the Lord.

Men are no different today. How many part with Christ at the crossroad of suffering! Like Orpah, they go a short distance only (Ruth 1:14). They profess the Gospel and name themselves heirs to the blessings of the saints. But when put to the test, they quickly grow sick of the journey and refuse to endure for Christ. At the first sign of hardship, they kiss and leave the Savior, reluctant to lose heaven, but even more unwilling to buy it at so dear a price. If they must resist so many enemies on the way, they will content themselves with their own stagnant cisterns and leave the Water of Life for others who will venture farther for it. Who among us has not learned from his own experience that it requires another spirit than the world can give to follow Christ fully?

Let this exhort you, then, Christian, to petition God for the holy determination and bravery you must have to follow Christ. Without it you cannot be what you profess. The fearful are those who march for hell (Revelation 21:8); the valiant are they who take heaven by force (Matthew 11:12). Cowards never won heaven. Do not claim that you are begotten of God and have His royal blood running in your veins unless you can prove your lineage by this heroic spirit: to dare to be holy in spite of men and devils.

JANUARY 2
YOU ARE PART OF CHRIST'S ARMOR

God Himself underwrites your battle and has
appointed His own Son "the captain of [your] salvation"
(Hebrews 2:10).

You should find great strength and encouragement in the
knowledge that your commission is divine. God Himself
underwrites your battle and has appointed His own Son
"the captain of [your] salvation" (Hebrews 2:10). He will lead
you on to the field with courage, and bring you off with honor.
He lived and died for you; He will live and die with you. His
mercy and tenderness to His soldiers is unmatched. Historians
tell us Trajan tore his own clothes to bind up his soldiers'
wounds. The Bible tells us Christ poured out His very blood as
balm to heal His saints' wounds; His flesh was torn to bind
them up.

For bravery none compares with our Lord. He never turned
His head from danger, not even when hell's hatred and heav-
en's justice appeared against Him. Knowing all that was about to
happen, Jesus went forth and said, "Whom seek ye?" (John 18:4).
Satan could not overcome Him—our Savior never lost a battle,
not even when He lost His life. He won the victory, carrying His
spoils to heaven in the triumphant chariot of His ascension.
There He makes an open show of them, to the unspeakable joy
of saints and angels.

As part of Christ's army, you march in the ranks of gallant
spirits. Every one of your fellow soldiers is the child of a King.
Some, like you, are in the midst of battle, besieged on every
side by affliction and temptation. Others, after many assaults, repulses, and rallyings of their faith, are already standing upon
the wall of heaven as conquerors. From there they look down
and urge you, their comrades on earth, to march up the hill after them. This is their cry: "Fight to the death and the City is
your own, as now it is ours! For the waging of a few days' conflict, you will be rewarded with heaven's glory. One moment of
this celestial joy will dry up all your tears, heal all your wounds,
and erase the sharpness of the fight with all the joy of your permanent victory."

JANUARY 3
HEAD AND HEART

If your heart is not fixed in its purpose, your principles, as good as they may be, will hang loose and be of no more use in the heat of battle than an ill-strung bow.

He who has only a nodding acquaintance with the king may easily be persuaded to change his allegiance, or will at least try to remain neutral in the face of treason. Some professing Christians have only a passing acquaintance with the Gospel. They can hardly give an account of what they hope for, or whom they hope in. And if they have some principles they take kindly to, they are so unsettled that every wind blows them away, like loose tiles from a housetop.

When Satan buffets and temptation washes over you like a tidal wave, you must cling to God's truths. They are your shelter in every raging storm. But you must have them on hand, ready to use. Do not wait until it is sinking to patch the boat. A feeble commitment has little hope of safety when caught in a tempest. While that flounders and drowns, holy determination, grounded in the Lord, will lift up its head like a rock in the midst of the highest waves.

Scripture promises, "The people that do know their God shall be strong, and do exploits" (Daniel 11:32). An angel told Daniel which men would stand up and be counted for God when tempted and persecuted by Antiochus. Some would be taken in by the bribery of corrupt men; others would fall victim to intimidation and threats. But a few, who were firmly grounded in the tenets of their faith, would do great things for God. That is to say, to flatteries they would be incorruptible, and to power and force, unconquerable.

Head knowledge of the things of Christ is not enough; this following Christ is primarily a matter of the heart. If your heart is not fixed in its purpose, your principles, as good as they may be, will hang loose and be of no more use in the heat of battle than an ill-strung bow. Half-hearted resolve will not venture much nor far for Christ.

THE CHRISTIAN'S CALL TO SERVICE

Those sins which have lain nearest your
heart must now be trampled under your feet.
And what courage and resolution this requires!

The soldier is summoned to a life of active duty, and so is the Christian. The very nature of the calling precludes a life of ease. If you had thought to be a summer soldier, consider your commission carefully. Your spiritual orders are rigorous. Like the apostle, I would not have you be ignorant on this point and will, therefore, list a few of your directives.

Those sins which have lain nearest your heart must now be trampled under your feet. And what courage and resolution this requires! You think Abraham was tested to the limit when called upon to take Isaac, "thine only son . . . whom thou lovest" (Genesis 22:2), and offer him up with his own hands. Yet what was that to this: "Soul, take the lust which is the child dearest to your heart, your Isaac, the sin from which you intend to gain the greatest pleasure. Lay hands on it and offer it up; pour out its blood before Me; run the sacrificing knife into the very heart of it—and do it joyfully!"

This is more than the human spirit can bear to hear. Our lust will not lie so patiently on the altar as Isaac, nor as the Lamb brought dumb to the slaughter (Isaiah 53:7). Our flesh will roar and shriek, rending the heart with its hideous cries. Indeed, who can express the conflict, the wrestlings, the convulsions of spirit we endure before we can put our heart into such a command? Or who can fully recount the cleverness with which such a lust will plead for itself?

When the Spirit convicts you of sin, Satan will try to convince you, "It is such a little one—spare it." Or he will bribe the soul with a vow of secrecy: "You can keep me and your good reputation, too. I will not be seen in your company to shame you among your neighbors. You may shut me up in the attic of your heart, out of sight, if only you will let me now and then have the wild embraces of your thoughts and affections in secret."

STAY ON COURSE TO THE END

*We have known many who have joined the army of
Christ and liked being a soldier for a battle or two,
but have soon had enough and ended up deserting.*

There are times when a saint is called to trust in a with-drawing God. "[Let him] that walketh in darkness and hath no light . . . trust in the name of the Lord" (Isaiah 50:10). This requires a bold step of faith—to venture into God's presence with the same temerity as Esther into Ahasuerus's. Even when no smile lights His face, when no golden scepter is extended to summon us to come near, we must press forward with this noble resolution: "If I perish, I perish" (Esther 4:16).

Which leads our faith one step further: We must trust also in a "killing God." We must declare with Job, "Though he slay me, yet will I trust in Him" (Job 13:15). It takes a submissive faith for a soul to march steadily forward while God seems to fire upon that soul and shoot His frowns like poisoned arrows into it. This is hard work, and will test the Christian's mettle. Yet such a spirit we find in the poor woman of Canaan, who caught the bullets Christ shot at her, and with a humble boldness sent them back again in her prayer (Matt. 15:22–28).

Your work and your life must go off the stage together. Persisting to the end will be the burr under your saddle—the thorn in your flesh—when the road ahead seems endless and your soul begs an early discharge. It weighs down every other difficulty of your calling. We have known many who have joined the army of Christ and liked being a solder for a battle or two, but have soon had enough and ended up deserting. They impulsively enlist for Christian duties, are easily persuaded to take up a profession of religion, and are just as easily persuaded to lay it down. Like the new moon, they shine a little in the first part of the evening, but go down before the night is over.

Taking up the cross daily, praying always, watching night and day and never laying aside our armor to indulge ourselves, sends many sorrowful away from Christ.

THE SOURCE OF THE SAINT'S STRENGTH

*God can overcome His enemies without help from
anyone, but His saints cannot so much as defend
the smallest outpost without His strong arm.*

The strength of an earthly general lies in his troops—he
flies upon their wings. If their feathers get clipped or their
necks broken, he is helpless. But in the army of saints, the
strength of the whole host lies in the Lord of hosts. God can
overcome His enemies without help from anyone, but His saints
cannot so much as defend the smallest outpost without His
strong arm.

One of God's names is "the Strength of Israel" (1 Samuel
15:29). He was the strength of David's heart. With Him, this
shepherd boy could defy the giant who defied a whole army;
without God's strength, David trembled at a word or two that
dropped from the Philistine's mouth. He wrote, "Blessed be the
Lord my strength, which teacheth my hands to war, and my
fingers to fight" (Psalm 144:1). The Lord is likewise your
strength in your war against sin and Satan.

Some wonder whether a sin is ever committed without Satan having a part. But if the question were whether any holy action is ever performed without involving the special assistance
of God, that is settled: "Without me ye can do nothing" (John
15:5). Paul put it this way: "Not that we are sufficient of ourselves to think any thing as of ourselves; but our sufficiency is
of God" (2 Corinthians 3:5). We saints have a reservoir of grace,
yet it lies like water at the bottom of a well and will not ascend
with all our pumping. First God must prime it with His awaken-
ing grace. Then it will gush forth.

Paul says, "To will is present with me; but how to perform
that which is good I find not" (Romans 7:18). Both the will to
do and the action which follows are of God. "It is God which
worketh in you both to will and to do of His good pleasure"
(Philippians 2:13). God is at the bottom of the ladder, and at the
top also, the Author and Finisher, assisting the soul at every
rung in its ascent to any holy action.

THE SIGNIFICANCE OF GOD'S STRENGTH

"God uses the conscience to give some knowledge of His righteousness to all, so that no one can stand before Him on the Day of Judgment and plead ignorance" (Romans 1).

God alone is the source and sustainer of all life; therefore, it is His constant regenerating power that keeps the conscience alive.

Conscience may be defined as that divine influence at work in man to restrain him from sin. One evidence of its origin is that it always speaks against sin and for righteousness. Therefore, it cannot be the product of our own hearts, which in their fallen state are "deceitful above all things, and desperately wicked" (Jeremiah 17:9). God uses the conscience to give some knowledge of His righteousness to all, so that no one can stand before Him on the Day of Judgment to plead ignorance (Romans 1). When you become a Christian and consecrate yourself —conscience and all—to Him, the Holy Spirit begins in earnest to perfect you in Christ.

It is said when God made the world He ended His work of creation—that is, He made no more new species of creatures. Yet to this day He has not ended His work of providence. "My Father worketh hitherto," Christ said (John 5:17). In other words, He continually preserves and empowers what He has made with strength to be and to act. A work of art, when complete, no longer needs the artist, nor a house the carpenter when the last nail is in place. But God's works on behalf of both the outer and the inner man are never off His hands.

If the Father's work is a preserving one, the Son's is a redemptive one. Both acts are perpetual. Christ did not end His work when He rose from the dead, just as the Father did not end His work when He finished creation. God rested at the end of creation; and Christ, when He had wrought eternal redemption and "by himself purged our sins, sat down on the right hand of the Majesty on high" (Hebrews 1:3). From there He continues the work of intercession for the saint, and thereby keeps him from certain ruin.

GOD'S PLAN FOR PROVISION

*"The Christian ought to rely on divine strength
because this plan results in the greatest advancement
of God's own glory" (see Ephesians 1:4, 12).*

If the provisions were left in our own hands, we would soon
be bankrupt merchants. God knows we are weak, like cracked
pitchers—if filled to the brim and set aside, the contents
would soon leak out. So He puts us under a flowing fountain of
His strength and constantly refills us. This was the provision He
made for Israel in the wilderness: He split the rock, and not
only was their thirst quenched at that moment, but the water
ran in a stream after them, so that you hear no more complaints
for water. This rock was Christ. Every believer has Christ at his
back, following him as he goes, with strength for every condition and trial.

The Christian ought to rely on divine strength because this
plan results in the greatest advancement of God's own glory
(Ephesians 1:4, 12). If God had given you a lifetime supply of
His grace to begin with and left you to handle your own account, you would have thought Him generous indeed. But He is
magnified even more by the open account He sets up in your
name. Now you must acknowledge not only that your strength
comes from God in the first place, but that you are continually
in debt for every withdrawal of strength you make throughout
your Christian course.

When a child travels with his parents, all his expenses are
covered by his father—not by himself. Likewise, no saint shall
say of heaven when he arrives there, "This is heaven, which I
have built by the power of my own might." No, the heavenly Jerusalem is a city "whose builder and maker is God" (Hebrews
11:10). Every grace is a stone in that building, the topstone of
which is laid in glory. Some day the saints shall plainly see how
God was not only the founder to begin, but benefactor also to
finish the same. The glory of the work will not be crumbled out
piecemeal, some to God and some to the creature. All will be
entirely credited to God.

DON'T TRUST IN YOUR OWN STRENGTH

"When we were without strength,
in due time Christ died
for the ungodly" (Romans 5:6).

I s the Christian's strength in the Lord, and not in himself? Surely then, the person outside of Christ must be a poor, impotent creature, helpless to do anything to effect his own salvation. If a living tree cannot grow without sap from the tap-root, how can a rotten stump, which has no root, revive itself of its own accord? In other words, if a Christian imbued with God's grace must continually rely on His strength, then surely the one outside of God's grace, dead in trespasses and sin, can never produce such strength in himself. To be unregenerate is to be impotent. "When we were without strength, in due time Christ died for the ungodly" (Romans 5:6).

The philosophy called humanism has long been a suitor to man's pride. It boasts in his natural strength and wisdom, and woos him with promises of great accomplishments now, and heaven later. God Himself has scattered such Babel-builders and proclaimed His preeminence for eternity. Confounded forever be such sons of pride, who trust in the power of nature as though man with his own brick and mortar of natural abilities were able to make a way to heaven! You who are yet in your natural state, would you become wise to salvation? Then first become fools in your own eyes. Renounce this carnal wisdom which cannot perceive spiritual things, and beg wisdom of God, who gives without rebuke (James 1:5).

Here is a word for Christians. Knowing your strength lies wholly in God and not in yourself, remain humble—even when God is blessing and using you most. Remember, when you have your best suit on, who made it and who paid for it! God's favor is neither the work of your own hands nor the price of your own worth. How can you boast of what you did not buy? If you embezzle God's strength and credit it to your own account, He will soon call an audit and take back what was His all along.

STAND IN THE HOUR OF TESTING

But if you conclude finally that God cannot
pardon or save, cannot *come to your rescue,*
this shoots faith through the heart.

Without God's strength, you cannot stand in the hour of testing. The challenge is beyond the stretch of human fortitude. Just suppose all your strength is already engaged to barricade your soul against temptation and Satan is steadily hacking away at your resolve; what will you do? You need not panic. Only send faith to cry at God's window, like the man in the parable asking his neighbor for bread at midnight, and He who keeps covenant forever will provide. When faith fails, however, and the soul has no one to send for divine intervention, the battle is all but over, and Satan will at that very moment be crossing the threshold.

When you are in the midst of testing, do not give up in despair. Faith is a dogged grace! Unless your soul flatly denies the power of God, this courier—faith—will beat a well-worn path to the throne. Doubt cripples but does not incapacitate faith. Indeed, even as you are disputing the mercy of God and questioning in your mind whether He will come to your rescue, faith will make its way, if haltingly, into His presence. And the message it delivers will be, "If thou wilt, thou canst make me clean."

But if you conclude finally that God *cannot* pardon or save, *cannot* come to your rescue, this shoots faith through the heart. Then your soul will fall at Satan's feet, too disheartened to keep the door shut any longer to his temptation. Remember this: The one who abandons faith in the midst of a spiritual drought can be compared to the fool who throws away his pitcher the first day the well is dry.

It has ever been and always will be the Father's will that we trust only Him. God demands to be called the Almighty; He insists we place our confidence in Him. That child is wise who does as his father bids. Man may be called wise, merciful, mighty; but only God is all-wise, all-merciful, almighty.

GOD'S DEAR LOVE FOR THE SAINTS

It is this image of God reflected in you that so enrages hell;
it is this at which the demons hurl their mightiest weapons.
When God defends you, He also defends Himself.

God's love for His saints sets His power in motion. He who has God's heart does not lack for His arm. Love rallies all other affections and sets the powers of the whole man into action. Thus in God, love sets His other attributes to work; all are ready to bring about what God says He likes. God considers all His creatures, but the believing soul is an object of His choicest love—even the love with which He loves His Son (John 17:26).

When a soul believes, then God's eternal purpose and counsel concerning him—whom He chose in Christ before the foundation of the world—is brought to term. Can you imagine the love God has for a child He has carried so long in the womb of His eternal purpose? If God delighted in His plan before He spoke the world into being, how much greater is His delight to witness the full fruition of His labor—a believing soul. Having performed His own will thus far, God will surely raise all the power He has in that believer's behalf, rather than be robbed of His glory within a few steps of home.

God showed us how much a soul is worth by the purchase price He paid. It cost him dearly, and that which is so hard won will not be easily given up. He spent His Son's blood to purchase you, and He will spend His own power to keep you.

As an earthly parent you rejoice to see your own good qualities reproduced in your children. God, the perfect parent, longs to see His attributes reflected in His saints. It is this image of God reflected in you that so enrages hell; it is this at which the demons hurl their mightiest weapons. When God defends you, He also defends Himself. Now knowing that the quarrel is God's, surely He will not have you go forth to war at your own expense!

WHEN YOU ARE WEIGHED DOWN BY SIN

If you fear you will one day fall
to temptation, grab hold of God's strength
now and reinforce yourself to resist.

You can be absolutely certain that no sin is powerful enough to overwhelm God's strength. One Almighty is more than many "mighties"! He has shown His eagerness to rescue you over and over again. Provoked to the limit by His people's sins, what does He do? He issues a sweet promise! "I will not execute the fierceness of mine anger," He declares. And why not? ". . . For I am God, and not man" (Hosea 11:9). It is as though he said, "I will show you the *almightiness* of My mercy!"

Who can doubt the omnipotence of God? We know he has power to pardon if He so chooses. But there is greater comfort than this for the believer; it rests in His *covenant* to pardon. As none can bind God but Himself, so none can break the bond He makes with Himself. These are His own words: "[I] will abundantly pardon" (Isaiah 55:7). In other words, "I will drown your sins in My mercy and spend all I have, rather than let it be said that My good is overcome by your evil."

So when Satan terrifies you with his awful accusations against your soul, you can say with confidence, "It is God and no other who justifies me. He has promised to restore my life if I submit to Him. Has He ever broken a promise? Therefore, I have committed myself to Him as unto a faithful Creator."

If you fear you will one day fall to temptation, grab hold of God's strength now and reinforce yourself to resist. Believe you will be victorious on the day you are tested. Your Father watches closely while you are in the valley fighting; your cries of distress will bring Him running. Jehoshaphat called for help when pressed by his enemies, and the Lord rescued him (2 Chronicles 20). You can be just as sure of His help when you are pressed to the wall. Remind Him often of His promise: "Sin shall not have dominion over you" (Romans 6:14).

GOD ACCEPTS YOUR WEAK FAITH

*Your heavenly Father is so eager to care for you, that while
you are timidly asking for a nibble of peace and joy, He is
longing for you to open your mouth wide so He can fill it.*

P erhaps you find the duty of your calling too heavy for your
weak faith. Look to God for strength. When you are sick of
your work and ready like Jonah to run away, encourage
yourself with God's words to Gideon: "Go in this thy might
. . . have not I sent thee?" (Judges. 6:14). Begin the work God
has given you, and you will engage His strength *for* you; run
from your work, and you engage God's strength *against* you.
He will send some storm or other after you to bring His runaway servant home.

Are you called to suffer? Do not flinch in fear. God knows
the limits of your strength. He can place the load so evenly on
your shoulders that you will scarcely feel it. But still He is not
satisfied. His watchful eye is always on you, and when you stagger He picks you up—burden and all—and carries you to your
destination nestled in the bosom of His promise: "God is faithful, who will not suffer you to be tempted above that ye are
able; but will with the temptation also make a way to escape . . ."
(1 Corinthians 10:13). How can you fret when you are wrapped
in His covenant? Your heavenly Father is so eager to care for
you, that while you are timidly asking for a nibble of peace and
joy, He is longing for you to open your mouth wide so He can
fill it. The more often you ask, the better; and the more you ask
for, the more He welcomes you.

Go quickly now. Search your heart from one end to the other and gather up all your weaknesses. Set them before the Almighty, as the widow placed her empty vessels before the
prophet. Expect a miracle of deliverance from the limitless resources of God. If you had more vessels to bring, you could
have them all filled.

God has strength enough to give, but He has no strength to
deny. Here the Almighty Himself (with reverence I say it) is
weak. Even a child, the weakest in grace of His family, who can
but whisper "Father," is able to overcome Him.

YOUR HEART SHOULD BE RIGHT WITH GOD

Because He loves you,
He will recall your ration of power
if it takes you out of fellowship with Him.

I f your heart is not set in the right direction when you appeal for deliverance, strength will not come. Ask yourself these questions when you feel shut off from God's power.

Am I really trusting God, and Him only, to meet my need? Or am I depending on my own resolve, my pastor, or some other outside source? All these things may be good, but they are only Christ's servants. Press through them to the Master Himself. Touch Him—and deliverance is yours.

Am I thankful for the strength I have? In a long-distance race, the contestants run at varying paces. Perhaps you are discouraged when you see so many strong ones pass you on the way to glory. Rather than cry after them, be thankful that you have the strength to run at all! Are you in the race? It is by God's grace and that alone; thank Him for the privilege. Remember this: Everyone (even the weakest saint) who finishes the race is a winner.

Has my pride stopped the flow of God's power? God will not keep supplying power if you use it for your own advancement. He knows how quickly you are carried away from Him on the wings of your pride. Because He loves you, He will recall your ration of power if it takes you out of fellowship with Him. All this He does for your own good, so that when your pride lies gasping, you will be forced back to Him.

God may call you to persevere in the face of overwhelming odds. Perhaps nothing that has been said answers your particular case. Your heart is clean before God; you have sincerely and prayerfully waited, yet God withholds His hand. Then you must resolve to live and die waiting, for that may be what He requires. What greater evidence of your faith and of God's grace at work in you than to persevere to the end!

THE CHRISTIAN MUST BE ARMED

"Put on the whole armor of God,
that ye may be able to stand against
the wiles of the devil" (Ephesians 6:11).

I f by negligence or choice you fail to put on God's armor and rush naked into battle, you sign your own death certificate.

The story is told of a fanatic in Munster who valiantly tried to repulse an invading army by shouting, "In the name of the Lord of hosts, depart!" But his unregenerate soul had no such commission from the General for whom he pretended to fight, and he soon perished. His example should teach us the high price to be paid for such folly. What brave but foolish language you hear drop from the lips of the most profane and ignorant among us! They say they hope in God and trust in His mercy; they defy the devil and his works. But all the while they are poor, naked creatures without the least piece of God's armor upon their souls. Such presumption has no place in the Lord's camp.

Paul's admonition to put on armor falls into two general parts. First, a direction telling us *what* to do: "Put on the whole armor of God . . ." And second, *why* we should do it: ". . . that ye may be able to stand against the wiles of the devil."

So to begin, every recruit in Christ's army should be properly fitted with armor. The first question that comes to mind is, What is this armor?

We are told, "Put ye on the Lord Jesus Christ" (Romans 13:14), where Christ is presented as armor. The apostle does not exhort the saints simply to put on temperance in place of drunkenness, or for adultery to put on chastity. Instead, he tells them to "put on the Lord Jesus Christ," implying that until Christ is put on, the creature is unarmed. It is not the man decked out in morality or philosophical virtues who will repel a full charge of temptation sent from Satan's cannon; it is the man suited up in armor—that is, in Christ.

I speak now of the "girdle of truth, the breastplate of righteousness," and so forth. We are instructed to "put on the new man" (Ephesians 4:24), who is made up of all the graces. The point is this: To be without Christ and His graces is to be without armor.

THE SAD STATE OF THE UNARMED SINNER

"Ye were without Christ, being aliens from the
commonwealth of Israel and strangers from the
covenants of promise" (Ephesians 2:12).

A person in a Christless, graceless state is naked and unarmed—totally unequipped to fight sin and Satan. In the
beginning, God sent Adam out in complete armor. But by
sleight of hand, the devil stripped him. As soon as the first sin
was completed, "[Adam and Eve] were naked" (Genesis 3:7).
Sin robbed them of their armor and left them poor, weak creatures. It cost Satan some fancy footwork to make the first
breach, but once man opened the gates to let him in, the devil
named himself king and brought to court a whole cortege of
deadly sins, without ever drawing a sword.

Here is what I mean: Instead of confessing their sin, Adam
and Eve tried to hide from God and became evasive in their
dealings with Him. They blamed one another, shifting the responsibility for their disobedience rather than appealing for
mercy. How quickly their hearts were hardened by deceit!
Man's basic nature has not changed since that day. This is exactly the condition of every son and daughter of Adam; naked
Satan finds us, and slaves he makes us until God, having bought
us with the blood of His dear Son, comes to reclaim each penitent soul for service in His own kingdom.

"Ye were without Christ, being aliens from the commonwealth of Israel and strangers from the covenants of promise"
(Ephesians 2:12). If you are not a kingdom child, you have no
more to do with any covenant promise than a citizen of Rome
has to do with the charter of London. You are alone in the
world, without God. If you get into trouble, you must plead
your own case. But if you are a citizen of heaven, God has power to grant you special immunity in any situation. And while the
devil's spite is directed toward you, he dare not come upon
God's ground to touch you without permission.

WARFARE WITHOUT CHRIST

Do not let anyone deceive you.
Spiritual darkness can never
be expelled except by union with Christ.

What a desperate condition, for a soul to be left to his own defense against legions of lusts and devils! He will be torn like a silly hare among a pack of hounds—no God to call them off, but Satan to urge them on. Let God leave a people, no matter how militant, and before long they lose their courage and cannot fight. A company of children could rise up and chase them out of their own front yard. When the Israelites panicked at news of invincible giants and walled cities, Caleb and Joshua pacified them with this assurance: "They are bread for us; their defense is departed from them" (Numbers 14:9). How much more must that soul who has no defense from the Almighty be as bread to Satan?

Only an ignorant soul is foolish enough to ride out of his castle unarmed during a siege. He obviously has not studied the enemy, or he would know what peril lies beyond his gates. To make matters even worse, if he fights without putting on Christ, he must fight in the dark. The apostle writes, "Ye were sometimes darkness, but now are ye light in the Lord" (Ephesians 5:8). As a child of light, you who are Christians may be in the dark from time to time concerning some truth or promise. But you always have a spiritual eye which the Christless person lacks. The unregenerate man is always too ignorant to resist Satan, whereas the Christian's knowledge of the truth pursues and brings back the soul even when taken prisoner by a temptation.

Do not let anyone deceive you. Spiritual darkness can never be expelled except by union with Christ. As the physical eye once put out cannot be restored by human means, so neither can the spiritual eye—lost by Adam's sin—be restored by the efforts of men or angels. This is one of the diseases Christ came to cure (Luke 4:18).

IMPOTENCY WITHOUT CHRIST

*Sometimes Satan and a carnal heart
appear to scuffle, but it is a farce—
like the parrying of two fencers on stage.*

When we were yet without strength, in due time Christ
died for the ungodly" (Romans 5:6). What can an unarmed soul do to shake off the yoke of Satan? No more
than an unarmed people can do to shake off the yoke of a conquering army! Satan has such power over the soul that he is
called the strong man who keeps the soul as his palace (Luke
11:21). If he has no disturbance from heaven, he need fear no
mutiny within. He keeps everything under his control. What the
Spirit of God does in a saint, Satan in a diabolical sense does in
a sinner. The Spirit fills the heart with love, joy, holy desires;
Satan fills the sinner's heart with pride, lust, lying. And like the
drunkard filled with wine, the sinner filled with Satan is not his
own man, but an impotent slave.

Friendship with sin and Satan is enmity toward God. A soul
that refuses to put on Christ declares himself a rebel and makes
himself the enemy of God. I think we can safely say that whoever is God's enemy must be Satan's friend—and how will you
make someone fight against his own friend? Is Satan divided?
Will the devil within fight against the devil without?

Sometimes Satan and a carnal heart appear to scuffle, but it
is a farce—like the parrying of two fencers on stage. You would
think at first they were in earnest, but when you see how wary
they are and where they strike one another, you soon know
they do not mean to kill. Any doubt is removed when you see
them after the match, making merry together with the proceeds
of their performance! Likewise, when you see an unrepentant
heart make a great show against sin, follow him off the stage of
good works where he has gained the reputation of a saint by
playing the hypocrite. There you will doubtless see him and Satan together in a corner as friendly as ever.

JANUARY 19

SATAN'S VAST EMPIRE

*If God's grace did not step in
and override the veto, the whole
world would be held in Satan's sway.*

When you look around and see the devil's vast empire and what a little spot of ground contains Christ's subjects— what heaps of precious souls lie prostrate under Satan's feet and what a tiny regiment of saints march under Christ's banner of grace—perhaps you ask yourself, "Is hell stronger than heaven? Are the arms of Satan more victorious than the cross of Christ?" But if you consider what I am about to tell you, you will wonder that Christ has any to follow Him rather than that He has so few.

Every son of man is born in sin (Psalm 51:5). So when the prince of this world first approaches a young soul with this or that wicked proposal, he finds the soul unarmed and in its natural state already familiar with his policies. Yielding to Satan's control will therefore not cause much of a stir in the naturally sinful heart. But when Christ campaigns for a soul, He proposes sweeping changes. And the selfish soul, which generally likes things as they are, answers Him with the same scorn as the rebellious citizens in the parable: "We will not have this man to reign over us!" (Luke 19:14). The vote is unanimous: All the lusts cast their ballots against Christ, and rise up like the Philistines against Samson, whom they called the destroyer of their country (Judges 16:23–24). If God's grace did not step in and override the veto, the whole world would be held in Satan's sway.

Satan's conquests are limited to ignorant, graceless souls who have neither strength nor sense to oppose him. They are born imprisoned to sin; all he has to do is keep them there. But when he assaults a saint, whose freedom was won at the Cross, once for all, then he is laying siege to a city with gates and bars. Sooner or later, he must retreat in shame, unable to pluck the weakest saint out of the Savior's hand. Doubt your own strength, but never doubt Christ's. In your gravest conflicts with Satan, trust Him to bring you out of the devil's dominion.

THE MALICE OF SATAN

*Do you wonder that Satan works
so hard to dispossess the Gospel
which dispossesses him?*

D
o not doubt for a moment that Satan will hurl all his fury
at those who love God's Word. His acquaintance with the
Good News of Christ goes back a long way, to the dawn
of the ages, in fact. He has seen its power demonstrated over
and over again, and he knows it houses an arsenal of arms and
aids for battered souls.

The very first assault the Gospel made against the kingdom
of darkness shook its foundation and put the legions of hell on
the run. They are fleeing still. When the seventy missionaries
commissioned by Christ returned with their reports that even
demons were subdued by the power of the Gospel, Christ replied, "I beheld Satan as lightning fall from heaven!" (Luke
10:17–18). In essence He tells them, "What you say is not news
to Me; I watched when Satan was cast out of heaven. How well I
know the power of the Gospel!"

Do you wonder that Satan works so hard to dispossess the
Gospel which dispossesses him? By the light of the Gospel
many who were once his friends find the way to truth and life.
By the same light, saints move with blessed assurance toward
their eternal home. Nothing torments the devil more than to
see his old companions neglect their former sinful pleasures
and spend time studying the Scriptures instead. He knows that a
saint without a knowledge of the Gospel is as vulnerable as an
army without ammunition. Therefore, he labors either by persecution to drive God's Word away, or by political policy to persuade a people to send it away from their coast.

For it is God's Word which teaches us how to put on Christ
and His graces so that we are fitly armed. Never flatter yourself
into thinking you can do without this priceless book.

FOLLOWING GOD'S ORDERS

*It was God's war they waged, and therefore
only reasonable they should be under His command.
They encamped and marched by His order.*

The Christian soldier is bound to God's orders. Though the army is on earth, the council of war sits in heaven and issues directives: "Here are your orders... these are your weapons." And those who do more or use other than God commands, though with some seeming success against sin, shall surely be called to account for their boldness.

The discipline of war among men is strict in this case. Some have been court-martialed and executed even though they have beaten the enemy, because they forgot their rank or acted without orders. The discipline of God is also very precise on this point. He will say to all who invent ways of their own to worship Him or who fabricate their own forms of penance, "Who has required this at your hands?" This is truly to be "righteous over-much," as Solomon says (Ecclesiastes 7:16), when we presume to correct God's law and add supplements of our own to His rules. God told Israel that the false prophets were wasting their time because they did not come on His errand (Jeremiah 23:32). You, too, are wasting your time if you are doing anything that is not by God's design.

God's thoughts are not like man's, nor His ways like ours. If Moses in his own wisdom had directed Israel's flight from Egypt, we would have expected him to plunder the Egyptians of their horses and arms. But God would have His people come out naked and on foot, and Moses kept close to His orders. It was God's war they waged, and therefore only reasonable they should be under His command. They encamped and marched by His order; they fought at His command. And the tactics and weapons they used were all prescribed by God. What are we to learn from their example? In our march to heaven, fighting with the cursed spirits and lusts that stand in our way, we too must go by God's rules, which are spelled out for us in His Word.

JANUARY 22

GOD MAKES HIS SAINTS' ARMOR

*Thus thousands perish who supposed they
were armed against Satan, death, and judgment—
when all along they were miserable and naked.*

Look closely at the label to see whether the armor you wear
is the workmanship of God or not. There are many imita-
tions on the market nowadays. It is Satan's game, if he cannot keep the sinner satisfied in his naked, lustful state, to coax
him into some flimsy thing or other that by itself will neither do
him good nor Satan harm. Perhaps it is church attendance, or
good works, or some self-imposed penance by which he intends to impress both God and man. Do such impersonators
believe in God? Oh, they hope they are not infidels. But what
their armor is, or how they came by it, and whether it will hold
up in an evil day, they never stop to question. Thus thousands
perish who supposed they were armed against Satan, death, and
judgment—when all along they were miserable and naked.
These people are worse off than those who have not a rag of
pretense to hide their shame from the world's gaze.

To most of us, a careful copy of a masterpiece looks quite as
good as the original. But when the master himself appears, he
can tell in an instant which is real and which the imposter. It is
the same with that self-righteous hypocrite who is a pretender
to faith and hope in God. Here is a man in glittering array with
his weapon in his hand. With the sharp sword of his tongue he
keeps both the preacher and the Word of God at arm's length:
"Who can say I am not a saint? Name one commandment I do
not keep, one duty I neglect!" he demands indignantly. Many
are impressed by his seeming piety. It takes the Spirit's discern-
ing eye to expose him, and even then it is harder to convict him
because Satan has so cleverly tampered with him already. He
must first be disarmed and unclothed of his own filthy self-righteousness, because God's armor can never be made to fit over
the suit he has fashioned for himself.

FAITH AND KNOWLEDGE

Satan is not particular what lie he tells you;
one will work as powerfully as another
if he can get you to believe it.

G od designs each part of the armor for a particular purpose; therefore, the saint must be properly attired. In
other words, it will not do to cover the heart with the
helmet, or to hold the buckler where the breastplate ought to
be. Indeed, there is a series of graces, each with a special func-
tion to bring life and health to the soul—much like the network
of veins and arteries which carries blood through the body.
Prick one vein, and the blood of the whole man may spill from
that outlet; neglect one duty, and the strength of all the graces
may be lost.

The apostle Peter urged Christians to increase the whole
body of grace. Is this not true health—when the whole body
thrives? *Faith* is the grace which leads the procession. If you
have faith, then add virtue: "Add to your faith virtue," says Peter
(2 Peter 1:5). These graces are of mutual benefit to one another.
Good works and gracious actions get their life from faith; faith,
in turn, fattens and becomes strong on works—so says Martin
Luther.

Your works may bear luscious-looking fruit, but you are not
safe from the devil's blight unless you add to your virtue knowledge. Knowledge is to faith as sunshine is to the farmer. Without it, faith cannot see to do her work. Nor can the work, once
finished, be adequately inspected in the dim light of half-truths.
If you do not ground yourself in the truth of the Gospel, Satan
will play upon your ignorance to thwart your spiritual growth.
He has a clever proposition for every occasion. In one instance
he may try to persuade you that you are not humble enough,
and cause the weeds of self-condemnation to choke out the assurance of your salvation. Another time, he will flatter you into
a false sense of pride in your humility, and the pestilence of
self-righteousness will wipe out the Spirit's crop of fruit in your
life. Satan is not particular what lie he tells you; one will work
as powerfully as another if he can get you to believe it.

JANUARY 24
TEMPERANCE AND PATIENCE

Satan will line the hedges with
a thousand temptations when you come
into the narrow lanes of adversity.

But knowledge is not the end of the work of grace. To it we must add *temperance*. Without it, both faith and reason may soon relinquish their rightful place to temporal pleasures. Temperance is an excellent steward. It regularly inspects the soul and sets the saint's affections in order so that he does not ignore holy duties to pursue his own entertainment. If you allow your love of creature comforts—or even your pleasure in family and loved ones—to outrun your love for the Lord, you cannot be a victorious soldier for Christ. Therefore, pray for temperance, which keeps the spiritual gauge of your heart well within the safety range.

Imagine yourself now well equipped and marching toward heaven while basking in prosperity. Should you not also prepare for foul weather—i.e., a period of adversity? Satan will line the hedges with a thousand temptations when you come into the narrow lanes of adversity, where you cannot run as in the day of your prosperity. You may manage to escape an alluring world, only to be flattened when trouble strikes, unless you know how to persevere. Therefore, the apostle commands, "to temperance [add] *patience*" (2 Peter 1:6).

Do you have patience? An excellent grace indeed, but not enough. You must be pious as well. So Peter continues, "to patience [add] *godliness*" (v. 6). Godliness encompasses the whole worship of God, inward and outward. Your morals may be impeccable, but if you do not worship God, then you are an atheist. If you worship Him and that devoutly, but not according to Scripture, you are an idolater. If according to the rule, but not according to the spirit of the Gospel, then you are a hypocrite. The only worship that leads to the inner chamber of true godliness is that which is done "in spirit and in truth" (John 4:24).

GOD PERFECTS HIS SAINTS

"Simon, Simon, Satan hath desired to . . . sift you,"
Jesus said to Peter (Luke 22:31).
The devil knew the disciples were weak at this time.

I n an army called to active duty, weapons are frequently battered and broken. One man has his helmet dented, another his sword bent, a third his pistol broken. So replacements are often necessary. In one temptation you may have your helmet of hope crushed or your charity trampled upon. You need an armorer's shop near at hand to make up your losses as quickly as possible, for Satan is most likely to attack when you are least prepared to repel his charge.

"Simon, Simon, Satan hath desired to . . . sift you," Jesus said to Peter (Luke 22:331). The devil knew the disciples were weak at this time. Christ, their captain, was about to be taken from the head of their regiment. They were discontented among themselves, arguing about who would have the best seat in heaven. And their supply of stronger faith, which the Spirit was to bring, had not yet come. Therefore, Christ sent them to Jerusalem to wait together until He could dispatch His Spirit to them (Acts 1:4). This example shows us, in the weakness of our graces, whom to ask for a fresh supply.

He is called "the old serpent," and for good reason: subtle by nature, yet ever more cunning; wrathful by nature, yet ever more enraged. Like a bull, the longer he is baited, the madder he grows. And considering what little time he has left, we who are to fight with him must enter the arena well equipped.

The end of all God's working is to perfect His saints in their virtues and comforts. He is the wise caretaker of our souls. When He uses afflictions to lop and prune our spirits, it is only to purge so we can bring forth more and better fruit (John 15:2). The same tribulation which yields bitter results in the arid soul of the wicked is used to produce the sweet fruit of the Spirit in the fertile soil of the saint.

Why is God so intent on perfecting His saints? To prepare a spotless bride for His Son, and complete His grand design!

THE ARMOR MUST BE KEPT ON

*He tells us to have our armor on, our grace
in action: "Let your loins be girded about,
and your lights burning" (Luke 12:35).*

The Christian's armor is made to be worn—no taking it off until you have finished your course. Your armor and your garment of flesh come off together. Then there will be no more need of shield or helmet, no more late night watches. Those military duties and field graces—as I may call faith, hope, and the rest—shall be honorably discharged. In heaven you shall appear, not in armor, but in robes of glory.

Nevertheless, for the present you must wear your assigned suit night and day. You must walk, work, and sleep in it or you are not a true soldier of Christ. Paul set himself a goal: "Herein do I exercise myself, to have always a conscience void of offense toward God, and toward men" (Acts 24:16). Here we see this holy man at his arms, training like a true soldier, his own heart the target range on which he practices all the graces in preparation for battle. We have ample reasons to conduct ourselves in like manner.

For one thing, Christ commands it. He tells us to have our armor on, our grace in action: "Let your loins be girded about, and your lights burning" (Luke 12:35). He speaks as a general to his soldiers: "Oil your armor; light your torch; be ready to march. Prepare to fight at the first alarm of temptation!" Again He speaks, this time as a master to his servants: "If the lord of the manor is called away and the hour of his return uncertain, will a faithful servant bolt the door, douse the fire, and retire? No, he will stand watch through the night, ready to greet the master whenever he comes." Meaning, it is not fit for the Master to stand at our heart's door knocking, and find our graces sleeping.

Every duty of the Christian demands this constant effort. Pray he must, but how? "Without ceasing." Rejoice, but when? "Evermore." Give thanks—for what? "In everything" (1 Thessalonians 5:16–18). We must hold our shield of faith and helmet of hope to the very end (Ephesians 6:16–17).

ALERT FOR THE ENEMY

"Surely," says Satan
when he sees a fervent Christian,
"this will not last long."

Where the soldier is placed, there he stands and must neither stir nor sleep till he is discharged. When Christ comes, only that soul whom He finds so doing shall have His blessing.

Why is Christ so insistent that His soldiers remain on alert? Because *Satan's actions demand it.* Satan's advantage is great when he catches our graces napping. When the devil found Christ so ready to repel his temptation, he soon had enough. It is said, "He departed . . . for a season" (Luke 4:13). But in his shameful retreat it seems he comforted himself with the hopes of surprising Christ unawares at another time more advantageous to his design. And we do find him coming again at the most likely time to have had his way—but only if his enemy had been man and not God (Matthew 27:42).

Now if this bold tempter watched Christ so closely, does it not seem likely he will scout you, too, hoping sooner or later to find your graces slumbering? What he misses now by your watchfulness he may gain later by your negligence. In fact, he hopes you will push yourself to exhaustion with continual duty. What fiendish pleasure he would derive from turning the tables on your sincere efforts for Christ. "Surely," says Satan when he sees a fervent Christian, "this will not last long." When he finds him most sensitive to the Spirit and scrupulous in conduct, he says, "This is but for a while; he cannot keep it up for long. Soon he will unbend his bow and unbuckle his armor, and then I will have at him." But this can never happen as long as we are continually applying to God for our strength.

Satan is not the only pitfall; *the nature of our graces makes diligence essential.* If not watched closely, they will play the truant. And a soul long absent from the school of obedience will not be eager to return and take up his old assignments.

SATAN'S SURPRISE ATTACK

*Perhaps you are a parent
with a family under your wing.
They fare much as you do.*

One of Satan's favorite maneuvers is the surprise attack. Imagine the confusion in a town if an alarm suddenly sounded in the dead of night, signaling the enemy was already at the gates—but all the soldiers were home in bed. What turmoil would ensue! One hunts his pants, another his sword, a third does not know what to do for ammunition. Thus in utter chaos they run up and down, spreading panic—which could never happen if the enemy had found them upon their guard. A similar uproar will occur if you do not keep your spiritual armor on. You will be feverishly searching for this grace and that when you should have already reported to Christ for active duty.

Not only are active graces necessary for your own protection, but also for the help and comfort of other Christians. Paul had this in mind when he disciplined himself to keep a good conscience so as not to be a scandal to other believers. He knew that the cowardice of one may make others run; that the ignorance of another may do mischief to many. How often has the waywardness of a saint seduced a fellow Christian to leave the narrow path for the broad road that leads to destruction? This is among the gravest of errors for we are commanded to do just the opposite! God told the Reubenites and Gadites to go before their brethren armed for battle, until the land was conquered. Thus you are to assist your fellow brethren who may not have the same measure of grace or comfort as you. Help such weak ones; be their shield bearer. This you will not be able to do unless your own grace is exercised, your armor buckled on.

Perhaps you are a parent with a family under your wing. They fare much as you do. If your heart is feasting on Christ, you will never find yourself in short supply when caring for their spiritual needs. On the other hand, if your own heart is malnourished, they will go hungry for spiritual food.

THE OBJECT OF GOD'S AFFECTIONS

*When was His ear deaf to
your cries or His hand short
from supplying your needs?*

H e who keeps you does not slumber. The psalmist assures us, "The eyes of the Lord are upon the righteous" (Psalm 34:15). He has fixed His gaze forever and with definite delight pleases Himself in the object of His affection. When was His ear ever deaf to your cries or His hand short from supplying your needs? Does not your welfare occupy the thoughts of God, and are there any other than thoughts of peace which He entertains? A few drops of this oil will keep the wheels of your faith in motion.

To better understand the nature of our enemy let us note the term Paul uses here: *wiles,* or methods. The word in the Greek connotes "that art and order one observes in handing an argument." Now because it implies extraordinary skill and a sharp wit to compose that kind of discourse, *wiles* is used to express the subtlety of Satan in planning his strategy against the Christian. The expert soldier is keenly aware of this order, as well as the scholar. He understands there is method in forming an army, as well as in framing an argument.

Because the devil is a very subtle enemy, the saint must always be on his guard. Satan is called the old serpent. The serpent is subtle above the other creatures; and an old serpent, above other serpents. If Satan was too crafty for man in his perfection, how much more dangerous to us now in our maimed condition—for we have never recovered from that first crack Adam's fall gave to our understanding. And as we have lost knowledge, so Satan has gained more and more experience. Granted, he lost his heavenly wisdom as soon as he became a devil, but ever since, he has increased his craft. And while he does not have wisdom enough to do himself good, yet he has knowledge enough to do others harm. God showed us where Satan's strength lies when He promised to bruise the *head* of the serpent; with his head crushed, he will soon die.

JANUARY 30
SATAN CHOOSES WHEN TO TEMPT

*Temptation is never stronger
than when relief seems to dress itself
in the very sin that Satan is suggesting.*

The devil especially likes to tempt when the Christian is newly converted. No sooner is the child of grace born than this vicious dragon belches forth white-hot temptations upon him. The first cry of the new creature in Christ startles all the legions of hell. They are as troubled by it as Herod and Jerusalem were when they sat in council to take away the life of the newborn King. Satan did not hesitate to tempt the apostles while they were yet infants in Christ. He knew grace within was weak and the nourishment promised at the Spirit's coming had not yet arrived. Is an enemy ever more likely to take a town than when only the children are home? Indeed, the disadvantages are so many that we would despair for every babe in Christ if we did not know he is wrapped in covenant grace and held tightly in the strong arms of God's promise.

Another time Satan attacks is when the Christian is enduring some great affliction. Satan first got permission from God to weaken Job in his temporal estate, then he tempted him to impatience. He let Christ fast forty days before he came, and then fell to his enticing work—just as an army blocks off a town and waits to negotiate until it is pinched for provisions and likely to agree to almost anything. If you wish to stand firm in the midst of suffering, forewarn yourself of this fact: Temptation is never stronger than when relief seems to dress itself in the very sin that Satan is suggesting. For example, suppose your family falls on hard times and you see no way out of your predicament. This is the very moment Satan will come to whisper in your ear, "What are you going to do? Surely God would not have your children starve! Your neighbor's garden is just beyond the hedge. He has enough and to spare. The night is dark. Who will see if you step across and take only what you need?"

SATAN AS TEMPTER TO SIN

*The more eminent your service for God, the greater
the probability that Satan is at that very moment
hatching some deadly scheme against you.*

S atan will come on the scene when you are on some nota-
ble errand for God's glory. He will raise himself up like a
snake in your path, hissing his venomous lies. This old serpent never was a friend to kingdom work. What a handsome excuse he served the Jews: "The time is not come!" God's time
was come, but not the devil's; and therefore he perverted the
sense of Providence, as if it were not yet time for the Messiah.

Two periods stand out in Christ's life: His entrance into
public ministry at His Baptism, and the culmination of it at His
Passion. At both He had a fierce encounter with the devil. This
should give you an idea of how the master tempter works. The
more public your place, and the more eminent your service for
God, the greater the probability that Satan is at that very moment hatching some deadly scheme against you. If even the cadet
corps need to be armed against Satan's bullets of temptation,
how much more the commanders and officers, who stand in the
front line of battle!

Satan will not always wait until you are on an important mission to tempt you, however; he will seize every opportunity
along the way to practice his enticing skills. His job is made a
little easier if he can find some object to enforce his temptation.
Thus he took Eve when she was looking with longing at the
tree. Since her own eye first enticed her, it was all the easier for
Satan to take the object of her affection, polish it to a high gloss,
and with it quicken a lust which lay dormant in her heart. If we
lean out the window to hear temptation's serenade, Satan is satisfied that his suit may in time be granted. If we do not wish to
yield to sin, we must take care not to walk by or sit at the door
of the occasion. Do not look on temptation with a wandering
eye if you do not wish to be taken by it, nor allow your mind to
dwell on that which you do not want lodged in your heart.

SATAN CHOOSES HOW TO TEMPT

They thought their zeal was kindled by a
holy fire until Christ told them, "Ye know not
what manner of spirit ye are of" (Luke 9:54–55).

Not only does he choose when he will tempt, Satan also chooses the best methods for displaying his temptations.

One strategy is to hang out false colors. He comes up to the Christian disguised as a friend, so that the gates are opened to him before his true identity is discovered. Paul says we should not be shocked to find false teachers masquerading as apostles of Christ, "... Satan himself is transformed into an angel of light" (2 Corinthians 11:13–14). Of all his plots, this is perhaps the most dangerous to the saints; when he appears in the mantle of a prophet and silver-plates his corroded tongue with fair-sounding language. In this manner he corrupts some in their judgment by interpreting gospel truth in such a way that God appears to condone questionable behavior. These Christians get caught up in the world's morality under the guise of Christian liberty.

Not everyone will swallow such heresy, so Satan tempts them with other wares, though still in the disguise of a saint himself. He desecrates Scripture by magnifying faith to the exclusion of every other grace. Or he labors to undermine repentance and overpraise good works. He pulls back in seeming horror at the corruption of church administrations, and thus draws unstable souls from the body of believers. Under the pretense of zeal, he kindles wrath in the Christian's heart and makes his spirit boil over into desires for revenge in situations where God would have him forgive. Luke records such an occasion where the disciples wanted "fire to come down from heaven." They thought their zeal was kindled by a holy fire until Christ told them, "Ye know not what manner of spirit ye are of" (Luke 9:54–55). How we need to study the Scriptures, our hearts, and Satan's wiles, that we may not bid this enemy welcome and all the while think it is Christ who is our guest!

OPPORTUNITIES FOR THE ENEMY

Satan is the greatest intelligence agent in the world.
He makes it his business to inquire into your
inclinations, thoughts, affections, and plans.

Another of the enemy's methods is to spy on the saint's affairs. Satan is the greatest intelligence agent in the world. He makes it his business to inquire into your inclinations, thoughts, affections, and plans. Then he sets to work accordingly—finding which way the stream goes, opening the passage of temptation, and cutting the channel to the fall of your affections. You can scarcely stir out of the closet of your heart without Satan knowing your destination. Some corrupt passion or other will betray your soul and be the informer to Satan, saying to him, "If you want to surprise such a one, you will find him in the wood of worldly employment, up to his ears in the desires and cares of this life."

Is ambition the lust the heart favors? Such pleasing projects he will put that soul upon! How easily, having first blown him up with vain hopes, he draws him into horrid sins. This is how he hurried Haman, who was willing to do anything to become the prince's favorite, into that bloody plot against the Jews, fatal at last to himself (Esther 7:9–10).

In his approaches to a sensitive soul, Satan uses an especially subtle strategy. When he comes to tempt, he is modest and asks for just a little. He knows he may get through several askings what he would be denied if he asked all at once. This is how he wriggled into Eve's bosom. He did not dare her to eat the fruit at first. He knew she would probably be frightened away by such a bold challenge. Instead, he asked a provocative question which would set the stage for his debut as man's archenemy: "Hath God said?"In other words, "Are you sure you are not mistaken? You know how generous God is! He lets you eat everything else in the Garden; why would He deny you the best of all?" Thus he digs about and loosens the root of her faith, and then the tree falls more easily with the next gust of temptation.

SATAN'S TACTICAL MOVES

*As the master workman, Satan cuts out the temptation
and gives it shape, but sometimes he has his journeymen
finish it. He carefully considers who can do the work.*

Another strategy Satan uses is his shrewd retreat. We read not only of Satan's being cast out, but of the unclean spirit going out voluntarily, with a purpose to come again and bring worse company with him (Matthew 12:43–45). Satan is not always beaten back by the dint and power of conquering grace; sometimes he retreats willingly, then lays his own siege. He waits until the Christian is out of his trench, intending to snap him up on the plains if he cannot take him in his fortification. When Satan seems to have conceded defeat, do not assume the battle is won. His flight should strengthen your faith, but not weaken your guard.

Satan chooses what or whom to use as instruments of temptation. We have seen that he decides when and how he will tempt; now we shall see that he decides what or whom he will use to do his work.

As the master workman, Satan cuts out the temptation and gives it shape, but sometimes he has his journeymen finish it. Knowing his work may be carried on better by others, he carefully considers who can do the work to the greatest advantage of his evil cause. Just as every politician is not fit to serve as an ambassador, so not just everyone qualifies for the devil's special service. He screens his prospects with care. In this he is unlike God, who is not at all limited by His choice of instruments, because He needs no one and is able to do as well with one as with another. But Satan's power is finite, so he must patch up the defect of the lion's skin with the fox's.

The ambassadors Satan prefers are chiefly of four sorts: persons of prominence and power; persons of superior intellect and diplomacy; persons of holiness, or at least reputed to be; and persons able to influence those in power.

SATAN ATTACKS LEADERS

*Satan also aims at those in office in the church.
What better way to infect the whole town than to
poison the cistern where they draw their water?*

S atan singles out persons of prominence and power. They may be either in the state or in the church. If he can, he will secure both the throne and the pulpit, as the two generals that command the whole army. A head of state may influence thousands; therefore, Paul said to Elymas, when he tried to dissuade the deputy from the faith, "O full of all subtlety and mischief, thou child of the devil" (Acts 13:10). As if he had said, "You have learned this from your father the devil—to haunt the courts of princes and wield your influence over rulers."

Satan doubles his leverage in gaining such leaders to his side. First of all, they have the power to draw others to their way. Corrupt the captain, and he will bring his troops with him. Let Jeroboam set up idolatry, and all Israel is soon in a snare. Second, should the sin stay at court and the infection go no further, yet a whole kingdom may pay dearly for the sin of its leader. David succumbed to Satan's temptation to number the people, but the entire nation suffered the plague of punishment with him (1 Chronicles 21).

Besides trying to infiltrate the ranks of government, Satan also aims at those in office in the church. What better way to infect the whole town than to poison the cistern where they draw their water? He takes special delight in corrupting the heart of a minister. If he can wiggle into a pastor's heart, then he is free to roam among God's flock undetected—a devil in shepherd's clothing. Who will persuade Ahab to go to Ramoth-Gilead and fall? Satan can tell: "I will be a lying spirit in the mouth of all [God's] prophets" (1 Kings 22:22). How shall sinners be hardened in their sins? Let the preacher place cushions under their consciences and sing a lullaby of "Peace, peace," and it is done. How may the worship of God be discredited? Let the world observe the scandalous conduct of a minister, and many, both good and bad, will reject the truth of the Gospel on the strength of the lie his life tells.

TARGETING PERSONS OF INFLUENCE

What you say and do, because you are a leader,
causes others to look less to themselves and
more to you to set the pace and make the rules.

D oes Satan prefer the company of persons of power and intellect? He also delights to entertain those who have a reputation for holiness. What works as well as a live bird to draw others into the net? Such is the craft of Satan—and the frailty of the best among us—that the holiest men have been his bait to snare others. That great patriarch Abraham tempted Sarah to lie: "Tell them you are my sister!" (Genesis 12:13). The old prophet of Bethel led the man of God out of his way, the holiness of the prophet's life and the reverence of his age lending authority to his counsel (1 Kings 13:18).

Oh, how this should make you watchful if you are one whose long travel and great progress in the ways of God have gained you a name of eminence in the church! What you say and do, because you are a leader, causes others to look less to themselves and more to you to set the pace and make the rules.

Satan chooses persons able to influence those in power. If he can win family or friends to his side, he has easy access to the real object of his desire. Some think this is why he spared Job's wife—so he could send by her own hands his cup of poison: "Curse God and die!" We know David would not have received from Nabal what he took from Abigail. Satan thought to send the apple to Adam by Eve's hand; he sent defeat to Samson by Delilah. And he used Peter, a disciple, to tempt Christ. Some martyrs have confessed that their hardest work was to overcome the prayers and tears of their friends and relatives. Paul himself expressed these same feelings when he said, "What mean ye to weep and to break mine heart? For I am ready, not to be bound only but also to die at Jerusalem for the name of the Lord Jesus" (Acts 21:13).

KNOW HOW SATAN PLAYS THE GAME

*This diabolical dealer will show you
how to slip your sins under the table,
telling you no one—not even God—will see.*

S tudy Satan's tricks, and acquaint yourself with his tactics. Paul takes for granted that every Christian understands them in some measure: "We are not ignorant of his devices," he says (2 Corinthians 2:11). Can this be said of you? Do you know how subtle and clever your enemy is? What pleasant company he can pretend to be?

"Sit down at my gaming table," says Satan. "Here are some tempting prizes: your earthly estate, your life, your liberty." Now you must agree, these things are good and lawful. But here is Satan's gimmick: he expands the rule of his game so that if you play for him, you will certainly violate the irrevocable and unchangeable laws of God. If you cannot have good things by plain dealing but must resort to sleight of hand, you know the prize is counterfeit and will turn to dung in your hands. How utterly foolish to fast shuffle with God by compromising His truth. You may think you have won a hand or two, but when the game is over, you will find yourself bankrupt.

If Satan can entice you to sin for what he assures you is a worthy prize, you are in serious trouble, but the worst is yet to come. Once he has you sitting at his table, he will begin in earnest to teach you the tricks of his trade. This diabolical dealers will show you how to slip your sins under the table, telling you no one—not even God—will see. He has been teaching this trick since Adam, who thought he could hide behind a fig leaf. What did Joseph's brothers do when they had left him for dead but hide their deed under the coat they had bloodied? And how did Potiphar's wife respond when Joseph turned away from her adulterous gaze? She hid her sin (again in his coat) and accused him of her own wickedness.

Beware of playing such games of chance with God. No coat is large enough to hide your sin; no hand is quick enough to slip it under the table and miss the all-seeing eye of God. If He does not call you to account for it in this life, you can be sure you will answer for it in the next.

KNOW YOUR STRENGTHS AND WEAKNESSES

*Know your heart. Be intimately acquainted
with yourself, and you will better
know Satan's design against you.*

Everything transacted in heaven or hell passes through
Christ's hands. The Son knows all the Father knows, and
He is ready to reveal to His saints all they need to know in
this life (John 15:15). We live in days of high political intrigue.
Only the few who stand on the upper end of the world understand the mysteries of state; the rest of us know little more than
what we read in the newspaper. It is the same with regard to
the plots which Satan is furtively weaving against the souls of
men. Only a few have an inkling as to the purpose of Satan's designs against them. These are the saints, to whom God's Spirit
reveals not only what He has prepared for them in heaven but
also the warp and woof of Satan's deadly schemes here on earth.

Know your heart. Be intimately acquainted with yourself,
and you will better know Satan's design against you. He takes
his method of tempting from the inclination he finds there. As a
general walks about the city and views it well, then directs his
assault where he has the greatest advantage, so Satan surrounds
and considers the Christian in every part before he tempts.

Read God's Word attentively. It gives a history of the most
remarkable battles between the great soldiers of Christ and
their adversary Satan. You can read how Satan has foiled them,
and how they recovered lost ground. There is not a lust of
which you are in danger, but you have it disclosed; there is not
a temptation which the Word of God does not arm you against.
It is reported that a certain man planned to poison Martin Luther, but Luther was forewarned by a faithful friend who sent
him a picture of the would-be murderer. The Bible shows you,
Christian, the faces of those lusts which Satan hires to destroy
your precious soul. "By them is thy servant warned" (Psalm
19:11).

SATAN ACCUSES YOU OF HIS OWN THOUGHTS

*Satan will probably throw a fit of jealous rage and
stoke the fires of his wrath seven times hotter until
the flames of his blasphemous emotions engulf you.*

When you see a snake creeping along, you can hardly tell which way it is heading. Satan moves in a similar fashion, turning this way and that to conceal his true intentions. Here are some of the methods he uses to accuse your soul and cloud your relationship with the Father.

He lays his own evil imaginings like foundling children at their door. How clever he is at this deception! When thoughts or inclinations contrary to the will and ways of God creep in, many dear Christians mistake these miserable orphans for their own children, and take upon themselves the full responsibility for these carnal passions. So deftly does the devil slip his own thoughts into the saint's bosom that by the time they begin to whimper, he is already out of sight. And the Christian, seeing no one but himself at home, supposes these misbegotten notions are his own. So he bears the shame himself, and Satan has accomplished his purpose.

What recourse does the child of God have? Stay in close fellowship with the Father. Then you will be able to repulse the devil's accusations by the sword of the Spirit. But be prepared for another assault. Like Nebuchadnezzar, Satan will probably throw a fit of jealous rage and stoke the fires of his wrath seven times hotter until the flames of his blasphemous emotions engulf you. By this he hopes to frighten you and so muddle your spiritual senses that you may yet be persuaded to draw a wrong conclusion—that you are no longer a child of God, for instance. The truth is, if you sin at all in this situation, it is because you doubt God's keeping power instead of doubting these mongrel emotions. My counsel in this case is to do with such feelings as you would with outlaw gangs who travel around the country harassing good citizens. While you may not be able to keep them from passing through your town, you can certainly see to it they do not settle there.

SATAN EXAGGERATES THE SAINT'S SINS

Satan is a clever investigator.
He closely observes the
relationship between you and God.

H is aim is to discredit not the sins but the saints. Here his chief tactic is to deliver his accusations as if they are an act of the Holy Spirit. He knows a charge from God's cannon wounds deeply; therefore, when he accuses a conscientious Christian, he forges God's name on the missile before he fires it. Suppose a child were conscious of gravely displeasing his father, and some spiteful person, to harass him, wrote and sent him a counterfeit letter full of harsh and threatening accusations, copying the father's name at the bottom. The poor child, already painfully aware of his sins and not knowing the scheme, would be overcome with grief. Here is real heartache stemming from a false premise—just the kind of thing Satan relishes.

Satan is a clever investigator. He closely observes the relationship between you and God. Sooner or later he will catch you tardy in some duty or faulty in a service. He knows you are conscious of your shortcomings and that the Spirit of God will also show distaste for them. So he draws up a lengthy indictment, raking up all the aggravations he can think of, then serves his warrant on you as though sent from God. This is how Job's friends reacted to his trouble. They gathered up all the evidence of his infirmities to use against him, implying they had been sent by God to declare him a hypocrite and denounce him for it.

While Satan is a master inquisitor, we know that not all our rebukes come from him. God's Word clearly states that "whom the Lord loveth he chasteneth" (Hebrews 12:6). How, then, can we discern the spiteful accusations of Satan from the loving reprimands of God and His Spirit?

Try this test: If such rebukes contradict any prior work of the Spirit in your soul, they are Satan's and not the Spirit's. Satan's purpose in emphasizing your sin is to try to unsaint you and persuade you that you are only a hypocrite.

THE ACCUSER OF THE BRETHREN

*Satan delights in taking your duties to pieces and so
disfiguring them that they appear superficial, though they
are truly zealous; pharisaical, though they are really sincere.*

The devil is at church as often as you are. And he stands outside your closet door and listens to what you say to God in secret, all the while studying how he may accuse you. The rebellious spirit who dared to criticize God's rule of heaven will not hesitate to pass judgment on the way you rule your soul. He is like those who listen to sermons only to find fault so they can call the minister an offender for some misplaced word or other. Satan delights in taking your duties to pieces and so disfiguring them that they appear superficial, though they are truly zealous; pharisaical, though they are really sincere. He will not rest until he can hand in a verdict of "Guilty!" against your soul.

When you have done your best, then this persuasive critic goes to work, "There," he will say, "you played the hypocrite—appearing noble, but really serving self. Here you wandered; there, you were lazy; farther along, puffed up with pride. What reward can you hope for at God's hands, now that you have spoiled His work?" Such constant nitpicking makes many poor souls lead a weary life. Are you one of these—spiritually exhausted? Does he snipe at everything you do until you know not whether to pray or not, to listen or not? And, when you have prayed and listened, whether it is to any purpose or not? Thus your soul hangs in doubt, and your days pass in sorrow, while your enemy stands in a corner and laughs at the trick he has played upon you. It is his master plan that if he cannot rob you of your righteousness, he will deprive you of your joy.

He comes to fetch you away from the green pastures of covenant comfort and drag you into the depths of despair. He does this under the false pretense that you are not humble enough over sin. The apostle knew what sophisticated mind-games the devil plays. He called them his "devices" (2 Corinthians 2:11), meaning his clever arguments. Here Satan relies heavily on his smooth tongue. Everything he says is flagrant lies and double-talk.

FEBRUARY 11

GOD'S SORROW IN PROPORTION TO SIN

Oh, tempted soul, when Satan says you are not humbled enough and tells you to keep wallowing in your own sorrow, see how you may be saved. Christ is the footbridge by which you may safely cross the raging river of your sins.

Manasseh was a great sinner, and an ordinary sorrow would not do for him. He "humbled himself greatly before . . . God" (2 Chronicles 33:12). "Now," says Satan, "weigh your sin in the balance with your sorrow; are you as great a mourner as you have been a sinner? For many years you have waged war against the Almighty, making havoc of His laws, loading His patience to the breaking point, wounding Christ with the dagger of your sins while you grieved His Spirit and rejected His grace. And now do you think a little remorse, like a rolling cloud letting fall a few drops of rain, will satisfy? No, you must steep in sorrow as you have soaked in sin."

To show you the flaw in his thesis, we must distinguish between two kinds of proportion in sorrow.

First, an exact proportion of sorrow to the inherent nature and demerit of sin. This is not feasible; the injury done in the least sin is infinite, because done to an infinite God.

Second, a relative proportion of sorrow to the law and rule of the Gospel. And what is the law of the Gospel concerning this? That genuine heart-sorrow is gospel-sorrow: "They were pricked in their heart"(Acts 2:37). This gospel sorrow is indeed repentance unto life, given by the Spirit of the Gospel for your relief. Oh, tempted soul, when Satan says you are not humbled enough and tells you to keep wallowing in your own sorrow, see how you may be saved. Christ is the footbridge by which you may safely cross the raging river of your sins. You are a dead man if you think to answer your sin with your own sorrow; you will soon be above your depth, and drown yourself in your own tears, but never be rescued from the least sin you have committed. The strength of your sorrow is not what carries you to heaven—but true heart repentance.

PROFITING FROM THE ENEMY'S ATTACKS

*First, he will point out that you are not perfect but are
expected to be; then he will tell you that since you are not
perfect, God will have nothing to do with our pitiful efforts.*

You may be asking yourself, "What can I do of a practical
nature to withstand Satan when he comes to criticize my
duties for Christ?"

This is God's purpose in allowing Satan to spy on you. Is a
child ever more circumspect than when the teacher has sched-
uled a conference with his parents? Likewise, if you know Satan
is watching and is sure to tell tales about you to God, you ought
to be more careful to keep your slate clean. This should challenge you to study your heart well and read God's Word faithfully. Then when Satan attacks, you will have a rebuttal ready to
counter every accusation.

To be honest with ourselves, we must admit that many of
his charges are all too true. If Satan, whose eyes of understanding are so darkened, can charge us with this much, what could
the light of God uncover! What a wonderful opportunity again
to acknowledge your own sinfulness, and the overriding mercy
of God! By this attitude, we take the very bricks Satan is throwing at us, and use them to build a monument to the glory of our
gracious Lord.

Then you can answer his criticisms wisely. The fallacy is
double. First, he will point out that you are not perfect but are
expected to be; then he will tell you that since you are not perfect, God will have nothing to do with your pitiful efforts.

To persuade you that your service and yourself are hypocritical, proud, selfish, etc., is generally not too difficult, because something of these sins is found in everyone—even
Christians! You must learn to distinguish between pride in a
work and a proud work, between hypocrisy in a person, and a
hypocrite. The best of saints have the stirring of such corruptions in them. Comfort yourself with this: If you find a voice
within your heart pleading for God and entering its protest
against evil, you and your efforts are acceptable in His sight.

God sees your failures as symptoms of your sickly state here
below and pities you are He would a lame child.

YOUR ACCEPTANCE IN CHRIST

*From the day of your salvation, your performance
and obedience are entered into a separate ledger
as tokens of your love and thankfulness to God.*

Note Christ's words in His prayer against Satan: "The Lord
rebuke thee . . . is not this a brand plucked out of the
fire?" (Zechariah 3:2). It is as though He said, "Lord, will
you allow this envious spirit to blame your poor child Joshua
for those infirmities of his old nature which still cling to his
perfect state? He is just newly plucked out of the fire. No wonder there are some sparks unquenched, some corruptions unmortified, some disorders unreformed." And what Christ did
for Joshua, He does incessantly for all His saints, apologizing to
the Father for their infirmities and pleading leniency on their
behalf.

The second distortion in Satan's argument is in reasoning
that because the residue of our old nature still clings to our
present efforts, God does not accept them. "Will God," he asks,
"take such broken coins from your hand? Is He not a holy
God?" Now here is where you must learn discernment. There
are two kinds of acceptance I want to discuss: the acceptance of
something in payment of a debt, and the acceptance of something offered as a token of love and gratitude. He who will not
take broken money or half of what is owed to satisfy a debt,
will, if his friend sends him only a bent sixpence as a token of
love, accept it joyfully. It is true the debt you owe God must be
paid in good and lawful money. But, for your comfort, Christ is
your paymaster. Send Satan to Him; have him bring his charge
before Christ, who is ready at God's right hand to open the
books and show the debit column blotted out with His own
blood, and the debt stamped "Paid in Full."

From the day of your salvation, your performance and obedience are entered in a separate ledger as tokens of your love
and thankfulness to God. And such is the gracious disposition of
your heavenly Father that He accepts your mite. Love refuses
nothing that love sends. Not the weight nor the worth of the
gift, but "the desire of a man is his kindness" (Proverbs 19:22).

BEWARE OF SATAN AS A SEDUCER

Another way to fortify yourself against Satan
is to study that grand gospel truth of
a soul's justification before God.

If you want to be protected from your enemy as a troubler, you must take heed of him as a seducer. You can be sure he takes heed of you! The handle of the hatchet with which he chops at the root of the Christian's comfort is commonly made of the Christian's own wood. Satan is only a creature and cannot work without tools. He can indeed make much from a little, but he cannot make anything out of nothing. We see this in his assault on Christ, where he troubled himself to no purpose because he came and found nothing in Him (John 14:30).

But when he comes to us he finds fossils of our old natures, which tell him much about the disposition of our hearts. These are the artifacts our carnal hearts once held so dear; our strength, our lusts, our pride. He holds them out to us, thinking to draw us away from our new-found grace in Christ. Beware of his enticements. Do not drink from his cup; there is poison in it. Do not even look on it as it sparkles in the temptation. What you drink down with sweetness, you will be sure to bring up again as gall and wormwood.

Above all sins, guard against bold or arrogant ones. You are not beyond the danger of such. If caught in the web of presumptuous sin, call quickly to God for help. If you hesitate, you only give Satan time to entangle you more tightly. But if you cry out to God in true repentance, He will come at once to rescue you. The sooner you yield to the Spirit, the less damage is done to your soul.

Another way to fortify yourself against Satan is to study that grand gospel truth of a soul's justification before God. Acquaint yourself with this truth in all its aspects: the free mercy of God's grace; the accomplishment of Christ's sacrifice; the effectiveness of faith in appropriating these blessings (Rom. 3:24–25). An effectual door once opened to let the soul in to this truth will spoil the devil's market.

FEBRUARY 15

DEALING WITH ADVERSE CIRCUMSTANCE

Every son whom He loves, He corrects.
Behind the travail of every affliction
is a blessing waiting to be born.

Satan will try to draw you off your steadfast course to heaven in still another way—by the presence of circumstances you cannot understand. With them Satan argues against God's love, and for your soul. First (by God's permission) he pillaged Job's earthly possessions, and then fell to work on his spiritual estate. He used every circumstance and everybody at his disposal. He had Job's wife blame God; he had Job's friends condemn the man himself. Satan convinced them all—except Job—that an afflicted condition and a state of grace could not live together in the same house.

Here is a timely warning when you find your soul adrift in a heavy fog of tribulation: Neither accuse God foolishly of your enemy's mischief, nor charge yourself with belonging to the enemy. God can chart a straight course in the worst storm. He can be righteous when He uses wicked instruments, and gracious when He dispenses harsh providences. Do not overreact to changes in your temporal estate. Christ told us to expect some rough sailing before we reach heaven's shore.

Your perspective should be very different from that of the unregenerate. Like naive children, they think everyone loves them who gives them plums. They do not realize that prosperity can be a curse to bind them in a deeper sleep of false security. Remember how Jael served Sisera (Judges 5:25–26). She gave him milk though he asked for water, that she might more surely nail him to the ground—milk having the property, it is said, to incline to sleep. But the Christian in an afflicted state has a key to decipher God's providence. The Spirit, through the Word, teaches you to read the shorthand of His dispensations: Every son whom He loves, He corrects. Behind the travail of every affliction is a blessing waiting to be born.

MAINTAIN ASSURANCE OF SALVATION

*Renew your repentance, as if you had never repented.
Put forth fresh acts of faith, as if you had never
believed, and you will beat Satan at his own game.*

Still another way to fortify yourself against Satan is to preserve the hope of your salvation, which is promised
through Christ's atoning sacrifice. Record God's special vis-
its to you in the memory book of your heart. Paste in keepsakes
of the occasions when He declared a holiday and came to you
in festive robes of mercy, holding forth the scepter of His grace
more familiarly than usual. Keep old receipts written in His
own hand for the pardon of your sins.

"But," the doubting soul may ask, "what if I cannot grasp
this assurance, or vouch for those evidences which I once
thought to be true?" Then try the following prescriptions as a
tonic for your ailing faith.

First of all, renew your repentance, as if you had never repented. Put forth fresh acts of faith, as if you had never believed, and you will beat Satan at his own game. Let him tell you
that your former actions were hypocritical, or that they are old
and worthless. What can he say against your present affirmation
of faith? In this way, the very accusations he uses to drive you
away from God, instead draw you closer to Him.

If he still haunts you with fears of your spiritual condition,
then apply to the throne of grace and ask for a new copy of the
old evidence, which you have misplaced. The original is in the
pardon office in heaven, of which Christ is the Master. And if
you are a saint, your name is on record in that court. Appeal to
God, and hear the news from heaven, rather than listen to the
tales your enemy brings from hell. If you would argue less with
Satan and pray more to God about your fears, they would soon
be resolved. Can you expect truth from a liar, or comfort from
an adversary? Turn your back on him and go to God. Try not to
worry. Sooner or later you will receive your certificate of
assurance.

COMFORT IN FELLOWSHIP WITH OTHERS

*Telling a trusting, godly friend of your struggles
often brings relief. Satan knows this too well,
so in order more freely to rifle the soul of its
peace and comfort, he frightens it into silence.*

If Satan continues to hound you, call in help and do not listen to the devil's counsel to the contrary. The very strength of some temptations lies in trying to keep them hidden. Telling a trusted, godly friend of your struggles often brings relief. Satan knows this too well, so in order more freely to rifle the soul of its peace and comfort, he frightens it into silence. "Oh, my," Satan says, "if your friends knew such a thing of you, they would cast you off. You had better hope they never find out!" He has kept many a poor soul in misery by swearing it to secrecy. You lose two blessings by keeping the devil's secret—the counsel of your fellow brethren, and their prayers. And what a serious loss this is!

You have the assurance of victory if you are armed. We have seen the perilous straits of the unarmed soul; turn your thoughts now to the glorious prospects of a soul fitly armed. Who would decline the honor of serving in the army of the King of kings—especially when victory has already been declared! This is the assurance Paul gives every saint who puts on the whole armor of God: "That ye may be able to stand against the wiles of the devil." With this statement he places the enemy's potential back in proper perspective. He never intended to scare the saints into cowardly flight or woeful despair of victory when he acknowledged the enemy's might. Rather, he hoped to rouse them to vigorous resistance by promising them strength to stand in battle, and a sure victory afterwards. These two ideas are implied in the phrase "to stand against the wiles of Satan." Sometimes to *stand* implies a fighting posture (Ephesians 6:14), sometimes a conquering position—"I know that my Redeemer liveth, and that he shall *stand* at the latter day upon the earth" (Job 19:25). The earth which today is the field for all the bloody battles between the saints and Satan, will one day be Christ's footstool, when not an enemy shall dare to show his head.

SATAN IS UNDER A CURSE

You will not find a faithful servant
sifted and winnowed by this enemy, who
did not come off with an honorable victory.

S atan, with all his wit and wiles, will never defeat a soul armed with true grace, nor will the contest ever end in a stalemate. Look into the Word. You will not find a faithful servant sifted and winnowed by this enemy, who did not come off with an honorable victory. Witness David, Job, Peter, and Paul, who were the hardest put to it of any upon record. And lest some should attribute their victory to their own inherent strength, the glory of the victories is attributable to God alone, in whom the weak are as strong as the strongest. There are two reasons why the Christian who seems to be so overmatched is yet so unconquerable (2 Corinthians 12:9; James 5:11).

The curse that lies upon Satan is God's curse. God's curse blasts wherever it comes. The Canaanite, along with their neighboring nations, were easy prey for Israel, though they were famous for war. Why? Because they were cursed nations. The Egyptians were a shrewd people. "Let us deal wisely," they said. Yet God's curse lay like a thorn at Egypt's heart, and was finally her ruin. In fact, when the Israelites, themselves children of the covenant, sinned and became the object of God's curse, they were trampled like dirt under the Assyrian's feet.

An irrevocable curse clings to Satan from Genesis 3:14–15: "And the Lord God said unto the serpent, Because thou hast done this, thou art cursed . . ." And as the curse works eternally against Satan, so it operates eternally in favor of the saints.

For one thing, it prostrates Satan under their feet: "Upon thy belly shalt thou go" (v. 14). This prostrate condition of Satan assures believers that the devil can never lift his head—his wily schemes—higher than the saints' heels. He may make you limp, but he cannot take your life. And the bruise which he gives you will be rewarded with the breaking of his own head—the utter ruin of him and his cause.

THE LIMITS GOD PLACES UPON SATAN

*When Satan tempts a saint, he is only serving as God's
messenger. Paul called his thorn in the flesh
"the messenger of Satan" (2 Corinthians 12:7).*

The devil may not tempt anyone unless God allows it. When Christ went into the wilderness, He was led, not by an evil spirit, but by the Holy Spirit (Matthew 4:1). All that transpired was by God's permission. And the same Holy Spirit that led Christ into the field brought Him off with victory. As soon as He had repulsed Satan, we see Him marching into Galilee in the power of the Holy Ghost (Luke 4:14).

When Satan tempts a saint, he is only serving as God's messenger. Paul called his thorn in the flesh "the messenger of Satan" (2 Corinthians 12:7). Another translation reads "the messenger Satan," implying that the messenger was sent by God to Paul. Indeed, the errand he came on was too good to be Satan's own, for Paul himself says it was to keep him humble. This tempter to sin never meant to do Paul such a service, but God let him go to Paul to accomplish His own divine will. The devil and his instruments are both God's instruments. We will be well advised to let God alone to wield the one and handle the other.

Let Lucifer choose his way; God is a match for him at every weapon. If he assaults the saint by persecution, God will oppose him. If he works by a subtlety, God is ready there also. The devil and his whole council are mere fools to God. The more wit and craft in sin, the worse, because it is employed against an all-wise God who cannot be outwitted. In Paul's words, "The foolishness of God is wiser than men" (1 Corinthians 1:25). God is wiser in His creatures' weak sermons than Satan is in his deep plots; wiser in His ignorant children than Satan in his Ahithophels and Sanballats. "[God] disappointeth the devices of the crafty" (Job 5:12). By displaying His wisdom in pursuing the saints' enemies, God adds a sweet relish to their ultimate deliverance. After He had hunted Pharaoh out of all his lairs and burrows, He broke the very brains of that wicked ruler's plots and served them up to His people.

GOD USES TEMPTATION

*God omnipotent sits in the devil's
council and overrules proceedings
there to the saint's advantage.*

S atan designs every temptation to bring as much discomfort
as possible to the saint, hoping to rob him of his peace and
create self-doubts about his sincerity.

But God does not sit idly by. We have a sure promise that
"the eyes of the Lord are upon the righteous" (Psalm 34:15).
First of all, He uses the temptations of Satan to one sin as a preventive against another. God omnipotent sits in the devil's
council and overrules proceedings there to the saint's advantage. He allows the devil to annoy the Christian with certain
troublesome temptations which He knows will drive the soul to
watchfulness. So Paul's thorn in the flesh prevents his pride.
God sent Satan to assault Paul on his strong side so that in the
meantime He might fortify the apostle where he was weak.

Second, God uses the temptation to sin as a purgative
against future sin. Peter never had such a conquest over his self-
confidence, never such an establishment of his faith, as after his
denial in the high priest's hall. This man, who recanted when
questioned by a serving maid, became a bold confessor of
Christ before councils and rulers. If you should trip over a
temptation and fall headlong into sin, do like Peter. Use the experience to discover your prevailing infirmity and take measures to overcome it.

Third, God uses temptation to promote the whole work of
grace in the heart. A good husband, seeing the roof leak in one
corner, will send for a repairman to check the whole house.
And a good wife, finding a stain on her husband's shirt, will
wash the whole garment. This kind of concern for one's spiritual condition distinguishes a sincere heart from a hypocrite,
whose repentance is only partial. Judas confessed his treason,
but not a word of his thievery and hypocrisy. If he had been truly repentant, his sorrow for one sin would have broken his
heart for the others also. David, when overcome by one sin, renewed his repentance for all (Psalm 51).

SATAN'S INTENTION TO DEFILE SAINTS

*If you fall to temptation and
come under Satan's rule for a time,
you learn what an evil taskmaster he is.*

S atan plants temptation in one saint, hoping it will blossom
into sin and its seeds will be carried to other hearts by the
winds of conformity or disillusionment so that they are either encouraged to sin by example, or discouraged in their own
walk by the scandal.

God once again fools Satan, by making such sins a season-
able warning to others to look to their standing. When you see
a meek Moses provoked to anger, you keep more careful watch
for such chokeweeds in your own unruly heart!

God also comforts His afflicted saints by showing them what
a rocky road some of His dearest children traveled on their way
to heaven. Is your conscience distressed by your sin? Is your
soul grief-stricken because Satan has convinced you there is no
hope of pardon? The lives of some of the greatest saints are an
indisputable rebuttal to Satan's accusations against you. David's
sins were great, yet he found mercy. Peter denied his faith, yet
he is now in heaven. Does God love you any less than them?
Has He not promised to pardon *all* who are of a contrite heart
(Psalm 34:18)?

Another way God uses Satan's attacks is as a training ground
for His saints. The saint who has been severely tested is best
equipped to help other suffering saints. The best drill sergeant
is not the general behind the desk but the man who has served
in the front line of battle. So here you put your faith to work in
earnest; all your graces are called into action. If you fall to
temptation and come under Satan's rule for a time, you learn
what an evil taskmaster he is. He wields an iron rod in one
hand and a cruel lash in the other, with which he intends to
drive all his subjects to hell. But the sincere child of God, when
he sins and feels the sting of Satan's whip, knows how to escape. He runs to the Word and to God Himself. And he yields to
the kind ministrations of the Spirit.

USING SATAN'S TEMPTATIONS

What did Satan get for all the energy
he spent on Job, but to let that holy man
know at last how dearly God loved him?

God makes Satan's temptations the courier of His love to the saints. The devil thought he had the game in his own hands when he got Adam to eat the forbidden fruit. He supposed he now had man in the same predicament as himself. But did he catch God by surprise? Of course not! God knew the outcome before the match was ever begun and used Satan's temptation to usher in that great gospel plot of saving man by Christ. At God's command, Christ undertook the charge of wrestling His fallen creatures from Satan's clutches and reinstating them to their original glory, with access to more than they ever had at first.

And what did Satan get for all the energy he spent on Job, but to let that holy man know at last how dearly God loved him? When he foiled Peter so shamefully, do we not find Christ claiming Peter with as much love as ever? Peter was the only disciple to whom Christ sent the joyful news of His resurrected by name—as if He had said, "Be sure to comfort Peter with this news. I want him to know I am still his friend, despite his cowardice." God never condones wickedness in His saints, but He does pity their weakness. He never sees a saint in mourning without planning to clothe him in the sunlight of His love and mercy.

God can, in fact, use His saints' failures to strengthen their faith, which, like a tree, stands stronger for the shaking. Times of testing expose the heart's true condition. False faith, once foiled, seldom comes on again; but true faith rises and fights more valiantly, as we see in Peter. Temptation is to faith as fire is to gold (1 Peter 1:7). The fire not only reveals which is true gold, but makes the true gold more pure. It comes out less in bulk, being separated from the dross that was mixed with it, but is greater in quality and value.

GOD'S HELP IN TEMPTATION

*Do you see now why God allows His children to meet
with temptation? He is in control! He holds the
reins on Satan and will not let him trample you.*

Faith before temptation has much extraneous stuff that
clings to it and passes for faith; but when temptation
comes, the dross is discovered and consumed by the fiery
trial. The quality of faith that emerges is like Gideon's handful
of men—stronger when all these worthless accessories to faith
are sent away than when they were present. And here is all the
devil gets: Instead of destroying the saint's faith, he is the means
of refining it, thereby making it stronger and more precious.

The love of tempted saints is enkindled to Christ by the fires
of temptation. Did you edge too close to the flames and singe
your soul? Where will you go for cleansing, if not to Christ? And
will His kindly aid not rekindle your love for Him above all others? Christ's love is fuel to ours; the more He puts forth His
love, the more heat our love gets. And next to Christ's dying
love, none is greater than His rescuing love in temptation. The
greatest opportunity a mother has to show her child how much
she loves him is when he is in distress—sick, poor, or imprisoned. Christ is both mother and nurse to our love. When His
children lie in Satan's prison, bleeding from the wounds of
their consciences, He hurries to reveal His tender heart in pitying, His faithfulness in praying, His mindfulness in sending help
to them, and His dear love in visiting them by His comforting
Spirit. No child is more dutiful in all the family than the one
who has repented of his rebellion. Jesus Christ, whom Satan
thought to shut out of the soul's favor, comes in the end to sit
higher and surer than ever in the saint's affections.

Do you see now why God allows His children to meet with
temptation? He is in control! He holds the reins on Satan and
will not let him trample you. If you never experienced the
mighty power of Satan arrayed against you, you could not know
the almighty power of God displayed for you.

GOD OUTWITS HIS OPPONENT

*All the plots of hell and commotions on earth
have not so much as shaken God's hand to spoil
one letter or line He has been drawing.*

Rest easy, worried Christian. The duel is not between the church and Satan, but between Christ and Satan. These are the champions of the two sides. Gather round and watch the all-wise God joust with His crafty opponent. You shall behold the Almighty smite off this Goliath's head with his own sword, and take this wicked knight in the trap of his own schemes. That faith which ascribes greatness and wisdom to God will shrink up Satan's challenge into a thing of nothing. Unbelief fears Satan as a lion; faith treads upon him as a worm.

Observe God at work, and be assured that what He is about will be an excellent piece. Man's wisdom may be leveled with folly, but God's design is never interrupted. None can drive Him from His work. A builder cannot work when night draws the curtain, and he is driven off his scaffold by a rainstorm. But all the plots of hell and commotions on earth have not so much as shaken God's hand to spoil one letter or line He has been drawing. The mystery of His providence may hang a curtain before His work so that we cannot see what He is doing, but even when darkness surrounds Him, righteousness is the seat of His throne forever. Where is our faith, saints? Let God be wise, and all men and devils be fools. Even if a Babel seems more likely to go up than a Babylon to be pulled down, yet believe God is making His secret approaches and will besiege Satan's stronghold.

What does it matter though the church be like Jonah in the whale's belly, swallowed up out of view by the fury of men? Do you not remember that the whale had no power to digest the prophet? Do not be too quick to bury the church before she is dead. Be patient while Christ tries His skill before you give it over. By your prayers, bring Christ to its grave to speak a resurrection word. The saints of old exhibited admirable faith in circumstances which were just as dire.

EVERYONE MUST BATTLE SATAN

*"For we wrestle not against flesh and blood, but
against principalities, against powers, against
the rulers of the darkness of this world, against
spiritual wickedness in high places" (Ephesians 6:12).*

Whether you like it or not, you must go into the ring with
Satan. He has not only a general malice against the army
of saints, but a particular spite against every single child
of God. As our Lord delights to have private communion with
His saint, so the devil delights to challenge the Christian when
he gets him alone. The whole issue of your spiritual destiny is
personal and particular. You give Satan a dangerous advantage
if you see his wrath and fury bent in general against the saints,
and not against you specifically: Satan hates *me;* Satan accuses
me; Satan tempts *me.* Conversely, you lose much comfort when
you fail to see the promises and providences of God as available for your own specific needs: God loves *me;* God takes care
of *me.* The water supply for the town will do you no personal
good unless you have a pipe that carries it to your own house.
Let it serve as both a caution and a comfort to know your spiritual combat is singular.

Second, wrestling is a close combat. Armies fight at some
distance; wrestlers grapple hand-to-hand. You may be able to
dodge an arrow shot from a distance, but when the enemy actually has hold of you, you must either resist manfully or fall shamefully at his feet. When Satan comes after you, he moves in close,
takes hold of your very flesh and corrupt nature, and by this
shakes you.

"We wrestle" encompasses everyone. You may have noticed
that the apostle changes the pronoun "ye" in the former verse,
into "we" in this, that he may include himself. He wants you to
know the quarrel is with every saint. Satan neither fears to assault the minister nor disdains to wrestle with the lowliest saint
in the congregation. Great and small, minister and people, all
must wrestle—not one part of Christ's army in the heat of battle
and the other at ease in their quarters.

THE LENGTH OF COMBAT

As long as his comrade,
your old nature, is alive within,
he will be knocking at the door without.

T he length of a man's combat with Satan measures the same
as the length of his life. He is, as Jeremiah said of himself,
born "a man of strife" (Jeremiah 15:10). And once he becomes a saint, the struggles increases. From your spiritual birth
to your natural death, from the hour you first set your face toward heaven until you set your foot inside the gate, you will
have wars with Satan, sin, and self. Israel's march out of Egypt
is, in a figurative way, our open declaration of war against the
forces of darkness. And when did they have peace? Not until
they reached Canaan.

No condition the Christian finds himself in here below is
quiet. Is it prosperity, or is it adversity? Here is work for both
hands—to keep pride and complacency down in the one, faith
and patience up in the other. The Christian has nowhere he can
call privileged ground. Lot wrestled with the wicked inhabitants
of Sodom, his righteous soul vexed with their filthy behavior.
Then what happened at Zoar? His own daughters brought a
spark of Sodom's fire into his bed, and he was inflamed with in-
cestuous lust (Genesis 19:30–38)!

Some have thought if they were only in such a family, under
such a ministry, removed from a certain temptation, then they
would not be such weak Christians. I confess a change of air is a
great help to an invalid, but do you think you can thus escape
Satan's presence? No! Even if you were to take the wings of
morning, he would pursue you. A change in circumstances may
make him change his method of tempting, but nothing temporal can make him lay down his designs. As long as his comrade,
your old nature, is alive within, he will be knocking at the door
without. This diabolical opponent will challenge you at every
opportunity. He delights to sneak up on you from behind, while
you are kneeling, trowel in hand, planting seeds for the
kingdom.

HOW NOT TO WRESTLE

Contention is always unfortunate—
whether with neighbors or friends,
wife or husband—but worst of all with God.

D o not wrestle against God's Spirit. Genesis 6:3 speaks of the Spirit as "striving" with man. This does not mean God is trying to overcome or destroy man. He could do that at a word, without any stir or scuffle. No, His striving is a loving contest with us. Seeing us run at such a gallop headlong to our ruin, He sends His Spirit to pull us back before we destroy ourselves. This is the same kind of strife you would witness if someone were attempting to take his own life and another intervened and struggled to take the weapon from him.

The lusts of men are those bloody instruments of death with which sinners are harming themselves. The Holy Spirit strives to get them out of our hands and replace them with Christ's grace and eternal life. When you repulse such loving strife, you are justly counted a fighter against Him. "Ye stiff-necked, and uncircumcised in heart and ears, ye do always resist the Holy Ghost," said Stephen (Acts 7:51). Do not wrestle against God's providence.

Questioning God's acts, whether of mercy or justice, is called contending or reproving Him (Job 40:2). He is a bold man for sure who dares to name himself the plaintiff and God the defender. No! God is the Judge, and He will find you in contempt of court for bringing such false accusations against Him. Contend with the Almighty? Reprove God? You had better cry with Job: "I am vile; what shall I answer thee? I will lay mine hand upon my mouth" (Job 40:4). Hear his plea: "Only pardon what is past, and you shall hear such language no more!"

Christians, take heed of this wrestling above all other. Contention is always unfortunate—whether with neighbors or friends, wife or husband—but worst of all with God. If God cannot please you and your heart rises against Him, what hopes are there of your pleasing Him? Love cannot think any evil of God, nor endure to hear any evil spoken of Him.

DO NOT WRESTLE BY YOUR OWN RULES

Others wrestle with sin but do not hate it.
They wrestle in jest, not in earnest. Until the love of
a sin is quenched in the heart, the fire will never die out.

We wrestle against God when we disregard His rules and substitute our own. Maybe you do not wrestle against God's providence, and you do wrestle against sin. This seems commendable, but God requires more: You must wrestle by His rules and His alone. Timothy tells us, "If a man also strive for masteries, yet is he not crowned, except he strive lawfully" (2 Timothy 2:5). Check your own conduct against the errors of some who have waged their own battle, and not Christ's:

Some, while they wrestle against one sin, embrace another. Our lusts are diverse and will fight for rank among themselves. When malice wants revenge, craft says, "Hide your wrath—but do not forgive." When passion sends out for whores, hypocrisy cancels the request but for the fear of the world, not God. The man who allows one sin to command another, and thus to rule his soul, cannot be God's champion.

Some wrestle because they are pressed into service. Their slavish fears frighten them and keep them from their lusts for the moment. But the real combat for such a wrestler is between his conscience and his will, rather than between his soul and his lusts. In such a case, the will at last prevails, for a lust held in check but not discarded grows as wild as a trapped stallion. Finally the conscience can no longer hold the reins nor sit in the saddle, but is thrown down. Then the lust ranges where it can have its fullest meal and will continue to gorge itself until conscience revives and runs to God for help.

Others wrestle with sin but do not hate it. They wrestle in jest, not in earnest. Until the love of a sin is quenched in the heart, the fire will never die out. How is this accomplished? Jerome says one love extinguishes another—that is, the love of Christ must quench the love of sin. Then and not until then will the soul's decree stand against sin.

TRAINING IN WARFARE

The object is to put your opponent on his back and keep him there. Do not so compliment sin as to let it breathe or rise.

Your bout with sin and Satan is not a weekend sport; it is the final conflict. So you dare not give your enemy a handhold. Wrestlers strive to fasten upon some part of the body which will let them more easily throw their adversary. To prevent this, ancient wrestlers used to anoint their bodies before a match. You should do likewise. Strive to put off the old man—that corruption. David called his own iniquity (Psalm 18:23). Observe what it is and mortify it daily; it is a favorite handhold of Satan's. He will beat a shameful retreat when he finds no iniquity in you to catch hold of—and he dare not touch that in you which is holy.

Is your flesh mortified? Now anoint your soul with the frequent meditation of Christ's love. It will help you disdain the offer of sin and, like oil, will make your spirit supple and your will agile to evade the enemy. Satan will find little welcome where Christ's love dwells. Love will kindle love, and flame as a wall of fire to keep him away.

Use your advantage wisely. If you are a smart wrestler, you will fall with all your weight upon your enemy when you have him on the ground. Though in most sports the referee would call "Foul!" if you were to strike when your opponent is down, this is not the case with wrestling. The object is to put your opponent on his back and keep him there. Do not so compliment sin as to let it breathe or rise. Do not repeat Ahab's sin and let the enemy loose when God has decreed his destruction.

Learn a little wisdom from Satan's brood. Though they had Christ on His back, they still took precautions. They never thought they had Him sure enough—not even when dead. So they sealed and watched His grave. You should do the same to hinder the resurrection of your sin: seal it down with stronger purposes and solemn covenants, and watch it by a wakeful, circumspect walk.

MARCH 2

WRESTLE WITH YOUR WHOLE HEART

Wrap your weary soul in this promise: There is a place of rest reserved for the people of God. You do not beat the air, but wrestle to win heaven and a permanent crown.

Perhaps you are discouraged, not only by the strength of the enemy, but by your own apparent weakness and the constant contention with sin and self. Be encouraged! There is strong consolation for the Christian who struggles with the truth of God's grace and his own inner conflicts with sin. Gideon cried out in despair, "If the Lord be with us, why is all this befallen us?" (Judges 6:13). We understand his perplexity because we identify with his sufferings. Our hearts, too, cry out, "Why do I find such struggling in me, provoking me to sin, pulling me back from that which is good?"

God has a ready answer if we will stop whining long enough to hear it. "Because," He says, "you are a wrestler, not a conqueror." It is as simple as that. Too often we mistake the state of a Christian in this life. He is not immediately called to triumph over his enemies, but is carried into battle to fight them. The state of grace is the commencement of your war against sin, not the culmination of it. God Himself will enter the battle in disguise and appear to be your enemy, rather than leave you no enemy to wrestle with. When Jacob was alone, He sent a man to wrestle with him until dawn.

Take comfort in the fact that you are a wrestler. This struggling within you, if upon the right ground and to the right end, only proves there are two nations within you, two contrary natures, the one from earth earthly, and the other from heaven heavenly. And for your further comfort, know that although your corrupt nature is the elder, yet it shall serve the younger (Genesis 25:23).

Wrap your weary soul in this promise: There is a place of rest reserved for the people of God. You do not beat the air, but wrestle to win heaven and a permanent crown. Here on earth we overcome to fight again. One temptation may be conquered, but the war remains. When death comes, however, God strikes the final blow.

OUR FLESHLY NATURE

All its desires, delights,
cares, and fears are wrapped
up in this present world.

The thoughts of the corrupt mind are incapable of perceiving the things of God. All its desires, delights, cares, and fears are wrapped up in this present world, and are therefore fleshly. Just as the sun hides the heavens above it while revealing the things beneath, so carnal reason leaves the creature in the dark concerning spiritual truths, while enlightening his carnal knowledge most excellently. Every creature has its proper diet: the lion does not eat grass, nor the horse, flesh. Just so, what is food to the carnal heart, is poison to the gracious; and what is tasty to the gracious, is odious to the carnal.

Now according to this interpretation of flesh and blood, the apostle is not saying that the war is over between your old and new natures. You know from experience this is not the case. The Spirit lusts against the flesh and the flesh against the Spirit throughout the whole course of a Christian's life. Were there no devils, you would still have your hands full resisting the corruptions of your own heart. What Paul wants you to see is that your old nature is only a private in the war against your new nature. Satan comes to the battle as an ally of the flesh and launches a massive attack. He is the general who marshals your sinful inclinations, exercises them mercilessly, and sends them out as a united front against the power of God in your life. Compare it to the following situation. Suppose that while a king is fighting to subdue his own mutinous subjects, some superior foreign troops should join with them and take command. Then the king no longer fights primarily against his subjects. but against a foreign power. You see the spiritual analogy: Even as the Christian is fighting against his own inner corruptions, Satan joins his power to the residue of the old nature and assumes command. It could be said that our sin is the engine, and Satan, the engineer.

This knowledge should make every one of us diligent to keep our lusts unarmed.

WE ARE "FLESH AND BLOOD"

The soul, though of divine extraction,
is so immersed in sensuality that it
deserves no other name than flesh.

We wrestle not with flesh and blood"—that is, not with other *men*. "Handle me, and see," Jesus said, "for a spirit hath not flesh . . ." (Luke 24:39). Now according to this interpretation, observe first of all how scornfully the Holy Spirit speaks of man, and second, where He lays the stress of the saint's battle: not in resisting flesh and blood, but in combating principalities and powers in the unseen world of spirits.

First of all, note that the Spirit reduces man to flesh and blood. Man has a heaven-born soul, which makes him kin to angels, and what is more, kin to God. But this is passed by in silence, as if God would not own that which is tainted with sin and no longer the creature as He first made it. The soul, though of divine extraction, is so immersed in sensuality that it deserves no other name than flesh to express its weakness and frailty. It is the word the Holy Ghost uses to express the impotence of a creature. For example, "They are men, and their horses are *flesh*"—that is, weak (Isaiah 31:3). On the contrary, when God wishes to emphasize the power and strength of a thing, He contrasts it to the flesh: "Our weapons are not carnal, but mighty" (2 Corinthians 10:4).

How this should humble you! The flesh, which you so often glory in, is but one step from filth and corruption. Your redeemed soul is the salt that preserves you, or else you would stink above ground. Are you proud of your beauty? It is the vanity of vanities! How soon will time's plow make furrows in your face, or illness so change your complexion that your doting lovers will abhor to look at you!

Is it strength you boast of? Alas, it is an arm of flesh that withers while you stretch it forth. Soon your blood, which is now warm, will freeze in your veins. Your marrow will dry in your bones, your sinews shrink, and your legs bow under the weight of your puny body.

PUT NO FAITH IN THE FLESH

"He knoweth our frame,
he remembereth that we
are dust" (Psalm 103:14).

Whoever you are, you are baseborn until born again. The same blood runs in your veins with the beggar in the street (Acts 17:26). We enter and leave the world alike; as one is not made of finer earth, so he does not disintegrate into purer dust.

If such is the composition of all flesh, why place your faith in any man? Do not trust in princes; they cannot keep their crowns on their own heads, nor their heads on their own shoulders. Neither trust in wise men, whose designs so often recoil upon themselves. Man's carnal wisdom may predict whatever it likes, but God turns the wheel and brings forth His own providence regardless. Nor trust too much in spiritual leaders. They, too, are flesh, and their judgment is not infallible. The holy man's mistake may lead you astray, and though he repents, you may go on and perish. Trust not in any man—not even yourself. "He is a fool," the wise man said, "who trusts his heart."

Just as you should not trust in the flesh, neither should you be afraid of the flesh. You have seen what a rusty bucket it is, how subject to decay. This was David's resolve: "I will not fear what flesh can do unto me" (Psalm 56:4). If you are a Christian, what is there to fear? You have no life to lose if you have already given yourself to Christ. And while God has not promised immunity from suffering, He has undertaken to bear your losses and pay you a hundredfold, though your reward may not come until another world.

One more comforting thought. Is man mere flesh? Our heavenly Father knows it and makes allowances for our weakness: "He knoweth our frame, he remembereth that we are dust" (Psalm 103:14). When you begin to faint under the weight of duty or temptation, God rushes to you as a mother to her distraught child, revives you with His own sweet breath, and will not let your spirit die.

OUR WAR WITH THE WICKED

When reproached and persecuted by wicked men,
look beyond them. Spend your wrath on Satan,
who is your chief enemy. Men are only his puppets.

Now in all the saints' wars with the wicked, Satan is commander-in-chief on the wicked side. It is their captain's work the wicked do, his lusts they fulfill. The Sabeans were the ones who plundered Job, but they went on Satan's errand. The heretic spreads corrupt doctrine and perverts the faith of many, but he is only a minister of Satan (2 Corinthians 11:15), who gives him his call, his wiles, and his wages. Persecutors, whether by their tongues or their hands, are but the devil's instruments (Revelation 2:9–10).

When you see people striving furiously against the truths or servants of Christ, pity them as the most miserable people on earth. Do not fear their power, nor admire their talents. They are emissaries of Satan. The martyrs of old called them his drudges and slaughter-slaves. Augustine said in a letter to Lycinius (a brilliant but wicked man who once had been his student), "Oh, how I weep to see such a sparkling wit as yours prostituted to the devil's service! If you had found a golden chalice, you would have given it to the church; but God has given you a golden head, talent, and wit, and with them you are drinking yourself to the devil!"

When you see men of power and intellect using their talents against God, weep for their souls. Better they had lived and died slaves and fools than to do the devil's business with their God-given abilities.

When reproached and persecuted by wicked men, look beyond them. Spend your wrath on Satan, who is your chief enemy. Men are only his puppets. They may be won to Christ's side and so become your friends at last. Anselm explains it in the following manner, "When the enemy comes riding up in battle, the valiant soldier is not angry with the horse, but with the horseman. He works to kill the rider so that he may possess the horse for his own use." Thus we must do with the wicked.

THE SAINTS' CHIEF ASSAILANTS ARE EVIL SPIRITS

They are not "flesh and blood," but a host
of evil spirits directed by the devil himself,
and sent out to war against the saints.

If the saints' battle only pitted flesh against flesh, some might be able to win it by their own efforts. But Paul dashes any silly notion of an independent victory when he describes the character of our greatest enemies. They are not "flesh and blood," but a host of evil spirits directed by the devil himself, and sent out to war against the saints.

Having been forever denied preeminence above the stars, Satan has determined to have it beneath them. Since the day he was thrown out of heaven, he and his followers have worked tirelessly to establish their dominion on earth. The epistle to the Ephesians reveals the scope of their influence: first, their system of government; second, the magnitude of their power; third, their territory; fourth, their inherent nature; and fifth, the subject of their dispute with God.

Their system of government is beyond our natural understanding. The word *principalities* is used to designate the territory which that usurper Satan has claimed belongs to him. To deny the devil's exalted position in the present wicked world is to contradict God Himself. Christ referred to him as "the prince of this world" (John 14:30). And as princes have a people and a province which they rule, so Satan has his.

An earthly dictator is fortunate if he has a handful of subjects he can trust. The rest he must control by force, or he may shortly lose his throne as well as his head. But Satan has no reason to fear an assassin's bullet. He can trust all his subjects and never has to worry about rebellion—except when the Holy Spirit intervenes. As a matter of fact, the wicked go beyond mere obedience to the devil; they willingly bend their knees and bow their heads to *worship* him (Revelation 13:4). It is, nonetheless, no more than he demands.

SATAN'S CHOSEN EMISSARIES

*As princes appoint ministers of state to
enforce their whims and wishes, so Satan sends
out special emissaries to carry out his plans.*

Satan knows he must have the cooperation of all his subjects in order for his kingdom to thrive, but he is especially pleased to use the most wicked. As princes appoint
ministers of state to enforce their whims and wishes, so Satan
sends out special emissaries to carry out his plans. He too has
his chosen disciples like Elymas, whom Paul called "full of subtlety . . . and child of the devil" (Acts 13:10). It is to this inner circle of dark hearts that he imparts the mysteries of iniquity and
the depths of degradation.

But even with these chosen few he does not share everything. He always holds his own purse and the sinner's too, so
that he is the investor and the sinner only the broker to trade
for him. In the end, all the ill-gotten gains drop into the devil's
pocket. Everything the sinner has—time, strength, intellect and
all—is spent to keep the devil on his throne.

"How," you may ask, "did such a low creature come to hold
such a mighty principality?" Not lawfully, you can be sure, though
he is clever enough to show a claim which appears legitimate.

For one thing, he claims the earth by conquest. It is to some
degree true that he won his crown by power and politics, and
that he keeps it the same way. Yet "conquest" is a cracked title.

A thief has no legal right to the wallet he takes from his victim simply because he puts it in his pocket and claims it is his
own. Nor is the wrong thus committed ever made right by the
passing of time. Years may go by before he is discovered; he
will be as guilty on the day of his arrest as on the day he perpe-
trated the crime. Now a thief on the throne is no different from
one in the alley. Satan has indeed kept his stolen title a long
time, but he is no less a criminal than on the day he first took
Adam's heart from God.

SATAN'S CLAIM IS LIMITED

*The devil is the prince of the world,
not by the preference of God,
but by His permission.*

S atan's claim to a democratic victory is flawed, for man was
created as God's subject, and has neither the power nor
the authority to oust the eternal King in favor of another.
We may choose to ignore God's sovereignty, but we cannot
strip it from Him. Though sin disabled us to keep God's law, it
does not excuse us from our need to keep it, or from the terms
of God's government.

Finally, Satan presents a counterfeit deed of gift from God
to claim the earth as his. This imposter is so brazen that he actually presented his worthless claim to Christ Himself, pretending to possess absolute power as the prince of this world. He
showed our Lord all the earthly kingdoms and said, "All this
power will I give thee, and the glory of them: for that is delivered unto me; and to whomsoever I will I give it" (Luke 4:6).

There was a truth here—yet more than the truth. In a sense
God did deliver this world to Satan, but not to do whatever he
pleases. The devil is prince of the world, not by the preference
of God, but by His permission. And God can revoke His permission at any time.

God's present concession to Satan's claim is temporary. From
our limited human perspective, we must wonder why God allows His apostate creature to hold such a principality in the
world. Why does He let this rebel parade with such pomp and
arrogance before men and angels? There are several reasons we
might consider.

First, to punish sin. Letting Satan crack his whip over man is
one way God punishes rebellion: "Because thou servedst not
the Lord thy God with joyfulness, and with gladness of heart
. . . therefore shalt thou serve thine enemies . . . in hunger"
(Deuteronomy 28:47, 49). Satan is an overseer given in God's
wrath. The devil is God's slave, and man the devil's. Sin has
chained the creature to Satan, and now he drives him mercilessly.

SATAN'S TEMPORARY REIGN

*If we had not been Satan's prisoner
first, we would not fully understand
or appreciate our deliverance at last.*

No one will doubt God's almighty power when they see Him flick this mighty dragon off the earth and into hell as though he were a gnat. Just as man alone is no match for the devil, so Satan with all his troops is no match for God. What a glorious name God will have for Himself when He has finished this war!

The workmanship of heaven and earth gave God the name of Creator. Providence gave Him the name of Preserver. But His triumph over Satan gives Him a name above every other—that of Savior. As Savior He both preserves rescued man from destruction and creates a new creature in him—a child of grace. Then the Savior nestles this babe in His bosom and carries him safely past all the commotions of Satan, until at last he reaches heaven.

There is no greater evidence of God's mercy than His plan of redemption. All His other majestic works will flow as rivers into this one mighty sea, on whose shores the saints will stand with great rejoicing. Know this for certain: If we had not been Satan's prisoner first, we would not fully understand or appreciate our deliverance at last.

God permits Satan's temporary reign in order to increase the saint's eternal joy. Does this sound like a paradox? Think about your own life, and you will find that often the occasions for the greatest joy arise from the ashes of suffering. Scripture gives three illustrations of great joy: the joy of a new mother, the joy of a prosperous farmer, and the joy of a successful soldier. The exultation of all three is harvested from hard soil. It costs the travailing woman great pain, the farmer many months of backbreaking labor, and the soldier grave peril, before they come to their reward. But at last they are paid in full. And it is a peculiar attribute of sorrow that its past remembrance so often adds a sweetness to our present joy.

CHRIST VERSUS SATAN

You belong to one camp, and only to one.
Christ will allow no equal, and neither will Satan;
therefore, you cannot side with both.

Christ and Satan create a spiritual dichotomy which you cannot ignore. It divides the whole world. You belong to one camp, and only to one. Christ will allow no equal, and neither will Satan; therefore, you cannot side with both. The test of your allegiance is really quite simple. You are the subject of the one you crown in your heart—not the one you flatter with your tongue.

To know if Christ is really your Prince, answer these questions:

How did your prince come to the throne? You are Satan's subject by birth, just like the rest of the human race. It stands to reason that Satan would not voluntarily resign his place in your heart. And you know you cannot resist his power by your own efforts. Only Christ by His Holy Spirit can bring a change of government to your heart. Have you ever heard a voice from heaven calling out to you as it did to Paul, prostrating you at God's feet and turning you about-face toward heaven? Has Christ come to you like the angel to Peter in prison, wrenching the chains of darkness from your mind and conscience, making you obedient? If so, you may claim to have your freedom.

But if in all this I seem to speak a strange language, and you know no such work to have been done upon your spirit, then I fear you are still in the old prison. Do you suppose for a moment that an invading nation could overthrow a government and the citizens not know? Can one king be dethroned and another crowned in your soul, and you hear no scuffle at all? When Christ is crowned, the joyous celebration at His coronation will resound throughout your whole being. When He comes to you and wrests your spirit from Satan, you will know it. You must say, like the man sent by Jesus to wash in the pool of Siloam, "Whereas I was blind, now I see" (John 9:25). Are you able to say it is thus with you?

OBEYING YOUR MASTER

*Now the same fear that drives the wicked man
away from God, encourages the gracious one
to throw open his heart to the Spirit's knock.*

W*hose law do you obey?* The laws of the prince of dark-ness and the Prince of peace are as contrary as their na-tures—one a law of sin (Romans 8:2), and the other a law of holiness (Romans 7:12). Unless sin has already blinded you so that you can no longer discern between the holy and the profane, you should have no problem resolving this issue.

When Satan comes to tempt you, observe your behavior. How do you respond to his enticements? Do you stand fast on the ordinances of God and refuse to be swayed? Or does your soul embrace the temptation as a bosom friend, glad for an ex-cuse to entertain it? If so, you are under the power of Satan! In the words of Paul, "Know ye not, that to whom ye yield your-selves servants to obey, his servants are ye?" (Romans 6:16).

Where do you go for protection? Who has your confidence? A good prince is eager to protect his subjects. He expects them to trust him with their safety. Obedient subjects therefore com-mit state matters to the wisdom of their prince and his council. When wronged, they appeal for justice; when guilty, they submit to the penalty of the law and bear their proper punishment.

Do you trust the wisdom of God to deal justly with you? An impenitent man is afraid to trust himself to God's care. He knows what a thorough housecleaning his soul needs, but he likes the filth and wants to keep it. So he locks the doors and windows to all that is pure and righteous, and spreads a lusty feast for his own sinful nature to devour in private. Now the same fear that drives the wicked man away from God, encour-ages the gracious one to throw open his heart to the Spirit's knock. He welcomes the prospect of a cleansed soul and under-stands that the purging God sends is to get rid of carnal refuse and make room for added blessings.

RUNNING THE RACE FOR GOD

Have you joined the troops that
fight to subdue the insurrections
of evil men spurred on by Satan?

With whom do you sympathize? He is your prince whose victories and losses you take to heart. What do you say when God's Spirit stands in the threshold of your will and blocks the sin Satan is soliciting? If on Christ's side, you will love Him all the more for keeping you from sin. But if otherwise, you will harbor a grudge against God because He kept you from your heart's real desire. When Satan returns, as he surely will, he will find you still pining for the lust that was turned away from your door. And he always gratifies the soul that longs for sin.

When you see God blessing the efforts of His children, how do you respond? Hearing that the Gospel thrives, does your spirit swell in songs of praise? If you are still a child of the devil, any triumph over sin is a defeat for your camp. The sound of the saints' rejoicing will clang in your ears like a miscast bell. You will go muttering to your house, like Haman, inwardly furious that some favorite sin of yours has been snatched away and given to Christ for destruction. But if God is truly your Father, your heart will leap to hear the bells of victory whenever sin is defeated by your fellow soldiers.

Have you joined the troops that fight to subdue the insurrections of evil men spurred on by Satan? Just standing on the sidelines and cheering other saints to victory is not enough. You too must run the race that is set before you. If you are a saint, you belong to God and you run, not for yourself, but for Him. His desires must come before your own. If subjects could choose where they would like to live, most would ask to stay in the palace with the prince. But usually this is not in the best interests of their lord. So those who love him most not only gladly deny themselves the delicacies of the court, but volunteer for service along the border where the enemy is strongest. And they thank their prince for the honor of serving him!

CITIZENS OF HEAVEN

You serve a prince who knows your heart. Nothing pleases Him more than for you to love Him completely.

Check your heart. If you find that a transfer of title has indeed been made out to Christ, praise God that you are a citizen of heaven and not of hell. Mark the day of your spiritual birth on the calendar of your heart and call for a celebration! It is your marriage day: "I have espoused you to one husband . . . Christ," Paul told the Corinthians (2 Corinthians 11:2). This same Christ has given you the promise of eternal life. Do you know that from the hour you come under His dominion, all the sweet fruit of the tree of life is yours? It is a perfect gift given in perfect love to the bride which He is even now perfecting.

Dear saint, remind yourself often of the change that God has made in you. Satan will tempt you to doubt the wisdom of choosing Christ as your sovereign, so nail God's promises on the upper doorpost of your heart. They will keep your soul in quarantine; Satan will run from them as from the plague. And don't let time erode the memory of the smoky hole where Satan kept you in the bondage of sin, or he may entice you back with his old lies and broken promises. Compare this horror to the taste of heaven you have already received and know that your greatest joy on earth is but a whiff of all that heaven holds.

Clinging to such a wonderful prospect should give you the courage you need to serve Christ faithfully while Satan's principality prospers all around you. You cannot excuse yourself from service. Even though you may not be called to preach and baptize, you can still be used to help those who are. Your prayers whet the minister's sword; they break down barriers so Christ's kingdom can be enlarged.

You serve a prince who knows your heart. Nothing pleases Him more than for you to love Him completely. How He longs to know that if you were free to choose your own king and to make your own laws, you would choose none other than Himself, nor any laws except those He has already decreed.

CHARACTERISTICS OF THE ENEMY

*Only the children of the most
high God dare to oppose him and,
if need be, resist to blood.*

The devils have names of great power ascribed to them in Scripture. Satan is singled out as the most powerful of all. He is called the "strong man" (Luke 11:21)—so strong that he keeps his house in peace, defying all the sons of Adam. We know from our own experience that flesh and blood is no match for him. Christ must come from heaven to destroy him and his works, or we would all die in our sins.

He is also called the "roaring lion" (1 Peter 5:8), the beast that rules the whole jungle. When a lion roars, the sound of his voice so petrifies his prey that he can walk calmly among them and devour them without resistance. Such a lion is Satan, who moves with ease among sinners, preying on them at will (2 Timothy 2:26). He takes them alive as easily as the fowler entices a bird into the net with a scrap of bread. If the truth were known, the devil finds most sinners so naive and spiritless that he needs only to appear with a proposition, and they yield without the slightest twist of the arm. Only the children of the most high God dare to oppose him, and if need be, resist to blood.

Another name for Satan is "the great red dragon," who with his tail (i.e., wicked men) sweeps down the third part of the stars of heaven (Revelation 12:3–4). He is also called "the prince of the power of the air" (Ephesians 2:2), because as a prince he can muster his subjects and call them to report for duty at any time.

But his most powerful title of all is "the god of this world" (2 Corinthians 4:4). It is given to him because sinners grant him a godlike worship, mistakenly holding him in reverence as the saints do God Himself.

The nature of demons also makes them mighty. Remember, these fallen creatures were once angels and have not yet been stripped of all their power. Scripture verifies the potency of angels: "Bless the Lord, ye his angels, that excel in strength," wrote David (Psalm 103:20).

ANGEL'S ROLE IN CREATION

*The devil lost much of his power in relation
to the holy estate in which he was created.
He is an angel still, and still has an angel's power.*

In the works of creation, the superior has power over the inferior: the beasts over the grass and herbs, man over the beasts, and angels over man.

Next, angels are superior because of the spirituality of their nature. The weakness of man resides in his flesh. His soul is made for great enterprises, but it is weighed down by a lump of flesh and must row with a strength suitable to its weak partner. Devils, being angels by virtue of creation, have no such encumbrance, no fumes from a fleshly intellect to cloud their understanding, no clog at their heel to retard their motion. They are as swift as a flame of fire carried on the wind. Being spiritual, they cannot be resisted with human force. Neither fire nor sword can hurt them. No one is strong enough to bind them except God, the Father of spirits.

By his fall the devil lost much of his power in relation to the holy and happy estate in which he was created, but not his natural abilities. He is an angel still, and still has an angel's power.

In addition to their names and nature, the vast number of devils adds to their power. What is lighter than a grain of sand? Yet number makes it weighty. What creature is smaller than lice? Yet what grief a plague of them brought the Egyptians! Think how formidable devils must be, who are by nature so powerful and by number such a multitude. Satan has enough devils to harass the whole earth; not a place under heaven where he has not stationed his troops; not a person on earth without some of these cursed spirits tracking him wherever he goes.

For special service Satan can send a legion to keep garrison in a single person (Mark 5:9). And if he can spare so many to attack one, how many must there be on the muster roll of Satan's whole army? Do not be surprised to find your march to heaven difficult, since you must pass through the very quarters of this demonic multitude.

SATAN'S REIGN

We cannot say there is love among them. Such a heavenly fire cannot burn in a devil's bosom. Yet there is unity and order in their common goal to overcome both God and man.

When God cast these rebels out of heaven, they became aliens on earth. Ever since, they have been wandering fitfully, seeking to do mischief to the children of men—especially those traveling on heaven's road.

Besides their vast number, the unity and order among devils makes their number even more formidable. We cannot say there is love among them. Such a heavenly fire cannot burn in a devil's bosom. Yet there is unity and order in their common goal to overcome both God and man. Knit together not by ligaments of love but of hatred and policy, they know their prospects are utterly hopeless if they do not all agree in their evil design.

How faithful they are to this wicked brotherhood! Our Lord testified to this when He said, "If Satan cast out Satan, he is divided against himself" (Matthew 12:26). Did you ever hear of a mutiny in the devil's army? Or that any of these apostate angels freely yielded one soul to Christ?

They are many, and yet there is but one spirit of wickedness in them all. "My name is Legion; for we are many," the devil said to Christ (Mark 5:9). Note he did not say, *"Our* name . . ."* These cursed spirits work together in their schemes and will enlist human cooperation whenever they can. Not content with bare obedience, they work on the darkest souls to extract an oath of faithfulness, as in the case of witches.

Yet another declaration of the power of devils is their mighty works. What dreadful effects this prince of the power of the air can produce in nature! He is no creator, so he cannot make the least breath of air, drop of water, or spark of fire. But let him loose in God's storehouse, and he will use the Creator's tools so deftly that no man can stand before them. He can hurl the sea into such a commotion that the depths boil like a pot, and fan the air into storms and tempests that threaten to bring the very heavens crashing down to earth.

THE BELIEVER'S SPIRIT IS SAFE

Satan is crafty and admires the wisdom
of God, so he works in the wicked in
much the same way God works in His saints.

Truly, if Satan had no other way to work his will on us except by taking advantage of our frail constitutions, he would still have a great advantage. I grieve to see the soul fallen so far beneath its divine origin! The body, which was intended to be its servant, has instead become its master, and rules with a merciless hand.

Regardless, Satan is not limited to harassing our bodies to get to our souls. He has a nearer way of access. When man first fell, he splintered his soul's barricade against sin and left the way wide open for the spirit Satan to enter, bag and baggage, and make himself at home. He would not leave a soul on earth uninhabited if God did not call a halt to the procession. Christ's saving and keeping power is the only thing that protects anyone from this intruder.

Satan is crafty and admires the wisdom of God, so he works in the wicked in much the same way God works in His saints. God works effectually in the saints (Galatians 2:8; 1 Thessalonians 2:13); Satan works effectually in the children of disobedience (Ephesians 2:2). But the fruits of their labor bear no resemblance at all. The Spirit brings knowledge and righteousness to the saint's heart (Ephesians 5:9), while Satan brings envy and all unrighteousness to the wicked. The Holy Spirit fills with comfort; Satan fills with terror—as with Judas, who first became traitor to his Master and later hangman to himself.

If you are a saint, you do not need to fear that Satan will infiltrate your soul. God will not permit it. But the devil can and does attack along the borders of your faith. Though you are not the proper subject of his power, you are and always will be the chief object of his wrath. He wrestles with you at every opportunity, and you will only overcome him as long as God supplies His strength in your behalf.

PURPOSE IN STUDYING SATAN

*By studying Satan, we see that power
is no basis for pride. Carnal pride
is the illegitimate offspring of power.*

All this study of Satan's power may cause you some discouragement, but that is not my intention at all. These are valuable lessons, which will help you on your march toward heaven and fit you for the kingdom.

By studying Satan, we see that power is no basis for pride. Carnal pride is the illegitimate offspring of power. It is a lust conceived in the womb of Satan, and though your heart may swell at its birth, it will be to your spirit as Cain to Abel—a deadly foe disguised as your next of kin.

Power is the rightful attribute of God alone. We mortals make a poor showing when we claim it as our own, and so does Satan. The devil, in fact, is the most miserable of all God's creatures, and all the more because he has so much power to misuse. Had he lost all his angelic prowess when he fell, he would have gained by his loss. Tremble, therefore, at any power you have unless you use it for God. A plague of locusts is no more destructive in a field of ripened wheat than prideful power is to a man's grace.

Are you powerful? How do you spend this gift from God? On His work, or on the satisfaction of your own lusts? Here is one of Satan's finest instruments of temptation. Power is a citizen of the world and is equal to the task Satan assigns. It dresses itself first in one fashion, then in another—all designed to impress the rest of mankind. And most are so nearsighted, they are taken in by its false show. Sometimes power parades in the finest silks and jewels, pretending that wealth is the key to greatness. Or it dons the robes of a respected profession and disdains to speak to those of meaner occupations. Then it may dress in military regalia and demand the instant obedience of hundreds and thousands of men beneath its rank. Yet for all its show of strength, power is an iridescent bubble floating on the wind. God need only nod His omnipotent head, and it will disappear into nothing.

PRESSING INTO THE KINGDOM

*The closer the Christian gets to heaven,
the more there are who will try to
cheat his soul and steal his crown.*

Happy would devils be, and happy would worldly poten-
tates be, if at the judgment they could appear in the garb
of some poor slave to receive their sentence. On that
day, all their titles and dignity and riches will be read no longer
for their honor, but for their eternal shame and damnation.

I do not doubt—nor should you—that Satan's power makes
it harder to gain heaven. If the devil is so mighty and the way to
heaven so crowded with his mischief-makers, then surely it will
cost us something before we can display our banners on the
walls of the new Jerusalem. If you see someone taking a long,
treacherous journey alone and unprotected, you conclude he
expects no thieves on the road and you might well question his
wisdom. Many pretenders to Christianity travel in a similar fashion. They tell you they are on their way to heaven, yet they
show little inclination to travel in the company of the saints—as
if they had no need of fellowship on the journey! Most of them
go unfortified, without anything even resembling armor. Others
brandish some vain, flighty hopes of the mercy of God, without
so much as a single Scripture for ammunition. Such "hope" is a
rusty pistol and will fly in the fool's face when he tries to use it.

These men, many of whom are highly successful by the
world's standards, never got their earthly fortunes with so little
effort as they expect to get to heaven. They know from experience that fortunes are not won while sleeping, nor are families
provided for by standing around with their hands in their pockets. The farther along the road to success, the more crooks
there are who will try to cheat you. And the closer the Christian
gets to heaven, the more there are who will try to cheat his soul
and steal his crown of glory if they can. Mark this well: You can
never defend yourself alone against Satan; nor with Satan,
against God. But align yourself with Christ, and you will be delivered from both self and Satan.

GOD WILL TAKE CARE OF YOU

All power is of God, whether on earth or in hell.
Get your faith to embrace this truth and you
can walk anywhere with absolute confidence
that Satan can do you no permanent harm.

Praise be to God! Satan's power is mighty, but no reason for you to despair. What a marvelous comfort God gives His children in allowing us to see that we do not need to fear Satan. Let them fear him who fear not God. What are his mountains of power before you, Christian? You serve a God who can make a worm thresh a mountain! (Isaiah 41:15). Surely, then, He can take care of you. The greatest blow Satan can strike at your courage is to cause you to nourish too great a fear of him in your bosom.

I have been told there are wild beasts that, though stronger than the lion, yet tremble when he roars. How many needless hours have you spent trembling at the appearance of Satan when you have the power, in Christ, to trample him under your feet! Strive for a proper perspective of Satan's power, and then this lion will not appear so fierce. Three considerations will relieve you when at any time you are in danger of thinking his power is omnipotent.

In the first place, it is a derived power. It is not his by right, but by permission from another and that other is God. All power is of God, whether on earth or in hell. Get your faith to embrace this truth and you can walk anywhere with absolute confidence that Satan can do you no permanent harm. Do you think for a moment your heavenly Father would give His archenemy a sword too mighty for you, His own child, to overcome? Since God provides the enemies' arms, you can be sure they will be of little use against you if you place yourself under God's protection.

When Pilate tried to frighten Christ by boasting of his power to pardon or condemn his prisoner, Christ replied that Pilate could do nothing ". . . except it were given thee from above" (John 19:11). In other words, "Do your worst, I know who sealed your commission." Satan buffets, man persecutes—but God is the One who gives them both power.

MARCH 22

GOD STANDS BY OUR SIDE

*Not only is Satan's power derived
and limited, it is also subservient
to the overruling power of God.*

There may be times when you feel that God has left you to fight alone. That is when your faith must do its hardest work. Hold fast to the assurance that God is watching every move of Satan and will not let him have the final victory. He can, when God allows it, rob the Christian of much of his peace and joy, but he is always under command. When God says "Stay!" he must stand like a dog by the table while the saints feast on God's comfort. He does not dare to snatch even a tidbit, for the Master's eye is always on him. You lose much comfort when you forget that God's hand is always raised above Satan, and His loving eye is always on you.

Not only is Satan's power derived and limited, it is also *subservient* to the overruling power of God. Whatever mischief he devises is appointed by God for the ultimate service and benefit of the saints. It is as true of the devil as of the proud Assyrian, that " . . . he intendeth not so, neither doth his heart think so" (Isaiah 10:7), for the devil's heart is always bent toward destroying all men.

But God's intention is otherwise, as many wise saints have learned through the ages. When told what had passed at the Diet of Nuremberg against the Protestants, Luther simply said, "It was decreed one way there, but otherwise in heaven." So for the saints' comfort, the thoughts God speeds to them are of peace and preservation, whereas Satan's are of ruin and destruction. Who will doubt that God's thoughts can outrun the devil's?

Know that while Satan is persecuting, God is purging (Daniel 11:35). Most of the stains on your graces get there while you feast on peace and prosperity, and they never recover their whiteness as well as when they have come from under Satan's scouring. He sends discouragement, or grief, or despair to swallow up the saint (as the whale swallowed Jonah). But God uses the tribulation instead to sand and polish your faith, so that in the end it is finer and more precious than ever.

THE DEVIL'S DOMAIN

*But when Christ calls for the final curtain at the end of
this age, Satan will be exposed before everyone, his crown
taken off and his sword broken over his head.*

If you are Christ's, nothing can come into your life without
the permission of God. The One who has given life to yours,
has given death also. The One who has given heaven for
your inheritance has also given the world with all its afflictions—including the prince of this world in all his wrath and
power. This, indeed, is love and wisdom in a riddle. But you
who have the Spirit of Christ can unfold it.

Satan would like nothing better than to convince you that he
is "lord over all," even though he knows this title belongs ex-
clusively to God. Satan is a ruler of the "darkness of this world"
only and is therefore God's subordinate. The boundaries of his
empire are circumscribed and limited. First, the time this
prince rules is "in this world," not hereafter. Second, the place
he rules is "in this world," not heaven. And third, the subjects
whom he rules are "the darkness of this world," not the children of light.

To begin, then, Satan's empire is bounded by time. "This
world" is that little spot of time bounded on either side by vast
eternity. On this stage Satan plays the role of a prince. But when
Christ calls for the final curtain at the end of the age, Satan will
be exposed before everyone, his crown taken off and his sword
broken over his head. He will be driven off the stage in utter
disrepute, to become the eternal prisoner of hell. No more will
he infest the saints or rule the wicked. Instead, both he and all
the members of his cast will lie under the immediate execution
of God's wrath. The long run of their vile acts will be over
forever.

To this very end Christ has His commission, and His work
will not be finished until "he shall have put down all rule and
all authority and power" (1 Corinthians 15:24). Then, and not
until then, He will deliver up His kingdom to the Father, "for
he must reign, till he hath put all enemies under his feet" (v.
25). The question is not *whether* Christ will subdue Satan—but
when.

SATAN'S DAYS ARE NUMBERED

Let the buyer be warned.
Time will show how
Satan has cheated you.

The fact that Satan's days are numbered is bad news for the wicked. Sinners at present have a merry time of it and seem to think it will go on forever. On any given day you can hear them laughing while Christ's disciples weep and mourn. They rustle by in their silks, while the saints shiver in rags. The devil is careful to gratify their sensuous nature, as a prince rewards his courtiers with pensions and preferments. "Am I not able indeed to promote thee to honor?" Balak asked Balaam (Numbers 22:37).

Oh, it is strange—and yet not strange, considering man's degenerate nature—to see how Satan leads sinners by the nose with his gilded hook. Let him but bait it with honor, or wealth, or pleasure, and their hearts strain after it as eagerly as fish for a worm. He can get them to sin for a morsel of bread. It happened to Demas, who forsook the Gospel for the world's pleasures.

An evil heart is so eager to collect the bonuses which the devil promises that it ignores the dreadful wages God threatens to pay for the same work. The men who fall into the devil's snare are those resolved to feast on the fruit of unrighteousness. How it glistens as it hangs on the tree of temptation. One bite, and you want more. But beware! Nothing Satan offers is free of his curse. His rewards are as contaminated as he is. They are poison to the souls of men (1 Timothy 6:9).

Would it not be wise, before you barter with the devil, to ask if his promises come with a warranty? Can he secure the bargain and keep you from a lawsuit with God? Can he guarantee that when you die you will not be left destitute in another world? Let the buyer be warned. Time will show how Satan has cheated you. "Oh, but I have already begun to collect on the pleasures he offers, I am enjoying them right now," the sinner says. "And I would have to wait until heaven for most of the things Christ promises."

THE STORM IS ONLY TEMPORARY

*The clouds that are presently rolling over
your head will pass, and then you will have
fair weather, an eternal sunshine of glory.*

Sinner, you are right to say your pleasure is now, for you cannot be sure it will last for another moment. Your present happiness is going, and that of the saints, though future, is coming, never to end. Will you, like Esau for a gulp of pottage and immediate gratification, part with the eternal inheritance of God's kingdom? What desperate madness makes sinners refuse a little hardship of the present? They foolishly choose to endure the eternal wrath of God hereafter in exchange for the short feast Satan spreads for them. If Satan keeps you royally entertained for a lifetime, what is that to eternity?

Let this encourage those of you who belong to Christ: The storm may be tempestuous, but it is only temporary. The clouds that are presently rolling over your head will pass, and then you will have fair weather, an eternal sunshine of glory. Can you not watch with Christ for one hour?

Bid faith look through the keyhole of the promise and see what God has laid up for those that love Him. You serve a God who keeps covenant forever. Having already bathed in the fountain of His tender mercies, how can you stand on this side of eternity, afraid to wet your feet with those short-lived sufferings which, like a little splash of water, run between you and glory?

Besides being bound by time, Satan's empire is also confined as to place. The devil rules in this world only. He cannot ascend to heaven, not even if he marshals all the power of all his demon hosts. The rebel who once shared intimately in God's glory has not dared even to look into that holy place since he was first expelled. So he ranges to and fro here below as a vagabond, excommunicated from the presence of God though not from the saints on their way to heaven. You can, if you will, take this fact as a source of great joy: Satan has no power where your eternal happiness lies!

YOUR NAME IN THE BOOK OF LIFE

*The devil's principality is bounded
not only by place and time, but also
by those he is allowed to govern.*

E ven while confined to this earth, you can be confident that your Father is watching over you. The devil took away Job's purse and left him temporarily destitute, but Job had a God in heaven who replenished his account. As a saint, you have some collateral: your stock of faith, and your deed of inheritance as a citizen of heaven. These are great security both now and for the future. Satan knows it, and will do his best to snatch them away from you. But no matter how hard he tries he cannot blot your name from the Book of Life. He cannot annul your faith, make void your relationship with God, or dry up the spring of your comfort though he may dam up the stream for awhile. Nor can he hinder the glorious outcome of your whole war with sin. God, who is said to preserve us by His power "through faith unto salvation ready to be revealed in the last time" (1 Peter 1:5), keeps all these things in heaven among His own crown jewels, well out of Satan's reach.

Satan's empire is also restricted as to subjects. The devil's principality is bounded not only by place and time, but also by those he is allowed to govern. They are described as "the darkness of this world" or, more simply, those who are in darkness.

The word darkness is sometimes used in Scripture to express the condition of a person in great distress (Isaiah 50:10), sometimes to describe the nature of all sin (Ephesians 5:11), and sometimes to refer to the particular sin of ignorance. It is often compared to the darkness of night or to physical blindness. To enlighten this particular passage, I will take the word in the two following interpretations: first, for the darkness of sin in general; and second, for the darkness of ignorance in particular.

Mark this distinction before we begin: The devil's rule is over those who are in a state of sin and ignorance, not over those who are sometimes sinful or ignorant.

A VEIL OVER THE WORD

*A man in a state of sin is under the
same plague. He can do nothing profitable
until God lifts the darkness from his soul.*

To a sinner, the light of truth is more blistering than a desert sun at mid-day (John 3:19). He shuns to walk where it is shining, and when exposed to it, will spare no expense to get relief. Satan is always at his elbow, ready to help him find a way to hide from its penetrating rays.

Does he hear the truth in a powerful sermon? Satan will sit alongside him in the pew and whisper nonsense to distract him. He may ask his plans for dinner, or what is on the docket for tomorrow. And if the sermon gets too hot, the devil will dull his senses and get him to doze until the service is over. Suppose a man's conscience strains toward the truth. Satan may then send him to hear a cool preacher, whose senseless prattle will tickle his fancy rather than prick his conscience. Oh, he may preach from the word of God, but he does it gingerly. He is too cowardly to use the Sword of the Spirit in all its might and power, lest he "offend" some members of his congregation. Many who dare to handle the truth and even admire it when encased in a scabbard would faint on the spot to see it drawn and bared.

Both sin and darkness cause distress. What could the Egyptians do under the plague of darkness but sit still and hope it would pass? A man in a state of sin is under the same plague. He can do nothing profitable until God lifts the darkness from his soul. The epitaph of every impenitent sinner could fitly read: "Here lies one who never did an hour's work for God."

And if he can do God no service while kept in darkness, neither can he help himself. Pity the man whose darkness hides the disservice he does to his own soul! He is like one who stands helplessly in a dark cellar, supposing himself trapped and doomed to die. But if a candle were lit, he would find the key to the door within easy reach. Christ is the candle that lights the way out of man's darkness.

LIGHT VERSUS DARKNESS

If you will cry out to Him,
He will hear and will come
to your rescue at once.

On this earth there is some mixture of darkness and light, even for the vilest sinner—some peace with trouble, some pleasure with pain, some hope of pardon. But in eternity there is darkness to the utmost. There the fire of wrath will burn without slacking, and sin keep pace with utter torment.

Satan is called the "ruler of the darkness of this world." All those in a state of darkness are therefore under his rule by God's decree. Scripture tells us sinners are the very dwelling place of the devil. Do you recall the account where the unclean spirit determined to "return into my house" (Matthew 12:44)? It is as though he said, "I have walked among the saints of God, knocking at this door and that, and no one will let me in. But I know who will. I will go back to my own house, where I am sure to rule with complete control." And sure enough, when he returns he finds it empty and ready for his enjoyment. Every inclination of the soul is employed to make the house trim and handsome for the master.

Those in darkness have no power to resist Satan. He rules the whole man, shaping his apprehensions and distorting his perceptions. If he reads the Scripture, Satan stands by with his own running commentary, twisting the truth into a maze of lies. If he shows any distaste for sin, Satan has him view it through the rose-colored glasses of compromise. And while the sinner may think his insight is greatly improved, in truth, he remains under manifold delusions. In fact, Satan is so gracious in lending this or that instrument of unrighteousness, he often is taken for a friend rather than a cruel master. But a man can no sooner cut the tether by which Satan keeps him pastured in sin than the woodsman's axe can chop a tree of its own accord.

Yet here is hope for everyone: Christ the Good Shepherd is standing by. If you will cry out to Him, though it be no louder than the pitiful bleating of the weakest lamb, He will hear and will come to your rescue at once.

SATAN'S INTERFERENCE

Let those who will, mock and scorn
your faith. What is heaven worth
if you cannot bear a little shame?

When Pharaoh observed the Israelites' thoughts turning back to God, he knew it was a dangerous sign. He supposed he could hinder their spiritual deliverance by increasing their physical bondage, so he intensified their workload. Satan does the same with his slaves, keeping them too busy to think of heaven or hell. He never leaves them, always working to intercept any thoughts of grace, mercy, peace, or repentance sent by the Holy Spirit.

Satan interferes with God's messengers. When God sent Moses to deliver Israel, Satan sent Jannes and Jambres to resist him (Exodus 7:11; cf. 2 Timothy 3:8). When Paul preached truth to the deputy, Elymas countered with lies (Acts 13:8). Satan has spies on every corner, watching the activities of the saints. When God sends His children on an errand of mercy to a sinner, these spies race to beat them and block their way.

Sinner, be especially wary of carnal friends and relatives when you decide to follow Christ. Resolve that if your own children grab you by the ankles and try to hold you back from Him, you will drive them away. And if your father and mother throw themselves in front of you, you will step over their backs if you must, to get to Christ. Let those who will, mock and scorn your faith. What is heaven worth if you cannot bear a little shame? If they spit on your face, Christ will wipe it off. They may laugh at you now, but not later. The final outcome has already been declared, and you have sided with the victor.

Satan distracts sinners with delays. He does not fear fleeting thoughts of repentance. I doubt there are many in hell who did not at one time or another give some thought to repenting, but Satan was always able to carry them away on some more urgent business. Sinner, if you ever hope to escape, run for your life —away from Satan, away from your lusts, away from your present joys if they are the handiwork of Satan. The devil says, "Tomorrow." God says "Today." Whom will you obey?

CONSCIENCE SHOULD SOUND THE ALARM

*Our omniscient God has known all along that the way
to heaven can never be found in the dark; that is
why He sent His Son as the Light of the world.*

Conscience is God's alarm to wake the sinner up, but it can only be a witness to what it knows. If not informed of the truth, it will not sound when heresy or sin creeps in and sets fire to your soul. And if you do not wake up and quench the flames with timely repentance, you will burn forever.

Ignorance locks out the means of rescue. Friends and ministers stand outside and cannot save a burning man if he will not let them in. Neither threats nor promises are of any use if you are counseling a willfully ignorant man. He fears not the one and desires not the other. Write "Danger!" as large as you can, and paint it red; it will no more serve as a warning to a blind man than to a dumb ox.

Yet there will be times in a sinner's life when, by the grace of God's Holy Spirit, he senses the oppression of his soul and longs for deliverance. So he feels around for an avenue of escape. There are some ways which at first seem right to him, and Satan will lead him on a merry chase down one dead-end street after another to keep him off heaven's road. "Try good works," he will say. "That will lift your spirits." Or, "Make some new resolutions and promise yourself to be a better person from now on. What more could God expect from you?" But at last, exhausted and disillusioned by all his misguided meanderings, the sinner looks up to find himself right back where he started —a slave to sin and darkness!

Our omniscient God has known all along that the way to heaven can never be found in the dark; that is why He sent His Son as the Light of the world. There is but one safe exit from your darkened state, one way of escape—through Jesus Christ our Lord. Let your faith join hands with His promise of eternal life for all who believe on Him, and He will lead you out of darkness and into the glorious light of the Gospel.

A WORD TO PARENTS

*I have never known a true saint who was
not deeply concerned about his child's
relationship with the heavenly Father.*

Parents, your children have souls which God expects you to nourish with at least as much care as you lavish on their physical needs. Who will teach them if not you? No one is surprised to hear that a ship put out to sea without a compass has sunk or run aground. Why should we be surprised to see children wander far from God, when they have received no spiritual direction?

We see a pattern set for us by the saints of old. David, busy king that he was, thought it his solemn responsibility to instruct his son in the ways of the Lord: "Know thou the God of thy father, and serve him with a perfect heart and with a willing mind" (1 Chronicles 28:9). And what need I tell you of Timothy's mother and grandmother, who taught him the Scriptures from the time he was a child? I believe a man calls in question his own Christianity if he does not bother to acquaint his child with God and the way that leads to Him. I will even go so far as to say I have never known a true saint who was not deeply concerned about his child's relationship with the heavenly Father.

You will give a poor account at the Last Day if all you can say is, "Lord, here are my children, I bred them gentlemen and left them wealthy." What a mocking witness to your own folly that you would do so much for that which rusts, and nothing for a knowledge of God unto salvation, which endures forever!

A careful study of the principles of God will show how serious this matter is. If we neglect the spiritual training of our children, we fail on many fronts.

You obviously fail your children when you leave them ignorant. Faith and disbelief are fundamentally different, not only by definition but in the way they operate as well. Faith will not grow without planting, and will die even where it is planted unless it is watered and fertilized with the Word of God.

TRAINING YOUR CHILDREN

*Do your best while they are young
and in your constant care, to win them
to God and set them on the road to heaven.*

Y ou also fail yourselves by leaving your children in a state
of ignorance, for you heap upon yourselves the consequences of their sins as well as your own. When a child
breaks one of God's commandments, it is his sin; but it is also
the father's if he never taught the child what the commandment
of God was. Wicked children become heavy crosses to their parents. When a father or mother must trace the source of wickedness to his or her own neglect in training the child, cross is laid
upon cross and the load becomes unbearable. Can there be a
greater heartache in this life than to see your own child running
full speed toward hell, and know that you were the one who
outfitted him for the race? Oh, do your best while they are
young and in your constant care, to win them to God and set
them on the road to heaven.

Most important, you fail God when you rear an ignorant
child. Scripture tells of those who hold the truth in unrighteousness. Among others, this includes parents who lock up the
knowledge of salvation from their children. Where is the parent
who will rob his own son's house? Yet this is what you do if you
neglect his spiritual education. For you keep in your own pocket the gold talent God intended you to give to your child. If you
leave no godly inheritance, what will happen when you die, and
the truth of the Gospel is buried alongside your rotting bones?

If you are God's child, then your children stand in closer relationship to the heavenly Father than the children of unbelievers. God depends on you to nurture them as you have been
nurtured, and to protect them at all costs from the devil's education. Training your children up in the ways of the Lord is no
casual suggestion. Your refusal to obey, whether the product of
deliberation or neglect, will pay you bitter wages when you
stand before the King of kings in the judgment.

IGNORANCE OF TRUTH

The less time you have,
the more diligence you
must use to gain knowledge.

E very ignorant soul is the willing slave of Satan!
Are you young? Inquire after God early, while your talents are fresh and your memory is strong. The feet of those lusts which have carried millions of others to perdition stand ready to carry you off the same way. How easy you make their task when you refuse to open the eyes of your understanding and fortify yourself with the knowledge of God.

Perhaps you intend to rouse up from the sleep of ignorance at the eleventh hour, which you suppose is many years away. How foolish! You cannot see the hands on God's clock; therefore, you cannot know how long your stay in the world will be. If you die ignorant of God and His law, what will become of you? The prospect is not pleasant. The small twigs and the old logs—supple young sinners and withered old ones—will meet and burn together.

Are you old and still ignorant? Perhaps you hear nature tolling the passing bell. You know you will shortly come to the end of the road that leads into eternity, but you cannot see what lies in the darkness beyond. The less time you have, the more diligence you must use to gain knowledge. Though knowing the truth of the Gospel is no guarantee of salvation, gross ignorance of it is a sure guarantee of damnation.

Are you poor and ignorant? Your sin is not your poverty, but rather your ignorance of where the true treasure lies. "Better is a poor and wise child than an old and foolish king, who will no more be admonished" (Ecclesiastes 4:13). If the princes of the world could only see the end from the beginning, they would beg to trade their ermine robes for the saints' rags. Christian, new robes are being made for you in heaven, which you shall put on—while they shall be left naked in their shame.

APRIL 3

USING THE KNOWLEDGE YOU HAVE

Do not hesitate to pray boldly.
God gives wisdom to all who ask,
and He gives generous, heaping portions.

Perhaps you have only a small light to lead you into truth. If so, follow it closely. When it casts a shadow on anything—even the smallest speck—convincing you it is sin, flee from it at once. Or if your light leads you into action for the Lord, follow eagerly and wholeheartedly. How else will your knowledge of the truth grow fat and healthy, unless you exercise it regularly?

Here is a word of caution: use your knowledge properly. God will not bless anyone who uses knowledge as an excuse to sin. Nor will He increase your knowledge of Him if you keep it shut up in your conscience, afraid to confess Him before men. The light of truth in a man's heart is like a candle flame—it must have air to flourish. If you keep it hidden for very long, what little knowledge you have will be taken away. Learn a lesson from what happened to the heathen described in Romans who "[held] the truth in unrighteousness . . . and their foolish heart was darkened" (Romans 1:18, 21).

Pray for more wisdom. God is the repository of all knowledge and wisdom. To excel in the school of divinity, you must study upon your knees. This is the way to place yourself under God's tutelage. You may attend lectures or study in the world's great universities to gain a knowledge of Scripture, but wisdom to apply its precepts comes from God alone. If you wish to be wise, pray, pray, pray! Holy conversing with Him yields sanctified knowledge.

Do not hesitate to pray boldly. God gives wisdom to all who ask, and He gives generous, heaping portions. Never be ashamed to go to Him in your ignorance. He is not like those rude, unfeeling teachers we have seen who seem to delight in mocking the ignorance of their pupils. He is a kind teacher, and your desire to learn pleases Him. While everyone does not achieve the same level of understanding in this life, all who come with earnest, open hearts will receive ample instruction to prepare them for the kingdom of heaven.

SEARCH THE SCRIPTURES

*Strive for wisdom, not so that men
will respect and admire you, but so
that they will celebrate God's greatness.*

The Word of God is called a light unto our feet—not to our tongues, merely to speak about—but to our feet, to walk by. Getting knowledge is *your* work; opening your heart to understand is the work of the Holy Spirit. But you must ask Him for wisdom and believe He will give it to you. God has promised wisdom to those who "ask in faith, nothing wavering" (James 1:6). Strive for wisdom, not so that men will respect and admire you, but so that they will celebrate God's greatness. The end of every human effort should be to magnify His name. Go to God with David's prayer on your lips: "Make me to understand the way of thy precepts: so shall I talk of thy wondrous works" (Psalm 119:27).

Do not give up when the lessons are long or hard to understand. Scripture promises, "Then shall we know, if we follow on to know the Lord" (Hosea 6:3). The mysteries of Christ are not learned in a day. Too many read a chapter or two in the Bible, then for lack of interest put it down for weeks at a time and never look at it. Bernard compares the study of the Word and the mere reading of it to the difference between a close friendship and a casual acquaintance. If you want genuine knowledge, he says, you will have to do more than greet the Word politely on Sundays or nod reverently when you chance to meet it on the street. You must walk with it and talk with it every day of the week. You must invite it into your private chambers, and forego other pleasures and worldly duties to spend time in its company.

Do you long for greater intimacy with your heavenly Father? Then meditate often and long on His Word. David likens the Word for sweetness to honey and the honeycomb. Like the honeycomb, the Bible is so rich and full that at first reading some wisdom will now and then drop from it. But unless you press it by meditation, you leave the most behind.

PRACTICE SPIRITUAL DISCIPLINE

*I sincerely believe a poor
foundation is the reason
many are not steadfast today.*

Christians who are not instructed in the fundamentals of Christianity are not likely to mature into solid saints. I sincerely believe a poor foundation is the reason many are not steadfast today. Dear saint, do not be too proud to go back and learn the basic precepts of the Gospel if you have not yet mastered them. Too many are more concerned about their reputation than their salvation.

Wait on the ministry of the Word. The apostle cautioned the Hebrew Christians not to neglect church attendance (Hebrews 10:25). If you say you want to know God's truth, but neglect to go where the Word is preached, you are as insincere as the man who says he wants to watch the sun set but will not bother to turn his chair toward the west.

To know God, you must come to where He has appointed you to learn. If there is a church, go. If there is none, study your Bible diligently and wait on the ministry of the Spirit at home. You can trust your heavenly Father to use extraordinary measures to honor your demand for spiritual food. He is like a father who, if there is no school in town, teaches his child at home and turns him into an excellent scholar. God, Paul tells us, "maketh manifest the savor of his knowledge by us in every place" (2 Corinthians 2:14).

God's Word is filled with good things for your soul. He wants you to have them all, so see to it that you are a wakeful and attentive student. Strive to be like Lydia, who "attended unto the things which were spoken by Paul" (Acts 16:14). When you go to church, try to fix your quicksilver mind and set yourself to hear the sermon. Above all, make sure your heart is consumed with love for God, and your will is in submission to His desires. The mind goes on the will's errand; we spend our thoughts on what our hearts propose.

THE NATURE OF EVIL SPIRITS

*Frequently the devil himself is
called a spirit: the "unclean spirit,"
"foul spirit," "lying spirit."*

The inherent nature of the devils themselves, as well as the character of their works, is included in the description, "spiritual wickedness." A literal rendering of the passage reads, "against the spirituals of wickedness." Some interpret this to mean "against wicked spirits." That is true, as far as it goes. But it overlooks an additional truth, in that the passage refers not only to the spiritual nature of devils but also—in fact, chiefly—to the nature and kind of sins they perpetrate. These sins are the apples of temptation which they most often use to poison the saints. Such sins are the "spirituals of wickedness." Not gross, fleshly sins which ignorant sinners, like swine, wallow in—but *spiritual sins,* which are much more subtle and perhaps even more despicable.

This brief phrase, "against spiritual wickedness," when taken in context, presents us with three doctrinal conclusions: (1) The devils are spirits; (2) The devils are consummately wicked spirits; and (3) These wicked spirits use spiritual wickedness both to persecute the saints and to provoke them to sin.

The devils are *spirits.* The word *spirit* has several meanings in Scripture. It is often used to describe angels, both good and evil ones (Hebrews 1:14; 1 Kings 22:21). Frequent the devil himself is called a spirit: the "unclean spirit," "foul spirit," "lying spirit."

What, then, are spirits? And, more particularly, what are the special characteristics of evil spirits?

First of all, they are *immaterial*—not made of matter like humans. "Handle me, and see," Christ said to His disciples, who thought they had seen a spirit, "for a spirit hath not flesh and bones, as ye see me have" (Luke 24:39). We have no evidence to indicate that sin altered Satan's basic substance. As Lucifer, son of the morning, his essence was immaterial; as Satan, prince of darkness, he is immaterial still.

THE NATURE OF EVIL SPIRITS

*The wisest human being is as far
from the angels' intelligence
as the earth is from the heavens.*

F allen man, helplessly immersed in the flesh, will not readily believe what he cannot see with his mortal eyes. On the same grounds, we might deny the existence of God Himself, because He is invisible.

What a clever trick on the part of Satan, to make us think that if we cannot see something, it does not exist! A sinner may carry Satan in his heart and walk all day long in his company, yet never notice him. Like a horse with blinkers, he feels the crack of the whip that drives him to selfish ambition or lustful desires, but never sees the face of the driver. But Satan is there—whether you see him or not. When your passions are on a runaway course, hell-bound for destruction, you can be sure it is the devil himself who spurs them on.

Another characteristic of spirits is that they are highly *intellectual.* They are smarter than other creatures because they come closest by creation to the nature of God. By diligent study, men have accumulated vast stores of scientific knowledge. Still, the wisest human being is as far from the angels' intelligence as the earth is from the heavens.

No doubt the fallen angels lost the use of much of their celestial knowledge—all their wisdom as holy angels, in fact. What they now know of God has lost its savor, and they have no power to use it for their own good. Jude's assessment of wicked men applies to them: They misuse the knowledge they have been given to corrupt themselves further (v. 10). They know the holiness of God, but do not love Him for it. They know the evil of sin, and do not love it the less. And though they are utter fools with regard to their own destiny, evil spirits are more than a match for all the saints on earth—except for one thing: We have Almighty God to play our game for us!

SATAN'S NATURE AS A SPIRIT

*Devils do not die. They will track you to your grave,
and if you die Christless, they will meet you in
another world to accuse and torment you there also.*

I n addition to being immaterial and highly intellectual, spirits
gain a distinct advantage by being immortal. Of other enemies, you may hear at last that "they are dead which sought
[thy] life," as the angel told Joseph concerning Herod (Matthew
2:20). Wicked men walk a turn or two upon the stage, then are
called off by death; so end their plots. But devils do not die.
They will track you to your grave, and if you die Christless, they
will meet you in another world to accuse and torment you there
also.

These wicked spirits are indefatigable. When the fight is
over among men, even the conqueror must sit down and catch
his breath. His strength has a limit. Other men, successful by
human standards but deprived of their own personal goals, lose
their will to fight and give up in despair. Tertullian said of Dio-
cletian that he threw down his scepter in a fit of pique when he
was unsuccessful at stamping out Christianity. He could not kill
Christ's followers as fast as they were being born into the kingdom, so at last he gave up altogether and sought some other
fiendish amusement.

But the devil never becomes dispirited, nor does he tire of
doing mischief to the souls of men. He has not stood still for a
moment since he first began to walk to and fro in the earth (Job
1:7). Indeed, God Himself must bind him hand and foot to stop
his feverish activities.

Not only are devils spirits, but they are *extremely wicked*
spirits. God is called the Holy One because none is as holy as
the Lord. The devil is called the "wicked one" because he is
uniquely evil (Matthew 13:19). What we know of him from
Scripture gives us a measure of the height of his wickedness,
and can be used to judge the degrees of sins and sinners among
men. The formula is simple. The more we are like God, the ho-
lier we are; the more like the devil, the more wicked.

LEADING OTHERS ASTRAY

*Those who tempt others plant their
own wickedness in fertile fields
and raise up new seed to the devil.*

To the end of the world, every age will exceed the previous one in its degree of sinning. Ishmael and the mockers of the old world will look like children and bunglers compared to the scoffers and cruel persecutors of the last days.

Think twice before you use your intelligence to invent new sins! You may provoke God to new punishments. Sodom devised a new way to sin, so God devised a new way to discipline them: He sent hell from above upon them.

These same demons who invented sin are likewise the chief *promoters* of it. The apostate angels were not only the inventors of sin, but are also its chief enterprisers. These spirits are therefore called "the tempter," and sin is called "the work of the devil," no matter who commits it—just as the credit for the design of a house goes to the architect, even though other men do the actual construction.

When you cause anyone to sin, you take the devil's office out of his hands. Let him do it himself if he can, but *never* allow him to use you as his hireling. Tempting someone else to sin is worse than sinning yourself. Those who tempt others plant their own wickedness in fertile fields and raise up new seed to the devil. To cultivate the devil's crop of sin with the evil in your own heart shows sin is mighty in you indeed. Parents, especially, must guard against such a heinous act. What are they but devils incarnate who, by their own example, teach their children the devil's catechism—to swear and lie and drink?

Do you not know what you do when you tempt? I will tell you. You do that which cannot be undone by your own repentance. You contaminate your family and friends with error, and send them rushing to join the devil's throng. Later, you may see your mistake and turn from your wicked way. But can you force those you have led astray to fight against the press of the worldly crowd to get to Jesus at all cost?

SATAN'S INCESSANT HATRED

If he could, he would not leave one of Christ's
flock alive. Such is the height of his malice
against God, whom he hates with a perfect hatred.

Your heart may break, like Lamech's, with the weight of your sorrow. But unfortunately their rescue is out of your hands. What a grief to your spirit to see them on the road to hell and know you paid the toll, yet not be able to call them back! Even after you are dead and gone, your sins may be perpetuated in those who are alive, generation after generation.

Devils are *maliciously and incessantly wicked.* Fallen angels are not just incidentally or occasionally wicked, but willfully and constantly wicked. The devil's name, "wicked one," denotes his spiteful nature, his desire to vex and harass others. He draws souls to sin, not because he tastes any sweetness or finds any profit in such enterprise. He has too much light to have any real joy or peace in sin. He knows his doom, and trembles at the thought of it. Yet his spiteful nature drives him mercilessly. He is as bloodthirsty for souls as a mad dog for sheep. The difference is that the dog will finally drop in exhaustion, whereas Satan never tires of his work as a butcher of souls.

Though he toils for the eternal damnation of every soul, the devil's open vengeance is most often directed toward the saints. If he could, he would not leave one of Christ's flock alive. Such is the height of malice against God, whom he hates with a perfect hatred. And because he cannot reach Him with a direct blow, he strikes at Him secondhand through the saints. He knows that the life of God is in a very real sense bound up in theirs. If you are even now feeding in God's green pastures and drinking from the well of His mercy, beware. Satan is sure to attack. He knows the honor God receives on this earth is directly related to the flow of His mercy. He therefore labors to build a dam with his wicked deeds that will stop the flow of mercy to the saints. This is the worst that can be said of these wicked demons: They maliciously spite God, and in God, the glory of His mercy.

GOD USES SATAN TO CONVICT

*The most sincere philanthropist or moral crusader has
within him the same seeds of corruption, the same
potential for wickedness as the devil himself.*

If the measure of a man's own good works compares favorably to everyone else's—i.e., if they are not noticeably meaner or viler than his neighbor's—he thinks he can pass God's
inspection. Before the Holy Spirit can convict such a person of
his need of Christ, he must agree with God that all his righteousness is but filthy rags. It may help him understand his own
wickedness if he sees how utterly polluted the spring is that incessantly feeds it.

Can you somehow get a mental picture of the monstrous in-
tensity of Satan's wickedness? Then you have an idea of every
man's potential for evil. The finest human being—the most sincere philanthropist or moral crusader—has within him the
same seeds of corruption, the same potential for wickedness as
the devil himself. If his true nature has not yet shown through,
it is because God's grace is intervening. For until you are made
a new creature in Christ, you are of the same brood as the Serpent; his seed is in you. And the devil can only beget a child
like himself.

Sinner, if you do not blossom into Satan's likeness here on
earth, you can be sure you will in hell. There the flames will
wash off the paint that hides your true complexion. In heaven,
the saints will be like the angels in alacrity, love, and constancy
to God; in hell, the damned will be like the devils, in sin as well
as in punishment. Before you excuse yourself by claiming
"good intentions," know this: If your heart is good, then so is
the devil's! His nature is wicked, and so is yours! The blemishes
which you think are so small and insignificant are symptoms of
a deadly disease within. Without Gospel medicine—the blood
of Christ—applied to you personally, you will die a leper. Sin is
a hereditary disease that increases with age: a young sinner will
be an old devil. And the malady is always passed on to the next
generation.

OUR INNER REBELLION

Do you think your pleasure or profit is his goal?
Not likely! His aspirations are all for himself.
He has a personal grudge against God.

C an you honestly say that when God first came to you your
thoughts were pure and your intentions holy? Were you
not already armed with the weapons of rebellion—a covetous spirit, a deceitful heart, a lying tongue? Oh, yes, you had a
nature fully charged with enmity against God. It lay like unfired
gunpowder, waiting for a flame! Fall on your knees in humble
gratitude to the One who sent His Spirit and grace to stop you,
even while your nature meditated on nothing but war against
God and His laws.

One reason we are so easily persuaded to sin is because we
do not understand Satan's purpose. He does with men in sinning as generals do with them in fighting. Captains beat their
drums for volunteers, promising pay and promotions to all who
enlist. The guarantee of such excellent benefits makes soldiers
come streaming it, with little or no thought as to whether the
ground of war is just. Satan entices to sin by giving golden
promises of rewards for entering his service—power, fame, or
fortune. Many foolish souls are won by his clever arguments
and the prodding of their own greedy natures. Few bother to
ask, "Why is the devil so eager to have me join his ranks?"

Shall I tell you? Do you think your pleasure or profit is his
goal? Not likely! His aspirations are all for himself. He has a personal grudge against God, and he brings you, by sinning, to join
his quarrel. What he fails to mention is that you jeopardize your
very soul to defend his pride and lust. But he is hardly worried
about your welfare. He loses no more sleep over your certain
damnation than a demented general does over the men he
sends on a suicide mission. Knowing this, why would you ever
join Satan in his fight against God? He sends you on a suicide
mission! This bloody Joab will order you where no one ever
came out of alive. If you stand where God's bullets fly, you are a
dead man, unless you throw down your arms and surrender at
once.

SPIRITUAL SINS

*Paul calls them "filthiness of the spirit"
and sets them apart from filthiness
of the flesh (2 Corinthians 7:1).*

Some sins are more specifically "spiritual sins" than others. Two kinds stand out especially: (1) sins kept within the confines of the heart; and (2) sins directly related to spiritual topics—idolatry, spiritual pride, atheism, heresy, and the like. Paul calls them "filthiness of the spirit" and sets them apart from filthiness of the flesh (2 Corinthians 7:1).

When the spirit or the heart is the stage whereon sin is enacted, it is a spiritual sin; such are all impure thoughts, vile affections, and desires which do not break forth into overt action but are nonetheless real acts of the inner man. As with all sin, Satan is the great, unseen instigator of every sin of the heart.

When thoughts and feelings overtake you that you know are not pleasing to God, what can you do? You do not want to be critical—but you are; you do not want to covet—but you do. How can you take these stones of offense and rocks of stumbling Satan hurls into the path of your thoughts, and use them to build a monument of glory to the Father? In two ways in particular: by keeping a close watch on your heart and by steadfastly resisting its sins.

First, keep a close watch on your heart. What welcome does Satan find when he comes with these "spirituals of wickedness" and asks you to dwell on them? I do not ask whether such guests step inside your door. If we had God's ability to look into man's heart, we would see the worst of sins stirring in every Christian. That they have been scattered on the field of our hearts, we already know, and by whom—the grim sower, Satan. What is important is whether he finds our hearts a fertile field or whether, with holy thoughts and earnest prayer, we pour oil upon them and light a match to them, so that they are consumed in a holy fire.

INNER THOUGHTS OF THE HEART

When wicked or unclean thoughts first force
their way into your mind, you have not
yet sinned. This is the work of the devil!

Most of us would never commit murder, but how often have we taken a neighbor into some dark alley of our thoughts and there torn him limb from limb with a desire for revenge over some petty quarrel?

Christian, this is imperative for you to realize: When wicked or unclean thoughts first force their way into your mind, you have not yet sinned. This is the work of the devil! But if you so much as offer them a chair and begin polite conversation with them, you have become his accomplice. In only a short time you will give these thoughts sanctuary in your heart. Your resolve—not to yield to a temptation you are already entertaining—is no match for Satan and the longings of the flesh.

Your confidence must rest on this fact: Unclean thoughts will not stay where the love of Christ reigns supreme. They are as panicked by overhearing your conversations with Christ as an escaped murderer would be upon realizing he has been spotted in town. And well they should be—for your holy thoughts will track down these evil thoughts and kill them on the spot. Both the trial and the sentence will be speedy.

Secondly, steadfastly resist sins of the heart, thereby showing where your loyalties lie. We need to be constantly reminded that heart sins are sins as much as any: "The thought of foolishness is sin" (Proverbs 24:9). Every point of hell is hell! Lust, envy, and murder are sins when committed in the heart, the same as in the outward act. Such thoughts cannot run rampant in a Christian without serious consequences. Your spirit is the dwelling place of the Holy Spirit; He takes up the whole heart for His lodging. When He sees you have leased out rooms to the lusts of the devil, it is time for Him to be gone. If you cherish His presence, declare your loyalty to Christ at Satan's first knock by renouncing every thought that is not a willing captive of God.

MONITORING YOUR THOUGHT LIFE

The bee will not sit on a flower that has no nectar.
Neither should the Christian entertain
a thought that does not feed his spirit.

Here is a quick way to check your heart. Are your thoughts good or evil? When good, do you give credit to Christ? When evil, are you appalled and determined to expel these nasty urchins? If so, you show that these spirituals of wickedness are more Satan's than your own.

Besides evil thoughts, there are others that should also be unwelcome. These are empty, frothy, vain imaginations. Though you may not find them so abominable in themselves, still they keep you from something better. And who among us has time to waste in this life? Like the water that runs beside the mill, every thought that does not help you do God's work is wasted. The bee will not sit on a flower that has no nectar. Neither should the Christian entertain a thought that does not feed his spirit.

Even your good thoughts are not impervious to Satan's tampering. For instance, you may be overcome with the guilt of your sins and honestly mourn before the Lord. Yet if you become consumed with remorse, you are in danger of losing your faith in God's glorious promise of redemption by His grace. Or perhaps your thoughts turn to the needs and care of your family. Providing for your own is certainly scriptural. But if you worry so much about this responsibility that you forget God is the real provider, you again show a serious deficiency of faith.

We are instructed to learn and observe the whole counsel of God. What will it profit to light upon one of God's commandments and show it to be your favorite, if you slight all the rest? You will be in as much trouble as the person whose surgeon restores the flow of blood in a minor vein, but in the process severs a major artery. Such carelessness is likely to maim the man, if not kill him outright. Your soul is a delicate creature, and requires the utmost skill to maintain its equilibrium. Be constantly on your guard against concentrating so hard on one or two of God's ordinances, that you have no time for all the others.

SPIRITUAL SINS

Why is Satan so obsessed with perverting God's principles?
For one thing, God highly honors His truth (Psalm 138:2).
He is more scrupulous about it than all His other works.

S ins may be labeled spiritual sins because of the topics they address. Like sins which are committed in your heart, these "spiritual wickednesses" corrupt the inner man rather than the body. Satan enjoys great success with them. For your edification, study the following two, which are favorites of his: errors involving spiritual principles, and errors resulting in spiritual pride.

First let us consider errors involving spiritual principles. Satan was at work in the first sowing of the Gospel, scattering his weeds among Christ's wheat. Notice how often the apostle had to root out pernicious errors that cropped up among the early Christians. Why is Satan so obsessed with perverting God's principles? For one thing, God highly honors His truth (Psalm 138:2). He is more scrupulous about it than all His other works. Jesus declared, "Heaven and earth shall pass away, but my words shall not pass away" (Matthew 24:35). God can make new worlds whenever He pleases, but He cannot make another truth. Therefore, He will not lose one iota of it. Satan knows this, and sets his whole heart on disfiguring that which is so precious to God.

It should also be precious to us. The Word is the mirror in which we see Christ and, seeing Him, are changed into His likeness by the Holy Spirit. If the glass is cracked, our conception of Him will be distorted, whereas the Word in its native clearness sets Christ out in all His glory. You can see, then, that not only does Satan strike at God when He attacks the truth, but he also strikes at the saints. If he can lead them into error, it will weaken—if not destroy—the power of godliness in them.

The apostle joins the spirit of power and of a sound mind together (2 Timothy 1:7). We are exhorted to "desire the sincere milk of the word, that [we] may grow . . ." (1 Peter 2:2).

SEARCH THE SCRIPTURES

*Do not pretend you want to be led
into truth if you will not bother
to study the whole Word of God.*

Christian, if you can once and for all break your engage-
ment to the flesh and become a free man in Christ, truth
will be your steadfast friend.

Study God's Word faithfully as well. Satan has a habit of
stopping the ears from hearing sound doctrine before he opens
them to listen to corrupt. He will, as often as he can, pull a saint
away from God's Word and talk him into rejecting some point
of truth. But he who rejects the truth of one doctrine, loses the
blessing of them all. Paul predicted how this would happen:
"They shall turn away their ears from the truth, and shall be
turned unto fables" (2 Timothy 4:3–4).

Do not pretend you want to be led into truth if you will not
bother to study the whole Word of God. You are no different
from a child who says he wants to learn, yet plays the truant.
Such a child must be disciplined. Because your heavenly Father
loves you, He will bring you back to the Word with shame and
sorrow, rather than leave you trapped in Satan's lies.

As you study and grow, be wary of new doctrine. Do not
hastily accept everything you hear, even from the pulpit. Now I
admit that to reject a doctrine simply because we have never
heard it before is foolish. But we have every right to wait and
inquire before embracing it. When you hear a new notion about
the truth, go to God in prayer and seek His counsel. Search the
Scriptures. Discuss it with your pastor and with other Christians
whose wisdom and maturity you trust.

The truth will stand up under scrutiny. It is a fruit that never
bruises or spoils from handling. But error, like fish, begins to
stink after a few days. Therefore, let new ideas sit before you
make a meal of them. You do not want to poison your soul with
rotting mackerel when you could be feasting on manna from
heaven!

THE POISON OF PRIDE

Satan knows better than anyone the damning
power of pride. Is it any wonder, then,
that he so often uses it to poison the saints?

A second type of error Satan sows among saints is pride. Pride was the sin that turned Satan, a blessed angel, into a cursed devil. Satan knows better than anyone the damning power of pride. Is it any wonder, then, that he so often uses it to poison the saints? His design is made easier in that man's heart shows a natural fondness for it. Pride, like liquor, is intoxicating. A swallow or two usually leaves a man worthless to God.

One of the perilous things about pride is that it uses both our good and our bad inclinations to draw its chariot. On the other hand, it works companionably with other sins. In fact, a multitude of sins will slave all day long and into the night, supposing they are their own masters, when all along they are the hirelings of pride. Watch someone cheating, deceiving, lying, oppressing others. What is his motive, if not to acquire an estate to maintain his pride?

Even worse than teaming up with other sorts of wickedness, this rascal pride will also harness itself to that which is good, and work alongside God's ordinances. When this happens, we see a person zealous in prayer or faithful in church attendance, and suppose him to be a mighty saint. But all the while pride is the master he serves, though in God's livery. Pride can take sanctuary in the holiest of actions and hide itself under the very skirt of virtue. Thus you may hear of someone giving generously to the poor, and be moved to admire his charity. Yet pride—not compassion—may be the reason he lavishes out his gold so freely.

Another may steadfastly resist every appearance of evil and be respected as a model Christian. And all the while, pride—not true heart conviction—may be the promoter of his circumspect walk. This was the case with the Pharisee, who flaunted his spirituality and bragged because he was not like the publican. Christ showed us in a word or two how He felt about that kind of pride!

BE CONTENTED WITH YOUR GIFTS

*Great gifts can lift a saint up a
little higher in the eyes of men,
but they also tempt him to pride.*

The Bible says *every* saint has been given gifts to benefit the
body of Christ.

Here is a word to you who think your gifts are inferior
to those of other members of the body: *Be content with your
condition.* Great gifts lift a saint up a little higher in the eyes of
men, but they also tempt him to pride. Do not envy those with
great gifts; instead, pity and pray for them. It is hard for them to
escape the error of supposing that God's grace in them is their
own doing. You have a real advantage over them, for you have
the help of their gifts but not the temptation of their pride.

Here, now, are some words of caution for you to whom
God has given more or better gifts than ordinary.

Pride wants to grow where the best gifts have been bestowed. So beware of pride! The only thing that will keep you
from it is your humility. Remember to whom you wrestle
with—spiritual wickednesses. Their ploy is to lift you up high in
order to give you a harder fall. They will try to convince you
that your spiritual accomplishments are a result of your own efforts and that you deserve the credit for them. Surely you know
this is not true! In case you have forgotten, think back to what
you were like before the Holy Spirit came to you with gifts from
God's storehouse. How can you be proud of another's bounty?
You may be able to impress other men with your gifts, but you
will not impress God. He knows where they all came from.

Where pride flourishes, the body of Christ suffers. Had God
given you gifts merely for your own pleasure or edification, the
sin of pride would not be quite so bad. But when you use your
gifts to lift yourself up, you tear down the body of Christ. Your
gifts are necessary to the health of the whole body, but they
must be administered properly. You must be careful to acknowledge that Christ is the Great Physician; you are only the
assistant who uses His instruments and carries out His orders.

GOD WILL CHASTEN PRIDE

*God stamps His image of holiness
on the face of your soul. This attribute
of beauty is what makes us most like God.*

P ride must have the most and best of everything to satisfy its appetite. This voracious lust will devour your spirit of praise. When you should be blessing God, you will be applauding yourself. It will eat up Christian love, and cause you to disdain the fellowship of other Christians. It will keep you from acknowledging the gifts of others, because that would take away some of the glory you want for yourself. Ultimately, pride so distorts our taste that we can relish nothing drawn from another's dish.

Where pride reigns, God chastens. God will not allow such a weed as pride to grow in His garden without taking some course or other to root it up. He may let you fall into a sin that will humiliate you before men and God, and force you to come crawling home in shame. Or He may use a thorn in the flesh to prick the balloon of your pride. If your pride has placed His honor in jeopardy, expect to feel God's rod of correction. Most likely it will be applied to the very spot where your pride is rooted. Hezekiah boasted of his treasure; God sent the Chaldeans to plunder him. Jonah was proud of his gourd; God sent a pestilence to destroy it. Can you expect God to wink at this sin in your life when He has dealt so firmly with it in His other children?

Where gifts are bestowed, God calls an audit. Suppose a friend died and named you executor of his estate. But instead of dividing up his inheritance according to the instructions left in his will, you took the money and put it in your own bank account, then went around town bragging about how rich you were! How long could you fool people with your false prosperity? Sooner or later the rightful heirs would show up and not only take what is theirs, but probably sue you as well. In a spiritual sense, you are only God's executor. He has given you gifts, and specific instructions on how to dispense them. By the time you have paid all the legacies, you will see little left for yourself to brag or boast of. Never forget for a moment that you will be held accountable for the talents left in your care.

ENVY AS SPIRITUAL PRIDE

*When your envy prods you to belittle
the gifts of other Christians,
you are really belittling God who gave them.*

Another indicator that you are caught in the trap of spiritual pride is envy of others' gifts. Keeping our hearts and envy separated is as difficult as keeping two lovers from meeting. It is the sin that shed the first blood: Cain's envy hatched Abel's murder.

Envy is an affront to the character and person of God. When you envy, you are questioning God's right to administer His gifts as He sees best. You are also maligning the goodness of God. You are angry that God wants to bless someone besides you. Would you not have God be good? You might as well say you would not have Him be God, for He can no more cease to be good than He can cease to be God! When your envy prods you to belittle the gifts of other Christians, you are really belittling God who gave them.

Envy, like its mother, pride, is the scout for a whole host of other sins. This sin of the heart goes before and sets the stage for all kinds of sins of the flesh. Saul, Israel's first king, fell so low as to plot the murder of the very man who had saved his kingdom. From the day he heard David preferred above himself in the women's songs, he could not get the sound out of his head. Envy brought him to hate, which carried him on to plot David's death.

Later on, what did envy do to David's heart but make him covet the wife of his trusted soldier, Uriah, and lead him through a maze of lust, lies, adultery, and murder? Not one of these would have been committed had it not been for that rabble-rouser, envy. It is a bloody sin—the womb wherein lies a whole litter of other sins is formed (Romans 1:29). Therefore, unless you are willing to welcome the devil and his whole train, resist the sin of envy.

To gain mastery of this sin, you must call in help from heaven. We have a sure promise that the foundation of our grace is stronger than that of our lust, but only if we enlist the Holy Spirit in our behalf: "The spirit that dwelleth in us lusteth to envy. But he giveth more grace" (James 4:5–6).

PRIDE IN OUR OWN STRENGTH

*When you see that your own cupboard
is bare and everything you need is in His,
you will go often to Him for supplies.*

What happened to Peter when he bragged of the strength of his own grace? "Although all shall be offended, yet will not I," Peter boasted (Mark 14:29). He set himself up to contest a race with the devil, and he fouled before he was even out of the gate. Christ in mercy let Satan trample Peter's own grace to show him its true nature and to dismount him from the height of his pride.

Pray that He will be as merciful to you if He sees you climbing the ladder of your own spiritual successes. Joab said to David, when he saw him growing proud of the strength of his kingdom, and wanting to take a census, "The Lord add to the number of thy people a hundred-fold, but why doth my lord the king delight in this thing?" (2 Samuel 24:3). Can a groom be proud when he rides his master's horse, or a garden boast because the sun shines on it? Should we not say of every dram of goodness, as the young man of his hatchet, "Alas, master! For it was borrowed" (2 Kings 6:5)?

Count on the strength of your own godly attributes, and you will grow lax in your duties for Christ. Knowing you are weak keeps you from wandering too far from Him. When you see that your own cupboard is bare and everything you need is in His, you will go often to Him for supplies. But a soul who thinks he can take care of himself will say, "I have plenty and to spare for a long time. Let the doubting soul pray; my faith is strong. Let the weak go to God for help; I can manage fine on my own." What a sad state of affairs, to suppose that we no longer need the moment-by-moment sustaining grace of God.

Not only does overestimating the strength of our own goodness make us shun God's help, but it also makes us foolhardy and venturesome. You who boast about your spirituality are likely to put yourselves in all kinds of dangerous situations, then brag that you can handle them.

JUSTIFICATION ASSAULTED

*Satan uses two types of pride to keep us trusting
in the worth of our own grace. One I call mannerly
pride, the other, a self-applauding pride.*

This doctrine of justification by faith has had more assaults
made against it than any other teaching in Scripture. Indeed, many other errors were but the enemy's sly approaches to get nearer to undermine this one. When Satan
cannot hide the truth, he works to hinder the practical applica-
tion of it. Thus you see Christians who speak in defense of justification by faith, yet their attitude and actions contradict their
profession. Like Abraham, when he went in to Hagar, they try to
accomplish God's purpose by a carnal plan. All these efforts that
seem so noble are really baseborn, for they are rooted in pride.

At bottom, pride in your own abilities is what keeps you
working for righteousness. You keep trying to pray harder,
working to be a better Christian, laboring to have more faith.
You keep telling yourself, "I can do it!" But you will soon find
your own grace insufficient for even the smallest task, and your
joy will run out at the crannies of your imperfect duties and
weak graces. The language of pride hankers after the covenant
of works. The only way out of this trap is to let the new covenant cut the cord of the old one, and acknowledge that the
grace of Christ supersedes the works of the law.

Satan uses two types of pride to keep us trusting in the
worth of our own grace. One I call a *mannerly pride;* the other,
a *self-applauding pride.*

Mannerly pride tiptoes in, disguised as humility. This is a
soul that weeps and mourns for its vile condition, yet refuses to
be comforted. It is true—not one of us can paint our sins black
enough to do them justice. But think how you discredit God's
mercy and Christ's merit when you say they are not enough to
buy your pardon! Can you find no better way to show your
sense of sin than to malign the Savior? Are you unwilling to be
in Christ's debt for your salvation, or too proud to beg His
forgiveness?

OUR GOODNESS IS INADEQUATE

You were "justified freely by
his grace, through the redemption
that is in Christ Jesus" (Romans 3:24).

Another form of spiritual pride that shows you are depending on the worth of your own grace is *self-applauding pride*. This is when the heart is secretly lifted up and says of itself, "I may not be perfect, but I'm certainly better than most Christians I know." Every such glance of the soul's eye is adulterous—in fact, idolatrous. Any time you give your own righteousness the inward worship of your confidence and truth, this is great iniquity indeed. You come to open heaven's gate with the old key, when God has put on a new lock.

If you are truly a Christian, you must acknowledge that your first entrance into your justified state was by pure mercy. You were "justified freely by his grace, through the redemption that is in Christ Jesus" (Romans 3:24). Having been reconciled, to whom are you now indebted—to your own goodness, to your obedience, to yourself—or to Christ? If Christ does not lead in all you do, you are sure to find the door of grace shut to you. "The righteousness of God [is] revealed from faith to faith... [for] the just shall live by faith" (Romans 1:17). We are not only made alive by Christ, but we live by Christ. Heaven's way is paved with grace and mercy from beginning to end.

Why is God so insistent that we use His grace instead of our own? Because He knows our grace is inadequate for the task. The truth is this: Trusting in our own grace only brings trouble and heartache; trusting in God's grace brings lasting peace and joy.

In the first place, trusting in your own goodness will eventually destroy it. Inherent grace is weak. Force it to endure the yoke of the law, and sooner or later it will faint by the wayside, unequal to the task of pulling the heavy load of your old nature. What you need is Christ's yoke, but you cannot take it until you shed the one that harnesses you to works.

ACKNOWLEDGE GOD'S GIFTS

*"We are the circumcision, which worship God in
the spirit, and rejoice in Christ Jesus, and
have no confidence in the flesh" (Philippians 3:3).*

I f you are one of those who have claimed for years to be a
Christian, but you see little fruit in your life, perhaps you
should dig down to the root of your profession and find out
whether the seed you planted was cultivated in the barren soil
of legalism. If so, pull it up at once, and replant your soul in a
fertile field—God's mercy. David gave an account of how he
came to prosper when some who were rich and famous suddenly withered and died: "Lo," he said, "this is the man that
made not God his strength; but trusted in the abundance of his
riches . . . But I am like a green olive tree in the house of God: I
trust in the mercy of God for ever and ever" (Psalm 52:7–8).

Not only do you crush your grace by making it carry the
burden of your salvation, but you also deprive yourself of true
comfort in Christ. Gospel-comfort springs from a Gospel-root,
which is Christ. "We are the circumcision, which worship God
in the spirit, and rejoice in Christ Jesus, and have no confidence
in the flesh" (Philippians 3:3). The first step to receiving the
Gospel comfort is to send away all comforters of our own. A
physician asks his patient to stop going to every other doctor
who has been tampering with his health, and trust him for a
cure. As your spiritual physician, the Holy Spirit asks your soul
to send away all the old practitioners—every duty, every other
course of obedience—and lean only on Him.

Does your soul cry out from its depths for inward peace?
Then check to see what vessel you are drawing your comfort
from. If it is the vessel of your own sufficiency, the supply is finite and will soon run dry. It is mixed, or diluted, and therefore
not very nourishing. Above all, it is stolen if you claim it as your
own and do not acknowledge it as God's gift to you. Now how
much comfort can you expect from stolen goods? And how foolish to play the thief when your Father has so much more and
better to give you than you could pilfer in a lifetime!

APRIL 26

USE COMFORTS WISELY

*Do not grow lax when you are being comforted.
Rather, use this time of blessing to work
harder than ever for the Lord.*

Do not measure your grace by your comfort. God does not necessarily send you an extra measure of comfort as a reward for being good. Such discoveries of His love do indeed bear witness to the truth of His grace in you, but they say nothing about the degree and measure of your inherent grace. The weak child may be—in fact, generally is—oftener in his parent's lap than the strong one.

Do not grow lax when you are being comforted. Rather, use this time of blessing to work harder than ever for the Lord. The manifestations of God's love are to fit us for our work. Basking in the light of His comfort is one thing; going forth in the power of the Spirit's comfort is quite another. How foolish is the man who spends all his time counting his money but never invests it; how wise is the one who puts his money to work for him and earns dividends. Spiritually speaking, the one who hoards his comforts will lose what he has, while the one who puts his comforts to work for Christ will increase his stock five, ten, even a hundredfold.

Do not think you are the source of your own comfort. Remember that you depend on God for your continued peace and joy. The smiles you had yesterday will not make you happy today, any more than the bread you ate then will keep you satisfied if you do not eat again. You will need new drafts of God's love every day to keep you satisfied. Let God hide His face just for a moment, and you will quickly forget the taste and lose sight of the comforts you had just a short time earlier.

How we would ridicule the man who, when the sun shines in at his window, tries to trap the sunbeams indoors by closing the shutters. But we are just as foolish to take our present joy, then turn away from God's presence, supposing that we have all we need. You can feel the heat from the sun only when you stand beneath its rays; you can feel God's comfort only as you keep your face turned toward Him.

OUR DIVINE CALLING

*God stamps His image of holiness on the
face of your soul. This attribute of beauty
is what makes us most like God.*

Heap all the riches and honors of the world upon a man—
they will not make him a Christian. Heap them on a
Christian—they will not make him a better Christian.
Again, take them all away. When stripped and naked, he will still
be a Christian, and perhaps a better one.

Satan could do the sincere saint little harm if he directed his
forces only against his outward enjoyments, because they mean
nothing to him in comparison with his spiritual inheritance. Indeed, Satan's attack on a Christian's earthly possessions should
do him no more harm than a robber does to a man if he strips
him naked and then proceeds to beat the man's clothes as they
lie on the ground in a heap! Insofar as the spirit of grace prevails in a saint's heart, he has put off his desire for the things of
the world. Therefore, his heavenly treasure is the booty Satan
waits for: his nature, his occupation, and his hopes.

The Christian's nature is heavenly, born from above. As
Christ is the Lord from heaven, so all His offspring are heavenly. The holiness of Christ in you reminds Satan of his own first
estate. He has lost the beauty of holiness for ever, and how, like
a true apostate, he endeavors to ruin it in you.

God stamps His image of holiness on the face of your soul.
This attribute of beauty is what makes us most like God. How
God longs to see His clear likeness reflected in His children,
and His true children long to be like Him! Satan knows this and
works tirelessly to disfigure the divine image. Marring the
Christian's nature brings shame to the saint and pours contempt
upon God in distorting His likeness. Is it not worth risking life
and limb against this enemy who would annihilate that which
makes us like God Himself?

OUR HOPE IS IN HEAVEN

The Christian's hopes are all heavenly.
He does not expect lasting satisfaction
from anything the world has to offer.

The Christian's occupation is heavenly. That is to say, God is our overseer. We may plant our seeds here on earth, but our crop will be harvested in heaven. This keeps our hearts and desires on a celestial plane. In a spiritual sense, the Christian's feet stand where other men cannot even see. He treads on the moon and is clothed with the sun. He looks down on earthly men as one from a high hill looks upon those living in a swamp. While he breathes in pure heavenly air, they are suffocating in a fog of carnal pleasures and profits. He knows one heavenly pearl is worth infinitely more than the earthly accumulation of a whole lifetime.

The great business of a saint's life is to be doing things that enlarge the kingdom of heaven. Not only is he interested in his own welfare, but he eagerly recruits his friends and neighbors to join in his eternal enterprise. Now this alarms hell. What! Not content to go to heaven himself, but by his holy example and faithful work will he try to carry them along with him also? This brings the lion raging out of his den. Such a Christian, to be sure, will find the devil in his way to oppose him.

The Christian's hopes are all heavenly. He does not expect lasting satisfaction from anything the world has to offer. Indeed, he would think himself the most miserable person to have ever lived, if the only rewards he could expect from his religion were on this side of eternity. No, it is heaven and eternal life that he anticipates. And though he is so poor that he cannot leave one cent in his will, yet he counts himself a greater heir than if he were a child of the greatest prince on earth.

Hope is the grace that shows us how to rejoice in the prospect of promised glory. It sits beside us in the worst of times. When things are so bad that we cannot imagine how they could possibly get worse, hope lifts our eyes from our immediate troubles and places them on our future eternal joys.

THE "PREACHING PRAYING" DEVIL

*Of all men, God strikes with greatest speed
the one who gilds over worldly and
wicked business with holy pretensions.*

S ome individuals make a lot of noise about their religion, but secretly have their hearts set on earthly goals. They pretend to be heaven-bound, but their hearts are full of hypocrisy. Such deceivers are like the eagle who, when he soars highest, has his eye fixed on some carnal prey on the ground.

Hypocrites have always been and ever will be a part of the crowd thronging into the church and mingling with the true saints of God. Their speech is pure, their service admirable; but their hearts are lined with deceit. Worst of all, they fool even themselves. The world may mistakenly call them saints, but Christ knows they are devils. What did He say about the master hypocrite, Judas? "Have I not chosen you twelve, and one of you is a devil?" (John 6:70).

Truly, of all devils, none is as bad as the professing devil— the preaching, praying devil. God has repeatedly shown His severe displeasure when His so-called people have prostituted sacred things to worldly ends. Of all men, God strikes with the greatest speed the one who gilds over worldly and wicked business with holy pretensions. God has made a solemn promise: "I will set my face against that man, and will make him a sign and a proverb, and I will cut him off from the midst of my people, and ye shall know that I am the Lord" (Ezekiel 14:8).

Among thieves, there is often a scout who searches out where the booty is to be had. He is the brains behind every illicit operation, but he never risks his own neck by actually committing a crime. The devil uses this same tactic by watching how a Christian walks, where he goes, whose company he enjoys. Then he decides the best way to rob him of his grace. When the plan is set, he sends someone else to carry it out. Thus he sent Job's friends and even Job's wife to tempt him; he sent Potiphar's wife to entice Joseph.

APRIL 30

USE EARTHLY GOODS FOR HEAVEN

*If you are a prominent member of your community,
how do you use your influence—for good or
for evil? For selfish or selfless ends?*

A true saint will be zealous in his daily affairs, but all his energies will be tuned to heaven. While his hands are busy at his tasks, his heart and head will be taken up with higher matters—how to please God, grow in grace, enjoy more intimate fellowship with Christ. The carnal man, in contrast, spends long, hard hours in his shop and then goes home and spends half the night plotting how to get ahead in business. He sweats in the shop, but grows cold in the prayer closet. No weather is bad enough to keep him from market, but if the road to church is a little slippery or there is a chill in the air, he begs his leave from the services. No inconvenience is too great if it fattens his pocket, but let the preacher keep him a minute or two past the hour, and he complains. In short, at work he keeps his eyes on the till; at church, he keeps them on his watch.

If anything I have said speaks to you, go quickly to God and petition for a thorough change of heart.

Perhaps you have a heavenly spirit in getting earthly things. But do you have the same spirit when you use them? The good wrestler uses his earthly estate for heavenly ends.

What do you do with the fruits of your labor? Do you bestow them on your own overstuffed paunch—or do you share them with the poor? If you are a prominent member of your community, how do you use your influence—for good or for evil? For selfish or selfless ends? To pray for "things" without a heavenly end in mind is close to idolatry. Use your material wealth with a holy fear, dear saint, lest earth should rob heaven, and your temporal enjoyments endanger your heavenly interests. As Job sanctified his children by offering a sacrifice out of fear that they might have sinned, so the Christian must continually sanctify his earthly enjoyments by prayer. In this way He will be delivered from the snare of them.

INDIFFERENCE TO EARTHLY THINGS

*You cannot labor for heavenly
possessions if your hands and heart
are loaded down with earthly pursuits.*

The Christian must practice the same indifference in keeping his earthly possessions as he did in getting them. God never signs the title of anything over to us, but merely gives us things to keep in trust. All will be left behind when He calls us home. If He sees fit to let us keep them until then, we bless and thank Him for His generosity; and if He takes them away sooner, we bless Him still.

God never intended, by His providence in bringing Moses to Pharaohs' court, to leave him there in worldly pomp and grandeur. A carnal heart would have reasoned that Moses could best help his people—slaves under Pharaoh—by using his position and power to influence the king, or perhaps even by aspiring to the throne. But when Moses renounced his place of privilege, his faith and self-denial were made more eminently conspicuous. It is for this obedient faith that Moses is given such honorable mention in the New Testament (Hebrews 11:24–25).

Sometimes God lavishes us with things, not so we can hang on to them, but so we will have something to let go of to show our love for Him. Was there anything better in the whole world Mary could have done with her precious oil than to anoint her Lord? What enterprise will pay more lasting dividends than to invest what you possess in the cause of Christ?

Christian, keep a loose grip on the material possessions you value most highly. Be ready at a moment's notice to throw them overboard, rather than risk the shipwreck of your faith. You cannot labor for heavenly possessions if your hands and heart are loaded down with earthly pursuits. In the end, if you can save anything, it will be your soul, your interest in Christ and heaven. If you should lose all your worldly goods, you should still be able to say with Jacob, "I have enough [all things]" (Genesis 33:11).

MATERIAL GAIN IS NOT SUCCESS

*If anyone pursues heavenly things and
does not get them, it is because he did not
follow God's instruction in the right manner.*

Suppose you do die penniless. What will it matter at all? But suppose you die graceless! Heaven and heavenly things are the kind that cannot be recompensed by anything else. Do not let Satan distract you with baubles and toys. While he is entertaining you with his clever illusions, his other hand is in your treasure, robbing you of that which is irreplaceable. It is more necessary to be saved, than to be; better not to be, than to have a being in hell.

No matter how hard you work for material gain, there is no guarantee of success. Men have been doing business for thousands of years, yet no one has come up with a fail-proof plan for getting rich. How few carry away the prize in the world's lottery! Most have only disillusionment and bitter memories for their trouble.

But now for heaven and the things of heaven, the plan is quite clearly laid out in the Bible: "As many as walk according to this rule, peace be on them . . ." (Galatians 6:16). If anyone pursues heavenly things and does not get them, it is because he did not follow God's instruction in the right manner.

If you want heaven but you also want your sins, do not expect to succeed. You must part company with one or the other. If you will not let go of your sins, God will have to let go of you. If you want heaven but insist on purchasing it with your own righteousness, you will fall short of the price. You are like the near kinsman in Ruth who wanted to buy Elimelech's land but was not willing to marry Ruth as the law required (4:2–4). All the good you do, all the duties you perform, are admirable if they are acts of love that follow your act of repentance. But if you offer them as the price you are willing to pay for heaven, God will not deal with you. You must close with Christ and Him alone, or lose the whole bargain.

ONLY HEAVENLY THINGS LAST

*You may lose every temporal comfort,
including family and friends, but if your treasure
is secure in Christ, you are a rich man still.*

E arthly things are uninsurable. Though God may have blessed you with wealth, you could be rich today and poor tomorrow. You could be in good health when you go to bed, but seized by pangs of illness or death before morning. Can you take enough precautions to guarantee that nothing will happen to wipe out your fortune? Can you become rich enough to buy good health or add one day to the span of your years?

Scripture compares the world's population to a mighty ocean. Kings and rulers sit upon this ocean. As a ship floats upon the waves, so their lives float upon the favor of the multitude. And what kind of security is there in riding the waves? For a while they will be lifted up to the heavens, only to fall down again into the deep. David knew how fickle the world's preferments are: "We have ten parts in the king," said the men of Israel (2 Samuel 19:43); and in the very next verse the tide had already turned: "We have no part in David, neither have we inheritance in the son of Jesse" (2 Samuel 20:1–2). Thus was David tossed up and down, almost in the same breath.

But heaven is a kingdom that cannot be shaken. Christ is an abiding portion which changes not. His graces and comforts are sure waters that spring up into eternal life. The quail that were food for the Israelites' greed soon ceased, but the rock that was drink for their faith followed them. This rock is Christ. You may lose every temporal comfort, including family and friends, but if your treasure is secure in Christ, you are a rich man still. Christ will come to you in your darkest hour with peace and a promise: "Fear not death nor devils. I will stay right here beside you until you breathe your last breath. My angels are waiting with Me. As soon as your soul is breathed out of your body, they will carry it to heaven and lay it in the bosom of My love. Then I will nourish you with those eternal joys that My blood has purchased and My love has perfected for you."

EARTHLY THINGS ARE UNSATISFYING

*Those who try hardest to please
themselves with earthly goods
find the least satisfaction in them.*

A man's wealth often breeds misery, but never contentment. How foolish to suppose it ever could! Our spirits are immaterial; they will not be satisfied with the perishable delights of flesh and blood. The earthly prizes we strive to win are far inferior to the nature of man. Therefore, we must look far beyond them if we want to be blessed—even to God Himself, who is the Father of spirits.

The possessions God allows us to have are intended for our use, not our enjoyment. Trying to squeeze something out of them that was never in them in the first place is a futile endeavor. A cow's udders, gently pressed, will yield sweet milk, nourishing and refreshing. Applying more and more pressure will not produce greater quantities of milk. We lose the good of material things by expecting too much from them. Those who try hardest to please themselves with earthly goods find the least satisfaction in them.

All our frustrations could be easily avoided if we would turn away from things and look to Christ for happiness. Here is what you can expect when you do:

First, the guilt of your sins all gone. Guilt is the pin that constantly pricks our joy. When Christ takes away your sins, He also takes the guilt.

Second, your nature renewed and sanctified. Holiness is simply the creature restored to the state of health which God intended when He created him. And when is a man more at ease than when he is healthy?

Third, adoption into the family of God. Surely this cannot help but make you happy—to be the son or daughter of so great a King.

Fourth, an eternal inheritance with Christ. We cannot begin to comprehend what this means in terms of everlasting joy. Our present conceptions of heaven are no more like heaven itself than an artist's painting of the sun is like the orb in the sky.

A BETTER DWELLING PLACE

No holiness, no happiness.
Take the whole offer,
or take nothing.

We can cling to the promise that what God has prepared for us is beyond our most extravagant dream (Isaiah 64:4; 1 Corinthians 2:9).

Find out for yourself whether you are devoted to heavenly or earthly things. You cannot pursue both. Earthly things are like trash, which not only does not nourish, but takes away the appetite from that which would. Heavenly things have no appeal for one corrupted by such trash. Only when you come to the end of yourself, like the prodigal, will you make the judgment that heavenly things are better. Then you will know bread is better fare than husks, and your Father's house a better place to dwell than with hogs in the field.

If you will have heaven, you must have Christ, who is all in all. And if Christ, you must accept His service as well as His sacrifice. No holiness, no happiness. Take the whole offer, or take nothing. One can compare holiness and happiness to those sisters, Leah and Rachel. On the surface, happiness, like Rachel, seems more desirable. (Even a carnal heart will fall in love with that.) But holiness, like Leah, is the elder and has a special beauty also, though in this life it appears at some disadvantage —the eyes red from tears of repentance and the face furrowed with the work of mortification.

Here is heaven's law: The younger sister cannot be bestowed before the elder. We cannot enjoy fair Rachel—heaven and happiness—until we first embrace Leah—holiness—with all her demanding duties of repentance and mortification. Will you live by this law? Marry Christ and His grace, then serve a hard apprenticeship in temptations both of prosperity and adversity. Endure the heat of the one and the cold of the other. If you will be patient, at last the fairer sister will be handed over to you. This is the only way to win the prize of heavenly things.

PRIMARY TRUTHS

*The fundamental truths of
the Gospel are landmarks to keep us
safely within the boundaries set by God.*

These are the truths everyone must know and believe for salvation, the verities upon whose shoulders the whole weight of Christianity weighs.

The fundamental truths of the Gospel are landmarks to keep us safely within the boundaries set by God. Suppose your grandfather owned some property which at one time had been carefully surveyed. He was there when they set the stakes and could have paced it off blindfolded. But he never took the time to show anyone else the markings. Over the years, the markers rotted, were rooted up, or washed away. Now your grandfather has died and left the land to you. But a dishonest neighbor claims it is his, and as proof of ownership points to the burgeoning crop of corn he has planted. You discover the deed and land description have been lost. Since you do not really know the proper boundary lines yourself, how will you defend your case in court? You will probably end up losing your property because no one ever told you where it ends and your neighbor's begins.

The spiritual parallel is this: Every fundamental truth has some evil neighbor (i.e., heresy) butting up against it, eager to plant a crop of lies upon the sacred ground of God's Holy Word and thus fool the saints. And the very reason that a spirit of error has encroached so far upon the truth in the last few years is because ministers have not walked the boundaries of the Gospel with their people and acquainted them with these primary truths.

We have both staples and luxuries in our religion, just as in our homes. Luxuries are wonderful and often enhance our appreciation of the staples, but they quickly lose their appeal when our basic needs go unmet. What pleasure is there in dining from fine china if you have no food to put on the plate? Of what value is a silk blouse in the winter if you have no coat?

BE ON YOUR GUARD

Either you destroy the power of Satan in
your life by putting on the whole armor of God
and keeping it on, or Satan will destroy you.

S atan is not challenging you to a mock battle; this war is a life-or-death struggle. If you do not believe me, look what he has done to God's servants in times past. Charging full speed ahead at many a dear saint, he has battered their armor until the grace of God in them was almost unrecognizable. All this he does when he catches a saint off guard.

Do you remember what happened to Jacob when he unbuckled his girdle of truth and sincerity, and used a trick to get his father's blessing? He got the blessing all right, but he also was repaid in kind when Laban switched Leah for Rachel. Think how much suffering he might have saved himself by keeping his whole armor in place!

What about David? Oh, the battering he took by removing his breastplate of righteousness in the matter of Uriah! He sustained a dreadful wound, being shot right through the heart. And Jonah, when God wanted to send him to Nineveh, got caught without his shoes on. By that I mean he lacked the preparation and readiness with which his mind should have been shod, to have gone at the first call. Then there was poor Hezekiah. He had his helmet of hope knocked askew and so badly dented that he cried, "I shall not see the Lord . . . in the land of the living" (Isaiah 38:11). Even Abraham had fits of unbelief and distrustful qualms that crept in at some rusty spots in his graces.

This war is a spiritual holocaust. Either you destroy the power of Satan in your life by putting on the whole armor of God and keeping it on, or Satan will destroy you. The great saints of every century have been tried in the fires of temptation. And to a man they have been singed whenever Satan found the smallest chink in their graces. Do not disregard what history has repeatedly shown to be true.

DECLINING IN GRACE

*When your relationship to Christ is set aright,
you and your brothers and sisters in Christ are alike
benefited, and your heavenly Father is glorified.*

When your graces are in a state of decline, you do feel far from God and heaven; you do begin to wonder whether you were ever really saved.

Imagine that you held an estate because of having custody of a child, upon whose death the estate would be taken away from you. I have no doubt that the child would be well looked after. You would never let him out of your sight, and the slightest headache would send you running for a physician. The only claim we have to our heavenly estate is the child of grace that comes to dwell within us when we accept Christ as Savior and Lord. So when this "child of grace" is sick or weak, we had better use every means to make it well again.

If God's grace in you is sickly, you will find little joy in life, present or future. A person with a chronic illness gets no pleasure from anything else. His food is tasteless; he sleeps fitfully; he has no energy to work or play. If the image of Christ in you has faded, you are chronically ill. You will not taste the sweetness of the promise, nor enjoy any rest in Him. You will limp painfully to every duty, wondering whether you have strength enough to see it through. All the while, your disconsolate heart will be crying out at the heavy load you make it carry.

How sad that our own carelessness so often gives Satan the advantage! By our own spiritual complacency we put a staff in his hand and an argument in his mouth which he uses to question our salvation. But how sweet is the promise to our faith when it is active and vigorous! How easy the yoke when the Christian is not galled with guilt, nor his strength enfeebled by declining grace! When your relationship to Christ is set aright, you and your brothers and sisters in Christ are alike benefited, and your heavenly Father is glorified.

RESISTING TEMPTATION

*It is not frequency of duty
but spirituality in duty that
causes a Christian's graces to thrive.*

Being able to resist temptation does not guarantee that God's grace in you is strong, however. Lest you grow complacent, ask yourself why you are resisting the devil's trap. Perhaps you remember a time when your love for Christ would have spit fire in Satan's face for tempting you to sin. But now that holy fire is so nearly extinguished that some base motive is the only thing that keeps you from sinning. If all you care about is your own reputation, for instance, and you have little or no regard for God's reputation, your grace is at a low ebb. After all, He is the one most offended by your sin. Every act of grace must be a building stone in the monument to His glory, or it becomes a stone of offense.

Perhaps at one time your heart eagerly answered the call of the Holy Spirit, bidding you to seek God's face: "Thy face, Lord, will I seek" (Psalm 27:8). You longed as much for the season of worship to come as the sinner does for it to be gone. You cherished time alone with your heavenly Father. To hunger and thirst after righteousness is a sign of health, for a craving soul is a thriving soul. On the other hand, the soul that does not constantly cry out to God for spiritual food will grow weaker by the day.

Those who commune most with God know best how to serve Him. A captain can lead his soldiers only if they stay within the sound of his voice. Your frequent retreats into the secret places of God assure that you will hear Him when He speaks and receive your orders direct from Him. It is not frequency of duty but spirituality in duty that causes a Christian's graces to thrive. Just to be busy doing something for the Lord is not enough; you must make certain your work is stamped with faith, zeal, and love. If you find yourself going about your spiritual tasks out of habit rather than love, it is time to repair your armor.

THE CARES OF THIS LIFE

*If we let them, the cares of this world will follow us
into our prayer closets and cleave to our spirits, giving
a stale, earthly odor to our prayers and meditations.*

Does your heart still receive the same generous portions
of spiritual nourishment when you go to commune with
God? This communion should strengthen both your faith
and your obedience. Or do you listen and pray, but no longer
find strength to keep a promise or power to win over temptation? How you dishonor the Lord when you come down from
the mount of communion and break the tables of His law as
soon as you are off the place! To find no renewed faith and no
renewed strength in your communion with Him is a sure sign
of spiritual decline.

How easy it is to let the responsibilities of job and family
leave us in a less spiritual frame of mind than we once possessed. If we let them, the cares of this world will follow us into
our prayer closets and cleave to our spirits, giving a stale, earthly odor to our prayers and meditations.

One way to become weighed down by the cares of this life
is to put too much stock in your worldly estate. Perhaps you
work diligently but receive little remuneration, or you preach
and receive little recognition. When you first became a Christian, all you cared about was getting to know Christ better. Estate and rank meant nothing to you, and life's disappointments
only drew you closer to God. But now, this hankering of your
heart after the world's treasures and esteem drives you relent-
lessly. How urgently you need to have your grace restored! If
you will labor less to promote your earthly account and pray
harder to improve your fund of grace, you will soon find your
soul at peace with God's providence.

The Christian's armor becomes damaged in two ways. The
first is by violent assault—when you are overcome by temptation to sin. The second is by neglect—when you fail to perform
those duties which, like oil, keep your armor polished and shining. So inquire which has been the cause; it is likely the two
agents have concurred.

PRAYER AND BIBLE READING

*Meditating often on the magnitude
of God's goodness teaches us to
rejoice even in times of trouble.*

Read your Bible. Perhaps you say, "Oh, but I do read God's Word." Then read it more! The Word shows your graces a perfect picture of the object of their affections—Christ. And just as a young man's heart leaps at the sight of his beloved, so your graces come to life when they behold the Christ who loved you and gave Himself for you. At the same time, when you see what your sins cost Christ, it should produce in you a godly sorrow and a hatred for sin.

Meditate. Meditation is to grace as bellows are to a fire. It revives the languishing soul with fresh thoughts of God. As you ponder over them, a holy fire will burn and your heart will grow warm within you. Resolve to spend time every day thinking about what has passed between God and you.

Think, first of all, about the mercies you have received from the Lord. Do not be like Pilate, who asked a question but did not wait for a reply (John 18:38). Stay until you have received a full report of God's gracious dealings with you, and you will find memories of mercies, both new and old, flooding your soul. Meditating often on the magnitude of God's goodness teaches us to rejoice even in times of trouble, for the little evil that is our portion is drowned in the sea of His abundant mercies on our behalf.

Second, reflect upon yourself and your own behavior. What has it been toward God and toward man during the day? Ask yourself, "Soul, where have you been? What have you done for God, and how?" In this reflection, do not make excuses for yourself nor pamper yourself, for ultimately, God will judge you with full justice.

Pray. A soul in meditation is on its way to prayer. The two duties join hands to bring the soul into close communion with God. Meditation lays the wood in order, but the spark to kindle it comes from above and must be fetched by prayer. How can your soul flame with love for God if you never get close enough to Him to catch that heavenly spark?

THE DAY OF AFFLICTION

The saints can have their greatest
portion of joy in affliction, for the
source of their joy is outside themselves.

Affliction is evil, or bad, in the sense that it may rob us of
our joy. Like bitter medicine, affliction has an unpleasant
effect on the senses. Therefore, Solomon, speaking of the
evil days of sickness, declares them to be so distasteful that we
shall say, "We have no pleasure in them" (Ecclesiastes 12:1).
Natural joy is a flower that flourishes in the sun of prosperity
and withers when that sun is hidden by a cloud of trials.

Nevertheless, the saints can have their greatest portion of
joy in affliction, for the source of their joy is outside themselves. God sends it, or else they would be as miserable as others are when trouble strikes. For comfort to spring from
affliction is no more natural than for grapes to grow on thorns
or for manna to appear in the wilderness. But God chooses this
season to make the omnipotence of His love the more conspicuous. When Elijah challenged the prophets of Baal, he first had
the wood and sacrifice drenched with water and the trench
around the altar filled to the brim. Then he prayed and brought
fire from heaven to lick it up. In like manner, God may allow a
flood of afflictions to pour upon His children; He then kindles
that inward joy in their bosoms to consume all their sorrows.
The very waters of affliction add a further sweetness to their
spiritual joy. Still, it is God who is good and affliction that is
evil.

It is a day when past sins are remembered. The day of affliction brings unwelcome reminders of what sinful evils have
passed in our lives. Old sins which were buried many years ago
in the grave of forgetfulness come back to haunt us. Their
ghosts walk in our consciences. And as the darkness of night
heightens our fear of the unseen, so the day when death approaches adds to the terror of our sins, then remembered. Never did the patriarchs' sin look so ghastly to them as when it
recoiled upon them in their distress (Genesis 42:21).

ARMOR IS NEEDED TO WITHSTAND THE EVIL DAY

The soul is a castle which we are each one to keep for God.
We have been warned that Satan will lay siege to it.
The time when he intends to come with all
his powers of darkness is that "evil day."

Since death is inevitable for every person, it behooves us, first of all, to prepare for this evil day in regard to our duty. Your faithful allegiance to God is what keeps you safe. Suppose a subject, entrusted with the care of one of his prince's castles, should hear a powerful enemy was coming to lay siege to the castle. Yet he took no precautions to lay in arms or provisions for its defense, and so it was lost. How could he be cleared of treason? Did he not through negligence betray his prince?

The soul is a castle which we are each one to keep for God. We have been warned that Satan will lay siege to it. The time when he intends to come with all his powers of darkness is that "evil day." Now in order to be found true to our trust, we must plan for our defense and equip ourselves for a vigorous resistance. We cannot, without shameful ingratitude to our God, waste those aids He provides for that evil day.

What would you say of a prisoner who was sent money for his release, but used it instead to amuse himself while in prison? This is in essence what we do when we take the talents God expects us to use in preparation for the hour of death, and instead bestow them upon our lusts. What profit will we find in our Bibles or our ministers if we do not use them to equip ourselves with God's armor?

In a word, why does God lengthen our days in the land of the living? Is it that we might have time to revel in the pleasures of this vain world? Are we to be chasing such butterflies as earthly riches and honor? It cannot be. Wise masters do not give their servants such tasks as will not pay for the candles they burn in doing them. And truly nothing less than glorifying God and saving our souls at last can be worth the precious time we spend here.

DIRECTIONS FOR PREPARING FOR THE EVIL DAY

*"All the promises of God in him are yea,
and in him, Amen, unto the glory of God
by us" (2 Corinthians 1:20).*

Are you wise enough to prepare for the day when you must stand before God? Would you like to live now without dreadful anticipation of that day? Then take theses directions:

Establish a covenant relationship with Christ. You cannot expect to face death without fear unless you have solid ground that Christ will claim you as His. The heirs of heaven are those who are in covenant with God. And how do you get into this covenant relationship? By breaking your covenant with sin! You are by nature a covenant servant to sin and Satan. If ever you are to be taken into a new covenant with God, you must break the old one. A covenant with hell and heaven cannot stand together.

Betroth yourself to Christ. God bestows the covenant of grace only upon Christ's spouse. Rebekah did not receive the jewels and costly raiment until she promised to become Isaac's wife (Genesis 24:53). "All the promises of God in him are yea, and in him, Amen, unto the glory of God by us" (2 Corinthians 1:20). When you receive Christ, you also receive the promises. He who owns the tree has a right to all the fruit it bears. See to it that there is found in you what Christ expects in every soul that He espouses.

Consider whether you can heartily love the Person of Christ. Look fondly on Him again and again, as He is set forth in all His spiritual perfection. Do His holy nature and perfect grace make you desire Him? Can you find it in your heart to forsake all others and cleave to Christ? Will you put the life of your soul in His hands, to be saved by the sole virtue of His blood and by the strength of His omnipotent arm? If you have sufficient faith in His care to provide for you now and in the life to come, you can be sure His promises are for you.

DO YOUR BEST AS HIS SERVANT

"Then shall I not be ashamed,
when I have respect unto all
thy commandments" (Psalm 119:6).

Heaven is not won with good words or a bold profession, but with "having done all." Sacrifice without obedience is sacrilege. His religion is in vain whose profession brings no letters of testimony from a holy life. The doing Christian is the one who shall stand when the boasting Christian shall fall. Such braggarts rob God of that which He values most. A great captain once smote one of his own soldiers for railing at the enemy, saying that his orders were not to rant and rave, but to fight and kill him. To cry out against the devil, to rail against him in prayer or conversation, is not enough. You must take action against him and mortify him if you want to please God.

Is claiming sonship to the King of heaven so small a matter that you think you can obtain it without giving a real proof of your zeal for God and hatred of sin? "Not a forgetful hearer, but a doer of the work; this man," says the apostle, "shall be blessed in his deed" (James 1:25). Notice he does not say by his deed, but in his deed. He shall meet blessedness as he walks obediently. The hypocrite disappoints others who, seeing the leaves on his tree, expect fruit but find none. And at last he disappoints himself. He expects to reach heaven, but will miss it entirely.

Observe also that God's mercy to His children is so great that He gladly accepts their weak efforts to please Him as long as those efforts are joined with sincerity and perseverance. When the heart is right, God accepts the works as if they were done in full obedience. This is why the saints are said to have "done all." Oh, who would not serve such a God! You hear servants sometimes complain that their masters are so unreasonable they can never please them, even when they do their best. Such a charge can never be brought against God. Only do your best, and God will pardon your worst. David knew the indulgence of the Lord when he said, "Then shall I not be ashamed, when I have respect unto all thy commandments" (Psalm 119:6).

THE ENEMY DOESN'T GROW WEARY

*The saint's crown stands
at the goal; he who comes to
the end of the race wins it.*

The persistence of the enemy requires perseverance. The devil never retreats or declares a truce. If an enemy repeatedly assaults a city and those within cease to resist, you know who will win. The prophet who was sent to Bethel did his errand well and withstood Jeroboam's temptation. But on his way home he was drawn aside by the old prophet and at last slain by a lion (1 Kings 13). Thus many flee from one temptation, only to be vanquished by another. Many precious servants of God, not making such vigorous resistance in their last days as in their first, have fallen miserably, as we see in Solomon, Asa, and others.

You know it is hard to hold anything in your hand for very long and not have your fingers grow numb. This is also true in a spiritual sense. Therefore, we are frequently admonished to hold fast the profession of our faith. And surely when we see our enemy always keeping watch to catch us when we fall, we will be challenged to strengthen our grip, not loosen it.

Our eternal reward is contingent upon perseverance. The saint's crown stands at the goal; he who comes to the end of the race wins it. "To him that overcometh will I grant," says Christ (Revelation 3:21). In his letter to Timothy, Paul said, "I have fought a good fight . . . henceforth there is laid up for me a crown of righteousness" (2 Timothy 4:7–8). Why "henceforth"? Was it not laid up before? Yes, but having persevered and come within sight of home, ready to die, he now takes surer hold of the promise. Indeed, in this sense, a gracious soul is nearer his salvation after every victory than he was before, because he approaches nearer to the end of his race, which is the time for receiving his promised salvation (Romans 8:10). Then, and not until then, the garland will be placed on his head.

A THOROUGH CHANGE OF HEART

A man engaged to the world may profess faith in Christ,
but he will quickly show his true colors when
forced to make a choice between Christ and Satan.

All that God chooses to give, He can also choose to deny. If you are not a Christian, you may have some knowledge of the things of God, but, even so, you may die without saving knowledge at last.

A man engaged to the world may profess faith in Christ, but he will quickly show his true colors when forced to make a choice between Christ and Satan. When Satan bribes him with worldly treasures to abandon his profession of the Savior, he will, like Demas, show where his love lies. Or if his lusts call him, he must go, in spite of profession, conscience, God, and all. Herod feared John the Baptist, but love is stronger than fear. His love for Herodias overcame his fear of John, and made him cut off not only John's head but the hopeful buddings of his conscience as well. If the complexion of the soul is profane, it will finally show itself, though for a while there may be some religious color in a man's face from some external cause.

The lack of a thorough change of heart is the root of all final apostasy. The apostate does not lose the grace he had, but only discovers he never had any. Many take up their sainthood upon a false pretense, and use the credit they have gained from others' opinions of them to establish their trade among God's true saints. These false professors assume they are Christians because others suppose them to be. Their whole reputation is built on an outward show of religion. The fact that they have no stock of solid grace within to maintain them in their profession proves their undoing at last.

Let us therefore consider upon what basis we take up our declaration of faith. Is there anything within us that is proportionate to our outward zeal? Have we laid a good foundation? Is the superstructure top-heavy, jutting too far beyond the weak foundation? The roots of a tree spread as far underground as the branches do above; so does true grace.

SATAN'S POWER IS LIMITED

*The same limitless power that overcame
your rebellious heart will overcome
all your enemies within and without.*

If you are a saint, you are wrapped up in the everlasting arms of almighty power. The devil, however, is wrapped up in chains of everlasting condemnation and cannot shake them off no matter how hard he tries. If he cannot free himself from God's chains, how can he tear you from God's grasp? The devil can tempt a saint only by God's permission. If you believe God loves you, then surely you can trust His wisdom when He releases Satan to assault you. Will it not be when he can be repulsed with the greatest humiliation?

To know that Satan's power is limited, and God's grace is limitless, should restore the spirits of weak believers who fear they will not hold out to the end. God has given Christ the life of every soul within the ark of His covenant. If you are His, your eternal safety is provided for. Was He not able to make you willing to march under His banner and join His quarrel against sin and hell? The same limitless power that overcame your rebellious heart will overcome all your enemies within and without. The God who can make a few wounded men rise up and overthrow a city can also make a wounded spirit triumph over sin and Satan (Jeremiah 37:10). The ark stood in the midst of Jordan until the whole camp of Israel was safely over into Canaan (Joshua 3:17). So does Christ's covenant, which is typified by the ark. Christ, covenant and all, stand to secure the saints a safe passage to heaven.

A word of caution must be given. There is a great danger of believers falling from this comfortable doctrine into a careless security and presumptuous boldness. Although the Christian is secure from a total and final apostasy, yet he may suffer a grievous fall which bruises his conscience, weakens his grace, and brings reproach to the Gospel. To know these dangers lurk in the shadows of this doctrine should be enough to keep the Christian upon his watch at all times.

RESULTS OF PERSEVERANCE

*For your eternal comfort, Christian, you can look
forward to a day when there will be a full and final
decision in the quarrel between you and Satan.*

I n earthly wars, not everyone who fights shares the spoils.
The gains of war are commonly put into a few pockets. The
common soldier, who endures most of the hardship, usually
goes away with little of the profit. He fights to make a few that
are great yet greater, and is often discharged without enough to
pay for the cure of his wounds. But in Christ's army, the only
soldier who loses is the one who runs away. Every faithful soldier receives a glorious reward, which is spelled out in this
phrase, "having done all, to stand." To stand implies these
things:

It means "to stand conquerors."

An army, when conquered, is said to fall before its enemy,
and the conqueror stands. At the end of this spiritual war, every
Christian shall stand a conqueror over his vanquished lusts and
Satan who headed them. Though the Christian enjoys many
sweet victories here over Satan, still the joy of his conquests is
interrupted by fresh alarms from the rallied enemy. He wins a
victory one day, only to be confronted with still another battle
on the next. And often, even his victories send him from the
conflict bleeding. Though he repulses the temptation at last, yet
the wounds his conscience receives in the fight cast a shadow
on the glory of the victory.

For your eternal comfort, Christian, you can look forward to
a day when there will be a full and final decision in the quarrel
between you and Satan. You will see your enemy's camp completely scattered, with not a weapon left in his hand to use
against you. You will tread upon the very fortresses from which
he fired so many shots. You will see them dismantled and de-
molished, until there is not one corruption left standing in your
heart for the devil to hide himself in. On that glorious day, the
enemy who has made you tremble will be trampled under your
feet.

HEAVEN IN VIEW

*You may as soon persuade a king to throw down his
royal diadem and wallow in the mud with his robes on,
as convince a saint to sin when his heart is filled
with the expectation of heaven's glory.*

H eaven is the royal city where God keeps His court. The
joy of angels is to stand there before God: "I am Gabriel,
that stand in the presence of God" (Luke 1:19). That is, "I
am one of those heavenly spirits who wait on God, and stand
before His face, as courtiers wait upon their prince." Every
faithful soul is promised this honor.

Nothing should have a more powerful effect upon a saint's
spirit than to consider his blissful estate in heaven as being the
reward of all his conflicts here on earth. This sword should cut
the very sinews of temptation and behead those lusts which
defy whole troops of other arguments. How can sin coexist with
the hope of such glory? It is when the thoughts of heaven are
long out of the Christian's sight, and he forgets his hope of that
glorious place, that he begins to set up some idol as Israel set
up the calf and worshipped it in the absence of Moses. Only let
heaven come into view, and the Christian's heart will be well
warmed with thoughts of it. You may as soon persuade a king to
throw down his royal diadem and wallow in the mud with his
robes on, as convince a saint to sin when his heart is filled with
the expectation of heaven's glory.

Sin is a devil's work, not a saint's. The saint waits every hour
for the summons that will call him to stand with angels and glorified saints before the throne of God. How this should cheer
and sustain his heart when the fight is hottest and the bullets fly
thickest! If he must go through fire and water to reach it, what
is that discomfort compared to the eternal comfort of heaven?
Keeping the joy of heaven always before you will help you to
run your race with patience. It will help you endure your short
scuffles with temptation and affliction. What is more, it will
make you reckon also that these afflictions "are not worthy to
be compared with the glory which shall be revealed in us" (Romans 8:18).

SERVING GOD LOYALLY

*Sometimes He tests our loyalty in hard service
and sharp temptations, so that through our
faithfulness and bravery He may triumph over Satan.*

The Roman general Pompey boasted that a nod of his head would send his soldiers scrambling up the steepest rock on their hands and knees, though they were knocked down as fast as they advanced. This is the kind of loyalty God wants from us. And while He is never reckless with the blood of His servants, sometimes He tests our loyalty in hard service and sharp temptations, so that through our faithfulness and bravery He may triumph over Satan.

Perhaps you recall the time Satan impudently accused God of "bribing" Job, charging that this choice servant really only served himself in serving God: "Doth Job fear God for nought?" (Job 1:9). He dared God to take away His blessing, insisting that Job would curse God to His face rather than submit to suffering. So God let the devil have his way—and what was the result? Because Job remained steadfast in adversity, we find the Lord boasting to Satan, "Still he holdeth fast his integrity, although thou movedst me against him" (Job 2:3). In essence, God said, "You see, I have some who will serve Me without a bribe, who will hold fast to their commitment when they can hold on to nothing else. You took Job's estate, his servants, and his children, and still he stands his ground. You have neither captured his will nor his integrity!"

To allow a well-armed fortress to fall into enemy hands would be a disgrace to the defending soldiers. Spiritually speaking, such a defeat is even more dishonorable, because God in Christ gives His soldiers all the power they need to resist the devil at every turn.

We should not be surprised when an unregenerate soul yields easily to a temptation that promises carnal pleasure or profit. Those without Christ have no armor with which to repel the enemy's attack; they know nothing of His sweetness. So it is natural that they—for want of better food—would sit at the devil's table.

DON'T GIVE THE DEVIL A FOOTHOLD

*If a man is not strong enough to resist Satan
in a lesser thing, how can he believe he will
be able to repel a greater temptation?*

Satan is an encroaching enemy. Therefore, you must resist him constantly. "Let not the sun go down upon your wrath," warns the apostle; "neither give place to the devil" (Ephesians 4:26–27). A soldier assigned to guard duty on the outskirts of a city must keep watch as faithfully as the king's personal bodyguard, or the enemy will break through the outer limits and thereby gain access to the heart of the town.

If you yield to temptation along the perimeter of your heart, you give the devil a foothold from which to create havoc in your inner spirit. For example, you may become angry and thoughtlessly spew out some bitter words. At the very moment this unholy language spills from your mouth, the devil finds the floodgates open and enters. Then come gushing forth such things as you never dreamed of saying! He is a cunning opponent and will not easily relinquish any ground he gains. The safest strategy, then, is to give him no ground at all from which to work. If you so much as hesitate as you walk by the door where sin dwells, you give Satan more time to entice you to enter. Then you are on his territory.

Who will stop by a tavern to enjoy the company drunkards, or frequent places of sin, and yet pretend he does not intend to partake? Who will prostitute his eyes to unchaste objects, and yet remain chaste? Who will lend his ears to any corrupt doctrine of the times, and yet be sound in the faith? Such a person is under a strong delusion. If a man is not strong enough to resist Satan in a lesser thing, how can he believe he will be able to repel a greater temptation? You say you cannot avoid being surrounded by deep waters of temptation, yet you think you have the strength to hold your head above water? Then give careful thought to some practical advice: It is far easier, when in the ship, to keep from falling overboard than, when in the sea, to get safely into the ship again.

YOUR FAITH MUST BE PRACTICAL

*"As the Lord has called
every one, so let him walk"
(1 Corinthians 7:17).*

Religion which has no practical impact on our daily lives quickly becomes a vague, abstract notion that amounts to nothing. Yet many have nothing more than an empty profession to prove they are Christians. They are like the cinnamon tree whose outer bark is more valuable than all else that remains. The apostle speaks of such people in his letter to Titus: "They profess that they know God, but in works they deny him, being abominable and disobedient, and unto every good work reprobate" (Titus 1:16).

What is meant by "good works" becomes clear in the following chapter (Titus 2:2–8), where the apostle presents the duties which Christians ought to perform. A good Christian but a nagging wife, a godly man but a negligent father—these are contradictions that cannot be reconciled. The man who does not walk uprightly in his own house is nothing more than a hypocrite at church. If you are not a Christian in your shop, you are not a Christian in your closet—even thought you may pray there. If your faith founders in one way, it cannot flourish in any other. Some professing Christians fail in their duties toward their fellow men, while maintaining an outward show of worship to God. Others falter in acts of worship while seeming to be steadfast in their duties to their fellow men. Both inconsistencies are destructive to the soul. The soldier who stands in order is conscientious toward the whole duty that lies on him in regard to both God and man.

Third, to stand in order means we must stay within the bounds of our place and calling. The Israelites were commanded every man "to pitch by his own standard" (Numbers 2:2). This meant they were to be "arranged in order," as in a military formation. God allows no stragglers in His army of saints. "As the Lord has called every one, so let him walk" (1 Corinthians 7:17).

GO WHERE GOD CALLS YOU

*When you are in any place or about any work
to which you are not called, you may be sure
God is not in that place or enterprise.*

If you love to walk in God's company, you must abide in your place and calling. Every step in a different direction is a departure from Him. How much more blessed to stay at home in a humble place and low calling and there enjoy God's sweet presence, than to go to a sumptuous palace and live without Him. Truly, when you are in any place or about any work to which you are not called, you may be sure God is not in that place or enterprise. And what a bold adventure it is to stay where you cannot expect His presence to assist or protect!

In doing the duty of our place we have heaven's word for our security; but if we wander, we have heaven's word for our peril. It is just as dangerous to do what we are not called to do as to neglect or leave undone the duty of our place. As the earth could not bear the act of Korah and his company in usurping another's authority (Numbers 16:30–33), so the sea could not harbor Jonah, the runaway prophet. Refusing to be his escape route from God's command, the raging sea caused Jonah to be cast overboard (Jonah 1:14—15). Nor would heaven harbor the angels once they had left their God-appointed place and office (Jude 6).

The ruin of many souls rushes in upon them at this door. First they break rank, then they are led further into temptation. Absalom first looked over the hedge in his ambitious thoughts: He would be a king! This wandering desire to go beyond his place let in the bloody sins of rebellion, incest, and murder, and these at last delivered him into the hands of divine vengeance. The apostle joins order to steadfastness: "I am with you in the spirit, joying and beholding your order, and the steadfastness of your faith" (Colossians 2:5). That army alone is invincible in which every soldier stands in close order, attending to his duty and content with his work.

STAND—DO NOT SLEEP

*Take heed that you do not indulge yourself in
laziness; stir yourself to action, as we tell
someone who is drowsy to stand up and walk around.*

Watchfulness is more important for the Christian soldier than any other. In temporal battles soldiers fight against men who need sleep the same as themselves, but the saint's enemy, Satan, is always awake and walking his rounds. Since the devil never sleeps, the Christian puts himself in grave danger by falling asleep spiritually—that is, by becoming secure and careless. Either the unregenerate part of his nature will betray him, or grace will not be alert to discover the enemy and prepare for the assault. Satan will be upon him before he is awake enough to draw his sword. You should be aware that the saint's sleeping time is Satan's prime tempting time.

Even a fly dares to creep on a sleeping lion; unless he wakes up, there is nothing to fear. The weakest temptation is strong enough to foil a Christian who is napping in security. While Samson slept, Delilah cut his locks. While Saul slept, his spear was taken from his side and he was none the wiser. A drunken Noah slept and his graceless son took pleasure in seeing his father's nakedness. Eutychus slept, nodded, and fell from the third loft, and was taken up for dead. Thus the Christian sleeping in false security may be taken by surprise. He may lose much of his spiritual strength—be robbed of his spear or armor (graces, I mean)—or have his nakedness uncovered by graceless men, and bring shame to his profession.

Sleep steals upon the soul as quietly as it does on the body. The wise virgins fell asleep along with the foolish ones, though not so soundly. Take heed that you do not indulge yourself in laziness; stir yourself to action, as we tell someone who is drowsy to stand up and walk around. Yield to idleness and sloth and they will grow upon you; busy yourself in your Christian duties and spiritual drowsiness will flee.

WATCH CONSTANTLY

*The devil, I am sure, begins to tempt when saints
cease to watch. So be consistent in your watchfulness;
otherwise you stand to lose everything.*

What is our life in this world from beginning to end but a dark night of temptation? Christian, it is so very important to make sure your sentry lamp does not go out in this darkness, and your enemy catch you unawares. If you drift off into spiritual slumber, you are an easy mark for his wrath. And you may be sure if you do let sleep overtake you, the devil will hear of it. He knew the apostles' sleeping time and desired to sift them like wheat (Luke 22:31). A thief is just getting up when honest men are going to bed. The devil, I am sure, begins to tempt when saints cease to watch. So be consistent in your watchfulness; otherwise you stand to lose everything.

Some Christians, having been injured by a serious fall into sin, will be very careful for a while as to where they walk and the kind of company they keep. But as the soreness of their consciences wears off, they forget to keep watch and become as careless as ever. A shopkeeper who has just been robbed is very careful to lock up his store thoroughly. He may even stay up late to watch it for several nights, but as time passes he relaxes his guard and at last gives it no further attention.

Josephus, in his *Antiquities,* tells us that the sons of Noah lived only on the tops of high mountains for some years after the flood, not daring to build houses on lower ground for fear of being drowned by another deluge. But as time passed and no flood came, they ventured down into the plain of Shinar where their former fear gave way to one of the boldest, most arrogant attempts against God that man ever pursued. They tried to build a tower high enough to reach heaven (Genesis 11:2–4). The very men who at first were so fearful of drowning that they would not venture down the hill, at last ventured on a plan to protect themselves against all future attempts from the God of heaven to judge them.

MAY 27

BE VIGILANT IN ALL AREAS

It behooves us in everything to watch, so that God
may not lose His praise. No action is so small but
that in it we may do God or the devil some service.

I f you want to be a true soldier for Christ, always remain
watchful without slacking. Do not lie down by the wayside
like a lazy traveler; reserve your resting time until you reach
home and are out of all danger. God did not rest until the last
day's work in the creation was finished; neither should you
cease to wake or work until you can say your salvation is complete. You must watch universally.

The honest watchman makes his rounds faithfully and com-
passes the whole town. He does not limit his care to only one
or two houses. You also must watch over your entire being. A
pore in your body is a door wide enough to let in a disease.
Likewise, any one faculty of your soul or member of your body
can let in an enemy that may endanger your spiritual welfare. It
is said that so few are watchful in every area. You may set a
watch at the door of your lips so that no impure communication
comes out; but do you also keep watch at the door of your
heart to see it is not defiled with lust (2 Chronicles 23:6)? Perhaps you keep your hand out of your neighbor's purse, but
does your envious heart begrudge him the blessings God has
given him? The Christian who is truly scrupulous in one duty
may be falsely secure in others.

If the apostle bids, "In everything give thanks" (1 Thessalonians 5:18), then it behooves us in everything to watch, so that
God may not lose His praise. No action is so small but that in it
we may do God or the devil some service. There is nothing in
all God's creation that is so insignificant His providence does
not watch over it—even to a sparrow or a hair. By the same token, no word or work of yours should be thought too inconse-
quential to be watched over. Jesus said we would be judged by
every idle word that we speak (Matthew 12:36).

BE WATCHFUL WHERE YOU ARE WEAK

*Was there ever less love,
compassion, self-denial, or
power of holiness than today?*

Lately there has been much attention given to the small de-
tails of worship, but who is looking after the little child—
that is, the main duties of Christianity? Was there ever less
love, compassion, self-denial, or power of holiness than today?
Unfortunately these cardinal duties, like the child, are in great
danger of perishing in the fire of contention and division which
a perverse zeal for lesser things has kindled among us.

Be especially careful to watch yourself in those areas where
you know you are weak. The weakest part of the city needs the
strongest guard; in our bodies, the most vulnerable parts are
covered and kept the warmest. I would think it most unusual if
the fabric of your grace was so consistently strong that you
could find no weakness of any point.

Take my advice in the matter, and watch most carefully the
area you find weakest. Is your head weak—your judgment I
mean? See to it that you do not keep company with those who
drink only the strong wine of "seraphic notions" and high-
flown opinions. Is your weakness in your passions? Watch over
them as one who dwells in a thatched-roof house is careful of
every spark that flies out his chimney, for fear one should land
on the thatch and set the whole house on fire. When our neighbor's house is ablaze, we throw water on our own roof, or cover it with a wet sheet. When flame breaks out at another's
mouth, throw water on your own hot spirit to prevent a fire
breaking out in you. You should always have available some
cooling, wrath-quenching scriptures for just such a situation.

These preventive measures will enable you to secure your
house against any attack by the devil. And when the enemy has
been put down, you will still be "standing."

THE IMPORTANCE OF DOCTRINE

Truth is loved and prized
only by those who recognize it
and know it personally.

Since Satan comes as a serpent concealed in false teachers and tries to deceive us with error for truth, every Christian needs an established judgment in the truths of Christ. The Bereans studied Scripture to satisfy their judgments concerning the doctrine Paul preached. They refused to believe anything he had said before they "searched the scriptures daily, whether those things were so" (Acts 17:11). They took the preacher's doctrine straight to the written word and compared it to that; and the result was "therefore many of them believed" (v. 12). As the Bereans dared not believe before, they could not help but believe now.

Tertullian described the preaching of heretics like this: "They teach by persuading, and do not by teaching persuade." That is, they court the emotions of their hearers without convincing their judgment. For instance, it would be hard for an adulterer to convince his companion that her prostitution is lawful. Instead, he works another way: by romantic overtones and appeal to the flesh. The question of law is soon forgotten. judgment is easily and quickly absorbed by burning lust.

Thus error, like a thief, comes in through the window; yet truth, like the owner of the house, enters at the door of understanding, and from there moves into the conscience, will, and affections. The man who finds and professes truth before he understands its excellency and beauty cannot fully appreciate the worth of its heavenly birth and descent. A prince traveling in disguise is not honored because people do not realize who he is. Truth is loved and prized only by those who recognize it and know it personally.

If we do not desire to know truth we have already rejected it. It is not hard to cheat a person out of truth if he does not know what he has. Truth and error are all the same to the ignorant man and so he calls everything truth.

WHERE ARE YOUR AFFECTIONS?

"Ye become followers of us, and of the Lord,
having received the word in much affliction,
with joy of the Holy Ghost" (1 Thessalonians 1:6).

The more steady the glass of understanding is, where the light of truth is beamed upon our affections, the sooner they are set on fire: "Did not our heart burn within us, while he opened to us the Scriptures?" the disciples asked on the Emmaus Road (Luke 24:32). No doubt they had already heard Christ preach what He was saying now, but they had never been so completely satisfied as when He opened their understanding and Scriptures together.

The sun sends influence and warmth into the earth even when the light does not shed visible beams upon it. But the Sun of righteousness gives His influence only where His light comes to spread truth into our understanding. And as a Christian abides under these wings, a kind of heart-quickening heat is kindled in his heart. While the Holy Spirit is a comforter, He is also a convincer: He comforts us by teaching us.

The eye directs the foot—a man cannot walk safely unless he can see where he is going. Nor can he walk when the earth quakes under his feet. The principles we have in our understanding are the ground our behavior moves upon; if they shift, our actions will stagger too. It is as impossible for a shaking hand to write a straight line as it is for a faltering judgment to exhibit acceptable behavior. The apostle links steadfastness and unmovableness with "abounding in the work of the Lord" (1 Corinthians 15:58).

The Gospel came to the Thessalonians "in much assurance" —that is, in evidence of its truth (1 Thessalonians 1:5). And notice how it prevailed in their everyday lives: "Ye become followers of us, and of the Lord, having received the word in much affliction, with joy of the Holy Ghost" (v. 6). They were assured that this doctrine was from God and that assurance carried them through times of affliction as well as rejoicing.

BEWARE OF CURIOSITY

*Pride can make you a stranger to the
throne of grace and turn humble praying
for truth into ambitious arguments.*

The person who listens to every new opinion and covets the newest religious novelties is walking dangerously close to error. The "itching ears" Paul warns about commonly form a nasty scab of error (2 Timothy 4:3). Tamar lost her virginity by being naive—and chastity of mind is its soundness in the faith. Thus people compromise this soundness if they give themselves to every doctrine which is preached.

We must first be hearers and then disciples. Curiosity concerning many sects and persuasions can make a person skeptical of settling on the truth. Augustine, for example, confessed that he had gone through so many delusions that the errors made him afraid of truth itself. If a person has too many experiences with quacks he will have a hard time trusting the skilled physician.

Humbly seek an established judgment of God. A traveler who is so sure he knows the way that he will not ask directions may be the first one to get lost. Watch out for pride—no matter how confidently it soars now, you will later find it wrecked in the ditch of error. This is the destination God has made for pride, and it must keep His appointment.

Pride can make you a stranger to the throne of grace and turn humble praying for truth into ambitious arguments. So it is necessary for prideful men to be left to shame so when their understanding does return—if God's mercy allows it—they may "bless the Most High" the way Nebuchadnezzar did (Daniel 4:34).

Guard this judgment deeply in your heart—the God who gives an eye to see truth also gives a hand to hold it. What we have from God we cannot keep without Him. Cherish your closeness with Him or truth will not keep her intimacy with you very long. God is light, but you head for darkness as soon as pride suggests that you turn your back on Him.

BOLDLY PROFESS YOUR FAITH

We must not, then, spread our sails
of profession in a calm but fold them
up as soon as the wind starts to rise.

A person becomes unconquerable when he is empowered with a holy boldness from heaven to draw forth the sword of the Spirit and embrace the naked truth by freely professing it in the face of death. This is to have our "loins girt about with truth."

Maintain a steadfast profession of truth. The apostle pressed this instruction upon all Christians when he said: "Let us hold fast the profession of our faith without wavering" (Hebrews 10:23). Paul spoke against those who avoided assembling together with saints for fear of persecution, for he believed men who staggered spiritually like this stood next door to apostasy. We must not, then, spread our sails of profession in a calm but fold them up as soon as the wind starts to rise.

Pergamos was commended for her bold profession: "I know thy works, and where thou dwellest, even where Satan's seat is: and thou holdest fast my name, and hast not denied my faith, even in those days wherein Antipas was my faithful martyr, who was slain among you" (Revelation 2:13). It was a time when the deceiver sat in the judge's seat and Christians often drew a sentence of death. Blood was spilled right before their eyes but it did not make them deny the truth of Christ's blood given for them.

Paul delivered a strict charge to Timothy concerning a steadfast profession of truth: "But thou, O man of God, flee these things; and follow after righteousness, godliness, faith, love, patience, meekness" (1 Timothy 6:11). While people all around you aim at the world, run after spiritual riches with a chase as hot as theirs.

But what if this business of seeking righteousness cannot be transacted peaceably? Should we close up shop, put our profession on the shelf and postpone holiness until favorable times have come again? Paul's solution is to "fight the good fight of faith" (v. 12). Do not abandon your profession of truth but put your life on the line to keep it.

PROFESSING OF TRUTH IN THE FACE OF DANGER

*Engines of death continually
grind out the thoughts of Satan
against professing believers of truth.*

W e have the truth at a cheap rate now; but how soon the market may rise we do not know. Truth is not always available at the same price. We must buy it at any cost but sell it on no terms.

There has always been, and always will be to the end of the world, a spirit of persecution in wicked hearts. And even as Satan researched Job before he laid his hands on him, persecution is working now in the spirits of the ungodly. Engines of death continually grind out the thoughts of Satan against professing believers of truth. They already know exactly what they will do if power and opportunity are provided for them to carry out their sinister desires.

Satan comes first with a spirit of error and then of persecution; he poisons men's minds with error and then fills their hearts with anger against believers. It is impossible for error to bring any kind of peace; it is a brat of hell that must favor its father. Whatever comes from below can be neither pure nor peaceable. God has let this sulfurous spirit of error remain but He has given us a girdle of truth for protection.

But not everyone who applauds truth will follow it when it leads him to prison. And not everyone who preaches it is willing to suffer for it. Arguments are harmless things—blunt weapons which bring no blood. But when we suffer we are called to fight with the enemies of truth. And this requires more than a sharp tongue and logical brain. Where will disputers be then? They will appear like cowardly soldiers, who, in basic training when no enemy was in sight, seemed to be as brave as decorated heroes. To be on truth's side then meant only recognition and reward, not danger and death. But God has chosen the foolish to confound the wise in this service—the humble Christian, by his faith, patience, and love for truth—to shame men of high standing and no grace.

MAKE YOUR HEART CONFORM TO TRUTH

*Now there is a new union between you
and truth—or between you and Christ—
which can never be broken.*

L ikeness is the ground of love. A carnal heart cannot like
truth because it does not resemble truth. How is it possible,
then, for an earthly heart to love pure heavenly truth? It is
sad when men's understandings clash with their affections,
when judgment and will are so unequally yoked. Truth in the
conscience scolding lust in the heart! Like a quarreling couple,
they may live together for awhile; but the discontent will soon
expel truth as Ahasuerus did Vashti, and espouse principles
which will not cross his heart in its bent for sin. This has parted
many men from truth in these licentious days—they cannot sin
in peace and keep sound judgment at the same time.

But if the power of truth has transformed you into its own
likeness by the renewing of your mind, and made you bear fruit
like itself, you will never separate yourself from it. Before this
could happen you would have to part with the new nature
which the Spirit of God has formed in you. But now there is a
new union between you and truth—or between you and
Christ—which can never be broken.

A mighty power goes along with wedlock; two persons who
have barely known each other can leave friends and parents to
enjoy each other after their affections have been knit by love
and their persons made one by marriage. But a mightier power
accompanies the mystical marriage between the soul and Christ,
the soul and truth. This is the same person who, before conversion, would not have given a penny for Christ or His truth; yet
now, knit to Christ by a secret work of the Spirit, he can leave
the whole world behind for oneness with Him.

A persecutor once taunted a martyr by asking him if he did
not love his wife and children too much to die. "Yes," answered
the Christian, "I love them so dearly that I would not part with
any of them for all that is the Duke of Brunswick—whose subject he was—is worth; but for Christ's sake and His truth, fare-
well to them all!"

GOD PRESERVES HIS TRUTH

*If truth were not so precious to God he would not
allow it to be purchased with the blood of His people—
or most important, with the blood of His Son.*

God has never let truth get lost. In shipwrecks men do not try to save lumber and trivia of little worth but only what is most precious to them. In all the great revolutions of kingdoms and churches, God has preserved His truth. Thousands of saints' lives have been taken away, but the devil despises truth more than all the saints. And this is what still lives!

If truth were not so precious to God he would not allow it to be purchased with the blood of His people—or most important, with the blood of His Son. In that great day when the earth's elements will melt in fire, God's truth will not even be singed: "The word of the Lord endureth forever" (1 Peter 1:25).

God is severe to the enemies of truth. A dreadful curse is pronounced upon anyone who adds to or takes away from truth. One pulls down all the plagues written in the Bible; and the other takes away his part out of the book of life and out of the holy city. It is no wonder that God values truth so highly when we consider what it is—truth is the substance of His thoughts and counsels from everlasting to everlasting. It is the fullest representation that God Himself could give of His own being so we might know and love Him.

Princes used to send their pictures by ambassadors to those they hoped to win and marry. God is such infinite perfection that no hand can draw Him to life but His own; and this is exactly what He has done in His Word—and because of this, saints of every century have joyfully given their hearts to Him.

As we accept or reject truth we accept or despise God. Although men cannot pull God from His throne and ungod Him, they come as close as possible when they attack the truth—they execute God in effigy. Yet God never stops wanting those of us who love Him to cleave to His truth.

JUNE 5

TRUTH IS SOLID

*The man who cleaves to it
is free: "The truth shall
make you free" (John 8:32).*

T ruth has a firm bottom; we can lay the whole weight of our
souls upon it and know it will not break. Cleave to truth
and it will cleave to you. It will go with you to prison and
anywhere else you must go for her sake. "Not one thing," said
Joshua, "hath failed of all the good things which the Lord your
God spake concerning you; all are come to pass unto you, and
not one thing hath failed thereof" (Joshua 23:14).

Whatever truth promises, count it as money in your pocket.
"Fourscore years," Polycarp said, "I have served God and found
Him a good Master." When men forsake truth to advance themselves they are asking for disappointment. They are flattered
away from truth by empty promises and fare no better than Judas after he betrayed his Master into the hands of the Jews.

The man who cleaves to it is free: "The truth shall make you
free" (John 8:32). But Christ bluntly told the Jews why they
were in bondage: "Ye are of your father the devil, and the lusts
of your father ye will do" (v. 44). All sinners are slaves to Satan.
The man who has lust living on him like a parasite finds no rest
as he serves and provides for it every day. But if all the devil's
lusts bolted a single sinner to his dungeon floor, and the truth
of Christ opened his heart, you would soon see the foundations
of the prison shaken, its doors thrown open, and the chains falling off.

Truth will not be bound. And neither will it stay in a soul
that is tied up in sin. Therefore, once truth and the soul agree—
Christ and the soul—the person can lift up his head and know
that his redemption and delivery from spiritual slavery draw
near. The key is already in the lock to let him out. It is impossible for us to know truth as it "is in Jesus" and remain strangers
to the freedom that comes with it (Ephesians 4:21).

SINCERITY COVERS WEAKNESS

*Sincerity is the strength of
every grace. The more hypocrisy
in our graces, the weaker they are.*

S incerity, or truth of heart, can be compared to a girdle in
the light of the dual purpose of a soldier's belt.

Here at the loins the pieces of armor which defend the
lower parts of the body are connected to the upper ones. And
because it is impossible for these to be perfectly knit together
there will be some gaping open between the pieces. Thus a
broad girdle is used to cover all the unattractiveness.

Sincerity does the same work for the Christian. The saint's
graces are not so uniform, nor his life so perfect, that there are
no defects and weaknesses in his warfare. But sincerity covers
them all so they cannot expose him to shame or leave him vulnerable to danger.

The more closely the belt is drawn to the body the more the
loins are strengthened. Thus when God purposed to weaken a
people He used this expression: "I will loose the loins of kings"
(Isaiah 45:1).

Sincerity is the strength of every grace. The more hypocrisy
in our graces, the weaker they are. It is sincere faith which is
the strong faith, sincere love which is the mighty love. But hypocrisy is to grace as the worm is to the oak—or as rust is to
iron—it weakens because it corrupts.

This kind of uprightness is like a wildflower which can grow
in the waste places of nature. It may demonstrate a measure of
truth in its actions, yet it does not have a single fiber of sanctifying, saving grace. For example, God Himself came in as a witness for Abimelech after he had taken Sarah: "I know that thou
didst this in the integrity of thy heart" (Genesis 20:6)—that is,
he intended no wrong toward Abraham since he did not know
Sarah was his wife.

While this moral honesty motivates a man to be kind in his
relationships, the Lord's counsel has not changed since He directed it to Samuel: "Look not on his countenance . . . for the
Lord seeth not as man seeth" (1 Samuel 16:7).

AIM YOUR HEART TOWARD GOD

I see One who is above me—
infinitely higher than I seem
to be above you; and I fear Him.

The world's true man is one who will not wrong another man. Some boldly remind God that they would not steal a dime from their neighbor; yet these same people are thieves in far greater matters than all the money their neighbor is worth. They steal time from God and consistently conform the Sabbath to their personal plans instead of His. They purpose to sanctify God's name and even pray often for His will but their unholy hearts insist on compromise even though they know His will is sanctification.

But God's true man desires to be first true to the Father and then to man for His sake. For example, when Joseph's brothers feared he might deal with them brutally he freed them from suspicion: "This do," he responded, "and live; for I fear God" (Genesis 42:18). He reassured them, "Do not expect anything from me except what is right. You might think because I am a man of authority you would have no one to intercede for you if I take advantage. But I see One who is above me—infinitely higher than I seem to be above you; and I fear Him."

One of the Greek words for sincerity is an emphatic metaphor picturing something examined by the light of the sun. For example, when you buy cloth you can take it out of the artificial light and hold it up to the sun; if there is the tiniest hole or flaw in the fabric you can see it there. Truly the godly soul looks up to heaven and wants every thought, judgment, affection, and practice to stand before the light which shines through Scripture. (This is the great lamp where God has gathered all light to guide Christians, as the sun in the sky directs our bodies in our earthly walk.) If these agree with the Word and can look on it without being put to shame, then we go on our way and nothing can stop us. But if any one of them shuns the light of the Word—as Adam tried to hide from God—then we are at journey's end.

SIN'S UGLINESS

Sincerity does not blind God so He cannot
see the saint's sin, but makes Him consider
it with compassion instead of anger.

The soul-master of sin has so marred man's sweet countenance that it is no more like the comeliness God created
than the fiend of hell's similarity to the holy angel which
he had been in heaven. But by His grace Christ has undertaken
to heal this wound which sin has given to man's nature. His
healing power is at work in his elect, but the cure is not yet so
complete that no scars remain; this, then, is the uncomeliness
which sincerity covers.

Pardoning mercy eagerly embraces sincerity. Christ is the
One who covers our failures and sins, but He throws His garment of righteousness only over the sincere soul: "Blessed is
he . . . whose sin is covered. Blessed is the man unto whom the
Lord imputeth not iniquity." Everyone likes to believe this, but
notice the requirement of receiving this mercy: ". . . in whose
spirit there is no guile" (Psalm 32:1–2). Thus Christ's righteousness covers the nakedness of our shameful unrighteousness, but
faith is the grace which puts this garment on.

God approves of the sincere man as holy and righteous
even though he is not totally free of sin. And just as God does
not mistake the saint's sin for sincerity, neither does He unsaint
him for it. For instance, Scripture recorded that Job fell into the
pit of sin, but God saw sincerity mixed with his transgression
and judged him perfect.

Sincerity does not blind God so He cannot see the saint's
sin, but makes Him consider it with compassion instead of anger. This is like the husband who knows his wife is faithful to
him so he pities her weaknesses and cherishes her as a good
wife. "In all this," God said, "Job sinned not, nor charged God
foolishly" (Job 1:22). And at the end of the combat God brought
Job through with the favorable testimony that His servant had
"spoken of me the thing that is right" (Job 42:7). Job himself
saw his own earnestness dashed with failures, and this made
him confess his sin rather than presume upon God's mercy. But
God saw the sincerity.

EVEN THE SMALLEST FAITH

Scripture does not say, "If ye have faith like a cedar," but "if ye have faith as a grain of mustard seed" (Matthew 17:20).

God cautions us to be tender to His lambs, but no one can ever be as gentle as the Father Himself. Scripture lists three ranks of saints—"fathers," "young men," and "little children" (1 John 2:12–14). The Spirit of God shows His concern by mentioning the young ones first and delivering the sweet promise of mercy to them: "I write unto you, little children, for your sins are forgiven you for my name's sake" (v. 12). In plain terms He says their sins are forgiven. And at the same time He stops the mouth of guilt from discouraging them and opposing the Gospel—forgiven for His name's sake, a name far mightier than the name of a person's worst sin.

Sincerity, then, keeps up the soul's credit at the throne of grace so that no sin or weakness can hinder its welcome with God. Regarding iniquity in the heart, not just having it, keeps God from hearing our prayer (Psalm 66:18). This is a temptation which Christians often wrestle with when they let their personal shortcomings turn them away from prevailing prayer—they cower like some poor people who stay away from church because their clothing is not as fine as they would like.

To take care of this problem God has provided the promises—which, in any case, are our only ground for prayer—and has made them to fit the tiniest degree of grace. And as a well-done portrait faces everyone who enters the room, so the promises of the Gospel covenant smile upon everyone who sincerely looks to God in Christ. Scripture does not say, "If ye have faith like a cedar," but "if ye have faith as a grain of mustard seed" (Matthew 17:20). Justifying faith is not beneath miracle-working faith in its own sphere. The least sincere faith in Christ removes the mountainous guilt of sin from the soul. Thus every saint is said to have "like precious faith" (2 Peter 1:1). In Genesis we can barely see Sarah's faith, but in Hebrews 11 God gives it honorable mention, alongside Abraham's stronger faith.

CHRIST OUR SURETY

*"If any man sin, we have an advocate with
the Father, Jesus Christ the righteous: And he is
the propitiation for our sins" (1 John 2:1–2).*

Conscience is set by God to judge for Him in the private court of our own hearts. It is bound up by the same law by which Christ Himself will acquit or condemn at the last day. When we go on trial for our lives, before Christ's bar, the great question will be whether or not we have been sincere. And as He will not condemn the sincere soul, though a thousand sins be brought against it, neither can our hearts condemn us.

But how can God accept such imperfect obedience when He was so strict with Adam that He pronounced one failure as unpardonable? In the covenant God made with mankind in Adam there was no surety to guarantee and stand responsible for man's performance of his part of the covenant, which was absolute obedience. Thus God, to recover His glory and pay Himself for the wrong which man's default would do to Him, stood strictly with Adam.

Yet in the Gospel covenant there is a surety—Jesus Christ the righteous—who stands responsible to God for all the sins of a Christian's lifetime. And the Lord Christ cancels not only the vast sums of those sins which Christians are charged with before conversion, but also all the dribbling debts which they contract afterward through weakness and carelessness. "If any man sin, we have an advocate with the Father, Jesus Christ the righteous: And He is the propitiation for our sins" (1 John 2:1–2). So then, without impeaching His justice, God can cross out His saints' debts for which He is paid by Christ. It is mercy to saints but justice to Christ that God should do this. What a precious oneness when mercy and justice kiss each other!

Also, God required complete obedience in the first covenant because man was in a perfect state, full of power and ability to perform it; so God expected to reap no more than what He had planted. But in the Gospel covenant God does not infuse the believer with full grace but true grace; and accordingly, He expects not flawless but sincere obedience.

SINCERITY MAKES THE SOUL WILLING

Even when failure is the
result of our best effort,
willingness speaks success to God.

Aperfect heart and a willing mind are joined together. David counseled his son Solomon to "serve God with a perfect heart and with a willing mind" (1 Chronicles 28:9). A false heart puts off its work as long as possible and deserves little appreciation for work done under the rod of correction. But the sincere soul is ready for responsibility. Though it may lack skill and strength it will always be eager. Such willingness is like a hawk perched upon a man's hand; as soon as the game is in sight she launches forward and would be in flight immediately, except for the tether holding her back.

"The Levites" were "more upright in heart to sanctify themselves than the priests" (2 Chronicles 29:34). Why? They were more willing to work. No sooner had the word come out of the king's mouth concerning reformation than the Levites arise and "sanctified themselves" (v. 15).

Reformation is an icy path which cowards prefer to have well beaten by others before they venture out on it. But sincerity is made of better metal. It is like a true traveler—no weather gets bad enough to stop him after he has determined to make the trip. And the upright man does not stand around looking for loopholes or letting discouragement fester, but takes his orders from God's Word. And once he has them, he will not be turned back by anything short of a counter-command from the same God. His heart is merged with God's will. When the Father says, "Seek ye my face," the heart echoes, "Thy face, Lord, will I seek" (Psalm 27:8).

Even when failure is the result of our best effort, willingness speaks success to God. When a father asks his small son to bring him something, an obedient child does not complain that the command is too hard but runs to do it. And even if he uses all his strength but miscarries the simple mission, his willingness stirs up the parent's pity to help him. Thus Christ throws this covering over His disciples' blunders: "The spirit indeed is willing, but the flesh is weak" (Matthew 26:41).

GOD HATES HYPOCRISY

*Sincerity is the life of
all graces and puts life
into all our duties.*

J ust as sincerity covers all defects, hypocrisy uncovers the soul and strips it naked before God despite the richest embroidery of other qualities. This scab grows on even the sweetest perfection and changes the persons' complexion in God's eye more drastically than leprosy destroys the fairest face.

It is interesting to see how Scripture portrays the different characters of Asa and Amaziah. The writer says of Asa: "The high places were not removed: nevertheless Asa's heart was perfect with the Lord all his days" (1 Kings 15:14). Like true gold, sincerity allows grains for lightness. Asa's infirmities were not mentioned as flaws to dim his honor but as a wart or mole which an artist might use to accent the beauty of his other features. Thus failures were recorded to give a greater attractiveness to his sincerity, which—in spite of his sins—won a good testimony from God's own mouth.

Yet it is said of Amaziah, "He did that which was right in the sight of the Lord, but not with a perfect heart" (2 Chronicles 25:2). His actions were good but his attitude was faulty—and this turned his right into wrong. Thus we see how Asa's uprightness supported him in the midst of many shortcomings, but hypocrisy condemned Amaziah as he did what was right.

Sincerity is the life of all graces and puts life into all our duties, as life keeps the body warm and beautiful. And prayer breathed from a sincere heart is heaven's delight. If sincerity is gone, God must say of prayers what Abraham said of Sarah, whom he had loved dearly while she was alive: "Bury my dead out of my sight" (Genesis 23:4).

"Bring no more vain oblations; incense is an abomination unto me; . . . your appointed feasts my soul hateth: they are a trouble unto me; I am weary to bear them" (Isaiah 1:13–14). The thing God loathed which made Him speak so coarsely against His own ordinances was hypocrisy.

J U N E   1 3

DECEPTION OF THE HYPOCRITE

*Hypocrites' false playing and false
worship make the sweet Spirit of God
angry and cause His fury to break out.*

T he hypocrite intrudes upon the holy worship of God. Judas confidently sat down with the rest of the apostles at
the passover and felt as welcome as if he were the holiest
guest of them all. The proud Pharisee stood in the temple beside the brokenhearted publican. Yet when men like these
pray, they sound to God like wolves howling or dogs barking.
David's skillful hand played the harp so peacefully that he
soothed Saul's rages. But hypocrites' false playing and false worship make the sweet Spirit of God angry and cause His fury to
break out against them.

The hypocrite mocks God. But God will not be mocked. Jesus illustrated this doctrine when He cursed the fig tree, whose
green leaves invited hungry men to find fruit but sent them
away without any. If this tree had lacked the leaves as well as
the fruit, it would have escaped Christ's curse.

Every lie mocks the person who hears it, because the liar
makes a fool of him by cheating him of the truth. Delilah asked
Samson why he had told her lies, as if she had said, "Why are
you trying to make a fool of me?" God's command is that none
should appear before Him empty; but this is just what the hypocrite does, and thus mocks God. He may come with a full
mouth but he has an empty heart.

As for the formality of religious service, however, the hypocrite often outdoes the sincere Christian. Of all people he may
be called a "master of ceremonies" because he tries to entertain God with his tongue and knee, with only words and outward ceremony. Yet God looks on the heart. If the wine is good
a man can drink it from a plain wooden cup. But if a goblet is
wonderfully gilded, but has no wine in it, the hosts mocks his
guest by offering it to him.

SEEKING WORLDLY ADMIRATION

*It is to our advantage not to sample the free gifts
and give-away graces of stageplay saints, applauding
and drinking ourselves drunk with their admiration.*

C hrist is not "ashamed to call" the poorest saints "brethren," but He despises to have His name seen upon a rotten-hearted hypocrite (Hebrews 2:11).

Of all sinners the hypocrite does the most harm in this
world and therefore will have the most torment in the other
world. And yet it is religion which has consistently proved to be
the most effective bait of hypocrites, as they seek to snare others into their error and sin while posing as children of God.
Ehud, for example, could not have chosen a better key to open
the doors into King Eglon's presence than to say he had
brought a message from God. This caused such expectation and
confidence that Eglon welcomed him. When the two were
alone, the king rose to hear the Word of the Lord from the deceiver—but what he received instead was brutal death (Judges
3:14–30).

I confess the hypocrite may act his part so well that he may
accidentally do some good. His glistening profession, heavenly
speech, and eloquent preaching might bring to the sincere
seeker a measure of real comfort. Like an actor at center stage
who stirs up passion in the audience by counterfeit tears, the
hypocrite, playing his religious role, may temporarily spark the
believer's true graces. But that is when the Christian may be in
the most serious danger, for he will not readily suspect the person who once helped him spiritually.

It would have been far better had Sisera the Canaanite done
without Jael's butter and milk than to be nailed to the tent floor,
having been fooled by that woman's seeming hospitality. Thus it
is to our advantage not to sample the free gifts and give-away
graces of stageplay saints, applauding and drinking ourselves
drunk with their admiration. Sometimes a calculated distance
from the hypocrite is the safest way to avoid having our heads
nailed by errors.

SINCERITY IS ESSENTIAL

Eternity depends on your sincerity.
Your worth and destiny hang
on whether or not you have it.

A nother injury inflicted by the hypocrite is the scandal brought upon the church when his mask slips. Scripture says of Samson, "The dead which he slew at his death were more than they which he slew in his life" (Judges 16:30). Truly the hypocrite does more damage when he is discovered than when he seemed to be alive in his profession of faith. The hypocrite then puts a big stick into the hands of the wicked who have been looking for a way to bruise the saints. How fast they can then cause division and smear the face of all believers with the grime they see upon one hypocrite's sleeve!

Accusers of Christianity point out a hypocrite in church and reason that the whole group of believers is just like him. This is as absurd, of course, as to say that no coin is worth anything because we see one brass shilling among the silver. But this language fits the mouth of the ungodly world. And woe to the man's hypocrisy which manufactures these arrows for them to shoot at the saints. It would be better if he had been thrown into the sea with a millstone about his neck than to live and provide occasions for God's enemy to blaspheme.

Because sincerity covers all a Christian's weaknesses, there are several important reasons why we should carefully search our own hearts to see whether sincerity or hypocrisy reigns there.

Eternity depends on your sincerity. Your worth and destiny hang on whether or not you have it. This is your making or marring forever. "Do good, O Lord, . . . to them that are upright in their hearts. As for such as turn aside unto their crooked ways, the Lord shall lead them forth with the workers of iniquity" (Psalm 125:4–5). The hypocrite will try to crowd in with the godly on that last day and pass for a saint, but God "shall lead him forth with the workers of iniquity," company which is more his kind.

SINCERITY AND ASSURANCE

"Being justified by faith,
we have peace with God through
our Lord Jesus Christ" (Romans 5:1).

Others severely judge faults in order to hide their own flaws, thus enabling them to carry on selfish designs with less suspicion. Absalom, for example, criticized his father's government as a stirrup to help himself into the saddle. And Jehu loved the crown more than he hated Jezebel's whoredoms, even though he swung a keen sword against them. False zeal thus becomes revenge and shoots at the person rather than at his sin; hypocrites can hate the tyrant while admiring his tyranny.

The better way is to test a person's boldness by his sincerity, and not sincerity by boldness. True confidence and a spirit undaunted at death and danger are glorious when the Spirit and Word of Christ stand by to fulfill them. And certainly it is good when a person can give some account of the hope that is in him, as Paul did when he showed people the source of it operating in his life. This was Christian courage, not Roman fearlessness.

But the Christian must pass many rooms before arriving at this place of assurance, which adjoins heaven itself. Faith is the key which lets him enter into all these rooms. First, it opens the door of justification and takes him into peace and reconciliation with God through Jesus Christ: "Being justified by faith, we have peace with God through our Lord Jesus Christ" (Romans 5:1).

Through justification the seeker passes on to another room —the chamber of God's favor—and is welcomed into His presence: "By whom also we have access by faith into this grace wherein we stand" (v. 2). Not only have we been pardoned from sin and reconciled to God by faith in Christ, but now we are brought into the royal court under Christ's wing as favorites of the Prince.

We not only enjoy God's grace and favor and communion now, but move on and open the door to a third room—a hope firmly planted in our hearts for heaven's glory later, "rejoicing in the hope of the glory of God" (v. 2).

GOD'S PURIFYING LOVE

*Are you not only sorrowful because of your
divided affections but now wholeheartedly
determined to fear the name of God?*

Has God ever cast you into His furnace? Has His Word, like fire, taken a hold on you and refined your impure spirit so the unbelief, pride, and hypocrisy have been made visible and been separated like dross from gold? Only then are you free to sever sin from your soul and confess what a wretched person you have been, even though your spiritual condition appeared attractive in man's eye. Do you grieve to recall the religious pageantry you produced for the community in the name of Christ while you privately entertained lusts inside the locked dressing rooms of your heart? But, even more vital, are you not only sorrowful because of your divided affections but now wholeheartedly determined to fear the name of God?

Do you have just one design, to love Christ and be loved of Him? If the mighty power of God's Spirit has renewed your heart and gathered your affections into this one channel, and caused you to run to Him with sweet violence, then you are greatly blessed of the Lord. Mountains and rocks of corruption may surface in your stream to hinder the free course of your soul as it rushes to God; but even with these windings and turnings to block the most direct way to Him, sincerity—like water to the sea—will never turn back until it carries you to Him.

A sincere heart is a simple heart. The hypocrite is bred by the serpent, and like him, shrinks up or lengthens himself out to his best advantage, unwilling to expose himself to others. He has good reason, too, because he has the most credibility where he is least known. Hypocrites "seek deep to hide their counsel from the Lord, and their works are in the dark, and they say, Who seeth us? and who knoweth us?" (Isaiah 29:15). The hypocrite's pious words and the evil motives of his heart are miles apart.

THE SINCERE SOUL SHOWS ITS SIMPLICITY

*Truth in the heart is an exact copy of the truth in
God's Word—they agree as the face in the mirror
corresponds to the face of the man who looks into it.*

W e have had our conversation," Paul said to the Corinthians, "in simplicity and godly sincerity, not with fleshly wisdom" (2 Corinthians 1:12). The Christian will not subject heart to head—conscience to his policy. Because he commits himself to God he does not fear other people; and neither does he risk putting a hole in his conscience to keep his skin whole, but openly trusts God no matter what happens.

The hypocrite, though, shifts his sails and flies whatever colors the world unfurls in front of him. If the coast is clear and no danger is in sight he will appear as religious as anyone else; but no sooner does he discover a problem than he changes his course, concluding that the right road is any one which leads to safety. But "the highway of the upright is to depart from evil" (Proverbs 16:17).

Truth in the heart is an exact copy of the truth in God's Word—they agree as the face in the mirror corresponds to the face of the man who looks into it. Therefore if truth in the Word is harmonious, then truth in the heart, which is nothing but the impression of it, must be also. There is a threefold uniformity in the sincere Christian's obedience. He is uniform as to the object, subject, and several circumstances which accompany his obedience.

The hypocrite may touch the law of God in one point—in some particular command which pleases him—but ignore all the rest; yet a sincere heart stays close to the whole law in desire and action. The upright man's foot is said to stand "in an even place"—he is sensitive to the will of God in its entirety (Psalm 26:12). But Solomon said "the legs of the lame are not equal" and cannot stand in an even place because one leg is long and the other is short (Proverbs 26:7).

The Pharisees, for example, pretended to have great zeal for some of the commandments. They fasted and prayed, but prayed for their prey; and when they had fasted all day they ate at the expense of the widow whose house they devoured.

PRESSING TOWARD THE MARK

*Paul said, "I press toward the mark
for the prize of the high calling of God
in Christ Jesus" (Philippians 3:14).*

The sincere Christian is progressive. He never comes to his journey's end until he gets to heaven. This keeps him always leaning into God, thankful for each little favor but not smugly content with great measures of grace. "When I awake," said David, "I shall be satisfied with thy likeness" (Psalm 17:15). He had enjoyed many sweet hours of communion at the house of God; and the Holy Spirit had brought him covered dishes of which the world knew nothing. Yet David realized he would never have enough until heaven gave him his full portion.

When the Gauls first tasted the wines of Italy, they were so impressed with their sweetness that they would not just trade for this wine but resolved to conquer the whole land which furnished the grapes! Thus the sincere Christian does not think it is enough to receive samples of grace and comfort from heaven on special occasions, doing long-distance business with God. No, he meditates on taking that holy and blessed place which is the source of these riches and looks forward to drinking the wine of the kingdom in the kingdom.

This kind of meditation raises the soul to climb nearer and nearer heaven. The man who aims at the sky shoots higher than he who intends only to hit a tree. Paul said, "I press toward the mark for the prize of the high calling of God in Christ Jesus" (Philippians 3:14). Other people admired the apostle's spiritual achievements and would have been happy with them; yet Paul would have been most unhappy had he never scaled new heights of God's grace. He admitted that he had not apprehended what he was running for. The prize does not appear at midway but at the end of the race; and Paul ran toward it with full speed.

GOD HEALS HYPOCRISY

*It is the thirsty soul who will be
satisfied, but we must be sure
our thirst is right and deep.*

Take hypocrisy to Christ, the physician whose skill and faithfulness can make you whole. If you must die, die at His door. But for your comfort, remember that no one has ever fallen out of His healing hand; and no case has ever been too hard for Him to handle. He blamed the hypocrites who were ready to trust any charlatan ministering in his own name without God's authority but who would not confess the One who had come in the Father's name. And He who blamed hypocrites for not coming cannot be angry with you if you come. It is His calling.

Christ came to be a physician to sick souls. Pharisees were so settled in their own conceit that the Savior spent His time with those who admitted they needed help. If you cannot do anything but groan under your weight of hypocrisy, and send those groans in prayer to God, your healer will soon come to you. Since His ascension into heaven Jesus has never once laid down His calling, but still practices, granting forgiveness as faithfully as ever.

For example, Christ counseled Laodicea how to be loosed from her deadly disease of hypocrisy: "I counsel thee to buy of me gold tried in the fire, that thou mayest be rich; and white raiment, that thou mayest be clothed" (Revelation 3:18). He warned, "Laodicea, you are deceiving yourself and others with appearances instead of realities, with counterfeit graces for true ones; your gold is impure and your robes are rotten rags. They do not cover your shame but expose it. Come to Me if you want real treasure." Although Christ mentioned buying, what he meant was a buyer's spirit, valuing Christ and His grace so highly that, if they could be bought, a person would be willing to spend all the money in his account and even the blood in his veins for it, yet still go home saying it was a bargain. It is the thirsty soul who will be satisfied, but we must be sure our thirst is right and deep.

INSTRUCTIONS TO THE SINCERE

"Do not my words do good to him that walketh
uprightly?" (Micah 2:7). But surely it is a dangerous
walk when there is no word from God to guide our way.

To those of you whose diligent inquiry has shown sincerity from a pure heart, I counsel you to gird the belt of truth close and walk in the daily practice of uprightness. You are not ever dressed in the morning until this girdle has been put on, for the proverb is true which says, "Ungirded, unblessed."

God's promises, like a box of precious ointment, are collected to be broken over the head of the sincere man; "Do not my words do good to him that walketh uprightly?" (Micah 2:7). But surely it is a dangerous walk when there is no word from God to guide our way. It is a foolish man who dares go on when God's Word lies across his path. Where the Word does not bless, it curses; where it does not promise, it threatens. But God's approval keeps an upright soul safe.

The sincere Christian is like a traveler going about his business from sunrise to sunset; if harm tries to touch him God Himself will take care of it. The promise is on the saint's side, and by pleading it he may recover his loss at God's expense, for the Father stands bound to keep him protected. With this assurance in mind, let us look at several ways to walk in the exercise of sincerity.

What Luther said is most true: all the commandments are wrapped up in the first one. He pointed out that every sin is contempt of God; and so if we break any commandment we have broken the first. "We think amiss of God before we do amiss against God." Thus the Father commended a sovereign word to Abraham to preserve his sincerity: "Walk before me, and be thou perfect" (Genesis 17:1).

Uprightness before God kept Moses' girdle close to his loins. He was neither bribed by the treasures of Egypt nor browbeaten out of his sincerity by the anger of such a powerful ruler, "for he endured, as seeing him who is invisible" (Hebrews 11:27). He could see One greater than Pharaoh and this vision showed him the right path.

WALK IN VIEW OF GOD'S CARE

"The eyes of the Lord run to and fro throughout
the whole earth, to shew himself strong in behalf
of them," or to unite with them "whose heart
is perfect toward him" (2 Chronicles 16:9).

God strengthened Abraham's faith when He told him to be upright: "I am the Almighty God; walk before me, and be thou perfect" (Genesis 17:1). He was saying, "Act for Me and I will take care of you." Once we begin to doubt God's protection, though, our sincerity will soon falter. Hypocrisy hides in distrust. The unbelieving Jews, for instance, stored up manna overnight against God's explicit instruction because they did not have faith to trust Him for the next meal. And we do the same thing—first we doubt His care and then we start to lean on our own understanding.

This is the same old weapon Satan has always used to cheat Christians out of sincerity. "Curse God and die," he taunted Job through his wife (Job 2:9). Her words rang with bitter distrust: "Why are you still holding the castle of your sincerity for God to live in? You have been besieged long enough with sorrows on every hand. And to this day you have not gotten any news from heaven that God cares anything about you. Why do you not just curse Him and die?"

Jesus Himself faced Satan's identical tactic when he tempted the Son of God to turn stones into bread. We see, then, why it is so important for us to strengthen our faith in the caring heart and hands of God. This is the very reason He has made such abundant provision to shut out all doubt and fear from the hearts of His people. God has placed His promises like safe harbors, so if a storm sweeps the sea or an enemy chases us through the darkest night, we can tie up in one of them and know the comfort of full protection.

"The eyes of the Lord run to and fro throughout the whole earth, to shew himself strong in behalf of them," or to unite with them "whose heart is perfect toward him" (2 Chronicles 16:9). God does not depend on others to keep watch; His own eyes do it. He watches over us in the same way a mother takes care of her own child.

GOD ALWAYS ACTS FROM SINCERITY

God is so sincere that He gives
His own glory as hostage
for His children's security.

Love is the principle of God's actions and the good of His people is His goal. He never swerves from these. The fire of love never goes out of His heart, nor their good out of His eye. Every time He frowns with His brow, chides with His lips, or strikes with His hand, even then His heart burns with love and His thoughts meditate peace to His children. "So will I acknowledge them that are carried away captive of Judah, whom I have sent out of this place into the land of the Chaldeans for their good. For I will set mine eyes upon them for good" (Jeremiah 24:5–6). This was one of the sharpest judgments God ever brought on His people, yet He designed mercy and projected good into the severest hours of it. When the Israelites cried out that Moses had brought them into the wilderness to kill them, they were more afraid than hurt. God had plans for their good which they could not even imagine; He purposed to humble them so they could at last receive His goodness.

God is so sincere that He gives His own glory as hostage for His children's security. His robes of righteousness are locked up in their salvation and prosperity. He will not, indeed cannot, present Himself in all His magnificence and royalty until His intended thoughts of mercy become realities in the lives of His people. He is pleased to postpone the time of His appearing in all His glory to the world until He has fully accomplished their deliverance so both He and His people may come forth together in their glory on the same day: "When the Lord shall build up Zion, he shall appear in his glory" (Psalm 102:16).

The sun is always glorious, even on the most cloudy day, but this glory is not apparent until it has scattered the clouds which hide its light from the earth. God is glorious even when the world cannot see Him, but the demonstration of His glory appears when the glories of His mercy, truth, and faithfulness break forth in His people's salvation.

THE UNMOVABLENESS OF HIS LOVE

*The most flaming affections can quickly cool
in the heart of the man. His love is like fire
in the hearth—it blazes, flickers, and then goes out.*

As there is no "shadow of turning" in God's being, so there is no turning away of His love for us. There is no vertical point—His love stands still. Like the sun in Gibeon, it does not go down or decline but continues in its full strength. "With everlasting kindness will I have mercy on thee, saith the Lord thy Redeemer" (Isaiah 54:8).

The most flaming affections can quickly cool in the heart of the man. His love is like fire in the hearth—it blazes, flickers, and then goes out. But God's love is like fire in the sun. It never fails. In the creature, love is like the waters of a river, rising and falling again; in God, like the waters of the sea, which is always full and knows no ebb or flow. Nothing can destroy or change His love where He has sent it; and neither can it be corrupted or conquered.

God's love cannot be corrupted. There have always been people presumptuous enough to bribe God to desert His people. Thus when Balaam tried to win God over to Balak's side he spared no cost. He built altar after altar and heaped sacrifice upon sacrifice, hoping to force a word from God's mouth against His people. Yet the Father stayed true to His children and branded displeasure upon that nation for hiring Balaam and sending him on such a foolish mission. All the while, God continued to persuade them of His steadfast love: "O my people, remember now what Balak king of Moab consulted, and what Balaam the son of Beor answered him." Why should they remember this? "That ye may know the righteousness of the Lord" (Micah 6:5).

This story is mentioned to remind us of God's faithfulness toward His chosen ones. If you want your love for God to be incorruptible, embalm it with the sweet spices of His sincere love for you, which is immortal and cannot see corruption. If you believe God is true to you, how can you ever be false to Him again? It is cruel to return falseness for faithfulness in love.

THE LOVE AND FEAR OF THE WORLD

Get above the love of the world.
This is a stubborn root
for hypocrisy to grow on.

A Christian's sincerity is not eclipsed without the intervening of the earth between God and his soul. Get above the love of the world. This is a stubborn root for hypocrisy to grow on. If your heart becomes attached to something else in the world, and chooses it above everything else, you will be sick with longing for it and vulnerable to take the first advice Satan offers for getting what you want most. Hunters do not care how they get in—over hedges and ditches and through marshes—just so long as they catch the rabbit.

It is a mystery how a saint, with the precious ointment of Christ poured upon his heart, could still have such a strong scent after the world. It would seem that the sweet perfume which comes from those beds of spices—God's promises—would spoil the Christian's desire for hunting earthly game. The breath from Christ in them should so fill the saint's senses that gross earthly enjoyments would no longer be pleasing to him.

This is true as long as the Christian's spiritual senses are open, but as a head cold stops up the nose from doing its job, so a Christian's negligence obstructs his heavenly graces. And when the saint cannot enjoy Christ's divine savor, the devil takes advantage and immediately sets some worldly attraction before him. Soon the flesh picks up the scent and takes the Christian into a chase which dead-ends in sorrow and shame. Get above the fear of the world.

Fear of man brings a snare. A coward will run into any hole, no matter how filthy, to save himself. And when the holiest saints are tempted, they are like all other men. When Peter's reputation seemed to be in a little danger, he did not "walk uprightly according to the truth of the gospel" (Galatians 2:14). Instead he took one step forward and another back again—sometimes he was willing to eat with Gentiles, but at other times he was not. Why? Because he feared "them which were of the circumcision" (Galatians 2:12).

COMFORT FOR THE SINCERE ONE WHO DOUBTS

*There is a treasure of sincerity hidden in
many souls, but the time has not come for them
to open the sack and know their true riches.*

You may be genuinely sincere but doubt persuades you otherwise. To you I have a few words of counsel, and I trust God to give His blessings to each one.

Do not conclude you are a hypocrite because you cannot now see evidence of your sincerity. The patriarchs had money bundled up in their sacks and traveled all the way to the inn, not knowing what they had until they opened them. There is a treasure of sincerity hidden in many souls, but the time has not come for them to open the sack and know their true riches. Thousands of saints whose voyages were marked by fears about whether or not God's grace was truly in them have crossed the gulf and safely landed in heaven. Faith unfeigned puts a believer into the ark with Christ and shuts the door; but it does not necessarily keep him from getting seasick in the ship.

It is the work of Christ which demonstrates itself in such a way that we can see and own it, whereas the truth of our grace may not so clearly show itself. God has put the Holy Spirit beside the truth of grace to lead the soul into the light and show His children that truth. He alone is the great messenger who is able "to show unto man his uprightness" (Job 33:23).

But even as the eye, which cannot see anything in complete darkness, is still a seeing eye where there is light, so there may be truth of grace where there is not a sense of that truth present. So the person may hunt passionately from one church service to another to get the sincerity he already has, as one who looks frantically throughout the house to find his hat, when all the time it has been on his head.

Mark this down as real truth: "I may be upright even if I am not able to see it clearly." Although this insight will not furnish full comfort, it can be support until assurance comes.

EVIDENCE OF YOUR CALLING

*"He that believeth on the Son of God hath the
witness in himself" (1 John 5:10). Christ and
the Holy Spirit live in your heart.*

L ook for evidence of your sincerity. This is the "white stone"
with the "new name" in it, "which no man knoweth saving
he that receiveth it" (Revelation 2:17). Paul had this white
stone sparkling in his conscience more gloriously than all the
precious gems in Aaron's breastplate: "Our rejoicing is this, the
testimony of our conscience, that in simplicity and godly sincerity . . . we have had our conversation in the world" (2 Corinthians 1:12).

And Job was not without this evidence either when he ap-
pealed to the very thoughts of God while He was ransacking every corner of his heart by His heavy hand—"Thou knowest that
I am not wicked" (Job 10:7). He did not say he was without
sin—this we hear confessed again and again—but he knew he
was not a rotten-hearted hypocrite. The Lord gave way to let
him be searched and brought to trial to stop Satan's mouth and
to shame him for laying a spiritual felony charge against one of
God's elect.

Paul and Job were saints of the highest form, it is true; but
the weakest Christian in God's family has the identical witness
in him which they had: "He that believeth on the Son of God
hath the witness in himself" (1 John 5:10). Christ and the Holy
Spirit live in your heart just as they abide in the most holy saint
on earth. And you have the same blood of Jesus and the water
of the Word to wash you. These will testify for your grace and
sincerity as they did for Job's and Paul's. But witnesses in a
court of law must wait to give testimony until the judge calls
them to the bench. And you can be certain God will call up the
right witnesses at the right time. But now let us examine three
ways to find the evidence of a true heart.

WAIT ON GOD

Go to God's Spirit and wait.
The fact that you are at the
right door is comforting in itself.

Y ou might search all over the field and still not discover the treasure hidden there. The only way we can "know the things that are freely given to us of God" is by God's Spirit (1 Corinthians 2:12). He lives in God's ordinances as a governor works in his graces—evidences for heaven—sealed to our consciences.

Go to God's Spirit and wait. The fact that you are at the right door is comforting in itself. Even if you knock for a long time but do not hear anyone coming, you should not feel ashamed. Eglon's servants waited for a dead man (Judges 3:25), but you are waiting for the living God, who hears from heaven every knock you have ever given on earth. He is a loving God who hears your prayers and sees your tears. And even if He seems like a stranger, as Joseph appeared to his brothers, He is so big with mercy that He will soon fall on your neck and ease His heart by acknowledging and accepting you, and His grace in you.

Lift up your head, then—but remember, you cannot set times for God Almighty. The sun rises at its own hour, no matter what time you decide it should come up. Sometimes God comes to you in an ordinance and His heavenly light radiates into your innermost being while He quickens His Word to you. But have you not spent other nights on your face wrestling with God, wondering why He did not satisfy your soul? When someone brings a candle into the dark room we stir around and look for the thing we have lost and soon find what we had groped for in the darkness for hours. We can gauge more of our spiritual condition in a moment of His revelation than in days or weeks of His withdrawal.

Carefully watch for the seasons when God comes to you; take advantage of them. But even if God chooses to hide the treasure from your sight, comfort yourself. He knows your sincerity is real whether you can see it or not.

FASTENING THE BELT OF TRUTH

In Scripture, girding implies strength:
"Thou hast girded me with strength
unto the battle" (Psalm 18:39).

We have seen why sincerity is compared to the soldier's girdle or belt. Now we proceed to the other use of this girdle, which is to strengthen his loins and to fasten his armor close to him. In Scripture, girding implies strength: "Thou hast girded me with strength unto the battle" (Psalm 18:39). He "weakeneth the strength of the mighty" (Job 12:21); in this passage the Hebrew meaning is "He loosens their girdle." It is a grace which establishes and strengthens the Christian in his whole walk; on the contrary, hypocrisy weakens and unsettles the heart: "A double minded man is unstable in all his ways" (James 1:8).

A soul has as much of heaven's purity and incorruption as it has sincerity. "Grace be with all them that love our Lord Jesus Christ in sincerity" (Ephesians 6:24). So, then, the strength of every grace lies in its measure of sincerity. But not only does sincerity cover all infirmities but strengthens the soul for Christian warfare.

"The integrity of the upright shall guide them: but the perverseness of transgressors shall destroy them" (Proverbs 11:3). Despite all his clever strategies to save himself the hypocrite eventually sinks into his own instability; but sincerity holds the Christian safe above all dangers.

Israel's hypocrisy was "a generation that set not their heart aright"; they had a spirit which "was not steadfast with God" (Psalm 78:8). Stones which were not set right on the foundation cannot stand strong nor long.

We see more of this bitter fruit from the hypocrite's branches in the same Psalm: they "turned back, and dealt unfaithfully . . . they were turned aside like a deceitful bow" (v. 57). Before a defective bow is bent, you cannot see anything wrong with it. But when you draw the arrow to the head it flies to pieces. This is exactly what happens to a false heart when it is put under stress.

Sincerity, however, keeps the soul pure in the face of temptation. "He that walketh uprightly walketh surely" (Proverbs 10:9).

A PURE HEART

The sincere man stumbles as any traveler
might do, but he gets up and resumes his journey
with more caution and speed than before.

Sincerity does not guarantee we will not ever fall but it helps us up again when we do. The hypocrite, however, lies where he falls until he dies. Thus he is said to "fall into mischief" (Proverbs 24:16). The sincere man stumbles as any traveler might do, but he gets up and resumes his journey with more caution and speed than before. But the hypocrite plunges as a man from the top of a mast who is engulfed past any hope of recovery in the devouring sea.

We see this principle in King Saul's life. When his false heart discovered itself, he tumbled down the hill and did not stop, but went from one sin to another. In just a few years he had plummeted far from the place where he first left God. Once he had been so ready to worship God that he could not wait for the prophet Samuel to arrive—but later he was so far from seeking God that he went to a witch for counsel. And in the last act of his bloody tragedy, Saul desperately threw his life into the devil's mouth by self-murder.

The reason Saul's sin crushed him to death was that his heart was never right with God in the first place. Samuel hinted at this truth when he told Saul: "The Lord hath sought him a man after his own heart" (1 Samuel 13:14). Of course David himself fell into a sin far worse than Saul's wickedness—for which God rejected that first king—but the difference was that in David's life sincerity was "the root of the matter" (Job 19:28).

There is a double reason for the recovering strength of sincerity. One stems from the nature of sincerity itself and the other proceeds from God's promise which settles into the sincere Christian's soul.

The restoring nature of sincerity itself kindles the soul. Sincerity is to the soul as the soul is to the body, a spark of divine life kindled in man's heart by the Spirit of God. It is the seed of God remaining in the saint.

JULY 1

LIGHT IN DARKNESS

*"Unto the upright there ariseth light in the
darkness" (Psalm 112:4), not only light when the
night is past, but light in the darkness also.*

The hypocrite hears, prays, and fasts, but all to his detriment. Every ordinance is a wide door to let Satan in more fully to possess him, as Judas found in the last supper.

Sincerity lifts the Christian's head above the water and makes him float on the waves of trouble with a holy presence and courageous spirit. "Unto the upright there ariseth light in the darkness" (Psalm 112:4), not only light when the night is past, but light in the darkness also. The affliction which eats out the hypocrite's heart becomes vigorous nourishment to the sincere man's grace and comfort.

The hypocrite's joy, like strings of a musical instrument, cracks in wet weather; but sincerity keeps the soul in tune through all seasons. Unstable people let circumstances control how they feel—cheerful in sunshine but depressed in rain. And this is the way of the unsound heart. A few trying situations weaken his spirit and destroy him as a cold winter kills feeble bodies. Afflictions, however, help the Christian grow by uniting him even more closely with Christ. Trouble sends him straight to the arms of the Lord, as the bee flies to her hive in a storm. He is glad who has such a comfortable pillow as the lap of Jesus.

Sincerity keeps the Christian's mouth open to receive the sweet consolations which drop from the Word and the Spirit. In fact, God directs every one of His promises here. But hypocrisy is like a man with a badly inflamed throat, he burns inside but cannot swallow anything to quench the fire which sin has kindled in his soul. When God offers precious promises the hypocrite's conscience tells him, "These cannot be for you; you are not right with God. Surely you can understand that God's Word comes to sincere men; but what are you?"

VICTORIOUS IN AFFLICTION

A good conscience and God's Spirit
work together to make a Christian
rejoice in time of reproach.

The Hebrew word for sorrow pictures a shield that covers over; according to one commentator it denotes the disease which doctors say restricts the heart as with a lid, blocking out all relief. This is the hypocrite's sorrow in affliction, once conscience revives and God fills him with an amazing awareness of his sin. But now let me explore some particular kinds of affliction and show what comfort sincerity offers in each one.

Sincerity supports the soul under reproach from men. These are not just petty trials; they are known among the saints' martyrdoms as "cruel mockings" worthy of being recorded in the sufferings of Christ (Hebrews 11:36). The matchless greatness of Jesus' spirit appeared not only in His enduring the cross but in "despising the shame" which the foul tongues of His bloody enemies unmercifully loaded upon Him (Hebrews 12:2). Man's ambitious mind cannot put up with shame; applause is the idol he reaches out for and pays unbelievably high prices to have.

Diogenes once stood naked holding a heap of snow and drew gawking spectators to admire his patience—until someone asked him whether he would do the same thing if no one were watching. The hypocrite feeds on credit; he lives on what the breath of man's praise gives him. When that fails, his heart aches with disappointment; but when acceptance turns to scorn he dies because he does not have the approval of God while being reproached by man.

Sincerity, however, supports the soul against the wind of man's vain breath because he has conscience and God Himself as his character witnesses at the trials brought against him. A good conscience and God's Spirit work together to make a Christian rejoice in time of reproach. It does not matter then if the hail of man's accusation batters the doors and roof. The Christian is secure inside.

EXPECT GOD'S BLESSINGS

"God has not thrown me away.
I am in His mind day and night, and
His thoughts are at work to do me good."

Sincerity enables the Christian to think and speak well of
God. A deceitful man's countenance droops and his heart
enlarges with venom against God. He dares not let it come
out of his mouth but it festers in his deepest thoughts. Because
the wretched man does not love God, he has no place in his
soul to reflect on God's goodness. He fumes and frets and forgets the abundant blessings God has brought in the past and
gives in to resentment because of his present problems. And he
would much rather curse God than take the blame himself.

But the sincere Christian cherishes such sweet thoughts of
God that his meditations unite him with peace and he would
not consider speaking unworthily of God's glory or goodness.
We see this in David: "I was dumb, I opened not my mouth; because thou didst it" (Psalm 39:9). Both his spirit and body were
afflicted at the same time; he was sad and sick, yet he remembered where the affliction came from. "This is from You, Lord,
and I love You dearly; so I can take it without fear. After all, You
might have thrown me into a bed of flames instead of a bed of
sickness; so let me accept my correction thankfully." Thus he
fielded the blow without sending words of resentment or anger
back upon God.

Sincerity enables the soul to expect good from God. It
would break a heart of stone to read the sad cries which David's
soul made when he was in anguish of flesh and agony of spirit.
Yet even in this storm he cast out his anchor until it took hold
of God: "In thee, O Lord, do I hope: thou wilt hear, O Lord my
God." (Psalm 38:15). His expectation of good from God absorbed the bitterness coming from his pain: "I am poor and
needy; yet the Lord thinketh upon me" (Psalm 40:17). His condition was pitiful but his comfort was even stronger: "God has
not thrown me away. I am in His mind day and night, and His
thoughts are at work to do me good."

JUDGMENT OF THE NATION

"Remember that I stood before thee
to speak good for them, and to turn away
thy wrath from them" (Jeremiah 18:20).

E ven when the righteous are men beloved of God like Noah and Daniel, sometimes God still denies bail for a people under the arrest of His judgment. Jeremiah, for instance, boldly testified against the sins of the times and interceded in earnest prayer for the people; but he could not convert them by preaching or divert God's wrath by praying. Finally the Jews asked him not to prophesy against them any more and God commanded him to stop praying for the nation.

Judgment hovered like an eagle closing in on her prey. And the only thing that eased Jeremiah's heart, swollen with grief for Israel's sins, was his memory of sincerity to God and man: "Remember that I stood before thee to speak good for them, and to turn away thy wrath from them" (Jeremiah 18:20). It is as if he had said, "Lord, I cannot make this rebellious generation repent of their sins, and I cannot seem to prevail with You to reverse Your decree of punishment; but I have been faithful in my place both to You and to them."

On the contrary, horror and a terrified spirit is the portion of hypocrites in seasons of judgments. Pashur, for example, was a bitter enemy of Jeremiah and of the prophet's message from God. He put in long efforts to soothe the king with vain hope of golden days just ahead. And all this against the Word of the Lord at the mouth of Jeremiah! When the storm began to fall in torrents of judgment, Jeremiah tore away all such imaginary shelter by telling Pashur he would carry a personal brand of God's anger, besides sharing in the common calamity of the people (Jeremiah 20).

Sincerity strengthens the Christian deprived of the chance to serve God. If a servant of Christ could choose any affliction, he would select everything else before he would endure the pain of being a broken instrument, unserviceable to God. A devoted servant values his life by the opportunities he has to glorify God.

ROBES OF RIGHTEOUSNESS

"I put on righteousness, and it
clothed me: my judgment was as
a robe and a diadem" (Job 29:14).

Crowns and royal jewels cannot be compared with sincerity in value because truth in you will make a heart after God's own likeness. Nothing can make you more like Him in the simplicity and purity of His nature. When Haman was asked what should be done to that man whom the king delighted to honor, he assumed the king referred to himself and flew as high as ambition would take him. When God gives you sincerity He clothes your soul with His own robes. "I put on righteousness, and it clothed me: my judgment was as a robe and a diadem" (Job 29:14). This robe of righteousness makes you a greater conqueror than Alexander, who overcame a world of men. But you have defeated a world of lust and devils.

Have you ever looked at a frog and felt thankful God created you a man instead of such an ugly creature? How much more grateful should you be that He has changed you from the hypocrite you once were by nature into an upright Christian? Lactantius asked, "If a man would choose death rather than have the face and shape of a beast—though he might keep the soul of man—how much more miserable is it for the shape of a man to carry the heart of a beast?" The hypocrite is in the worst shape of all, for he carries a beastly heart in the disguise of a saint.

As we have noted before, sincerity shall not always keep you from stumbling or doubting—but your blood covenant with Christ will preserve you from final apostasy. Because the supply of grace in your hand is small, it is easy to question your security. "Can these weak legs really bring me to my journey's end? Can these few pennies—the little grace in my heart—possible pay all the charges to heaven, the many temptations and expensive trials of faith?"

DON'T GLORY IN SINCERITY

Can you ever starve, then,
when he who has fullness of grace
has undertaken to provide for you?

The loaf in your bread box is not enough to feed you the rest of your life. But you have a covenant! Has not God taught you to pray for your "daily bread"? If you diligently follow His calling every day, His blessing supplies everything you need.

And you have a Provider of spiritual "daily bread" as well. You have a precious Brother, a Husband who purposely has gone to heaven, where there is plenty of grace, so He can sustain our soul in this demanding world of stress and pressure. All power is in His hands: He goes to the Supply and sends whatever you need. Can you ever starve, then, when he who has fullness of grace has undertaken to provide for you?

The two coins which the Samaritan left were not enough to pay for the board and recovery of the wounded traveler: so he left his word that he would pay whatever was required when he came again. Christ does not just give a little grace from His hand, but "more grace" (James 4:6), as much as necessary to take us to heaven with Him. "The Lord will give grace and glory: no good thing will he withhold from them that walk uprightly" (Psalm 84:11).

You should not glory in your sincerity. It is true—sincerity empowers you to resist temptation and will lift you out of sin; but who empowers sincerity? Where does the root grow which feeds your grace? Not in your own ground but in heaven. It is God alone who gave it and will keep it. The Lord is your strength; let Him be your song. What can the axe do, even a sharp one, without the workman? Shall the axe brag that it has cut down something? Or the chisel boast that it has carved? Is it not the skill and art of the workman? When you resist temptation there is only one truth you can speak: "If the Lord had not been on my side I would have fallen."

EVANGELICAL RIGHTEOUSNESS

*This gift is a supernatural principle of new life
planted in the heart of every child of God
by the powerful operation of the Holy Spirit.*

This righteousness is twofold—imputed and imparted. Imputed righteousness is what Christ works for the believer, the justification which lets him stand righteous before God. This is called "the righteousness of God" (Romans 3:21). By way of distinction, imparted righteousness is what Christ works in the believer.

Although this righteousness is not inherent in God's children, we receive the benefit of it by faith, as if we had effected it ourselves. This is why Jesus is called "the Lord our righteousness" (Jeremiah 33:16).

God ordained imputed righteousness to be the basis for our justification and to be also the ground of acceptance of imparted righteousness. This righteousness belongs to the fourth piece of armor, "the shield of faith" and is called "righteousness of the faith" because it is applied by faith to the soul (Romans 4:11). The righteousness therefore which is compared to the breastplate here is the righteousness of sanctification imparted by Christ into the spirit of the believer. This gift is a supernatural principle of new life planted in the heart of every child of God by the powerful operation of the Holy Spirit. It is the only way Christians can seek God's approval and man's and is the only way we can perform what His Word requires us. We shall now study this work of God's Spirit in more detail.

If God's Spirit is not at the root, no "fruit of the Spirit"—holiness—can be found on the branches (Galatians 5:22). "Sensual" and "having not the Spirit" are inseparably coupled (Jude 19). When man fell he lost both God's love to him and his likeness to God.

Christ restores both losses to God's children—the first, by His righteousness imputed to them; and the second, by His Spirit re-imparting the image of God, which consists of "righteousness and true holiness" (Ephesians 4:24).

OUR DUTY TO GOD

*"Pray for us: for we trust we have a
good conscience, in all things willing
to live honestly" (Hebrews 13:18).*

Mary demanded, "Tell me where thou hast laid him"
(John 20:15), implying she wanted to carry the body of
Jesus with her, on her shoulders—a desire she was not
physically able to perform. Her affections were much stronger
than her back.

The principle of holiness in a saint, then, makes him try to
lift a duty which he can barely move; he can do little more than
desire with all his heart to see it done. Paul sketches his own
character from the sincerity of his will and efforts, not from the
perfection of his works: "Pray for us: for we trust we have a
good conscience, in all things willing to live honestly" (Hebrews 13:18). He was so willing to follow God into holiness that
he did not hesitate to claim "a good conscience," although he
could not accomplish everything he wanted to do.

True holiness will not divide what God joins: "God spake all
these words" (Exodus 20:1). There God gave together the four
commandments concerning Himself and the six concerning
man. And a truly sanctified heart does not want to skip over or
blot out one word God has written but desires to be a doer of
the whole will of God.

"To God and man"—first to God and then to man; this is
the sequence of a sanctified life. Paul said the Macedonians first
gave "their own selves to the Lord, and unto us by the will of
God" (2 Corinthians 8:5). A sanctified person first obeys God
and then, out of obedience to His will, serves his fellow man.

In Christianity we cannot write a right line without a rule, or
with a false one. And every standard except the Word is a false
rule—"to the law and to the testimony: if they speak not according to this word, it is because there is no light in them" (Isaiah
8:20). Whatever the Word of God requires is the rule of God's
Spirit; apocryphal holiness—doubtful, marginal, or extraneous
—is not true holiness at all.

DO NOT SIN IN LIGHT OF TRUTH

When God sees men scorn His truth by imprisoning it from having any command over their lives, this sight kindles the fire of His wrath into a consuming flame.

I f you are a slave to the devil it does not matter where the chain fastens you to him, the head or the foot. He holds you just as surely by the foot—in your actions—as he would by the head—in your blasphemy.

Christian, your wickedness is greater because it is committed in the face of truth. Many men are betrayed into unholiness by mistakes of faulty judgment; but your judgment lights another path for you, unless you intend to heap up more sin by fathering your unholiness on truth itself.

Sinners miss their way to heaven in the dark, or are misled by erroneous judgment, which, if corrected, might bring them back to the path of holiness. But you sin in the broad daylight of truth and boldly head for hell at high noon. This makes you favor the devil himself, who knows truth from error as well as any angel does—but he refuses to be ruled by it.

If a soloist sang to a sweet melody with her voice but with her hand played a different tune, the dissonant chords would offend the hearer more than if she had sung what she played. Thus, to sing to truth with our judgment but play wickedness with our hearts and hands is more abhorrent to God than the harmony of poor judgment and an unholy life.

Hanun, for example, would not have enraged David so much if he had charged him with twenty thousand men as he did by abusing his ambassadors in such a base way. The open hostility which sinners express by their lives does not provoke God so much as the vile dishonor they give to His truth, which He sent to make them free. When God sees men scorn His truth by imprisoning it from having any command over their lives, this sight kindles the fire of His wrath into a consuming flame. It is a dangerous choice to walk contrary to the light of God's truth.

CHOSEN BEFOREHAND BY GOD

*If men had kept the righteousness which God originally
created in him, Christ's pain would have been spared,
for it was man's lost holiness He came to recover.*

Why did God choose some men and leave others to sink in torment and misery? The apostle tells us "He hath chosen us in him before the foundation of the world, that we should be holy" (Ephesians 1:4). Not because God fore-saw that we of ourselves would ever be holy, but because He resolved He would make us holy. It was as if a highly skilled carpenter saw a forest of trees growing on his own ground—all alike, not one better than another—and he marked a certain number and set them apart in his mind, determining to make of them some wonderfully crafted objects.

Thus God chose some out of all mankind and set them apart to carve His own image of righteousness and holiness upon them. This is workmanship of such high quality that when He has finished it, and will show it to men and angels, it will out-shine the universe itself.

In sending His Son into the world He made us holy. Glori-ous angels who behold the face of God continually are ready to fly immediately wherever He assigns them. But God has such an important work to be done that He would not trust His servants, but rather His only Son, to accomplish it. And note the motive, the bottom of His heart in this great undertaking: He "gave him-self for us, that he might redeem us from all iniquity, and purify unto himself a peculiar people, zealous of good works" (Titus 2:14).

If men had kept the righteousness which God originally created in him, Christ's pain would have been spared, for it was man's lost holiness He came to recover. Neither God's glory nor man's happiness could be attained until this holiness was restored. As God is glorious in the holiness of His own nature and works, so He is glorified by the holiness of His people's hearts.

GOD'S EXALTED PURPOSE

*Scripture says it is better for us not to vow and
dedicate ourselves to Him than later to scheme so
we can sidestep that promise (Ecclesiastes 5:5).*

A regenerate heart is the "workmanship" of God Himself (Ephesians 2:10). And why has He been such a compassionate Artisan? We read that His saints are "created in Christ Jesus unto good works, which God hath before ordained that we should walk in them" (v. 10).

God's exalted purpose for man, then, underscores the unrighteousness of a saint and hands down a more serious verdict upon his sin than upon the sin of others because it has been committed against such a mighty work of His Spirit. A sin in the temple was more grave than that same sin committed by a Jew in his house, because the temple was a consecrated place. Because the saint is a consecrated person, then, his unholy acts profane God's temple. The sin of a natural man is theft because he robs God of the glory due to him; but the sin of a saint is sacrilege because he robs God of the sacredness which his profession of faith has vowed to Him.

Surely it is better not to repent at all than to repent of our repentance. Scripture says it is better for us not to vow and dedicate ourselves to Him than later to scheme so we can sidestep that promise (Ecclesiastes 5:5). To do this, the person must tell the world a baneful lie—that he has found some weakness or iniquity in God which changed his mind about following Him.

In a word, the Holy Spirit has consecrated the saint to God and also endues him with new life from God: "You hath he quickened, who were dead in trespasses and sins" (Ephesians 2:1). When God breathed a rational soul into man, he purposed that he should live up to His principles of holiness and righteousness and not follow the ways of life of carnal men. God clearly spoke His mind—"As ye have therefore received Christ Jesus the Lord, so walk ye in him" (Colossians 2:6).

GOD'S SOVEREIGN DIRECTION

*God loves purity in His children so much that He
will rub as hard as He has to in order to
get out the dirt ingrained in our natures.*

I n all His providences God is at work. "All things work together for good to them that love God" (Romans 8:28). As
God uses all seasons of the year for the harvest—the ice and
cold of winter as well as the heat of summer—so He uses both
good and bad, pleasing and unpleasing providences, for pro-
moting holiness. Winter providences kill the weeds of lust and
summer providences ripen the fruits of righteousness.

Even when God afflicts it is for our good, to make us partakers of His holiness. Bernard has compared afflictions to a sharp,
scratching burr called a teasel, which was used to make cloth
more pure and fine. And God loves purity in His children so
much that He will rub as hard as He has to in order to get out
the dirt ingrained in our natures; He would rather see a hole
than a spot in His child's garment.

But sometimes God's sovereign direction is more gentle,
and when He lets His people sit under the sunny bank of comfort, sheltered from the cold gusts of affliction, it is to draw
forth the sap of grace and hasten their growth in holiness. Paul
understood this when he urged the Roman saints "by the mercies of God" to present their bodies "a living sacrifice, holy, acceptable unto God" (Romans 12:1). He implied that God
expects a reasonable return on the mercies, mercies which have
all come from Him.

When the farmer lays his compost on the ground, he intends to receive it again at harvest in a fuller crop; and so does
God, by His mercies. Thus He firmly indicted Israel for her un-
thankfulness: "She did not know that I gave her corn, and wine,
and oil, and multiplied her silver and gold, which they prepared for Baal" (Hosea 2:8). God was angry because Israel embraced adultery at His expense.

SATAN WANTS CHRISTIANS TO BE UNHOLY

Christian blood is sweet to Satan
but the blood of the Christian's
godliness is far sweeter.

S imple holiness, then, is the flag which the soul hangs out to declare open defiance of Satan and friendship with God, even as the devil strives to shoot it down. And here is the ground of that quarrel, which will never end as long as Satan is an unclean spirit and the saint a holy child of God: "All that will live godly in Christ Jesus shall suffer persecution" (2 Timothy 3:12).

Persecutors often try to disguise their malice under the pretense of good works; but the Spirit of God looks through their hypocritical mufflers and knows the instructions they have from hell. God's Spirit tells us that godliness is the target at which Satan levels his arrows. Of course there are more kinds of godliness in the world than one, but Satan opposes only the true one: "all that will live godly in Christ Jesus."

Christian blood is sweet to Satan but the blood of the Christian's godliness is far sweeter. He prefers to sever the saint from his godliness rather than butcher him for it. Yet so he will not be too conspicuous, he often plays at small game and expresses his cruelty upon saints' bodies; but this happens only when he cannot capture their souls; "They were sawn asunder, were tempted, were slain" (Hebrews 11:37). What the persecutors wanted more than anything else was to entice them into sin and apostasy; thus they tempted Christians severely before they killed them. The devil considers it a complete triumph if he can strip away the saint's armor and bribe him away from steadfastness in his holy profession.

The devil would rather see Christians defiled with sin and unrighteousness than defiled in blood and pain, for he has learned that persecution only trims the church, which soon comes back up all the thicker; it is unrighteousness which ruins it. Persecutors, then, only plow God's field for Him and all the time He is sowing it with the saints' blood.

FOLLOWING SPIRITUAL ORDINANCES

*"If we say we have fellowship
with him, and walk in darkness,
we lie" (1 John 1:6).*

We must either renounce our hope of going to heaven or resolve to walk in the only path that will lead us there. It is vain breath which does not set the sails of our affections and the movement of our feet in the direction of our desired destination.

It empowers us for communion with God. Communion with God is so wonderful that many pretend to have it when they do not even know what it is. It is like the man who brags about knowing the king but never has seen his face or met him. God's Spirit calls it a lie when a man says he knows the Lord but entertains unrighteousness too: "If we say we have fellowship with him, and walk in darkness, we lie" (1 John 1:6). Communion is rooted in union, and union in likeness. "Can two walk together, except they be agreed?" (Amos 3:3). There is a big difference between communion with God and familiarity with ordinances. A man may live with ordinances every day but still be a stranger to God. Not everyone who walks around in the palace talks with the prince.

Ordinances are a kind of exchange where holy saints trade with God by His Spirit for heavenly treasures, an enriched filling of grace and comfort. But because an unholy heart has nothing to trade with God, the Father will not communicate His pure grace to him. Even the holy person under the power of a temptation is unfit to have communion with God until he overcomes the sin.

Solomon explained it like this: "A righteous man falling down before the wicked is as a troubled fountain, and a corrupt spring" (Proverbs 25:26). How much more true when a saint falls before the wicked one and yields to temptation, his spirit clouded with impurity! If we know better than to drink from a troubled spring, though wholesome in itself, but wait until it settles and becomes clear again, how can we expect God to taste communion with a godly person before his stream runs clear with repentance for sin?

JULY 15

THE EFFECT OF HOLINESS

Therefore God has given us a strict charge:
"Follow peace with all men, and holiness, looking
diligently lest any man fail of the grace of God;
lest any root of bitterness springing up trouble you,
and thereby many be defiled" (Hebrews 12:14–15).

When a Christian sees holiness sparkle in the life of another believer, the grace within him springs up as the baby in Elisabeth leaped at the sound of Mary's voice. Truly, one holy man is enough to put life into a whole society; but on the contrary, the looseness of a single professing Christian endangers the entire group of people who know him. Therefore God has given us a strict charge: "Follow peace with all men, and holiness, looking diligently lest any man fail of the grace of God; lest any root of bitterness springing up trouble you, and thereby many be defiled" (Hebrews 12 14–15).

A scab on the wolf's back is not dangerous to the sheep because they cannot easily be lured to spend time with him. But if the sore spreads into the flock, among Christians who feed, pray, hear, talk and walk in fellowship together, then there is a great fear and danger it might spread. Thus a careless Christian helps the devil with more efficiency than whole troops who never profess to believe. In fact, Satan had a whole fistful of sins and errors that he did not know what to do with until he found a way to hire unholy professors of the faith as his brokers to recommend and dispense them to others.

In a word, then, the man who will not keep up the power of holiness in his life, in some measure, makes himself useless to Christ. Do you want to pray for others? A heathen could tell an evil man to hold his peace and not let the gods know he was aboard the ship when a storm swept in. Is it comfort you want to speak to a grieving person? Or counsels to a friend? They will think you are only joking until your commendation of holiness is joined by holiness in your own life; that is to say, until you commend it to yourself.

HOLINESS IS ON THE WANE

*The power of holiness has
deteriorated among us, compared
to what it was a generation ago!*

W hen Josiah came to the crown he found Judah crumbling to pieces; yet because his heart was turned to God, and prepared to walk before Him, God accepted Josiah's plea for a people under arrest and at the prison door. Their safety was linked to the ruler's life, for soon after Josiah died the nation tumbled into ruin again (2 Kings 23:25–17).

When Martin Luther foresaw the black clouds of God's judgment coming toward Germany he told friends that he would do his best to keep it from falling in his lifetime; and he believed that it would not. But he concluded, "When I am gone, let them that come after me look to it."

The power of holiness has deteriorated among us, compared to what it was a generation ago! Christianity runs unclean and full of dregs, murky and unholy among professing believers in Christ. And we know God will not put up with it much longer. If Egypt knows a drought is coming by the low ebbing of the Nile, surely we can see judgment hovering by the fall of the power of godliness.

We hear many people mourning for what they have lost—some for the lives of friends in war, others for their wealth and possessions. But the group who must claim first place among mourners are churchgoers who have lost their first love. Thorough decay has set in because they have forfeited their compassion for Christ, His truth, worship, fellow servants, and their holy walk before God and man.

We are a people redeemed from countless dangers and deaths. It is a poor time for a rescued man to start stealing and cheating again, as soon as the rope is cut from his neck. Surely it added to Noah's sin to be drunk almost as soon as he had safely landed on shore, after he had seen the whole earth sinking before his eyes. Here was the one righteous man God had left to plant His world again with a godly seed.

FIGHTING SIN

*When we are unselfish and kind to others, though,
a "cup of cold water" given "in the name of
a disciple" is more valuable in God's sight than a
cup of gold for selfish purposes (Matthew 10:42).*

The person who saunters out into the appearance of evil in the name of "freedom in the Spirit" may find himself committing gross sin under some appearance of good. Combat sin for God's reasons.

Some people resist sin for such shallow motives that God hardly notices their victory. When we have fasted and prayed He asks, "Did ye at all fast unto me, even to me?" (Zechariah 7:5). When we are unselfish and kind to others, though, a "cup of cold water" given "in the name of a disciple" is more valuable in God's sight than a cup of gold for selfish purposes (Matthew 10:42).

God wants it to be His love which constrains us to renounce sin. Princes prefix documents with their coat of arms and royal names before sending them out; and God sets His glorious name before His commandments too—"God spake all these words" (Exodus 20:1). God would have His children to sanctify His name in everything they do.

Just as the Father commands His family to turn away from evil, it is for His sake that He wants us to mourn over those sins we do commit. Sometimes grief can be so selfish that a man is satisfied to snatch his soul from eternal damnation even if this somehow defamed the glory of God. But a gracious soul's mourning runs in another channel: "Against thee, thee only, have I sinned" (Psalm 51:4).

There is a vast difference between a man who works for another person and one who is his own boss. The independent person assumes all his losses himself, but the servant who trades with his master's stock must put every loss on that account. Christian, you are a servant. All you have is not really yours, but God's. And when you fall into sin, your sorrow must be for the way you have wronged Him: "I have dishonored my God and wasted the talents He has given me; I have wounded His name and grieved His Spirit."

PURITY IN WORSHIP

*The Holy Spirit sometimes gives more blessing
in some duties than He does in others, to fill
the Christian with extraordinary refreshment.*

The same light which shows us there is a God shows us He must be worshiped in holiness. Under the law, God was particular about every facet of worship. The tabernacle, for example, had to be made of the best materials; the workmen were gifted with rare talent; only the most excellent sacrifices were acceptable; and the persons who ministered to the Lord had to be holy in a peculiar way. God is wonderful in His worship!

Be consistent in all ordinances. God hates partiality, especially in ordinances of worship, all of which have their origins in Him. And surely we must not reject anything God chooses as a blessing to His children. He communicates Himself with amazing variety to keep our hearts encouraged. The spouse looks for her Beloved in secret at home but does not find him; so she goes to the public places and meets him whom her "soul loveth" (Song of Solomon 3:4).

No doubt Daniel had been to the throne of grace often, but God reserved the fullness of His love, and the opening of some mysteries to him, when he added fasting to his prayers. Only then did God send a messenger from heaven to let Daniel know His mind and heart.

The Holy Spirit sometimes gives more blessing in some duties than He does in others, to fill the Christian with extraordinary refreshment. Sometimes the baby takes milk from one breast and then from the other. While David was meditating, a heavenly heat kindled in his heart until at last the fire caught and spread. The eunuch was reading the Word when God sent Philip to join his chariot. Christ revealed Himself to the apostles as they were breaking bread. And He joined the two disciples on the road to Emmaus as they were having fellowship with each other. Cornelius was praying in his house when a vision from heaven directed him in the way he should walk.

DO NOT NEGLECT WORSHIP

Homage to our sovereign Lord is His just due.
If there were no worship, how could we declare that
it is in Him that we live and move and have our being?

B e careful, then, Christian, not to neglect any one privilege of worship—it might be the door where Jesus stands waiting to enter your soul! The Spirit is free. Do not bind Him to one duty only; but wait on Him in every one of them. It is not wisdom to let any water run past your mill which might be useful to send your soul moving toward heaven.

Maybe you do not receive as much enlightenment as you want when you seek God in public services. Let me ask you this—what kind of communion do you have with Him in secret? Here is a hole wide enough to lose everything you get in public, if you do not repair it. Samuel would not sit down to the feast with Jesse and his sons until David—the youngest of the family—was brought in to join them. If you want God's presence in any of the ordinances you must bring back the one you sent away; it might be the least important in your way of thinking but the one God has chosen to crown with His most special blessing to your soul.

Seek God's goals. God has two purposes in worship. First, He intends for us to honor Him as sovereign Lord. And second, worship is the way He communicates His presence and blessings to His children.

Homage to our sovereign Lord is His just due. If there were no worship, how could we declare that it is in Him that we live and move and have our being? One of the first things God taught Adam and his children was divine worship. And the holy person makes it the most important thing in his life to sanctify God's name and give Him glory. A subject may offer a present to his prince in such a ridiculous fashion that the ruler may be more scorned than honored; the soldiers bowed their knees to Jesus but their hearts mocked the holy God.

THE CHRISTIAN'S VOCATION

*Holiness must be written upon
the Christian's vocation as well
as upon his religious services.*

The holy Christian is stirred up by the Spirit of God to go from one aspect of worship to another, as a bee flies from flower to flower, to store up more grace.

The holy man does not seek God for an admirable reputation among Christians or for some sort of excitement. Instead, he is like the merchant who sails from port to port, not for sightseeing but for taking in costly pearls as he discovers them. And a Christian should be even more ashamed than the trader who returns home from his search empty, with no treasure.

Are you watching others grow rich in grace through their part in God's ordinances while you come away as a beggar? God sees a precious hunger in those who value Christ and His grace as the strongest need in their lives. "Ho, every one that thirsteth, come ye to the waters, and he that hath no money; come ye, buy, and eat; yea, come, buy wine and milk without money and without price" (Isaiah 55:1).

The Spirit of God alludes here to a custom in maritime towns—when a ship came into port, her traders went about the village crying out the arrival of their goods: "All who want certain commodities, let them come to the waterside, where they can be bought for a price." Thus Christ calls everyone who sees his need of Him and of His graces to come to the ordinances, where these gifts can be had freely.

Holiness must be written upon the Christian's vocation as well as upon his religious services. The construction superintendent who observes the building code is as exact in framing the kitchen as he is the parlor; so by the law of Christianity we must be as precise in our worldly business as in the duties of worship. "Be ye holy in all manner of conversation" (1 Peter 1:15). We must not leave our religion, as some people leave their Bibles, on the pew at church.

SUCCESS AND CONTENTMENT

*Faith is what teaches the saint to enjoy
the supplies of providence with sweet
complacency as the will of God concerning him.*

T he worldly person who does not go to his business every
morning by way of a prayer closet rarely returns home in
the evening to give thanks to God. He begins the day without God and it would be unusual for him to end it with Him.
The spider that spins her web out of her own body dwells in it
when she is through; and the person who operates his enterprises by his own ingenuity entitles himself to recognition as a
"self-made man." Thus it is easier for such a person to worship
his own wisdom than to worship God.

Once a man overheard his neighbor thanking God for the
rich stand of corn in his field and reacted to this praise: "Thank
God? Why I would rather thank my manure-cart!" It was the
speech of a sewer-spirit, more filthy than the load on his cart. If
you want to be a Christian you must acknowledge God in all
your ways and not lean unto your own understanding (Proverbs
3:6). This selfless attitude will lead you to crown God with
praise when success crowns your work.

Jacob worked as long and hard as any other businessman
for his wealth; yet the foundation of his diligence was in prayer
and in the expectation of blessing from heaven. He attributed
his valuable holdings to the truth and mercy of God, who promised to provide for him when he was still a poor pilgrim on his
way to Padan-aram (Genesis 28:2–4).

Necessity was the heathen's schoolmaster to teach contentment; but faith is the Christian's. Faith is what teaches the saint
to enjoy the supplies of providence with sweet complacency as
the will of God concerning him. This is godliness that triumphs
—when the Christian can carve contentment out of God's providence, no matter what dish it sets before him.

CHOOSING OUR AUTHORITIES

*How often do employers throw away all thoughts of
Christianity because their Christian employees
turn in performance of pride and carelessness?*

Sometimes we have no choice about our relationships—a child cannot select his own father or the parent his son. But when God does allow us freedom to choose, He expects a wise choice every time.

Select spiritual masters. Be careful to show your holiness in the authority you put yourself under. First, find out if the air inside the doors is as healthful for your soul as it is for your body outside. Will you voluntarily submit to ungodly men? It is hard enough to serve two masters, even when both have similar personalities; but it is impossible to serve a holy God and an ungodly man and please them both.

If you are already under the roof of wicked authorities, though, do not forget your responsibility to them even if they forget about God altogether. Your faithfulness might cause them to seek God for your sake as Nebuchadnezzar did for Daniel's. Besides, sinners would undoubtedly take the ways of God more seriously if there were more beauty upon Christians' lives to invite them into the kingdom.

We are more likely to choose a book if the print is attractive and clear and to ignore one with dull or tiny lettering. How often do employers throw away all thoughts of Christianity because their Christian employees turn in performance of pride and carelessness? The natural conclusion inevitably follows: "Is this what comes of your belief? Well, God keep me from such a religion!" Christian, your blameless behavior is the best way for ungodly or carnal employers to see the ways of God. But let me add a practical suggestion—maybe you are doing everything you can to bring God's truth into that place but the soil is so hard and cold that there is no visible hope of planting for Him there. Then it is high time to think about transplanting yourself; for if the field is too bad for you to sow Christianity in, it cannot be very good for you to grow in either.

SELECT SPIRITUAL SERVANTS

A godly servant, however, is a great
blessing. He can work hard and then
seek God to work for your good also.

When you hire an employee, choose for God as well as for yourself. How can he fit in with your plans if he does not fit in with God's? Of course you want his work to be successful. But on what ground can you anchor that hope if the hand that does your labor insists on sinning as he performs it? "A high look, and a proud heart, and the plowing of the wicked, is sin" (Proverbs 21:4).

A godly servant, however, is a great blessing. He can work hard and then seek God to work for your good also: "O Lord God of my master Abraham, I pray thee, send me good speed this day, and show kindness unto my master" (Genesis 24:12). Surely this prayer helped Abraham as much as the servant's good judgment did.

If you were to plant an orchard you would find the best-quality fruit trees instead of wasting your acres cultivating thistles. There is far more loss in a graceless person in your employ than a fruitless tree in the orchard. While David was at Saul's court, for example, he saw the disadvantage of having ungodly servants. No doubt his recognition of evil in a disordered house made him determine to have the highest standards when God would make him head of that royal family: "He that worketh deceit shall not dwell within my house: he that telleth lies shall not tarry in my sight" (Psalm 101:7).

Select a godly mate. There is no one area wherein Christians, even those recorded in Scripture, have betrayed their weakness more often than in choosing ungodly husbands or wives. "The sons of God saw the daughters of men that they were fair" (Genesis 6:2). You would think the sons of God would have looked for grace in the heart rather than for beauty in the face; but even they are quite capable of being turned aside by a pretty outward appearance without first looking into the person's spirit.

TAKING INSTRUCTION FROM GODLY RELATIVES

*If there is a holy person in your family, see what you can
learn from watching how he behaves under affliction,
how he worships and receives God's mercies.*

Let me remind you to be as careful to protect yourself from
receiving infection from your family as of breathing it on
them. You have a strong love for your wife, and that is
good. But do not let it make the apple of temptation more desirable, when her hand holds it out to you. You love yourself
and God too little if you sin for her sake. Even if you wives are
submissive to your husbands, obey "in the Lord": do not turn
the tables and put the seventh commandment before the first
one. Obey God before you obey your husband. You might need
to question your soul in this process: "Is it possible for me to
keep God's command in obeying my husband's wishes?"

In business we first pay the biggest debts which are already
due. Are you more deeply indebted to God or to your mate?
Travel as far as you can with your relatives in God's company,
but no farther—because you do not want to leave holiness and
righteousness behind. No one—family or otherwise—can ever
repay you in the loss of those treasures.

A holy father, a gracious husband or wife—even a godly
maid or gardener—the good from their holiness is like precious ointment which betrays itself wherever it lingers. Christian, if there is a holy person in your family, see what you can
learn from watching how he behaves under affliction, how he
worships and receives God's mercies, and how he directs his
daily life.

Elisha asked the widow to bring all the vessels she could
find or borrow to hold what would flow from the pot of oil in
her house. Those who are poor in grace must take advantage of
the holy oil of grace which drops from the lips and lives of
their godly relatives. Set your memory, conscience, heart, and
affections to receive all the expressions of holiness that pour
from them.

HOLINESS MUST RELATE TO OTHERS

*It is common for men to
wrong Christ and yet treat their
neighbors with respect and fairness.*

Outward obedience to the law is a road where Jews, Christians, and heathens may be found walking along together. How can we distinguish the Christian from these others, when heathens and Jews also are obedient children, loyal citizens, and loving neighbors?

The motive and goal make all the difference. It is common for men to wrong Christ and yet treat their neighbors with respect and fairness; they choose right behavior but not because love for Christ has constrained them. And without this love you may be an honest, moral heathen but you can never be a Christian.

Suppose a man trusts his employee to pay a certain creditor a sum of money. The person does this, not out of respect to the command or love for his boss but out of fear of being called a thief. As far as the creditor is concerned he has done his job but that is all—his attitude has wronged his employer. Men scorn Jesus like this every day; they are exact and righteous in their transactions with their neighbors and associates, but insulting to Him. Love carries out righteousness because it wants to please God's holy Son.

Christ called evangelical love to our neighbor "a new commandment" (John 13:34). This love to our brother takes fire from God's love to us. It is impossible to perform any commandment unless we first love Christ and then do it for His sake. "If ye love me, keep my commandments" (John 14:15).

Just as God set His name before His Ten Commandments, for the same reason Christ set His name before the Christian's obedience to those Ten Commandments. That is, we are to keep them because they are Christ's word and law, and so that we may illustrate our love to Him who has redeemed us from the curse and brought us out of a far worse kind of bondage than Egypt was for Israel.

JULY 26

LAY A GOOD FOUNDATION

*The soul that really loves Christ,
then, delights in holiness and
spends all his strength on it.*

Y ou must be holy before you can live a holy life. If a ship
has not been constructed right it will never sail properly;
and if your heart has not been molded again by the Spirit's
workmanship and fashioned according to the law of the "new
creature," you will never have a holy walk (2 Corinthians 5:17).
It is grace in the vessel of the heart which feeds profession in
the lamp—holiness in the life! This thorough change of heart
needs to be examined through two questions.

There was a time when sin looked as good to you as it did
to Adam when Eve offered him the forbidden fruit. And unless
you change your mind it will always seem pleasant. Circumstances might keep you from expressing that secret longing for
sin, but inwardly your heart will be continually hankering after
it. When two lovers are kept apart by their friends one will
eventually break loose and escape to the other, as long as their
affection stays strong. Thus lust will lure you back again and
again unless you are convicted to hate it as much as you once
loved it.

Are you content to live in Christ? There is no reason to fear
degeneration after Christ has tied you to His service by the
heartstrings of love. The devil finds it easy to separate a person
from kingdom work when the person never really liked doing it
anyway. A student learns more in a week when he is pleased
with the sweet taste of learning then he will in a month when
he attends a class merely to please his teacher. A man is diligent
about the thing that satisfies him. If a person's heart is turned to
his garden, for instance, it will become a beautiful place. Out of
his excitement he spends hours of hard work growing rare, delicate flowers that please him.

The soul that really loves Christ, then, delights in holiness
and spends all his strength on it. If only this man can be more
holy, he does not mind if he is behind in every other race.

KEEP YOUR MOTIVE PURE

If you really want to be holy,
be humble, because the two
are clasped together.

Satan's policy is to crack the breastplate of righteousness by beating it out farther than the metal can bend. And every time you trust in this distortion you destroy the very nature and purpose of the armor—your righteousness becomes unrighteousness and your holiness degenerates into wickedness.

Is anything worse than pride, such a pride which runs rampant over the way which God Himself has made for saving souls? If you really want to be holy, be humble, because the two are clasped together. "What doth the Lord require of thee, but to do justly, and to love mercy, and to walk humbly with thy God?" (Micah 6:8). God has not asked you to earn heaven by your holiness but to show love and thankfulness to Christ who earned it for you. Thus we have insight into the way Christ persuaded His disciples to walk in holiness: "If ye love me, keep my commandments" (John 14:15). It is as if He had said, "You know why I came and why I am going out of the world—I lay down My life and take it up again to intercede for you. If you value these deeds and the blessed fruit you reap from them, prove it by loving Me enough to keep My commandments."

When everything the saint does through Christ is offered up as a thanksgiving sacrifice to Him, then this is gospel holiness bred and fed by this love. Because Christ has loved us with "love . . . strong as death," our response is that of a bride: "I will give thee my loves" (Song of Solomon 8:6; 7:12). And this bride explains what is in her expression of love: "All manner of pleasant fruits, new and old, which I have laid up for thee, O my Beloved" (v. 13).

The saint in Solomon's Song had confessed her faith in Christ and had drunk deeply of His love for her. And now to return His love in thankfulness, she stirred herself to entertain Him with the pleasant fruits of His own graces, gathered from her holy behavior. She did not lay these fruits up to feed her pride and self-confidence but reserved them for her Beloved, so He could have all the praise.

CHRIST AS YOUR EXAMPLE

*"Am I like Him in my thoughts and in the way
I spend my time? If He were physically living on
earth right now, would He do what I am doing?"*

The good soldier follows his platoon leader only when he
himself marches after his captain. Paul commanded, "Be
ye followers of me, even as I also am of Christ" (1 Corinthians 11:1).

A doctrine must be followed no further than it agrees with
God's Word. The teacher of handwriting not only provides
ruled paper for the student but also writes him a copy in his
own hand. Christ's command is our rule and His life is our
copy. If you want to live a holy life you must not only do what
Jesus commands; you must do it as He did. You must shape every letter in your copy—each action in your life—in a holy imi-
tation of Christ. By holiness we are the very image of God's Son,
representing Christ and holding Him forth to all who see us.

Now two things make one thing an image of another—first,
likeness; and second, source. Milk and snow are both white but
we cannot say they are images of each other because in neither
is the likeness derived from the other. But a picture which is
drawn line by line of a man's face can be called the image of
that person. Thus true holiness is derived from God's Son,
when the person sets Christ in His word and Christ in His example before him.

What a sweet way to keep the power of holiness! When you
are tempted to walk toward vanity, look at Christ's holy walk
and ask yourself, "Am I like Him in my thoughts and in the way
I spend my time? If He were physically living on earth right
now, would He do what I am doing? Would He not choose His
words more carefully than I do? Would silly speech come from
His lips? Would He enjoy my friends? Would He spend a fortune
pampering His body, and swallow enough food at one meal to
feed hungry people for a week? Would He be fashion-con-
scious, even if that made His appearance ridiculous and offensive? Would His hands be busy with games that drive time away?
Should I do anything that would make me unlike Christ?"

ACCOUNTABILITY TO BELIEVERS

*Sometimes self-love binds us so we cannot see
a single fault; and at other times, self-condemnation
makes us appear worse than we really are.*

A spectator sometimes sees more than the actor himself. And a man with an open-hearted friend who dares speak honestly has a wonderful source of encouragement for the power of holiness. Sometimes self-love binds us so we cannot see a single fault; and at other times, self-condemnation makes us appear worse than we really are. Therefore, keep your heart soft and ready to receive a reproof with real meekness.

A person who cannot face plain dealing and straightforwardness hurts himself more than anyone else, for this reason: he seldom hears the truth. If you do not have enough humility to accept a rebuke you are "a scorner" (Proverbs 9:8). On the other hand, a man who does not have enough love to give reproof in season to his brother is not worthy to be called a Christian and proves himself a "hater of his brother" (Leviticus 19:17).

David said he would take it as "a kindness" for the "righteous to smite" him (Psalm 141:5). He accepted reproof as if the brother had broken a box of precious oil upon his head—a high expression of Jewish love. And his actions backed up his word. Indeed, both Abigail and Nathan knew Godspeed in their mission to reprove David. Abigail warned him about his treacherous intentions against Nabal and his family; and Nathan reproved him for his sin against Uriah. Whereas Abigail prevented the king from sinning by her reproof at the right time, Nathan forced him to come out of hiding and repent of the dismal murder he had already committed. And notice this—not only did these two saints prevail in their unpleasant errands but actually endeared themselves to David by being obedient to God and faithful to their friend. David took Abigail as his wife and Nathan as his private counselor (1 Samuel 25; 2 Samuel 12).

GUARD AGAINST DISCOURAGEMENT

*The devil works to picture a holy life
with such an austere, sour face that a person
could not possibly be in love with it.*

Depression is one of Satan's most dynamic weapons to divert you from God's purpose for your life. If he can scatter a little dejection here and there in your thoughts—and even in your prayers—he can convince you to remove your breastplate of righteousness because it is too cumbersome and will go against your material and temporal interest. Do not give in that easily! First let me describe some of the devil's weapons for wearing down the saints. Then I want to lend you a little help in making him drop his weapons at your feet. God wants you to know that because of the breastplate of righteousness He has provided, "no weapon that is formed against thee shall prosper; . . . this is the heritage of the servants of the Lord, and their righteousness is of me, saith the Lord" (Isaiah 54:17).

Satan says righteousness hinders pleasure. The devil works to picture a holy life with such an austere, sour face that a person could not possibly be in love with it. "If you intend to be this righteous, then say good-bye to joy," the deceiver skillfully counsels. "People who do not have such straight-laced consciences enjoy all kinds of good times—but you are missing them all." The truth is, Christian, if you want to see the countenance of holiness in its actual color and vitality, do not trust Satan's carnal talents to paint the portrait.

Now I agree that some pleasures are inconsistent with the power of holiness; and whoever purposes to live righteously must know what these are.

IMPROPER USE OF PLEASURE

Fruit eaten out of season is bad.
Scripture speaks of "a time to embrace, and a time
to refrain from embracing" (Ecclesiastes 3:5).

No one can live righteously without living soberly too. Godliness might allow you to taste of these pleasures as garnish but not to feed on them as solid meat. Sad to say, some live in pleasures as if they could not live without them.

Once the aroma of enticements rises to the brain and intoxicates a man's judgment, he is so enchanted that he cannot think of parting with them. When the Jews started to thrive on Babylonian soil, for example, they were willing to lay down their bones there rather than return to godliness in Jerusalem. A master never minds his servant having plenty of food and drink, but he does not appreciate it if that servant becomes drunk just when he has a responsibility to perform. Yet this drunken man can do his master's business about as well as a Christian overcharged with creature-comforts and worldly fascination can serve his God in holiness.

Fruit eaten out of season is bad. Scripture speaks of "a time to embrace, and a time to refrain from embracing" (Ecclesiastes 3:5). In certain seasons the power of holiness will not allow something which is acceptable at another time.

The Lord's day is an example—all carnal pleasures are inappropriate then. God calls us to higher pleasures and expects us to put aside everything else so we can taste His goodness. "If thou turn away thy foot from the sabbath, from doing thy pleasure on my holy day; and call the sabbath a delight, the holy of the Lord, honorable; and shalt honor him, not doing thine own ways, nor finding thine own pleasure, nor speaking thine own words; then shalt thou delight thyself in the Lord" (Isaiah 58:13–14). It is impossible to taste the sweetness of communion with God and honor Him in sanctifying His day unless you deny yourself carnal pleasures.

PLEASURES AT HIS RIGHT HAND

Your joy and pleasure are the same substance
which God delights in: "Thou shalt make them
drink of the river of thy pleasures" (Psalm 36:8).

God takes pleasure in the graces of His saints; but how much more in His own inherent holiness, from whence those graces, those beautiful beams of righteousness, were first sent forth! Thus you are doing something God Himself cannot do if you can wrest any true pleasure out of unholiness. And let me ask this—is it not the lowest of blasphemies for you to say that the path of righteousness is an enemy to true pleasure? In that accusation you are saying God Himself lacks joy, because true pleasure does not exist outside of holiness.

Even the devils who hate God with a perfect hatred dare not declare that He is without joy. They know God is "glorious in holiness" and the Christian's bliss consists in sharing the same holiness which makes God Himself so blessed (Exodus 15:11). This, Christian, is the ultimate expression of happiness, either on earth or in heaven—the same thing that makes you glorious is what has made God glorious. Your joy and pleasure are the same substance which God delights in: "Thou shalt make them drink of the river of thy pleasures" (Psalm 36:8). Mark those words—"the river of thy pleasures." God has His pleasures, and He causes saints to drink of them!

Whenever a king commands his servants to take a visitor down into the cellar so he can drink wine with them, the person is highly honored by his host's generous gesture. But for the king to set the man at his table and let him drink his own wine is an even more cherished experience. Thus when God gives a man the creaturely pleasures of property, corn, wine, and oil, He entertains him in that common wine cellar. But when His grace and mercy beautify a soul with holiness, He gives the most precious gift the person can receive. He never clothes a man with the robe of righteousness unless He means to seat him at His own table in heaven's glory.

DOES RIGHTEOUSNESS WASTE PROSPERITY?

*Although the devil's words are
deadly weapons, he does not have the
last word in spiritual warfare—God does.*

E ven if you did not falter at the first stone Satan hurled—
the lie that holiness hinders pleasure—he has another in
hand ready to throw at you. He is not such an inexper-
ienced hunter that he goes into battle with a single shot; expect
him to aim another at you as soon as he sees that he has missed
you with the first one.

Here is how the second runs: "You really should not get involved with this holy kind of life unless, of course, you are willing to lose everything you have worked hard to get. And do not
forget, people are depending on you. Just look at the most
prominent men in the world—did their wealth and affluence
come from being holy? Why, if they had been as strict in their
consciences as you are, and tied to the rules of a holy life, they
could never have arrived at such success. Now if you want some
of their prosperity the first thing you must do is to take off the
breastplate of righteousness—or at least unbuckle it so it will
hang loose enough to give your ingenuity some room. If you do
not, you may as well close up shop, for all the profit you will
show for your hard work."

Although the devil's words are deadly weapons, he does not
have the last word in spiritual warfare—God does. Let us study
four facets of it from His point of view.

You can fly to heaven without a penny in your pocket but
you will not get there at all without holiness in your heart and
life. And wisdom urges you to take care of that more important
requirement first.

There is a remnant of people who gratefully accept God's
gift of salvation, if only they can arrive at heaven's glorious city.
And God does not have to bribe them with prosperity and a
problem-free walk; they resolve to be holy at all costs. Do not
even consider what you might be missing—if you loved God,
you would abandon the whole world anyway rather than part
with Him.

WEALTH AND RIGHTEOUSNESS

*"Let your conversation be without covetousness; and be
content with such things as ye have: for he hath said, I will
never leave thee nor forsake thee" (Hebrews 13:5).*

I f He sees that wealth will not profit your soul, than He will
pay you another way. "Let your conversation be without covetousness; and be content with such things as ye have: for
he hath said, I will never leave thee nor forsake thee" (Hebrews
13:5).

If God gives you wealth but later asks you to part with it for
His name's sake, He hands you His bond along with His request
to recover the loss with "a hundredfold" advantage in this life,
besides eternal life in the world to come (Matthew 19:29). Only
a fool will part with God's promises for any security the devil
can give.

A heavy curse always cleaves to unrighteous gain. "The
curse of the Lord is in the house of the wicked" (Proverbs
3:33), but "in the house of the righteous is much treasure"
(Proverbs 15:6). You may visit a righteous man's house and find
no money, but you are sure to find a treasure. Yet in the wicked
man's house there may be much gold and silver but never treasure—the curse of God eats up all his gains. God's fork follows
the wicked man's rake.

The ungodly bring shame into their houses, "for the stone
shall cry out of the wall, and the beam out of the timber shall
answer it" (Habakkuk 2:11). And what man who cherishes his
life would live in a haunted house like this, even for tons of
gold? The cry of his unrighteousness follows him into every
room of the house and echoes until he can hear the stones and
beams groaning under the weight of sin that put them there.

This sin is so hateful to the righteous God that not only the
man who gathers unrighteous gain, but also the instruments he
uses to advance his project, are cursed. Thus the servant who
cooperates with his masters's fraud collects God's wages too. "I
will punish all those that leap on the threshold, which fill their
masters' houses with violence and deceit" (Zephaniah 1:9).

LOSING THE WORLD'S LOVE

*When we lose the world's love we gain its reverence and
honor. The people who will not love you because you are
holy cannot help but respect and fear you.*

When we lose man's love we gain God's blessing.
"Blessed are ye, when men say all manner of evil against
you falsely, for my name's sake" (Matthew 5:11). God's
providence is a perfect roof over our heads to defend us from
the storm of man's rage. But it is a different story when a saint
is caught in sin and gives the ungodly opportunity to speak evil
of him. Man reviles and God frowns. His Word does not open
its shelter then to hide you from the assault of reviling tongues.
But when the wicked hate you for your holiness, God is bound
by promise to pay you love for their hatred and blessing for
their cursing. Can we ever complain about man's disrespect
when obedience and holiness advance us to a higher place in
the King's favor?

When we lose the world's love we gain its reverence and
honor. The people who will not love you because you are holy
cannot help but respect and fear you for that same reason. But
every time you give up a little holiness to gain false love from
sinners, you forfeit the reverence which their consciences secretly paid to your life. Like Samson, a Christian walking in the
power of holiness is greatly feared by the wicked; but if sin exposes an impotent spirit, he is captured and falls under the lash
of their tongues and the scorn of their hearts.

Poverty and a low class in society cannot make you con-
temptible as long as you keep on the breastplate of righteousness. Majesty can reign in a holy heart even when it is dressed
in rags. For instance, the righteousness of David commanded
reverence from Saul, and the king paid homage to his exiled
subject: "He wept, and said to David, Thou art more righteous
than I" (1 Samuel 24:16, 17). And this is as it should be—carnal
men must admit that they are overpowered by the holy lives of
saints. And this shall happen as you behave in that distinctive
and singular manner called for by God, doing things that even
the best of our unbelieving neighbors cannot do.

HOLINESS AND DECEPTION

*"Put on the new man, which after God
is created in righteousness and
true holiness" (Ephesians 4:24).*

Some hide behind counterfeit holiness. There are men who are just as unholy as the ones contented in sin—but these wear something like a breastplate, a counterfeit holiness to save their reputation in the world. "Verily I say unto you, they have their reward" (Matthew 6:2). And what a measly reward! You are doing the devil a double service, and God a double disservice, to march into battle armed with hypocrisy. First you draw the prince's expectations towards you as a soldier who will attempt courageous duties for him. But then when you do nothing he sees only a traitor taking up the place of a faithful subject armed for victory. You do your prince more harm than the coward who stays home, or rebelliously runs over to the enemy's camp and tells him plainly what he intends to do.

Be serious, friends. If you are after holiness make sure it is true holiness. "Put on the new man, which after God is created in righteousness and true holiness" (Ephesians 4:24). Observe two phrases in that passage. Holiness is called the "new man after God"—that is, according to the likeness of God. Such a sculpture is drawn from God's being, as an artist copies the face of a man. Also, "true holiness" means a holiness of Scripture truth, not pharisaical and traditional doctrine; as well it means a holiness which has as its point of reference the heart, which is the seat of truth or falsehood.

In order to have true holiness then, the Christian must have righteousness and holiness in his heart. Many people have beauty of holiness which is like the attractiveness of the body— skin deep and all on the surface. If you tear open the most beautiful body on earth you will not find much except blood and stench; so also, when counterfeit holiness is exposed, it will have only an abundance of spiritual impurities and filth inside.

MANY MOCK RIGHTEOUSNESS

*The very hint of holiness works up such a strong
opposition inside the person that is causes him to
vomit out the gall and bitterness of his spirit.*

Some men are so far from being holy themselves that they
ridicule those who are. These think the breastplate of righteousness is so foolish that they laughingly point to the
saint who wears it in his daily behavior: "Look! There goes a
holy brother, one of the pure ones!" But their mocking language does more than scorn the saint's holiness—it betrays the
wickedness of their own hard hearts.

A further degree of ungodliness appears in mocking the holiness of another person rather than only harboring unholiness
in oneself. How desperately wicked is that man who not only
refuses to partake in the divine nature himself but cannot bear
the sight of others choosing to follow the holiness of Christ.
The very hint of holiness works up such a strong opposition inside the person that is causes him to vomit out the gall and bitterness of his spirit against it.

God's Spirit reserves the chair for this kind of sinner and
seats him above all his brethren in iniquity. "Blessed is the man
that walketh not in the counsel of the ungodly, nor standeth in
the way of sinners, nor sitteth in the seat of the scornful" (Psalm
1:1). In this case the scorner is set as chairman at the counsel-
table of sinners.

Some read the word scornful as "rhetorical mockers," for
there is indeed a devilish cleverness in some of these jeerers.
Such scorners take pride in polishing the darts they shoot
against saints. The Septuagint translates the phrase as "the chair
of the pestilent ones." As the plague is the most deadly of diseases, so is the spirit of scorning among sins. Very few recover
from this sin, for the Bible speaks of sinners almost synony-
mously with the dead. God warns us not to waste our healing
balm of reproof—"reprove not a scorner, lest he hate thee"
(Proverbs 9:8). All we can do is write "Lord, have mercy" on his
door—pray for him, but do not try to reason with him.

BLESS GOD FOR FURNISHING THE BREASTPLATE

*Now through His grace you are able to defend
yourself with the continual comforts which
heaven sends to withstand Satan's power.*

People are destroyed by the devil every day because they do not have the breastplate of righteousness to defend their hearts against his murdering shot. If God had made you famous and rich in the world, but not holy, He would have given you nothing more than fuel for hell. How then can we forget to thank God for His precious breastplate of righteousness?

When an enemy approaches a city without walls or arms for defense, the wealthier the city the worse the destruction. And each time Satan comes to a man who has much of the world but nothing of God in his soul to defend him, he makes a miserable wreck of the person. He takes whatever he pleases and does whatever he wants with such souls. The devil's plundering possession is so thorough that the captive would not think of postponing or denying a lust. Although he knows what this fulfillment will cost him in hell, he goes ahead and damns his soul rather than stand against the burning demands of temptation.

Herod threw down half his kingdom at the feet of a malicious wench; and when she decided this was not enough, he sacrificed everything he had. But if the blood of John the Baptist cost Herod his throne in this life, surely it was nothing compared to the wages of divine providence paid immediately when he met death.

But let the saints humbly shout "Hallelujah!" When God made you a holy man or woman He gave you gates and bars to your city. Now through His grace you are able to defend yourself with the continual comforts which heaven sends to withstand Satan's power. Once you were a timid slave to him but now he is under your feet. The day you became holy God firmly planted your foot on the serpent's head. Your lusts—mighty strongholds which gave him easy control—have been taken out of his hand. Satan has been dislodged and can never again set himself up as king of your soul.

KEEP YOUR BREASTPLATE ON

*Faith is a shield. Will a soldier
drop his protection unless
he has been seriously wounded?*

David expressed keen sorrow for the unholiness in his life: "O spare me, that I may recover strength, before I go hence, and be no more" (Psalm 39:13). He did not want to die until holiness ruled his heart again. Ungodliness is a poison which drinks up all serenity of conscience and inward springs of joy. If you throw a stone into a clear brook it will soon become muddy. "He will speak peace unto his people, but let them not turn again to folly" (Psalm 85:8).

Carelessness in the walk of holiness dangerously exposes your faith, which is kept in good conscience as a jewel is protected in a cabinet. Faith is an eye, and sin casts a hazy mist before it. To faith, a holy life is like pure air to the eye; we can see farther on a clear day. Thus faith sees further into God's promise when it looks through a holy well-ordered life.

Faith is a shield. Will a soldier drop his protection unless he has been seriously wounded? If faith fails, what will happen to hope, which cleaves to faith and draws strength from her as a nursing child takes nourishment from its mother? If faith cannot see pardon in the promise, then hope cannot look for salvation. If faith cannot claim sonship, hope will not wait for the inheritance. Faith informs the soul it has "peace with God" and then the soul rejoices "in the hope of the glory of God" (Romans 5:1–2).

Are you trying to use the sword of the Spirit? How can you hold it when unholiness has seriously maimed the hand of faith that must carry it? This sword has two edges—one side heals but the other wounds. With one it saves and with the other it damns. The Bible does not speak a single kind word to the person who practices sin. Now—think and then think some more—is any sin worth all this confusion which will inevitably strangle and smother your soul?

MEDITATE ON THE HOLINESS OF GOD

"Now mine eye seeth thee.
Wherefore I abhor myself,
and repent" (Job 42:5–6).

The holiest man in the world, once he sees God's infinite holiness, knows himself as he really is and is humbled. Isaiah's vision revealed God sitting on His throne surrounded by heavenly ministers covering their faces and crying, "Holy, holy, holy is the Lord of hosts." But the heavenly scene also opened up to the prophet his own vileness; when he heard the seraphim crying "holy" before God, he cried out "unclean" regarding his own spirituality (Isaiah 6:3, 5).

Job was another man who realized the impurity of his soul when he glimpsed God's holiness. "Now mine eye seeth thee. Wherefore I abhor myself, and repent" (Job 42:5–6). In a darkened room we seem clean enough; but if we could surround ourselves with beams of God's glorious majesty and holiness, the sun's rays could not discover more specks of dust in the air than God's holiness would convict us of our sin. But the policy of pride is not to appear where it can be outshined; it prefers to go where it will be adored in the muted light of self-exaltation.

If you are a believer you have a principle of holiness planted in you. But what about the nature you had before Adam sinned? The Israelites who saw the second temple, but could not remember the first one, thought it was a splendid structure. Yet those who had also seen the walls of the first one, Solomon's Temple, had tears mixed with their rejoicing as they recalled its destruction. "Many of the priests and Levites and chief of the fathers, who were ancient men, that had seen the first house, when the foundation of this house was laid before their eyes, wept with a loud voice" (Ezra 3:12). Let this remind us, then, of what man in all his glory fell into by Satan's design. In heaven you will realize the same pleasures Adam enjoyed in paradise, but many weary steps through obstacles of lust, temptation, and sin lie between you and the top of that hill.

THE CHRISTIAN'S SPIRITUAL SHOE

*"And your feet shod with
the preparation of the gospel
of peace" (Ephesians 6:15).*

Here is the third piece of armor in the Christian's protection—a spiritual shoe, fitted to his foot and designed to be worn as long as he battles sin and Satan. "And your feet shod with the preparation of the gospel of peace." Let us now study three distinct terms from Scripture concerning this shoe: first what is meant by the Gospel; second, what is meant by peace; and third, what the word feet means here, as well as the grace intended by the preparation of the gospel of peace.

Gospel, according to the meaning of the original word, signifies good news or joyful message. Usually in Scripture the word is reserved for the doctrine of Christ and His salvation. "I bring you good tidings of great joy," said the angel to the shepherds (Luke 2:10). And then he added, "Unto you is born this day in the city of David a Saviour, which is Christ the Lord" (v. 11). Thus Gospel in the New Testament generally carries the connotation of joy and good news, and we shall use that same meaning here.

The revelation of Christ and the grace of God through Him is, without compare, the best news a sinner can hear. It is such a unique message that no good news can come before it nor bad news can follow. God's mercy precedes His blessing to sinners: "God be merciful unto us, and bless us; and cause his face to shine upon us" (Psalm 67:1).

Until God mercifully pardons our sins through Christ He cannot look kindly on us sinners. All our benefits are but blessings in bullion until Gospel grace—pardoning mercy—stamps them with salvation and makes them current. God cannot show any good will until Christ makes peace for us; "On earth peace, good will toward men" (Luke 2:14). And what joy would it be, even to the sinner who inherited a kingdom, if he could not claim it from the joy and favor of God's heart?

THE NEWS OF THE GOSPEL IS JOYOUS

*"Jesus Christ, who hath abolished death,
and hath brought life and immortality to
light through the gospel" (2 Timothy 1:10).*

If we hear insignificant news we will probably forget it. But if it is both important and very good, it causes rejoicing. The angel of the Lord said, "I bring you good tidings of great joy" (Luke 2:10). It has to be great joy because it is all joy; the Lord Christ has brought news of such fullness that He left nothing for anyone else to add. If you think something might be missing from the Gospel you must look higher than God, for He gives Himself through Christ to believers in the covenant of grace. We are fully persuaded the apostle Paul's argument will hold: "All things are yours; and ye are Christ's; and Christ is God's" (1 Corinthians 3:22–23).

The Gospel places our vessels close to the fountain of goodness itself; and surely we must have all if we are united to the One who has everything. Can any good news come to glorified saints which heaven does not give them? We have proof of that glory in the Word: "Jesus Christ, who hath abolished death, and hath brought life and immortality to light through the gospel" (2 Timothy 1:10). The sun in the sky hides heaven from us while it shows the earth to us! But the Gospel enlightens both at once—godliness has the "promise of the life that now is, and of that which is to come" (1 Timothy 4:8).

The audience must have a personal interest before an announcement can be good news. While we can be happy to hear about something good happening to another person, it affects us more when it is poured directly into our own hearts. For example, a sick man does not feel the joy of another's recovery as strongly as he would his own.

The Gospel does not report what God has done for angels but for us. "Unto you," the angel said, "is born . . . a Saviour, which is Christ the Lord" (Luke 2:11). If angels rejoiced for our happiness, surely our benefit gives even deeper reason to be glad.

THE WORLD'S REJECTION OF THE GOSPEL

They like to keep the Gospel at a comfortable distance,
assuming there will be time enough to take care of
it when they are about to enter the next world.

When the news of the Savior's birth was told in Jerusalem, it should have caused every heart to beat for joy, to see the blessed Messiah fill the hope of every generation. But just the opposite was true—Christ's coming alarmed these men as if an enemy, not a Savior, had arrived.

But, one might reason, even though men faltered at accepting Christ's lowly birth and parentage, surely they would worship Him when the rays of His divinity started shining through all the miracles and wonders that followed this Man. When His own lips showed His authority and told the joyful message He brought from the Father, would they not thirstily drink in the salvation preached to them? No, they persisted in cursed unbelief and obstinate rejection of the Christ.

Although the Scripture, which the Jews seemed to adore, so fully testified for Christ that it accused them to their own consciences, they still refused Jesus. Christ warned, "Search the scriptures; for in them ye think ye have eternal life: and they are they which testify of me. And ye will not come to me, that ye might have life" (John 5:39–40). They did want life, but chose to lose it rather than come to Him for it.

Has the world changed much since then? Does Christ in His Gospel meet with any kinder welcome today? The invitation He offers is still the same: "Come unto me, all ye that labor and are heavy laden, and I will give you rest" (Matthew 11:28). The worst that Christ does to those who come to Him is to put them into a place of life and salvation; yet thousands somehow expect to hear better news from the world and relegate the Gospel to a foreign language which does not concern them, at least for the present. They like to keep the Gospel at a comfortable distance, assuming there will be time enough to take care of it when they are about to enter the next world.

AUGUST 13

THE PATH IS NARROW

*Most of Christendom is
made up of old disciples,
not new converts.*

Only a remnant will embrace the Gospel. If it were put to a vote, would not thousands carry the decision to get rid of Christ and His Gospel? History itself prophesies the future of such great odds. Each time God has withdrawn from a people, there have been a few holy ones mingled among the ungodly. Sardis, for example, has several names which had not "defiled their garments," but the candlestick was removed nevertheless. All they had was a promise for themselves—"They shall walk with me in white"—but no protection was pledged for the whole church (Revelation 3:4). God can pull down a house and at the same time provide safety for His saints whom He finds inside.

A few voices are easily drowned in the screams of a crowd and a dozen cups of wine are hardly tasted in a whole cask. Thus a remnant of Christianity sometimes can do little to save the wretched millions of unbelievers surrounding them. When disease controls a weakened body, nature tries with her utmost strength but cannot heal the sickness—perhaps her best efforts will only prolong life for a while. So then a few saints, shut up in a wicked age of Christ-despising men, may gain a reprieve from judgment. But if the unbelievers themselves do not choose to change, ruin inevitably will break in on them.

Most of Christendom is made up of old disciples, not new converts. The womb of the Gospel has been shut up from bringing forth souls in a solid work of conversion. Of course, if you count those who baptize themselves into new religious feelings with good intentions and wholesome opinions, there are plenty of "Christians." But in this age of withering professions of faith and an even weaker practice of holiness, it is hard to find a real convert!

ENJOYING GOD

*When unbelievers see Christians sad as they hold
the cup of salvation in their hands, they suspect
the wine is not so good as preachers say it is.*

A feast is made for laughter," Solomon wrote (Ecclesiastes 10:19). I am sure God intended His children to be joyful in the feast of Christ's Gospel. In the Old Testament, mourners were not allowed to sit at God's table. Since a saint's gloom reflects unkindness on God Himself, how can we recommend His satisfying love if it does not satisfy us? The world thinks the Christian life is depressing anyway, a dry meal where very little wine of joy is tasted. Why will you confirm their deception, Christian? Why should they have your example as evidence against Jesus and His Word, which promises peace and joy to everyone who comes to this table?

God forbid that your behavior, which should hold forth "the word of life" and demonstrate the reality of it in the eyes of the world, ever disagree or throw doubt on His Word (Philippians 2:16). It is a gross error for Rome to teach that we cannot know Scripture as God's Word except by the testimony of the church. Yet a practical testimony from Christians' lives has great authority over the consciences of men to persuade them of Gospel truth. They can believe it is good news when they can read it clearly in a cheerful life.

When unbelievers see Christians sad as they hold the cup of salvation in their hands, they suspect the wine is not so good as preachers say it is. If traders to the Indies returned poorer than they were when they began, it would be hard to convince others to venture to that place, regardless of how many golden mountains might tower there. Christian, do not give unbelievers reason to imagine, by seeing you limping through the race, that they must forfeit happiness if they become Christians and spend the rest of their lives in a house of mourning, with a team of losers.

Is Christ's Gospel full of abundant life or not? Then do not go into debt with the world to soak up its carnal benefits; you need never leave God's house to be made glad.

THE POISON COUNTERFEIT

*Once the mind is confused by error and begins
to malign the truth, it affects the heart,
poisoning it with carnal affections.*

Why do so-called Christians forsake the pure wine of Gospel joy for the adulterated poison which the whore of the world smilingly holds out to them in her golden chalice? Is it because the message of the Gospel, which once sparkled in the preached Word and furnished comfort to mourners, has now grown stale? Or has that stream of spiritual joy which has run through the lives of saints for so many generations, without mingling with the world's polluted pleasures, at last fallen into them and lost its divine nature? No, the Gospel stays the same; and the joy it brings is as refreshing and restoring as it has always been. It will be lovely as long as God and Christ continue to be life, for it flows and is fed from their heart.

The problem is not in Scripture; it lies in those who say they hold to it. Those who insist they obey this Gospel are not like holy men and women of earlier times. The world has grown callous and men's priorities and affections have chilled and become cold. Our palate is no longer chaste; it no longer prefers the heavenly foods served in the Gospel. The cheer is as lively as ever but the guests are deadened by constant contact with the world. We have grown debauched in our judgments and corrupt in our principles; no wonder that our joys are carnal.

Error is a whore that lures the heart away from Christ and His spiritual joys. Once the mind is confused by error and begins to malign the truth, it affects the heart, poisoning it with carnal affections. And carnal affections only keep company with gross and carnal joys. Here, then, is the root of the misery of our times.

Satan has played his game cunningly among us in that he has often changed his instruments into angels of light and made gullible souls think they might find more grace and power in this artificial light than in the revelation God provides.

GOD'S DISPLEASURE WITH SIN

*At every door where
sin enters, the anger
of God meets it there.*

Not only is man in arms against God, but God is against wicked man also. "God is angry with the wicked every day . . . he hath bent his bow and made it ready. He hath also prepared for him the instruments of death" (Psalm 7:11–13). God has set up His royal standard in defiance of all the sons and daughters of Adam, who are traitors to His crown. And He has taken the field as with fire and sword against everyone who rebels against His Word. God gives sufficient testimony of His wrath by revealing how He judges sinners—they are crushed to death by His righteous foot, a fate suited to their viperous master in sin.

At every door where sin enters, the anger of God meets it there. Because each faculty of the soul and member of the body is used as a weapon of unrighteousness against God, so every one, even to the tip of the tongue, receives its portion of divine wrath. And just as man is sinful all over, so he is cursed all over—inside and outside, soul and body alike. Curses and punishments are written over him so closely together that there is not room for one more to be added to those God has already written.

In a word, the Lord's displeasure against sinful man is so fiery that all creation must share in it. Although God takes aim at man, and levels His arrows primarily at him, yet they wound other creatures as well. God's curses, then, blast the whole creation for man's sake; and part of the misery of man is paid to him through the fallen creation, through all the forces and creatures of the natural world which originally were ordained to minister to man and to provide contributing drops in the filling of his cup of joy.

We can compare God's plagues to an enraged army which spoils all the enemies' land—destroying their supplies, poisoning their water, and burning their homes. Nothing escapes the fury of it. The very bread we eat, air we breathe, and water we drink are poisoned with God's curse, so that even the oldest, healthiest living man will eventually die.

PURCHASING PEACE WITH GOD

*We will be swallowed up in adoring the abyss of His
wisdom, who laid the foundation of all this peace
according to the eternal counsel of His own will!*

Some say God did not know any other way to do it. But how pitiful is any attempt of created understanding to fathom the unsearchableness of God's omnipotent wisdom—to say what He can and cannot do! Yet we can say, in full reverence for the Majesty of heaven, that God could not have found a better way of exalting His own glorious name and purchasing sinners' peace, than by reconciling them to Himself by Christ the precious Peacemaker.

This mysterious exchange has in itself the ability to solve all the difficulties of the enmity between man and God, and for wonder it exceeds even God's workmanship in creating the world. Now this creation is so perfect and glorious that it tells every creature that its Maker is God, a knowing which puts the atheist to shame in his own conscience because he will not believe. Even so, the plan of reconciliation excels the creation of heaven and earth as greatly as the watch surpasses the crystal which covers it. Indeed God intended, by this way of drawing sinners to Himself, to cause both angels and saints to admire the mystery of His wisdom, power, and love in it—from now through eternity.

When at last all angels and Christians meet together in heaven, the whole beautiful counsel of God will be unfolded to them! At that time we shall see how the seas of unbelief were dried up and what rocks of impossibilities were cut through by the omnipotent grace of God, before a sinner's peace could be secured. We shall learn how the Father worked to bring it all to completion. Surely we will be swallowed up in adoring the abyss of His wisdom, who laid the foundation of all this peace according to the eternal counsel of His own will! As the sun exceeds the strength of our natural vision, the glory of God's peace will stretch beyond our capacity to understand it.

JESUS PAID THE PRICE

*Picture a father who has only one son—and can
have no more—sending that child to prison
and with his own lips sentencing him to death.*

The whole curse of sin met in Jesus, as all streams run to the ocean—a collection of all the wages of sin and death merged in Him. "The chastisement of our peace was upon him; . . . and the Lord hath laid on him the iniquity of us all" (Isaiah 53:5–6). But take another step and consider God's unspeakable love for His beloved Son as He watched Him—alone —enter the stage of bloody tragedy. Be still here and know the painful price both God and His Son paid for you to be one with Him. I think you are at the highest stair God's Word can lead you to ascend into the meditation of His love.

Picture a father who has only one son—and can have no more—sending that child to prison and with his own lips sentencing him to death. And then, to guarantee the execution be completed with the most horrible torment possible, he watches his child's death with eyes brimming not with grief but with anger. If you study this parent's countenance you conclude that surely he hates his son or the sin he committed. This is what you see in the Father towards His Son, for it was God, more than men or devils, who caused Christ's death.

Jesus knew the warrant for His death was signed and sealed by His Father's hand, for He prayed, "O my Father, if this cup may not pass away from me, except I drink it, thy will be done" (Matthew 26:42). Yet the spirit of the Man of Sorrow rejoiced in obeying God and His blood was the only wine which made the Father's heart glad: "It pleased the Lord to bruise him" (Isaiah 53:10). When Christ suffered death on the cross, God was pleased—not because He did not love His Son and not because He had disobeyed Him, for Jesus never once disappointed God. But God hated sin, and in His determination to exalt His mercy toward sinners, He satisfied His justice on His only Son.

Our Dependence upon His Work

*God would never have allowed His first workmanship to
be so scarred by sin if He had not planned to build
a more magnificent structure out of its ruins.*

God chose to give this treasure of reconciliation to humble us, so our haughtiness might bow and God could be exalted in our day of salvation. "The bread of God is he which cometh down from heaven, and giveth life unto the world" (John 6:33). And notice why God chose that method to feed His children in the wilderness: "Who fed thee in the wilderness with manna, which thy fathers knew not, that he might humble thee" (Deuteronomy 8:16).

Let us examine this humbling process more carefully. Naturally we assume that the Israelites would have become wise as well as humble when God Himself fed them with "angels food" (Psalm 78:25). Yet man is proud and wants to be his own provider; he does not enjoy a meal sent in by charity, at another's expense, nearly so much as he does food which he earned himself. This pride made the children of Israel wish for the onions of their Egyptian gardens—inferior food but food bought with their own money instead of brought to them by God. God's reconciliation to sinners was aimed at a more perfect union than He had with Adam.

God would never have allowed His first workmanship to be so scarred by sin if He had not planned to build a more magnificent structure out of its ruins. Because He intended to print man's happiness in the second edition with a more perfect type than the first, He used Christ as the only fit instrument to accomplish this design: "I am come that they might have life, and that they might have it more abundantly" (John 10:10). He did not come to give the dead and damned a bare peace—naked life—but a more abundant life than man ever had before sin separated him from God.

AUGUST 20

THE SAINT'S CELEBRATION

*Certainly the prodigal who is received again into
his father's arms has more reason to return that
father's love than the brother who never left home.*

In order for those on earth not to fear that Christ's reclaimed
royalty might crowd them out of His heart, He proves He is
the same in the zenith of His honor as He was in the depth
of His humiliation. And He demonstrates this unchangeableness
by going back to heaven's glory in the same clothes He had borrowed from their nature. Thus God's Son makes those clothes
part of His glorified life and gives a pattern of what the saints'
own bodies will be like in the kingdom. None of this identifica-
tion of Christ with man was present in God's dealings with
Adam. Adam did not have this lump of sugar in his cup—he
knew about the love of a giving God, but was a stranger to the
mercy of a forgiving God. The reconciled sinner experiences
both.

A father's love is a great comfort to an obedient child, but
this demonstration of tenderness cannot be compared to the
compassion of a father toward his rebellious child. Certainly the
prodigal who is received again into his father's arms has more
reason to return that father's love than the brother who never
left home. Without a doubt, then, God's pardoning mercy and
the love of Christ which procured it are the sweetest, most
wholesome fruit a saint here on earth can meditate upon.

But who can conceive of the splendid music which glorified
saints will make on this note of God's mercy and love? Surely
the song their harps are tuned to is "the song of the Lamb"
(Revelation 15:3). The saints' fulfilled celebration in heaven's
glory is a composite of all the finest ingredients possible—so
arranged by the hand of God that not one of them can be left
out; and the taste of one cannot be lost in another. Yet pardoning mercy, and the unsurpassable love of God through Christ,
give a sweet topping to the feast and can be tasted above all the
rest.

DO NOT REFUSE PEACE WITH GOD

You cannot be happy with anything less than
peace but you do not need anything more
than peace to fill you with true joy.

Satan's quarrel with God is too advanced for him to give you a second glance. Besides, can he give you armor to quench the fiery blasts of God's judgment? How could he, when these burning bullets are embedded inside his own heart, causing unspeakable torment? And will he send sympathy when at last you have destroyed yourself by following his advice? Of course not—no more than the ravenous wolf pities the sheep after he has torn her into pieces and drunk her blood.

So that you can never say you did not understand how to find peace with God through the Gospel, carefully weigh these next four thoughts. This peace is both indispensable and comprehensive. You cannot be happy with anything less than peace but you do not need anything more than peace to fill you with true joy. Of all the varieties on God's spiritual menu, His serving of peace can least be spared. If you take this away the feast is spoiled, even if a brightly garnished outward peace replaces it at the center of the prince's table.

Sinner, listen to me! Is not this controversy between you and God like a swollen toad at the bottom of your cup of honey? Your sins are unpardoned and you are condemned to die for them, no matter how much you may be dancing in the shadows of your prison. What would you think about a man who spent his last hours before being hanged playing at his favorite sport? Truly God is merciful if He stays your execution one more day!

I confess, when I see a man whose life proves him an unforgiven sinner, and whose pleasure comes by dressing in expensive clothing and entertaining with the prideful air of affluence, I am amazed that he cares neither about God nor himself. How much longer do you think the Lord will watch him pile up all this trash around himself before He tosses a torch to the bottom of it?

THE JOY IN PARDONING SINNERS

*The motive which prevails
with God to forgive the ungodly
is that "he delighteth in mercy."*

God's strictness emphasize the seriousness of delivering His message faithfully. Paul trembled at the very thought of laziness: "Woe is me if I preach not." And Christ reached deep into His own heart to persuade Peter: "Lovest thou me? . . . Feed my sheep" (John 21:16). It is as if He had said, "Peter, you are crying and feeling guilty because cowardice made you deny Me; but there is still a way to demonstrate your love—feed My sheep. Do this and stop worrying about that traitor of the past." Once again, Christ showed more care for His sheep than for Himself.

God expresses joy when sinners accept His peace. Joy is the highest testimony which can be given to our peace. Love is to joy as fuel is to fire. If love gathers only a few scraps of kindling—only small desires in the heart—then the flame of joy that comes out of it will not be very hot. Now because God takes such great joy in pardoning sinners, His affection is also great in His offer of peace. In fact, the motive which prevails with God to forgive the ungodly is that "he delighteth in mercy." "Who is a God like unto thee, that pardoneth iniquity, and passeth by the transgression of the remnant of his heritage? He retaineth not his anger forever, because he delighteth in mercy" (Micah 7:18).

If you ask a fisherman why he stands with his hook in the water all night he will tell you it is because he enjoys fishing. Now you know why God waits for sinners—months, years—preaching to them; He delights in forgiving them by His grace and mercy. Now and then a government official will pardon an offender more to please others than himself; but God forgives to make His own heart glad. Thus when Christ came to reconcile sinners to God, His ministry was called "the pleasure of the Lord" (Isaiah 53:10).

THE COST OF REFUSING

*"There is no peace,
saith my God, to the wicked"
(Isaiah 57:21).*

Y ou might own all the empires of the world, and have nations creeping to your feet, as the animals came to Adam;
and your lease on life might be twice as long as Methuse-
lah's span to enjoy all this, without one cloud of trouble. But if
you lack peace, I would rather be the worm under your shoe or
the toad in the ditch than you in your palace. Just one small
thought of approaching death and the torment waiting for you
can immediately destroy all your present happiness.

This refusal to accept God's peace on Gospel terms makes
the great leaders of the world—in fact, all unreconciled sinners,
high and low—go to their graves as bears go down a hill—back-
wards. One glance forward might cause them to die of fright as
they see where they are going. They are headed there without a
breastplate, the persuasion of peace with God.

What should you do next then? Shut yourself up as a condemned sinner, apart from flattering friends who would lullaby
your soul into senseless security—the cradle which the devil
rocks souls in, to their utter destruction. Instead, send for those
who dare to be faithful, like Samuel, to tell you every word God
has against you, hiding nothing.

Read your own sentence with your eyes on the Word; take
your condemnation from God's mouth, not from man's. "There
is no peace, saith my God, to the wicked" (Isaiah 57:21). Meditate on that Scripture until it cleaves to your soul like a plaster
to a sore and draws out the core of pride and carnal confidence
which have hardened your heart. By this time the anguish of
your own spirit will prompt you to want peace with God more
than anything else in the world. This is what God has been waiting to hear from you.

RECONCILIATION IS ESSENTIAL

"Come now, and let us
reason together, saith
the Lord" (Isaiah 1:18).

It is plain to see today that many who pursue peace expect God to pardon them, although they care nothing for His honor and remain totally ignorant of Him and of His Son Jesus. They want God to make peace with them while they make war with Him and His Word. Like a thief at the bar, this kind of person implores the judge to spare his life by whatever means, right or wrong, legal or illegal. What difference does it make as long as he is pardoned? Does this man consider the honor of the judge? Well, do not be deceived, because God will not make war among His own attributes to make peace with you.

Reconciliation must seek to have fellowship with God. Suppose God should confide, "I am your friend—I have commanded that you will never go to hell. And My hand holds your discharge so you can never be arrested for indebtedness to Me. But as for fellowship, do not expect any. I am through with you now and you will never know Me better." If you heard the Father say this, how excited would you be about your peace? Even if the tormenting fires were put out, the anguish of a hell would remain in the dismal darkness without God's presence.

Absalom saw no middle ground between seeing his father's face and being killed. "Let me see the king's face; and if there be any iniquity in me, let him kill me" (2 Samuel 14:32). "If I am not worthy to enjoy my father's love and presence," he pledged, "I do not want to live." On the other hand, an ungodly heart gropes for peace without any longing after fellowship with God. Like the traitor, he is ready to promise the king anything, if only he will save him from execution. God will not talk with you as long as your sword is in your hand. "Come now, and let us reason together, saith the Lord" (Isaiah 1:18).

TAKE FIRM HOLD OF CHRIST

*The Father's essential goodness
is a powerful persuasion to rely
on the promise in Christ for pardon.*

L et him take hold of my strength, that he may make peace
with me" (Isaiah 27:5). And where is God's saving strength
but in Christ? The Father has laid strength upon His Mighty
One who is "able also to save them to the uttermost that come
into God by him" (Hebrews 7:25). Do not let natural reasoning
mislead you—it is not God's absolute power or mercy that will
help you, but His covenant strength and mercy in Christ. Take
hold of Christ and you hold God's arm.

Indeed, the Father's essential goodness is a powerful persuasion to rely on the promise in Christ for pardon, when the
person considers that God's very nature is forgiving and merciful. But if there were no promise to apply this mercy to sinners
through Christ, the fact of God's goodness would be only cold
comfort. After all, He could have damned the whole stock of
Adam and not impaired His goodness in the least.

It is certainly no blot to the almightiness of God's power
that He does not do everything in the spectrum of His divine
ability. He could make more worlds if He wanted to; but He is
no less powerful because He does not. And He could have
saved the fallen angels with the sons of lost man had He
thought such a design was fitting. But, having brought forth no
promise for such a thing, the essential goodness of God affords
the devils little hope that He will do it.

Yet God's goodness continues. Those who, out of simple ignorance of the Gospel or proud reasoning away from it, reject
God's way of making peace through Christ's satisfaction and
then depend on God's absolute mercy and goodness at the last
day will, it seems, find as little benefit from this Christless mercy as the devils themselves have found. And their final destination will only confirm the futility of neglecting such a great
salvation through the blood of God's Son.

PLACE COMPLETE CONFIDENCE IN HIM

Now you are not a new creature in Christ—
you are not saved—if you let go your hold on the
living Christ to rely on something within yourself.

Now the Lord has enacted a law, called the law of faith, for saving sinners through Christ; and He is under an oath to make it good both in the salvation of everyone who believes on Christ and in the damnation of everyone who does not. To make sure this plan works perfectly, God has given His Son an oath to be faithful, trusting Him as a priest to procure redemption and as a judge to pronounce the sentence at the great day of victory or condemnation.

So do not let anything draw you away from placing complete confidence in Christ the Son of the Most High—God and man in one Person—who laid down His life to atone for the sin of the whole world. Now He offers this blood as a price for you to carry in the hand of faith to the Father for pardon and peace.

Even if false teachers should come and call you from one Christ to another, from Christ outside you to a Christ within you, know this direction is not from God. The mouths of these reputed saints may quote Scripture, but their design is as dangerous as it is clever. When someone calls you from a Christ without to a Christ within, strip the doctrine of its pleasing disguise. In plain English, the false teacher calls you from trusting the righteousness of Christ (His objective work done for you and made yours by faith for your justification) to trusting in an alleged work of the Spirit within you. Now you are not a new creature in Christ—you are not saved—if you let go your hold on the living Christ to rely on something within yourself—on some creature, even if it is the "new creature." Unless your conscience has already been given over to believing a lie, you can tell that this "new creature" is only a vein of gold enclosed in much dirt and imperfection; and these outward trappings will never fully be purged until you have been put into the refining pot of the grave.

TRUST GOD FOR YOUR NEEDS

"All things are yours," and "ye
are Christ's" (1 Corinthians 3:21, 23),
God assures the Christian.

I f God has made peace with you and has forgiven your sins, you can always afford to trust Him completely for everything you need. Two things will help your faith as you exercise it.

God gives His children more than they will ever need. When God pardoned you He gave you His Son. And "how shall he not with him also freely give us all things?" (Romans 8:32). When a father gives his son the whole orchard, it is absurd for the child to ask for one apple. "All things are yours," and "ye are Christ's" (1 Corinthians 3:21, 23), God assures the Christian.

On the other hand, a wise father may bequeath a huge estate to his child—but not let him control any more of this inheritance than he can manage properly. In the same way, God gives believers a right to all the comforts of life, but His infinite wisdom proportions out smaller amounts for their actual use according to the needs of each soul. Thus if you should have much less than someone else, this does not mean God loves that person more, but that He cares enough to supply according to your ability to profitably use. We pour a drink according to the size of the cup; the wine which fills the whole cup would be spilled if poured into a smaller vessel.

Though unbelievers will soon stumble into hell, His providence reaches them while they are still on earth. Does He really feed these unclean ravens? And cause His rain to fall on their fields too? Then how can He neglect a believer? If the king regularly feeds the traitor in his prison cell, surely the child in his castle shall not starve either.

In a word, if God in His providence takes such good care of the ungodly, if He "so clothes the grass of the field"—a symbol of wicked man—"which today is, and tomorrow is cast into the oven, shall he not much more clothe you, O ye of little faith?" (Matthew 6:30).

WITNESS TO OTHERS

*Peace of conscience is to the soul what health is
to the body. Even a suit of gold cloth does not feel
comfortable on a diseased man's shoulders.*

What an acceptable work it is to win men to Christ! A doctor is never angry with a man who brings a patient to him, because through the cure his dedication and skill will be publicized. And this is the great design Christ has had for a long time, and prayed for—"that the world may believe" that God sent Him (John 17:21). His aim in gathering souls by the grace of the Gospel is "to take out . . . a people" from the heap of sinners "for his name" (Acts 15:14)—to choose a peculiar people, show mercy on them, and allow His glorious name to be exalted.

Peace of reconciliation reconciles a man to God; but peace of conscience reconciles him to himself. Since man broke peace with God he has not been able to be a friend to his own conscience. This second kind of peace is so necessary that the person cannot taste the sweetness of reconciliation with God, or of any other mercy, without it.

Peace of conscience is to the soul what health is to the body. Even a suit of gold cloth does not feel comfortable on a diseased man's shoulders. And neither does anything seem joyous to a distressed conscience. When Moses brought good news to the troubled Israelites in Egypt "they hearkened not" to him "for anguish of spirit" (Exodus 6:9). Hannah went up to the festival at Jerusalem with her husband but "she wept, and did not eat" (1 Samuel 1:7). Thus the wounded soul goes to the sermon but does not partake of it; she hears many precious promises but cannot receive the life they offer.

A royal banquet spread before a deeply troubled man does not make him happy; he would rather go off in a corner by himself and cry. "A wounded spirit who can bear?" (Proverbs 18:14). Diseases which are incurable are called the physician's reproach. And the spiritual perplexity of an accusing conscience puts all the world to shame for their vain attempts to apply a cure.

A COMFORTABLE CONSCIENCE

*Sin causes the convulsions of
horror which distort and
torment a person's conscience.*

Peace of conscience is the blessing of the Gospel and only the Gospel. Conscience knows Jesus, and the Gospel of Jesus; it refuses to obey anyone or anything else. Two particular themes will demonstrate this truth—first, what satisfies the conscience; and second, what applies this satisfaction to the conscience.

What satisfies the conscience? Sin causes the convulsions of horror which distort and torment a person's conscience. If this little word—but such a deadly plague—could ever be blotted out of men's minds, the storm would soon be stilled and the soul would immediately become a calm sea, quiet and smooth, without the least wave of fear to disturb its face. But sin is the Jonah which stirs up the tempest; wherever it comes, war is sure to follow.

When Adam sinned he drank away this sweet peace of conscience in one unhappy swallow. No wonder it almost choked him as soon as it was down his throat—"and they knew that they were naked" (Genesis 3:7). Now, whatever is to bring true peace to the conscience must first prostrate this Goliath of sin before the war can end and peace can heal.

It is true—the poisoned head of sin's arrow which burns and throbs in the sinner's conscience is guilt. It robs the person of his rest by giving the alarm that judgment is coming and punishment is inevitable. Because that man dreads what will happen when this infinite wrath of the eternal living God comes for him, he lives in fear and agony of that expectation.

Now if you want to comfort a conscience which roasts on the burning embers of God's anger, kindled by his own guilt, you must first quench those coals and present the news that God forgives sin and that He will make reconciliation with sinners who repent and believe. Nothing but this Gospel can offer the man true peace with his own thoughts.

OUR ALLEGIANCE TO CHRIST

"I am persuaded, that neither death, nor life,
nor angels, nor principalities, nor powers . . .
shall be able to separate us from the love of God,
which is in Christ Jesus our Lord" (Romans 8:38–39).

W ho shall separate us from the love of Christ?" (Romans 8:35). The apostle continues to challenge death and devils, with all their attendants, to step forward and do the worst they can against believers armed in God's breastwork. Finally he leaves the battle, filled with the holy confidence that none of them—no matter what they do—can ever hurt Christians: "I am persuaded, that neither death, nor life, nor angels, nor principalities, nor powers . . . shall be able to separate us from the love of God, which is in Christ Jesus our Lord" (Romans 8:38–39). In a word, the Christian fastens all his flags of allegiance to Christ and places all his confidence in Him. If I have spent much time on this subject, my brothers, it is because it is the richest vein in the whole mine of Gospel treasure.

What applies satisfaction to the conscience? Conscience is a lock which is not easily opened. Even if the key fits, a weak hand cannot make it turn in the lock. Thus when a mere man holds the key of comfort, conscience refuses to open; its doubts and fears will not be resolved until there is a work of God's Spirit.

Conscience is God's officer; and although the debt is paid in full from heaven, this official will not let the soul go free until the Spirit of God authorizes and brings a divine warrant. "When he giveth quietness, who then can make trouble? And when he hideth his face, who then can behold him?" (Job 34:29). Now follow me as I demonstrate why an abundant peace of conscience cannot be found apart from the Gospel and the working of the Holy Spirit.

Only the Gospel presents God's Spirit as the Comforter. The comfort of the Holy Spirit rests in the satisfaction of Jesus Christ. After He had shed His blood and paid the full price of the sinner's peace with God, He returned to heaven and asked His Father to send the Comforter.

THE SPIRIT'S WORK IN THE SOUL

When the Holy Spirit Himself comes,
all disputes will end. Satan cannot
pull rank or his false logic on Him.

T his blessed Holy Spirit has all the characteristics of a comforter. He is so pure and holy that He cannot deceive; He
is called "the Spirit of truth" (John 14:17). If He says your
sins are forgiven, you can believe Him; He will not flatter. If it
were not so He would have told you, for He can chide as well
as comfort—He can convince of sin as well as of righteousness.
And the Spirit of God is so wise that He cannot be deceived; He
never knocks at the wrong door nor delivers messages to the
wrong person, but knows the exact purpose which the heart of
God holds for each person on earth. "The Spirit searcheth all
things, yea, the deep things of God" (1 Corinthians 2:10).

These "deep things of God" which the apostle mentions are
God's counsels of love which lie deep in His heart until the
Spirit draws them out and shows them to men and women. And
He also knows perfectly the frame of man's heart. It would be
strange if the cabinet maker did not know every secret compart-
ment in the cabinet. Despite their long study, neither man nor
the devil have anything even approaching a full knowledge of
that little world, the microcosm of man's soul. But as in everything else, God knows this field perfectly and cannot be deceived.

In a word, God's Spirit is so irresistible that no one can
stand against the power of His peace. For example, the pardon
Nathan took to David was not all that he had hoped for; so David begged the Comforter to ease his pain. He went on his
knees and prayed hard to have his lost joy restored and his soft-
ened heart established by the free Spirit of God. You might baffle man, and through your own melancholy manipulation, even
evade the truths which Christians bring for comfort; but when
the Holy Spirit Himself comes, all disputes will end. Satan cannot pull rank or his false logic on Him. Confusion vanishes and
our fears with it, as darkness disappears before the sun.

SEPTEMBER 1

SOME DO NOT WALK IN GOSPEL TRUTH

*The saint's true joy is not a
giggling lightheadedness like
the world's; true joy is real.*

As many as walk according to this rule, peace be on them"
(Galatians 6:16). When peace is absent, then, can we blame
the Gospel? No matter how superior the pen is, even in
the hand of a skilled scribe, it will not write on wet paper. It is
not the pen's fault, nor the hand's—the problem is the paper.

If the heart of the saint—no matter how famous and respected—is defiled by a lust which has not yielded to repentance,
God's promise will not speak peace. This person has become a
disorderly walker, and no joy and peace can reach him in his
self-made prison. The Spirit knows how to use His rod of
correction.

Many misunderstand the meaning of peace. As for those
who walk as close to the Gospel as they can but still see no
comfort, they may have peace and not realize it. The saint's true
joy is not a giggling lightheadedness like the world's; true joy is
real. The parlor where the Spirit of Christ entertains the Christian is an inner room, not a porch next to the street where everyone who passes by can smell the banquet. "A stranger doth
not intermeddle with his joy" (Proverbs 14:10). Christ and the
Christian may be having supper within, even though you have
not seen a single dish go in, or heard the music which sounds
so splendid to believers. You might assume this soul does not
have peace because he has not hung out a conspicuous sign on
his countenance announcing the peace which he has inside.

On the contrary, sometimes there is never more inward
peace and comfort in a saint's heart than when his face is covered with tears. If you should hear a Christian moaning and
sobbing about his sins you might go home thinking that Christianity is a melancholy, dismal religion. And yet the one you pity
would not part with his sorrow for all the giddy joy the world
gives away. There is a mystery in these tears which human understanding cannot resolve.

A HARVEST TIME OF JOY

*"Light is sown for the righteous,
and gladness for the upright
in heart" (Psalm 97:11).*

Now God promises to bless His people with both outward and inward peace. It would be a sad place to have quiet streets but the cutting of throats inside our homes. Yet it would be even worse to have peace both in our streets and houses but war in our guilty consciences. Therefore Christ purchased the peace of pardon to obtain peace of conscience for His forgiven ones; and then He willed it to us in the promise: "Peace I leave with you, my peace I give unto you" (John 14:27). There He both writes and executes His own will—to give out with His hands what His love has bequeathed to believers. There is no fear, then—His will shall be performed to the fullest, seeing that He lives to get that done by the power of His Spirit.

"Light is sown for the righteous, and gladness for the upright in heart" (Psalm 97:11). It is planted in the believer when principles of grace and holiness are dropped into it by the Spirit of God. Thus it is called "the peaceable fruit of righteousness" (Hebrews 12:11). It sprouts up as naturally from holiness as any fruit does from seed of its own kind. It is true that this seed ripens into fruit sooner in some than it does in others—spiritual harvest does not take place at the same time in everyone. But here is the security—whoever has a seed-time of grace in his heart will also have his harvest-time of joy.

God would not be keeping His promise if even one saint should go without his reaping time. "He that goes forth and weepeth, bearing precious seed, shall doubtless come again with rejoicing, bringing his sheaves with him" (Psalm 126:6). Now if you think the Gospel might be defective because a certain Christian's peace has not matured, know this—it is on the way, and when it does come it will be everlasting. Do not focus on how the saint begins but how he ends. "Mark the perfect man, and behold the upright: for the end of that man is peace" (Psalm 37:36).

THE NEED FOR REPENTANCE

*"We are the circumcision, which worship God in
the spirit, and rejoice in Christ Jesus, and have
no confidence in the flesh" (Philippians 3:3).*

Now as for laying a sure foundation for solid peace in your
heart, you cannot complete it without prayers and tears—
I mean repentance. But by themselves, these remedies
will never provide peace with God. Peace of conscience is nothing more than the echo of pardoning mercy which brings the
soul into sweet rest as its pleasant music sounds in the conscience. This echo is only the same voice repeated; so if tears
and prayers and good works cannot purchase our peace of pardon, they cannot effect the peace of comfort either. Remember
what I have said—you cannot have inner peace without these;
but you cannot have it by them alone.

A common wound will hardly heal unless it is wrapped up
from the open air and kept clean; yet these measures do not
cure it—the medicine does. I do not want you to stop praying
and serving; just do not expect peace to grow only from their
root. If you do rely on this you isolate yourself from any benefit
of true peace which the Gospel offers. One resists the other like
two famous rivers in Germany, whose streams will not mingle
when they meet.

Gospel peace will not merge with any other peace. You
must drink it pure and undiluted or not at all. Speaking for himself and for all other believers, Paul testified, "We are the circumcision, which worship God in the spirit, and rejoice in
Christ Jesus, and have no confidence in the flesh" (Philippians
3:3). He was declaring, "We do not fall behind in any holy duty
or service. No, we go beyond them, because we worship God in
the spirit; but even this is not the tap where we draw our joy
and comfort. We rejoice in Christ Jesus, not in the flesh." Thus
anything which opposes Christ and our rejoicing in Him, Paul
calls flesh.

GODLY SORROW BETTER THAN FALSE JOY

*The soul realizes that nothing stands between it
and hell except Christ; and rather than die she
cries out to Him, willing to follow His direction.*

I hope you do not think I limit the Holy One of Israel in working to the same degree and measure in everyone. But in all cases the humbling work of the Spirit must convince a person before peace and comfort come to empty the soul of false confidence which she has stored up. Then the heart becomes like a vessel whose bottom has been beaten out until all the water spills out. It hates sin it once loved. The hopes which pleased and sustained her are gone and the person is left in a desolate and solitary condition.

The soul realizes that nothing stands between it and hell except Christ; and rather than die she cries out to Him, willing to follow His direction. The soul is like a patient who is thoroughly convinced of her doctor's personal skill and care. This is what I call "the broken heart."

I beg you, though, not to rest until your conscience answers some questions. Was your wine once water? Does your light arise from darkness? Is your peace the product of soul-conflict and trouble? Did you bleed before you were healed? If so, bless God who has turned your mourning into dancing.

On the other hand, if you drank wine before your pots were ever filled with water; if your morning dawned before there was evening; if your peace was settled before your false peace was broken; if your conscience was sound and whole before it was lanced and drained of pride and carnal confidence—you may possess short-lived peace. But Jesus denies all this to be His cure. It requires far more power to work true godly sorrow than false joy. You would be happier mourning from distress of a troubled conscience than dancing around the devil's idol of peace.

"As many as walk according to this rule, peace be on them" (Galatians 6:16). Now "this rule" is the holy walk of the "new creature" according to God's Word (v. 15). The principles of grace planted in the believer's soul are as appropriate to it as the agreement between the eye and light.

RESTORED THROUGH PEACE WITH GOD

*"Uphold me with thy free Spirit. Then will
I teach transgressors thy ways; and sinners
shall be converted unto thee" (Psalm 51:12–13).*

Why should we expect peace without seeking God? We would not think of harvesting before plowing and sowing. If we were like Israel in the wilderness, where the opportunities were taken away, and if we strove against pride and laziness, then I would not be surprised to see comforts falling on the soul as thick as manna around Hebrew tents. But God no longer rained bread once the Israelites grew corn to make their own bread. Neither will the Lord comfort by a miracle when the soul may obtain it through the ordinances: worship, preaching, the Lord's Supper, and so on. God certainly could have taught the eunuch Himself and satisfied him with a light from heaven. Instead, He send for Philip to preach the word, no doubt to honor the ministry of His Gospel.

Gospel peace strengthens and restores the Christian. This peace makes the Christian strong enough to fight against sin and Satan. The saint is revived when he tastes only a little of this honey, but what a slaughter he makes of his spiritual enemies when he has had a full meal! He can go into battle like a giant refreshed with wine—no one can stand before him.

Peace also strengthens the Christian to work. Paul, for instance, remembered God's mercy and the awareness of His love glowed in his heart until it infused him with a zeal for the Gospel above his fellows. This same kind of peace made David pray hard to drink again of this wine which had been locked up from him for so long. "Restore unto me the joy of thy salvation; and uphold me with thy free Spirit. Then will I teach transgressors thy ways; and sinners shall be converted unto thee" (Psalm 51:12–13). His fervent longing for the sweet taste of this wine was not the main reason he asked for peace—he desired power to do God's work.

AFFLICTION OVERCOME BY PEACE

*The less joy he has from awareness of
God's love, the more earnestly he will
grieve for the sin which clouded that joy.*

D oes your peace go with you only as far as the prison
door? Or the hospital bed? It is easy to be confident of a
salvation as long as your health is good; but as soon as
death is in sight, does your conscience point out the serious
symptom that your peace is a mere pretense?

I know that affliction is a trying time. Even the most sincere
Christian may, for a season, be beaten away from his artillery
and Satan seem to capture his confidence. Some precious saints
have been carried down the stream of violent temptations so far
that they question whether their former peace was from the
Holy Spirit the Comforter or from the evil spirit the deceiver.
Yet there is a vast difference between the two.

They differ in their causes. The darkness which sometimes
comes upon the sincere Christian's spirit in deep distress
comes from the withdrawing of God's countenance of light. But
the horror of the deceived man's torment proceeds directly
from a guilty conscience which prosperity and preoccupation
have lulled to sleep. As God's hand upon this man awakens his
numb conscience, it reveals the falseness of his profession of
faith. It is true that the saint's conscience may justly accuse him
of carelessness or compromise through strong temptation, but
it cannot accuse him of a hypocritical motive behind his whole
spiritual walk.

They differ in the things which accompany them. Lively
workings of grace are visible even as the Christian sorrows. The
less joy he has from awareness of God's love, the more earnestly he will grieve for the sin which clouded that joy. The farther
Christ is gone out of his sight, the more he clings to his love for
the Savior and cries after Him with the prayer of Heman: "Unto
thee have I cried, O Lord"; his heartfelt supplication rises to
God early in the morning hours (Psalm 88:13).

THE GOSPEL ARGUES FOR PEACE AND UNITY

*"There is one body," not a
philosophical or natural entity
but a mystical one—the church.*

T he cords of love are not woven in nature's loom; they are textured only by divine revelation. Thus Paul confidently exhorts Christians "to keep the unity of the Spirit in the bond of peace" (Ephesians 4:3).

The apostle then reminds God's people that "there is one body," not a philosophical or natural entity but a mystical one—the church—which consists of many saints (v. 4). If it is not normal for one member of a man's body to battle another, when they are all preserved in life by their union together, so much less in the mystical body.

Again, there is "one Spirit" who quickens all true saints, and He is to the whole body of Christians as the soul is to the whole man (v. 4). Now it is a strange violence against nature for members of a man's body to war against one another and drive out the soul, which gives life to them in their oneness. Surely it would be even more perverse for Christians to force the Holy Spirit to leave because of their contention and strife. A wider door cannot easily be opened for Him to go.

Further, the apostle persuades Christians to preserve unity because of the "one hope of your calling"—the bliss which we all hope for in heaven (v. 4). There is a day coming—and it cannot be far away—when we shall lovingly meet in heaven and sit at the same feast together, with no envy at what is on our neighbor's plate. Full fruition of God will be the feast, and peace and love the sweet music that accompanies it. How senseless it is, then, for us to fight on earth when we shall feast together in heaven. Now it is the Gospel which invites us to this feast and calls us to this unity. Other truths are engraved on the same holy invitation and command—"one Lord, one faith, one baptism" (v. 5)—but I shall leave these for your own study.

GRACE FOR CHILDLIKENESS

*"We ourselves also were sometimes foolish, disobedient,
deceived, serving diverse lusts and pleasures, living in malice
and envy, hateful, and hating one another" (Titus 3:3).*

Only the Gospel can form a plaster to draw out the very
core of contention from the heart. The apostle Paul testi-
fies how he and his brothers were healed of malicious
attitudes: "We ourselves also were sometimes foolish, disobedient, deceived, serving diverse lusts and pleasures, living in malice and envy, hateful, and hating one another" (Titus 3:3). And
then Paul writes in some detail how that healing came: "But after that the kindness and love of God our Savior toward man
appeared, not by works of righteousness which we have done,
but according to his mercy he saved us, by the washing of regeneration, and renewing of the Holy Ghost" (Titus 3:4–5). He
was saying, "If this love of God to us in Christ had not appeared, if we had not been washed by His regenerating Spirit,
we would still be paralyzed under the power of our lusts."

Mortification is a work of the Spirit. "If ye through the Spirit
do mortify the deeds of the body, ye shall live" (Romans 8:13).
And the Gospel is the sacrificing knife in the hand of the Spirit,
the "sword" God uses to kill sin in the hearts of His people
(Ephesians 6:17).

Just as the Gospel lays the axe to strife and digs it up by its
bitter roots, so it fills the hearts of men who embrace it with
principles leading to peace and unity. Some of these tenets are
self-denial, long-suffering, and gentleness. Self-denial prefers
that another be honored before himself. Long-suffering is that
which makes one not easily provoked. And if gentleness is pushed
by a wrong, it holds the door open for peace to come in again.

We can see a whole bundle of these sweet herbs growing in
one bed: "The fruit of the Spirit is love, joy, peace, long-suffering, gentleness, goodness, faith, meekness, temperance" (Galatians 5:22–23). Now this fruit does not crop up in just every
hedge, but only from Gospel seed.

TRUE FELLOWSHIP WITH GOD

*"And I will give them one heart,
and I will put a new spirit
within" (Ezekiel 11:19).*

Centuries ago a heathen said that true love and friendship can appear only between good men, but unfortunately he did not know what makes a good man. When God's mercy intends to accomplish oneness, He first makes the people new. "And I will give them one heart, and I will put a new spirit within" (Ezekiel 11:19). Genuine peace is a fruit of the Spirit—it inevitably sanctifies before it unites.

Finally, we see that every part and purpose of the sinner's love is carnal, not spiritual. Augustine pitied Cicero for not having Jesus Christ in his life far more than he admired him for his eloquence. This, then, is what draws a heavy black line through the carnal man's peace and unity—there is nothing of God and Christ in it.

Do carnally minded people aim at the glory of God? Is it Christ's command which binds them together? No, there is still a voice involved—but it is not God's. Their own relaxation or fleshly favor is the primary motive. Peace and unity are such welcome guests, and pay so well for their lodging, that they motivate men with no grace at all to keep up an external peace among themselves. In a word, the peace of the wicked will not last long because it lacks strong cement. Stones may lie together for a while without mortar, but not for long. The only lasting cement for love is the blood of Jesus.

The Gospel of peace is a strange text to preach contention from, yet Paul speaks of this very thing: "Some indeed preach Christ even of envy and strife" (Philippians 1:15). These men seem to have forgotten that their Lord who sent them is Himself the Prince of peace! Their work is not to blow a trumpet of confusion or sound an alarm to battle but rather to call for a joyful retreat from the dreadful fight against God and one another.

SEPTEMBER 10

THE MEAT OF THE WORD

*But as grace strengthens, and the Gospel
prevails in the hearts of Christians,
love and a spirit of unity increase with it.*

Can Christians be soldered together in unity, as long as they are not fully reconciled to God in regard to their sanctification? The less progress the Gospel has made in our hearts to mortify lust and strengthen grace, the weaker the peace and love among us.

From the contentions among Christians at Corinth, Paul concluded that they had not grown in grace beyond the spoon-feeding stage. "I have fed you with milk, and not with meat: for hitherto ye were not able to bear it, neither yet now are ye able. For ye are yet carnal" (1 Corinthians 3:2–3): he conceived their behavior to be clear evidence. "For whereas there is among you envying, and strife, and divisions, are ye not carnal, and walk as men?" But as grace strengthens, and the Gospel prevails in the hearts of Christians, love and a spirit of unity increase with it.

We say "older and wiser"—when children are very young they quarrel and fight, but age and wisdom furnish strength to overcome petty differences. For instance, in the controversy between the servants of Abraham and Lot, Abraham—the elder and stronger Christian—was determined, no matter what it cost him, to have peace with his nephew, who was inferior to him in every way. And Paul is another example. As a Christian who was head and shoulders above the others, he said of himself, "The grace of our Lord was exceeding abundant with faith and love which is in Christ Jesus" (1 Timothy 1:14).

Calvin points out that Paul's faith opposed his former obstinate unbelief as a Pharisee; his love in Jesus overcame the cruelty he expressed against Christians on his persecuting errand to Damascus. He was as full of faith as he had been of unbelief before; and as full of fire-hot love as he had been of hatred. This is what I want you to see—this pair of graces thrive and grow together; a Christian who has abundant faith will also have abundant love.

DIVISION AMONG BRETHREN

There is nothing, next to Christ and heaven,
which Satan begrudges believers more
than their peace and mutual love.

Now if the Gospel will not allow us to pay our enemies back in their own coin, returning anger for anger, then certainly it forbids a brother to spit fire into the face of another brother. When such embers of contention begin to smoke among Christians, we can be sure Satan planted the spark; he is the one great kindle-coal of all strife.

Whenever there is a storm in the spirits of saints, and the winds of their emotions are high and loud, it is easy to see who has stirred up the tempest. The devil practices his black art on unmortified lusts, that enable him to raise easily many storms of division among believers. Paul and Barnabas, for instance, set out in a calm together, but Satan sent a storm to part them in the middle of their journeyings: "And the contention was so sharp between them, that they departed asunder one from the other" (Acts 15:39).

There is nothing, next to Christ and heaven, which Satan begrudges believers more than their peace and mutual love. If he cannot separate them from Christ, and stop them from getting to heaven, he takes sinister pleasure in watching them get there in a storm. He would have them be like a shattered fleet separated from one another, saints deprived of the comfort and help of other Christians along the way. And when the devil can divide, he hopes to ruin also, knowing well that one ship is more easily taken than a squadron.

Now I love clear, calm air; but most of all I enjoy it in the church. I confess I am more aware of the greatness of this mercy when I see the dismal results of divisions that have troubled believers during these last years. What can I compare error to, better than smoke? And contention, than to fire? It is an emblem of hell itself, where darkness and flames meet to intensify the horror. But let me give you three reasons why a believer should give himself to peace and unity.

SEPTEMBER 12
UNITY WAS HIS LEGACY

*"Father, has there ever been any discord
between You and Me? Then why should these
who are Yours and Mine disagree now?"*

As soon as Christ finished His sermon He went to prayer for His disciples. Unity and peace was the legacy He wished so much to leave with them, and this was the request He now asked God to give them: "Holy Father, keep through thine own name those whom thou hast given me" (John 17:11). And then He added, "that they may be one, as we are." It is as if He had asked, "Father, has there ever been any discord between You and Me? Then why should these who are Yours and Mine disagree now?" Again, Christ continues to plead hard for the same mercy, not because it was so hard to wrest this blessing from God but because His desire for His people's unity and love was for their sakes. Notice also that Jesus did not speak a word for His own life while He redoubled His prayer for this unity. How can we thus miss its value?

He told His children what they must look for at the world's hand—all kinds of tribulation. Yet He did not pray so much for their immunity from suffering as He did against contentions amongst them. He knew that if His saints could agree in compassion, this heavenly fire of love would quench the flames of their persecutors' fire, or at least the terror of them. In a word, saints who live in strife and contention are sinning against the strong prayers which Christ Himself uttered on their behalf.

The price Christ paid for peace was great. Just as Jesus went from preaching peace to pulling down peace from heaven by prayer, so He went from praying about it to paying for it, but His prayers were not the petitions of a beggar, as ours are. He prayed that God would give Him only what He had paid for. And He was on His way to the place of payment, Calvary, where His blood was the price He willingly laid down for peace. Now this was principally our peace with God but Christ had this other peace in mind also—love among the brethren.

CONSIDER WHOSE TERRITORY YOU ARE IN

A person's soul cannot prosper
when it is inflamed with strife any more
than a physical body can enjoy a fever.

Are you not living in the midst of enemies? The rivalry between Abraham's herdmen and Lot's was aggravated by the presence of neighboring heathens: "And there was a strife between the herdmen of Abraham's cattle and the herdmen of Lot's cattle: and the Canaanite and the Perizzite dwelled then in the land" (Genesis 13:7). For God's people to quarrel while idolaters look on provides vulgar street talk which dishonors both them and their religion.

Now tell me—who are these people who have been in our land all the time God's men have been scuffling among themselves? Satan's spies have curiously observed every shred of uncomely behavior among Christians and have told the whole world about it. And these carnal ones are equipped with plenty of malicious ability to use this contention for their own ungodly purposes. They stand on tiptoes, in fact, to get on with the work of completely disabling saints who have wounded one another. They sincerely hope to undo us in this way; then they will cure us of our own wounds by inflicting one so deep that it pierces the heart of our life, Gospel and all.

O Christians, will you let Herod and Pilate disgrace you? They joined forces in a facade of peace to strengthen their hands against Christ. Are you unwilling to unite against the common enemy of the Lord Jesus? It is a tragic time for shipmates to argue when an enemy is drilling a hole in the bottom of the ship. Consider the consequences of contention.

It is now time for us to examine the major results of Christian contention. You put a stop to the growth of grace. A person's soul cannot prosper when it is inflamed with strife any more than a physical body can enjoy a fever. Just as this fire in the bones must be quenched and brought down to a normal temperature again, so must the unkindly fire among Christians be put out.

SEPTEMBER 14
SEEK PEACE FOR OTHERS' SAKE

*Do you not fear God too much
to lay a stumbling block for
men to break their necks over?*

We can pave a way for the salvation of the ungodly by letting them see the truth and ways of God in our love toward our brothers and sisters in Christ.

People are afraid to live in a place haunted with evil spirits. But can hell itself possibly house anything worse than the spirit of division? Christians, agree with one another, and your numbers will increase. The early Christians continued "daily with one accord in the temple, and breaking bread from house to house, did eat their meat with gladness and singleness of heart" (Acts 2:46). And notice what followed their fellowship—they had "favor with all the people and the Lord added to the church daily such as should be saved" (v. 47).

The world was such a stranger to real love that it was probably amused at first and then curious as to what kind of heavenly doctrine could soften men's hearts, plane their rugged natures, and join them into this family of love. And these things helped to persuade many out of the world and into the church. But tragically, the gold dulled—I mean, peace among the Christians faded—and gaping holes were seen in the church. These flaws were so obvious that passers-by were afraid to enter it. Here and there Gentiles were almost persuaded to embrace the Jewish religion, but became cautious because of the divisions and offenses embedded in it.

O Christian, do not let such sins as divisions and strifes harden your life! Do you not fear God too much to lay a stumbling block for men to break their necks over? To roll the stone over a sinner's grave and seal him down in it? Well, even as you keep yourself free of the blood of those who die in their sin, be careful not to contribute to the hardening of impenitent souls through dissensions in the body of Christ.

PREPARATION FOR TRIALS

*Just as Christ's whole body was
lifted up on the cross, no member of
His can expect to escape the cross now.*

It is our duty as believers to be prepared to endure any hardship and trial which God lays out for us in our Christian walk. And saints will never be without these trials. As Christ said of the poor, they will always be with us. Augustine said the bloody sweat which Christ felt signified the sufferings which He would endure in His mystical body. Just as Christ's whole body was lifted up on the cross, no member of His can expect to escape the cross now. When it comes to each of us, it will not speak glory for the Savior if we merely yield passively to God's will; we must be ready with an active and holy patience to obey, to be led down into the very chambers of death itself, if that is God's choice.

I heard about an epitaph which should never be engraved on a Christian's gravestone: "Here lies one against his will." Paul had the holy mind of Christ when he confessed: "I am ready not to be bound only, but also die at Jerusalem for the name of the Lord Jesus" (Acts 21:13). Skeptics might think the apostle's boldness flourished only when the enemy was far away, but faded into fear when he had to look death in the face. No, Paul stood on his earlier profession even then: "I am now ready to be offered, and the time of my departure is at hand" (2 Timothy 4:6).

If you listen closely you will hear Paul speaking as if his death had already happened. And he was dead before the stroke was given—not from fear, but from complete resignation to it. A criminal is dead in the sense of the law as soon as the judge speaks the sentence, although the condemned man may survive weeks afterwards. In a Gospel sense, then, we say those are dead who have willingly put themselves under the authority of their Father and are ready for death.

A YIELDED ATTITUDE

*Christ gives the believer a
cross to "take up" before
He gives him a crown to wear.*

G od expects us to keep our hearts pure from the defilement of sin, but with our affections rising to Him: "If a man therefore purge himself from these, he shall be a vessel unto honor, sanctified, and meet for the master's use, and prepared unto every good work" (2 Timothy 2:21).

God calls His redeemed ones to prepare not only for service but also for suffering: "If any man will come after me, let him deny himself, and take up his cross daily, and follow me" (Luke 9:23). These words may be called the Christian's contract sealed by the Spirit of God, for everyone who will be Christ's servant must agree to this relationship before he can call Him Master. The main provision the Lord has made for His servants is for them to suffer in peace. Christ has been careful to reach for the hearts of His servants, for if they love Him deeply they will not merely endure hardships in His service but show their readiness in it. Accordingly, God has included passages in Scripture for this very purpose.

Christ asks a saint to take his hands off his own will and give it up to Him. From the day he enters Christ's service he must answer the Savior's call with "I will."

Christ gives the believer a cross to "take up" before He gives him a crown to wear. He intends that Christians not only "bear" it—for the ungodly manage to do this against their wills—but to "take it up." Of course He does not mean for us to make our own cross and run headlong into trouble, but He does want us to take up that cross He has made for us. We should not step out of the way by any deceitful shift to escape trouble but accept the burden God has chosen as if He were doing us a favor to let us suffer for Him. No one stoops to pick up something that is worthless; but Christ asks His people to take up the cross the way a person takes up a pearl which lies on the ground in front of him.

SEPTEMBER 17

HE CONSOLES THOSE WHO SUFFER

*"In the day when I cried thou
answerdst me and strengthenedst me
with strength in my soul" (Psalm 138:3).*

The part of an army that sees action on the front lines is sure to have its pay—more compensation than those who wait behind in the quarters. I am sure, then, that there is more silver and gold—joy and comfort—in the camp of Christ's suffering ones than in the hearths of prosperity and ease.

God's promises are like strong wine stored up for a time of need: "Call upon me in the day of trouble," He says (Psalm 50:15). Certainly we can call on God in seasons of quiet peace, but He would have us be the boldest in the "day of trouble"— no one finds such fast help at the throne of grace as the suffering saint. David testifieth to this truth when he says: "In the day when I cried thou answerdst me and strengthenedst me with strength in my soul" (Psalm 138:3). We might not welcome a visit from a friend when it is past midnight, but we do not mind if a such person needs us at that late hour. In such emergencies we gladly go with the messenger who comes for us—and so does God. Peter knocked at the gate of the assembly who prayed for him almost as soon as their supplication knocked at the gate of heaven in his behalf.

The temptations of an afflicted person are great; to him every delay seems like neglect or oversight. Therefore God chooses to show marvelous measures of kindness at these times: "As the sufferings of Christ abound in us, so our consolation also aboundeth by Christ" (2 Corinthians 1:5). As man struggles with trouble, Christ supplies comfort. Both tides rise and fall together.

Just as we relieve the poor in their most extreme needs, Christ comforts His people as their troubles multiply. Now tell me, does not our Lord deserve a ready spirit in you to meet any suffering which brings His sweetest grace? And this, when you might expect the pains of severest sorrows to overcome you?

SEPTEMBER 18

FREEDOM BOUGHT WITH A PRICE

*The assurance which comes is especially soothing
when the landlord of hell tries hard to use the
saint's affliction as evidence to disprove his sonship.*

The apostle tells us that surrender to God's afflicting hand exhibits a son's spirit within: "If ye endure chastening, God dealeth with you as with sons" (Hebrews 12:6). Notice that He did not say "if you are chastened" but "if you endure chastening." Naked suffering never proves sonship. But to endure it with a full supply of courage, with the shoulder ready to carry it patiently, and with the expectation of future reward—these things show a childlike spirit. And the assurance which comes is especially soothing when the landlord of hell tries hard to use the saint's affliction as evidence to disprove his sonship. Here is the answer to stop the lies of this accuser's mouth: "Satan, if I am not God's child, why do I so readily yield myself to His family discipline?"

Freedom is bought with a price. Birds would rather fly among the trees of the wood, even in the cold, lean seasons, than live in a golden cage with an abundance of pampering. Some men are so attached to their lifestyle on earth that they soon let it order them about and dictate standards of happiness. Before long they become enslaved to materialism—"Their heart goeth after their covetousness" (Ezekiel 33:31); and because money is their master, their hearts wait for it like a dog at his owner's feet.

Others bow to their own reputation; they cannot enjoy anything unless they capture the place of honor everywhere they go. Haman was like this—he was the court favorite who got the king's ring to seal a decree for massacring thousands of innocent persons merely to satisfy his ambition. And it so upset his proud heart to see one poor Jew refuse to bow that his other achievements did not seem to matter. "Yet all this availeth me nothing," Haman said, "so long as I see Mordecai the Jew sitting at the king's gate" (Esther 5:13).

PREPARATION FOR DEATH

"I will fear no evil"—
even in the "valley of the
shadow of death" (Psalm 23:4).

Murderers can kill only once, but by meditating on his miseries a man kills himself a thousand times over, as often as the fear of death steals into his mind.

Once the Christian wears this armor called "the gospel of peace" (Ephesians 6:15) his soul is prepared for both danger and death. He sits at the feast which God in His providence has now given him and thoroughly enjoys it with no fear of a messenger of bad news knocking at the door. He can even talk about his dying hour and not spoil a crumb of his joy, as carnal men assume it must. To them the mere mention of death in the course of their "normal" interchange is like the wet cloth that Hazael slapped on to a king's face. The very shock of the subject scatters all the pleasant thoughts which may have dominated the conversation only minutes before.

On the other hand, the saint whose heart is prepared never tastes more sweetness in the comforts of life than when he dips these morsels into meditations of death and eternity. It causes him no more grief to think of losing his life, than it does to have the first serving of food taken away to make room for the main course. David, for example, was so little tied to this world that he could declare "I will fear no evil"—even in the "valley of the shadow of death" (Psalm 23:4).

And what about Peter? Did he know the secret of peace or not? He slept calmly, bound "between two soldiers" in a prison on the night before Herod "would have brought him forth" to his execution. And while these are certainly not the usual conditions for rest, he was so sound asleep that the angel had to strike him on the side to wake him (Acts 12:6). I seriously question whether Herod himself slept as well that evening as his prisoner did! No doubt this "preparation of the gospel of peace" (Ephesians 6:15) brought Peter to such divine rest. Because he was ready to die he was able to sleep.

CHRISTIANS SHOULD BE READY TO SUFFER

"Strive to enter—fight and
wrestle, risk life and limb
rather than fall short of heaven."

Genuine readiness to suffer thins out the number of true Christians from the ranks of professing believers; it eliminates those whose walk goes no further than a cheap profession. A person who looks into the crowded sanctuaries of Christendom today and finds multitudes who flock after the Word might wonder why ministers say that this company of Christians is such a small one, and he might think that they who say such things cannot see the forest for the trees. This very situation made one of the disciples question Christ: "Lord, are there few that be saved?" (Luke 13:23). At that time Christ "went through the cities and villages, teaching, and journeying toward Jerusalem" (v. 22). When his followers saw Christ preaching so freely in every town, and people thronging after Him with expressions of hope, it seemed almost incredible to think that only a few of them would have been saved.

Now mark how our Savior solved this riddle: "And he said unto them, Strive to enter in at the straight gate: for many, I say unto you, will seek to enter in, and shall not be able" (v. 24). Christ said His disciples were measuring by a wrong rule. "If following after sermons and testimonies and excitement were enough to save, heaven would already be full," He was saying. But do not sift the pure from the impure by such a coarse sieve. "Strive to enter—fight and wrestle, risk life and limb rather than fall short of heaven." "For many shall seek, but shall not be able"—that is, they are looking for a cheap religion through an easy profession.

Almost anyone is willing to walk through heaven's door if he never has to risk his pride in public or hazard his everyday interests by any inconvenience or opposition of the world. But "they shall not be able" to enter because their hearts are not willing to strive even unto blood. If we take the standard to be striving, not merely seeking, then the number of Christian soldiers will shrink, like Gideon's army, to a little troop.

SUFFERING MAY COME SUDDENLY

"Take now thy son, thine only son, Isaac,
whom thou lovest"—not in a year, not a
month or week, but now (Genesis 22:2).

Sometimes soldiers do not have as much as an hour's warning before they must take the field. And so you, too, might be called out to suffer for God or from Him before you expect it. Abraham, for example, had very little time to deal with his heart and persuade it to obey God by offering his child. "Take now thy son, thine only son, Isaac, whom thou lovest"— not in a year, not a month or week, but now (Genesis 22:2). This command came during the night and "early in the morning" he was on his way to the mountain (v. 3).

How could Abraham have handled such a shock had he not already wrestled with his own willingness or unwillingness to endeavor to be obedient to God in all things? Thus God already had His servant's whole heart and all Abraham was left to do was to obey. Sometimes God makes very sudden changes in our personal lives. For example, how would you receive a death bulletin like the one God gave Moses? He did not have the gradual preparation of a lingering illness but heard the message while he still enjoyed perfect health: "Get thee up . . . And die in the mount . . ." (Deuteronomy 32:49–50). Are we and our feet really ready for a journey like that?

But God can change the scene of public affairs as quickly as He can change personal situations. Maybe authority smiles on the church right now; yet it might frown again soon. "Then had the churches rest throughout all Judaea" (Acts 9:31)—it was a blessed time for the saints. But it did not last long: "About that time Herod the king stretched forth his hand to vex certain of the church" (Acts 12:1). In this persecution James the brother of John died by the sword and Peter was thrown into prison. The entire church was driven into a corner to pray in the night; and those who had had rest on every side now were threatened by violent death at every turn.

S E P T E M B E R   2 2
WEARING THE SPIRITUAL SHOE

Ask yourself why you practice Christianity
as you do. If faith's working hand is sincere
then its fighting hand will be valiant.

The question I expect from a true Christian reader now is not how to escape these troubles, but how to get this shoe on so you can wade through them in true peace with cheerfulness. It is right for the Christian soldier to ask for armor so he can fight the good fight; but the coward throws down his protection and asks which way he can run. Now I will give you the best counsel I can in the wearing of the spiritual shoe.

Examine the sincerity of your obedience. The same sound motives which take a Christian into Christ's service will guide him through suffering whenever God calls for that to happen. When the children of Ephraim took the field they were fully armed but "turned back in the day of battle" (Psalm 78:9). This seems strange until you read the preceding verse—they were "a generation that set not their heart aright, and whose spirit was not steadfast with God" (v. 8).

Soldiers can wear a complete suit of armor and live in a castle whose foundation is rock and whose walls are brass, yet if their hearts are not right with the prince, the slightest storm will throw open the gate and drive them from their place of duty. Sincerity is the only bolt that holds the gate secure.

We have all seen how honest hearts with very little support from without have held the town, while no walls have been thick enough to defend against treachery and the betraying of trust. Ask yourself why you practice Christianity as you do. If faith's working hand is sincere then its fighting hand will be valiant. The power of faith which enabled saints in days of old to "work righteousness"—that is, to live holy lives—is evidenced by the sufferings they endured. "Who through faith subdued kingdoms, wrought righteousness, obtained promises, stopped the mouths of lions, quenched the violence of fire, escaped the edge of the sword" (Hebrews 11:33–34).

CONSIDER SUFFERING

"God's promises are our fortress in times of danger; but it is not easy for us to run to them in a crisis unless we know them in times of comfort as well."

The pupil who performs best on a test is the one who has thought a great deal about the lesson before the teacher even gives him the test. In fact, we can discover an important principle when we watch porters carrying heavy loads. They lift them over and over again before they actually take them on their backs. And you can do this, too. In your meditation, lift up the troubles which might come for Christ's sake and see if you can carry them should God require it.

Set poverty, prison, isolation, and fire before you on the one hand, and the precious truths of Christ on the other, along with God's sweet promises for those who will hold fast the word of patience in such an hour of temptation. Suppose you had to choose right now which hand you would take; study this question seriously until your conscience can give a clear answer. Do this often so the self-pity which flesh and blood indulge will not be satisfied, nor the encouragements from Scripture be treated with doubt. You must make sure a promise is true before you stake your life on it.

Augustine summed up the urgency of being prepared before a battle: "It is hard to find the needed troops during war if we have not sought for and known them during peace." "God's promises are our fortress in times of danger; but it is not easy for us to run to them in a crisis unless we know them in times of comfort as well." A stranger who runs to a house for refuge in the dark night will probably fumble to open the door unless he has located the latch in the daytime—and his enemy may well destroy him while he is struggling to open the door. But one who lives inside that place, or is familiar with it, can get in easily. "Come, my people," said God, "enter thou into thy chambers" (Isaiah 26:20). He shows us our abiding place in His promises long before sufferings come so we can readily find our way to them in the dark.

REMAIN DEAD TO SIN

*"If a man therefore purge himself from these, he shall be a
vessel unto honor, sanctified, and meet for the master's use,
and prepared unto every good work" (2 Timothy 2:21).*

Now, Christian, put the gains of worldly men on the weighing scales with what is promised you if you deny yourself for Christ's sake and ask yourself how embarrassing it is to see them so freely give up comfort for an uncertain, temporary goal. All the while, you reluctantly forsake a few short-term pleasures which God will repay more than a hundredfold here —and inconceivable riches besides, whenever you come into heaven's glory!

Leave worldly lusts behind. It is the sap in the wood which makes it hard to burn, and unmortified corruption in the saint which makes him slow to suffer. But a heart drained and free of the lusts of the world will endure anything for Christ; it kindles as fast as dried wood. Paul points us toward Christians who were "tortured, not accepting deliverance; that they might obtain a better resurrection" (Hebrews 11:35). They did not love the world so much that they wanted to turn back from their journey to heaven—however hard it had become. So be careful not to leave any unmortified lust in your soul; it will never consent for you to endure the smallest suffering for your Savior.

Very few ships sink at sea; they are split by rocks and shallow places in the water. The man who can get off the jagged rocks of pride and unbelief and escape the sands of fear of men and love of the world will pass safely through the greatest storm that overtakes him. "If a man therefore purge himself from these, he shall be a vessel unto honor, sanctified, and meet for the master's use, and prepared unto every good work" (2 Timothy 2:21). If only we could know the heaven in a soul which has been crucified to the lusts of the world!

A man dead to sin lives above all disturbances of carnal passions. And when he comes to communion with God there are no intrusions of rude, sinful thoughts between him and the Father.

CHRIST'S PEACE PREPARES THE SAINT FOR TRIALS

*Only Christ can make a shoe fit the Christian's
foot so he can easily walk a hard path,
because he lines it with the peace of the Gospel.*

The peace which the Gospel brings to the heart makes a saint ready to wade through any trouble that might meet him in his Christian course. And the man who lives in this peace is the only one who stands shod, prepared for every trial. Only Christ can make a shoe fit the Christian's foot so he can easily walk a hard path, because He lines it with the peace of the Gospel. Then even when the way is covered with sharp stones, this shoe goes between the boulders and the foot—and obstacles are never much felt.

Solomon tells us that the ways of wisdom—that is, Christ— "are ways of pleasantness." But how can this always hold true when we know from experience that some of these paths lead to suffering? Scripture answers: "And all her paths are peace" (Proverbs 3:17). Because of peace with God and peace with conscience, the righteous man lacks no pleasure. David, for instance, went to bed satisfied when he had nothing for supper but the gladness God had given his heart. In fact, he promised himself a better night's rest than those full of the world's cheer: "Thou hast put gladness in my heart, more than in the time that their corn and their wine increased. I will both lay me down in peace, and sleep: for thou, Lord, only makes me dwell in safety" (Psalm 4:7–8).

The peace which David's conscience enjoyed comforted his body as well: "I laid me down and slept; I awaked, for the Lord sustained me" (Psalm 3:5). And David had this sweet rest not only when he lay in the stately palace in Jerusalem but also when he fled for his life from his unnatural son Absalom, and may have lain in the open field. It must have been a good pillow that made him forget personal peril when such a disloyal army hunted him from behind.

This Gospel peace is so transcendent that it causes the believer to lie down and rejoice to sleep in the grave as well as on the softest bed.

SEPTEMBER 26

BECOMING HIS CHILD

*"For I reckon that the sufferings of this present
time are not worthy to be compared with the glory
which shall be revealed in us" (Romans 8:18).*

Once a Christian experiences God's precious love he does not dread suffering or affliction; he knows the Father will not hurt His own child. I have often wondered about Isaac's peace and patience in submitting to be bound for a sacrifice when he saw the knife so near his throat. We know he was not a mere child because Abraham asked him to carry the load of wood. Some say he may have been more than twenty years old, certainly mature enough to be apprehensive of death. Yet the son had such complete confidence in the authority of his father that he did not struggle, but put his life into his hands. If anyone else had held the weapon he could not have trusted as he did. We must remember whoever may be the instrument of trouble to a saint, the sword is always in God's control. Because Christ saw the cup in His Father's hand He took it willingly.

A soul with God's peace is an heir of God. Kinship to heaven carries this benefit: "If children, then heirs, heirs of God, and joint-heirs with Christ" (Romans 8:17). Such a privilege lifts the Christian above any fear of suffering he might have had. For example, a few sweet meditations on this truth raised Paul's soul into a place where the troubles of this life could not discourage him: "For I reckon that the sufferings of this present time are not worthy to be compared with the glory which shall be revealed in us" (Romans 8:18). He refused to let himself or any other Christian undervalue the inheritance or the love of God that settled this glory on him by dwelling on the severity of suffering. It is as if he asked, "Has God made us His heirs, and given us heaven, for us to sit down and moan about a few minor problems in our short lives?" How important can suffering be, compared to the vast circumference of eternity that we will spend worshiping at the feet of Jesus?

PEACE WITH GOD ENCOURAGES SELF-DENIAL

*There is no other key
like love to open the heart.*

Self-denial is a grace so necessary to suffering that Christ lays the whole weight of the cross on its back: "Whosoever will come after me, let him deny himself, and take up his cross, and follow me" (Mark 8:34). Some Christians, like Simon of Cyrene, may be compelled to carry Christ's cross after him only a short way. But the self-denying saint will stoop to his knees and wait for Christ to lay this burden on him. Now there are two ways that peace with God empowers the Christian in the kind of self-denial which prepares him for suffering.

Sin may well be called self because it cleaves as close to us as our human body. It is as hard to mortify a lust as it is to cut off an arm or leg. Yet when Christ and the Christian feast together with the "hidden manna" of pardon and peace, he can ask for the head of the proudest lust of all, and take it with less regret on the part of the saint than Herodias felt as she demanded the head of John the Baptist.

There is no other key like love to open the heart. When love knocks at the door and expresses kindness, there is little reason to fear rejection. Esther, for example, persuaded her husband's heart against Haman her enemy as she showed strong love to Ahasuerus at a banquet. And God demonstrates His love to Christians each time He entertains at the feast of His Gospel. Surely this is the time He prevails with His children to send the cursed Amalekite to the gallows—that is, lust to its execution.

After Jesus' blessed words of forgiveness fell into Mary Magdalene's grieving heart, do you think she could have been persuaded to leave the embraces of His love and open the door to any of her former lovers and to whoredom again? She would have chosen martyrdom first! That one love which makes the saint deny a lust causes him not to deny a cross.

PRESUMPTUOUS SINS

*Be careful, then, to defend
yourself against these thieves
called presumptuous sins.*

When the Christian boldly walks in sinful choices and then thinks he can console his aching conscience with his pardoned state and interest in Christ, he finds the cellar door to God's comforting promises locked fast. Christ has withdrawn and taken the keys with Him. Because of pride, uncleanness, and earthly-mindedness he may even cry out in strong tears as Mary did when she could not find Jesus' body: "They have taken away my Lord, and I know not where they have laid him" (John 20:13).

Be careful, then, to defend yourself against these thieves called presumptuous sins. "The spirit of man is the candle of the Lord" (Proverbs 20:27). Has God lighted your candle and warmed your spirit with a sense of His love? If a robber from hell is allowed to touch this candle, your comfort will be snuffed out. Have you fallen into the hands of presumptuous sins which have stolen your peace? Then do not waste any time sending sincere repentance after them and raising a strong spirit of prayer and supplication to God.

As I have already warned, there is no time for delay. The farther you let these sins go without repentance, the harder you will find it to recover your peace and joy out of their hands. Yet know this—as you humbly return to God He is ready to restore to you the joy of His salvation and exact justice upon the enemies of your soul by His mortifying grace.

It is impossible for the Christian who is careless in his walk, infrequent or negligent in his communion with God, to enjoy true peace and comfort very long. Maybe you are not pouring presumptuous sins upon your joy to quench it. Well, you are not to be praised; your failure to feed it the oil of communion with God is enough to eat the heart out of your comfort. You can murder your own peace by starving it as well as by stabbing it.

THE SHIELD OF FAITH

"Above all, taking the shield of faith,
wherewith ye shall be able to quench all the
fiery darts of the wicked" (Ephesians 6:16).

The fourth piece in the Christian's armor presents itself in this verse—the shield of faith. It is a grace of graces, and is here fitly placed in the midst of its companions. It stands as the heart in the midst of the body; or as David when Samuel "anointed him in the midst of his brethren" (1 Samuel 16:13). The apostle, when he speaks of this grace, anoints it above all its fellows—"Above all, take the shield of faith."

We discover the kind of faith the apostle commended if we consider the use and end for which it is prescribed to the Christian—to enable him to "quench all the fiery darts of the wicked"—that is, of the wicked one, the devil. Now, consider the several kinds of faith. Among them must be the faith which empowers the Christian to quench all of Satan's fiery darts.

Historical faith cannot do this. This kind is so far from quenching Satan's fiery darts that the devil himself, who shoots them, has this faith. "The devils also believe" (James 2:19).

Temporary faith cannot do it. This is so far from quenching Satan's fiery darts that it is quenched by them. It displays a goodly blaze of profession and endures "for a while" (Matthew 13:21) but soon disappears.

Miraculous faith falls as short as the others. Judas's miraculous faith, which he used alongside the other apostles, enabled him to cast out devils from others but left him possessed by the devils of covetousness, hypocrisy, and treason. A whole legion of lusts hurled him down the hill of despair into the bottomless pit of perdition.

There is only one kind of faith which remains, and that is justifying faith. This indeed is a grace which makes him who has it a match for the devil. Satan has not so much advantage of the Christian by the superiority of his natural abilities, as the Christian has of Satan by this faith, his weapon. The apostle is so confident that he gives the victory to the Christian before the fight is fully over: "Ye have overcome the wicked one" (1 John 2:13).

JUSTIFYING FAITH

*The person who knows the truth of the
promise only intellectually, without
clinging to it, does not believe savingly.*

When the Devil tempted Christ he did not dispute against Scripture, but from Scripture, drawing his arrows out of this very quiver (Matthew 4:6). And at another time, he makes as full a confession of Christ as Peter himself did (Matthew 8:29; cf. Matthew 16:17). Assent to the truth of the Word is but an act of the understanding, which reprobates and devils may exercise. But justifying faith has its substance both in the understanding and the will; therefore it is called a believing "with the heart" (Romans 10:10). "Philip said, If thou believest with all thine heart, thou mayest" (Acts 8:37). It takes in all the powers of the soul.

There is a double object in the promise, which relates to both the understanding and the will. As the promise is true, so it calls for an act of assent from the understanding; and as it is good as well as true, so it calls for an act of the will to embrace it. Therefore, the person who knows the truth of the promise only intellectually, without clinging to it, does not believe savingly. That man no more receives benefit from the promise than a person who realizes food is nourishing but refuses to eat.

Justifying faith is not assurance. If it were, John might have spared himself the trouble of writing to "you that believed on the name of the Son of God, that ye might know that ye have eternal life" (1 John 5:13). His readers might then have said, "We already do this. Is it not faith to believe that we are among those pardoned through Christ, and that we shall be saved through Him?" But this cannot be so. If faith were assurance, then a man's sins would be pardoned before he believes, for surely he must be pardoned before he can know he is pardoned. The candle must be lighted before I can see it is lighted. The child must be born before I can be assured it is born. The object must be before the act.

RESTING IN CHRIST

Christ did not redeem and save man
by sitting in majesty on His heavenly throne
but by hanging on the shameful cross.

Just as redemption is impossible without Christ's blood neither can the church exist without it: "The church of God, which he hath purchased with his own blood" (Acts 20:28). The church is taken out of the dying Jesus' side, as Eve was brought from Adam's body. Christ did not redeem and save man by sitting in majesty on His heavenly throne but by hanging on the shameful cross, under the tormenting hand of man's fury and God's wrath. Therefore the person who wants his sins pardoned is directed to place his faith not only on Christ, but on the bleeding Christ: "Whom God hath set forth to be a propitiation through faith in his blood" (Romans 3:25).

Faith, then, becomes active when it rests on Christ crucified for pardon and life. There are many acts of the soul which must precede this, for a person can never truly exercise this faith unless he first has knowledge of Christ and relies on His authority. Only then can he say, "I know whom I have believed" (2 Timothy 1:12). Most people are reluctant to trust a complete stranger. Abraham did not know where he was going, but he knew with whom he was going! God worked with Abraham to teach him the knowledge of His own glorious self—who He was—so that His child could rely on His word, assenting to the truth of it no matter how harsh and improbable and impossible it seemed, "I am the Almighty God; walk before me, and be thou perfect" (Genesis 17:1).

God also wanted Abraham to recognize his own emptiness and inadequacy. He means us to see what we deserve—hell and damnation. But He also intends us to recognize our own impotence and how little—indeed, nothing—we can contribute to our own reconciliation. I join them together, because one arises out of the other. Our sense of emptiness comes from the deep apprehension we feel as we see God's fullness and our own insufficiency.

WHY FAITH IS COMPARED TO A SHIELD

*Satan will dispute truth and, if he can, will make
a Christian question the validity of faith merely
because his understanding cannot comprehend it.*

The apostle compares faith to a shield because of a double resemblance between this grace and that particular piece of armor.

The first likeness is that the shield is not for the defense of any one part of the body, as most other pieces are. The helmet is fitted for the head and the plate designed for the breast, but the shield is intended for the defense of the whole body. Therefore it was to be made very large and was called a "gate" or "door" because it was so long and large that it covered the whole body. And if the shield was not large enough to cover every part at once, the skillful soldier could turn it this way or that way, to stop the swords or the arrows, no matter where they were directed. This resemblance reminds us of the importance of faith in the life of a Christian. It defends the whole man—every part of the Christian is preserved by it.

Sometimes the temptation is leveled at the head—at the saint's reasoning. Satan will dispute truth and, if he can, will make a Christian question the validity of faith merely because his understanding cannot comprehend it. And sometimes he prevails, blotting out a person's beliefs in the deity of Christ and in other great and profound truths of the Gospel. But faith intervenes between the believer and this arrow, coming to the relief of the Christian's weak understanding.

Abraham, "being not weak in faith . . . considered not his own body now dead" (Romans 4:19). If reason had had the upper hand in that business, if that holy man had put the promise to a test of sense and reason, he would have been in danger of questioning the truth of it, although God Himself was the messenger. But faith brought him through the test. "I will trust the Word of God," says the believer, "not my own blind reason."

THE IMPORTANCE OF THE SHIELD

*It was the charge which one mother laid upon her son
going into war: "Either bring your shield home
with you or be brought home upon your shield."*

In old times the shield was prized by a soldier above all other pieces of armor. He counted it a greater shame to lose his shield than to lose the battle; and therefore he would not part with it even when he was under the very foot of the enemy, but esteemed it an honor to die with his shield in his hand. It was the charge which one mother laid upon her son going into war: "Either bring your shield home with you or be brought home upon your shield." She would rather have seen her son dead with his shield than alive without it.

The apostle further attached another noble effect to faith. We are commanded to take the girdle of truth, the breastplate of righteousness, and so on, but it is not specified what each one of them could do. Yet when the apostle spoke of faith he ascribed the whole victory to it. This quenches "all the fiery darts of the wicked" (Ephesians 6:16). And why is this true? Are the other graces useless, and does faith do everything? If so, why must the Christian arm himself with more than this one piece?

I answer that every piece has its vital use in the Christian's warfare. No one part can be spared in the day of battle. But the reason that no single effect is attributed to each of these, but that all is ascribed to faith, is to let us know that these graces— their power and our benefit from them—must operate in conjunction with faith.

Plainly it is the design of God's Spirit to give faith the precedence among all those graces entrusted to our keeping. But be careful not to become indifferent or careless in your dealings with the other graces just because you are more excited about getting and keeping this one. Could we warn a soldier to beware of a wound at his heart but forget to guard his head? Truly, we would deserve cracked crowns to cure us of such foolishness.

FAITH AND AFFLICTION

*Afflictions are a spade which God
uses to dig into His people's hearts
to find the gold of faith.*

C hrist further illustrates the preeminence of faith in the account of His restoring sight to the blind man by the pool
of Siloam. This healing so enraged the malicious Pharisees that they excommunicated the man for no fault other than
giving glory to his merciful Physician. And the presence and
tenderness of Jesus more than compensated for this man's sudden new role as an outcast. But to our present purpose, let us
note Christ's words to this person at their first meeting: "Dost
thou believe on the Son of God?" (John 9:35). The man had already expressed some enthusiasm in vindicating Christ and in
speaking favorably of Him to the bitterest enemies He had on
earth. But the one thing which Christ prized even more highly
than the man's loyalty was his faith, a fact which we find in His
Inquiry: "Dost thou believe?" It is as if He had said, "All this
zeal in speaking for Me, and your patience in suffering, are
worth absolutely nothing if you do not have faith."

As we see in Jesus' encounter with the blind man, most of
God's dealings with His people are questions concerning their
faith, either the presence or the strength of it. And even when
He afflicts, it is for "the trial of your faith" (1 Peter 1:7).

Afflictions are a spade which God uses to dig into His people's hearts to find the gold of faith. Not that He does not seek
out the other graces also, but faith is the most precious of them
all. Even when God delays and seems to withdraw His hand before coming with the mercy He promises, it is so that He can
explore our faith.

Jesus carefully but thoroughly examined the Canaanite
woman's faith while she struggled to believe: "O woman, great
is thy faith: be it unto thee even as thou wilt" (Matthew 15:28).
In answering this woman's plea for Him to heal her daughter,
Jesus gave her the evidence of her faith and more mercy by far
than she had expected.

THE PRICE OF HIS BLOOD

"Therefore being justified by faith,
we have peace with God through our
Lord Jesus Christ" (Romans 5:1).

I ndeed the Christian's most priceless riches are held in faith's hand. "Hath not God chosen the poor of this world rich in faith?" (James 2:5). Why does God say "rich in faith" rather than rich in patience, rich in love, or any other grace? When a sinner claims pardon for sin, favor of God, and heaven itself, it is not love or patience but faith alone which lays down the price of all these benefits. Not, "Lord, pardon and save me—here are my love and patience for it"; but, "Here is Christ and the price of His blood, which faith presents for the full payment of them all." This understanding, then, leads to a third reason for the preeminence of faith.

"Therefore being justified by faith, we have peace with God through our Lord Jesus Christ" (Romans 5:1). We are not justified by love, repentance, patience, or any other grace besides faith. "Justifying patience," "justifying repentance"—how jarring these words sound to a Christian. Rather, we find that justification is appropriated by faith and the rest of the graces hedged out from this act, although they are included and assumed in the person who is justified.

Paul's job was to prove that faith justifies without works. But the faith which justifies is not idle or dead but a lively working faith, which seems to be James's design in the second chapter of his epistle. As God singled out Christ from all others to be the only mediator between Himself and man, and His righteousness to be the worthy cause of our justification; so He has singled out faith from all the other graces to be the instrument for appropriating this righteousness of Christ to us. This righteousness is called "the righteousness of God' as opposed to our "own righteousness," although it is worked by God in us (Romans 10:3). It is wrought for us by Christ.

OCTOBER 6

FAITH FREES US FROM FEAR

There was a time when your hearth was cold—
not a spark of this fire could be found.
How is it that you love God so much now?

Faith supplies all the graces with work. Faith is like a wealthy owner of wool who supplies material to men who weave cloth. When the tradesman does not furnish supplies, the spinners must stop their production. They have nothing to work with except what the tradesman gives them. Thus faith gives out to each grace what it must have to act upon.

Let us review one or two graces as an example of all the rest. Repentance is a sweet grace but faith has to make it work. For instance, Nineveh's repentance can be traced to faith: "The people of Nineveh believed God, and proclaimed a fast, and put on sackcloth" (Jonah 3:5). Their repentance may have been nothing more than legalism, but it was as good as their faith. If their faith had been better, their repentance would have been of a deeper quality too.

In the same way as light causes the eye to focus on an object, faith uncovers sin in the conscience. Thoughts soon arise like clouds and thicken into a storm until they fill the soul with heavy black horror and trembling for sin. But at this point the person is at a loss and cannot go any further into repentance until faith sends in more support from the promise of pardon. When the sinner hears and believes the promise, repentance can continue. And finally, the cloud of terror which the fear of wrath had gathered in the conscience dissolves into a soft rain of evangelical sorrow.

Love is another heavenly grace, but faith finds the fuel that makes it blaze. Was your soul always flaming with love for God the way it is now? Undoubtedly there was a time when your hearth was cold—not a spark of this fire could be found. How is it that you love God so much now? Surely you have heard some good news from heaven!

Faith is the only messenger which can bring good news from heaven to the heart. It is faith that proclaims the promise, opens Christ's riches, and pours out His name to increase love in believers.

FAITH DEFENDS THE CHRISTIAN

*A saint may be humble, patient, and devout, Satan can
easily tear a hole in . . . and break in if faith
does not completely cover each piece of armor.*

If faith should fail, then every grace will be put to flight. Job's
patience was wounded when his hand got too tired to hold
up his shield as a covering.

Similarly, no grace is safe if it is out from under the wing of
faith. At a time when Peter's zeal surpassed his faith, Christ kept
him from falling from all grace by saying, "I have prayed for
thee, that thy faith fail not" (Luke 22:32). Peter's faith was the reserve that the Savior took care should be kept in order to recover his other graces when the enemy foiled him, and to
deliver him, bruised and broken, from that encounter.

Christ could not do many miracles for His own countrymen
"because of their unbelief" (Matthew 13:58). And neither can
Satan harm the Christian seriously when faith is in its place. It is
true that the devil skillfully aims to fight faith above all, because
it is the grace which keeps him from conquering the rest of the
graces. Although a saint may be humble, patient, and devout, Satan can easily tear a hole in these graces and break in if faith
does not completely cover each piece of armor. But God's design is still our best defense; He causes faith to be the grace
which makes Satan turn and run.

Faith alone gains acceptance with God for all the other
graces and their works. Even the obedient Christian who works
hard all day does not expect to take his accomplishment home
at night and find God's acceptance for the sake of his human effort. It is only by faith that he can present it though Christ to
God. We "offer up spiritual sacrifices, acceptable to God by Jesus Christ" (1 Peter 2:5)—that is, by faith in Christ. Faith can so
prevail with God that He will take even the smallest broken
pieces of human effort from its hand. But He takes nothing unless the hand of faith brings it to Him.

OCTOBER 8

THE GOD OF HOPE

*"Now the God of hope fill you with all joy and
peace in believing, that ye may abound in hope,
through the power of the Holy Ghost" (Romans 15:13).*

Of all the graces, faith is the Christian's cupbearer. The
Christian takes the wine of joy out of faith's hand, rather
than from any other grace. "Now the God of hope fill
you with all joy and peace in believing, that ye may abound in
hope, through the power of the Holy Ghost" (Romans 15:13).

The apostle Paul gives preeminence to faith, attributing the
Christian's joy to his faith rather than to his love. "Whom having
not seen, ye love; in whom, though now ye see him not, yet believing, ye rejoice with joy unspeakable and full of glory" (1 Peter 1:8). Mark the key word in that passage: "believing, ye
rejoice." Here is the door where the Christian's joy comes in.
God allows us to rejoice only in Christ. "For we are the circumcision, which worship God in the spirit, and rejoice in Christ Jesus, and have no confidence in the flesh" (Philippians 3:3).

Christ's blood is the only wine which gladdens God's heart
and satisfies his justice at the same time. Therefore it is all that
can bring true gladness into the heart of man. When Christ
promises the Comforter, He tells His disciples about the vessel
He will use to draw the wine of joy. "He shall take of mine, and
shall shew it unto you" (John 16:15). No grape of our own harvest is pressed into this sweet cup. It is as if Christ says, "When
He comes to comfort you with the forgiveness of your sins, He
will take of mine, not anything of yours. I purchased your peace
with God with My blood, not by your tears of repentance or
mourning for your sins."

The Christian's joy flows from Christ alone, not from any human source. But faith discovers unsearchable riches in Christ
and reveals to the Christian all that it sees and knows of Him.
And it is faith that makes an opening in our hearts for the promises and then pours in the sweet realities of God's Word (see
Romans 10:17).

THE PREEMINENCE OF UNBELIEF

The devil sets up a blind of unbelief between the sinner and God so that he will not fear the Father's warning and chastening aimed at his heart.

Unbelief deserves as high a place among sins as faith has among graces. Unbelief is the Beelzebub, or prince of sins, which makes others sin. God branded Jeroboam as one "who did sin, and who made Israel to sin" (1 Kings 14:16). Unbelief is a sin-making sin.

The first poisonous breath which Eve took in from the tempter was sent in these words: "Yea, hath God said, Ye shall not eat of every tree of the garden?" (Genesis 3:1). It is as if he had said, "Think about this now. Do you really believe God would keep back the best fruit in the whole garden from you?" This was the traitor's gate whereby all other sins rushed into Eve's heart; and even now Satan continues to hold this same gate wide open.

The devil sets up a blind of unbelief between the sinner and God so that he will not fear the Father's warning and chastening aimed at his heart. Then once there is a barricade between him and these merciful bullets, the sinner can be bold with his lust. Unbelief not only diverts the bullets of wrath which are sent out of the law's fiery mouth, but it also retards the actions of grace coming from the Gospel. All the offers of love which God makes to an unbelieving heart fall like sparks into a river; they are put out as soon as they fall into it.

"The word preached did not profit them, not being mixed with faith in them that heard it" (Hebrews 4:2). The secret of sin's strong hold upon a person is unbelief. There is no mastering a sinner while unbelief overpowers him. This sin will break down all reasoning as easily as Samson did the doors and posts, bar and all, from the city of Gaza (Judges 16:3). It is a sin which holds out last on the battle field, the one which the sinner is least aware of, and which the saint ordinarily conquers last. It is one of the chief fortresses to which the devil retreats when other sins are routed.

LEGITIMATE CHILDREN

*The judgment scene itself should
be enough to stir our earnest
determination to have true faith.*

When you come to the bar of judgment, God will demand that you pay the debt you owe Him or writhe painfully in hell's prison. If you hold false faith in your heart, He will not accept your payment, even though it is Christ Himself you believe in. He will give you over to the tormentor's hand not only for not believing but for counterfeiting the King of heaven's coin and placing His name on your false money. The judgment scene itself should be enough to stir our earnest determination to have true faith.

As your faith is, so are all your other graces. As a man's marriage is, so are all his children—legitimate or illegitimate. Thus, as our marriage is to Christ, so all our graces are. Now it is faith by which we are married to Christ. "I have espoused you to one husband," said Paul to the Corinthians (2 Corinthians 11:2). It is by faith that the soul gives consent to take Christ for her husband. If our faith is false, then our marriage to Christ is also false; and if the marriage is illicit, then all our assumed graces are illegitimate also.

No matter how handsome an illegitimate child may be, he is still illegitimate. Our humility, patience, temperance—they are all illegitimate. Just as "a bastard shall not enter into the congregation of the Lord" (Deuteronomy 23:2), no bastard grace can enter the congregation of the redeemed in heaven. A man who has children of his own will not make another's illegitimate child his heir. God has children of His own to inherit heaven's glory. And by His Spirit he has begotten heavenly graces in their hearts which resemble His own holy nature. Surely, then, He will never give His glory to mere strangers, counterfeit believers who are the devil's brats.

JUDGING TRUE FAITH

*Be careful not
to let Satan cheat you
with false faith.*

It is not hard for the ignorant sinner to admit he deserves nothing but hell, but the man who pretends to have faith lives a lie. Satan delights in stalling this man's search for fulfillment by cheating him along the way with a counterfeit faith. The Israelites longed for the true worship of God in Jerusalem, but Jeroboam kept them from going there by setting up something like religious worship at home. He substituted golden calves and satisfied many Israelites to such a degree that they never took the first step to Jerusalem.

Be careful not to let Satan cheat you with false faith. Everyone, I know, would have the living child, and not the dead one, to be hers. All of us want true faith. But do not be your own judges; appeal to the Spirit of God and let him decide the controversy by using the sword of His Word. You say you have faith, but which kind is it—false or true?

By this time you may want to know what your faith is and how you can judge the truth of it. In your search there are two directions you can take—one, how the Spirit works faith in the soul; and the other, the characteristics of this faith.

The Spirit works faith in the soul. Faith is the greatest work which the Spirit of Christ accomplishes in the human spirit. The apostle calls it "the exceeding greatness of his power to us-ward who believe" (Ephesians 1:19). Notice the expressions of the Spirit of God describing this work of the Spirit: "power," "greatness of power," "exceeding greatness," and "exceeding greatness of his power." What angel in heaven can understand the command of faith's power in the human spirit?

God assigns His whole being to this work. It is compared to "the working of his mighty power, which he wrought in Christ, when he raised him from the dead, and set him at his own right hand in the heavenly places, far above all principality, and power" (Ephesians 1:19–21).

CHANGING THE REBELLIOUS WILL

*Has the Spirit of God put His golden key
into the lock of your will, to open the door of
your heart and let Christ the King of glory in?*

The sinner who is thoroughly convicted by the Spirit sees himself like a condemned prisoner held by so many irons that escape is impossible. It is not their disease but their physician that kills sinners. They think to cure themselves; and this deception leaves them incurable. If you cling to the self-confidence of repentance and reformation, they will betray you into the hands of God's justice and wrath. But if you have turned away from this religious self-confidence, you have escaped one of the finest snares that the wit of hell can weave.

Not only is the convicted sinner so convicted that he knows he is helpless, but he welcomes the full provision laid up in Christ for him. And this attitude is a necessary antecedent to faith. Without it the soul convicted of sin is more likely to go to the gallows with Judas, or fall on the sword of the law, than to run to Christ.

The Spirit powerfully but sweetly renovates the rebellious will so it can deliberately choose Christ as Lord and Savior. During a storm a person may run under an enemy's shelter which he would not have even glanced at in fair weather. Do you take pleasure in choosing Christ? Do you go to Him not only for safety but also for delight? As the lover said of her bridegroom, "I sat down under his shadow with great delight" (Song of Solomon 2:3). This must be a deliberate choice, wherein the soul seriously weighs the covenant Christ offers and then chooses Him. Even when Naomi spoke the worst she could to discourage her daughter-in-law, Ruth enjoyed her mother's company too much to give it up regardless of the potential hardships involved in her decision.

Has the Spirit of God put His golden key into the lock of your will, to open the door of your heart and let Christ the King of glory in? Has He opened the eye of your understanding, as He awakened Peter asleep in prison, and caused the chains of dullness to fall off your conscience?

FAITH AND PRAYER

Faith is the wrestling grace.
It comes up close to God, reaches out to
Him, and will not easily take a denial.

aith puts forth an assisting act in prayer. And it does this in
two ways. First, it assists the soul with persistence. Faith is
the wrestling grace. It comes up close to God, reaches out
to Him, and will not easily take a denial. Faith is the soul's eye
by which it sees the filth and hell in every sin. It is this insight
which makes the heart sorrowful when the soul spreads its
abominations before the Lord. Tears come as freely as water
from a flowing spring when faith finds Jesus in His love and
graces reflected in the mirror of promise.

Never before could the Christian know what to do with a
promise in prayer until faith teaches him to press in to God
with it, humbly yet boldly. "What wilt thou do unto thy great
name?" asks believing Joshua (Joshua 7:9). It is as if he had said,
"You are so inseparably bound to Your people by promise that
You cannot leave them to die unless Your name suffers with
them."

The second way faith assists in prayer is that it empowers
the soul to persevere. As the wheel wears out with turning until
it breaks, the hypocrite prays until he gets tired. Sooner or later
something will make him abandon the duty which he never
really liked anyway. But it is impossible for the sincere believer
to stop praying unless he also stops believing. Prayer is the very
breath of faith. Stop a man's breath and where is he then?

Are you compelled to pray? As a baby cannot help but cry
when it is hurt or wants something—because there is no other
way to get help—so the Christian's wants, sins, and temptations
return to him and he cannot do anything but pray about them.
"From the end of the earth will I cry unto thee," says David
(Psalm 61:2). He was saying, "Wherever I am I will find You. Im-
prison me, banish me, or do with me what You will—You will
never be rid of me." "I will abide in thy tabernacle for ever"
(Psalm 61:4).

UNBELIEVERS NEED THE SHIELD OF FAITH

*"I will not give sleep to mine eyes, or slumber to mine
eyelids, until I find out a place for the Lord, an habitation
for the mighty God of Jacob" (Psalm 132:4–5).*

Is there any way to have Christ except by faith? There is a
generation of men in the world who would almost make
one think so. Their corrupt, profane life-styles have been
decorated with flowers of morality, leaving a sweet reputation
among their neighbors. Yet why do they continually ignore the
Gospel of Christ? Surely it is not because they are more willing
to go to hell than other people, but because they think their
"morality" will get them into heaven. They are deceived.

Did Christ come to help only the sensual, defiled sinners
such as drunkards, liars, and prostitutes find heaven? And are
civil, moral men left to walk there the best way they can? God's
Word opens only one way to heaven. There is but "one God,
and one mediator between God and men, the man Christ Jesus"
(1 Timothy 2:5). And since Christ is the only bridge over the
gulf between earth and heaven, judge what will happen to the
self-righteous man and his sweet-scented life if he misses this
one bridge.

The man who thinks he does not need faith to accept
Christ's offer of salvation as much as the bloodiest murderer or
filthiest Sodomite in the world is treading in hopeless deception. If a group of men and children were to wade through a
brook no deeper than a man's head, the men would have a definite advantage over the children. But if they tried to cross the
ocean, the men as well as the children would need a ship to
carry them. And only the insane would try to wade through
without the help of a ship just because they are a little taller
than the rest.

Nothing deserves precedency before faith in your thoughts.
David resolved, "I will not give sleep to mine eyes, or slumber
to mine eyelids, until I find out a place for the Lord, an habitation for the mighty God of Jacob" (Psalm 132:4–5). The habitation which pleases God most is your heart; but it must be a
believing heart, "that Christ may dwell in your hearts by faith"
(Ephesians 3:17).

OPPOSITION TO THE SPIRIT'S WORK

*There is more hope for a sick man when his
disease is discovered than when it is hidden
in the heart and cannot be seen outwardly.*

Beware of opposing the Spirit. Does He beam light from His Word into your understanding? Be careful what you do with this candle of the Lord that lights your mind; do not pride yourself in this new insight, or it may be snuffed out in an instant. If the Holy Spirit confirms the light in your understanding so that it sets your conscience on fire with the awareness of sin, do not resist Him. He is mercifully kindling fire in your soul to keep you out of a hotter fire in hell. But you must expect Satan—whose house is on fire over his head—to do everything he can to quench it; your greatest danger is listening to him. Instead, draw water freely from God's Word to control this blaze.

Satan longs for you to quench the Spirit by trying to calm your own conscience. There is more hope for a sick man when his disease is discovered than when it is hidden in the heart and cannot be seen outwardly. Satan is so afraid of losing his throne inside you that he tries to smother your conscience with carnal lukewarmness and extinguish the Holy Spirit's convicting work. But it is God's goodness which sends these convictions to effect your spiritual delivery, and you should welcome them as much as a woman in labor welcomes every pain. Without the travail she could not be delivered of her child, and neither can God bring forth the new creature in your soul without repentance.

Sometimes the Spirit of God not only furnishes light for your mind and hell-fire in your conscience, but heaven-fire in your affections. From the Word He makes Christ so visible in His excellencies and sufficiency for all your needs that your affections begin to desire Him. These glimpses of Jesus and of God's mercy through Him are so luscious that you begin to taste sweetness in hearing of them, which stirs up further desire in you so that finally you must have the desire of your heart: "I must have Christ!"

OCTOBER 16

YOUR PRAYERS ASCEND TO GOD

How glad God must be to
answer prayer which fulfills
His highest purpose for you.

D o not be afraid to pray for faith. God will not reprimand me for sending such customers to His door. You have a Friend in God's own breast who will ensure your welcome. He who could give Christ before anyone ever prayed is more than willing to give faith to you when you ask. Remember that what you ask God to give, He commands you to do: "This is his commandment, That we should believe on the name of his Son Jesus Christ" (1 John 3:23). How glad God must be to answer prayer which fulfills His highest purpose for you.

By this time you can promise yourself a joyful return on your prayer sent to heaven. But so that you can be even more hopeful, remember that this grace which you want so much and ask God for is the main part of Christ's purchase. His blood, which is the price of pardon, is the full price of faith also. Not only has He canceled man's debt of sin but He has also made a way for us to approach Christ's bank of grace for sinners who see they have nothing of their own. "Thou hast ascended on high, thou hast led captivity captive: thou hast received gifts for men; yea, for the rebellious also, that the Lord God might dwell among them" (Psalm 68:18).

Scripture tells us the reason these gifts are given: "that God may dwell among them." Nothing but faith can make a soul who has been rebellious an acceptable place for the holy God to dwell. This is the gift He received all other gifts for. Now let this understanding give you boldness to humble yourself and press God for that which Christ has already brought: "Lord, I have been a rebellious person; but did not Christ receive anything for such? I have an unbelieving heart; but I hear there is faith paid for in Your covenant. Christ shed His blood so You could pour out Your Spirit on a sinner like me."

While you are pleading like this with God and using His Son's name in prayer, Christ Himself can hear, agree, and give favor to your prayer.

FAITH PRESERVED WITH GREAT CARE

He prefers security in his spiritual life
to stability in his natural life, which he is
willing to lose and count himself no loser.

All other graces are to be measured by our faith; and if these are not fruits they have no true worth. This is the difference between a Christian and an honest heathen. The heathen values himself by his patience, temperance, liberality, and other moral virtues. While he lives he brags about his morality; and he expects God to commend him and to guarantee him happiness after he dies. But the Christian has found Christ, whose righteousness and holiness by faith become his; and he values himself by these more than by inherent traits.

Let me illustrate this by two men—the one a courtier, the other a countryman and stranger to court—both having sizable estates, but the courtier the greater by far. Ask the country gentleman, who has no relation to the court or place in the prince's favor, what he is worth, and he will tell you the sum of his lands and monies. He values himself by these. But ask the courtier what he is worth, and although he has more property and money than the other, he will tell you he values himself by the favor of his prince more than by all his other assets. He says, "What my prince has is mine, except his crown and royalty, his treasure mine to take care of me, his love to embrace me, his power to defend me."

The poor heathen—strangers to God and His favor in Christ —bless themselves only by their natural resources and the stockpile of moral values which they gather with great effort. But the believer, having access by faith into this grace because he stands high in God's favor by Jesus Christ, values himself by his faith rather than by any other grace. And he cherishes this grace of God in himself above all the world's treasure or pleasure—he had rather be the ragged saint than the robed sinner. He prefers security in his spiritual life to stability in his natural life, which he is willing to lose and count himself no loser.

OCTOBER 18

PRESERVE A GOOD CONSCIENCE

*The sheep may fall into
a ditch, but it is the
swine that wallow in it.*

If only Christians who complain about their weak faith would turn their murmuring into an investigation of why it is so weak! It is because faith has missed its meals from the Word. In earlier days you went through many pressures to keep yourself in the fellowship of God's Word; and you were always rewarded for the time taken from other schedules. But now that you have gradually stopped coming to God in His Word, there is a sad change. It is not easy for you to trust Him; and you have little authority over your unbelief.

The best counsel I have is what doctors recommend for healthy bodies. They find out where a patient was born and send him back there. Let me ask you—if you ever had faith, where was it born and brought up? Was it not in the sweet air of hearing, meditating, and praying over the Word? Go as fast as you can into your native air, where you drew your first Christian breath, where your faith thrived and grew from the beginning.

Look to your conscience. A good conscience is the vessel faith sails in. If the conscience is wrecked, how can faith be safe? Now you know what sins destroy the conscience—sins deliberately committed or impenitently repeated. Guard against these deliberate sins! Like a stone thrown into a clear storm, they will so muddy the conscience that you cannot see the reflection of the promise.

But even if you have fallen into the pit of sin, do not stay there. The sheep may fall into a ditch, but it is the swine that wallow in it. Therefore, how hard will it be to stir up faith in the promise when your garment is filthy and your countenance smeared with sin? It is dangerous to drink poison, but far more lethal to let it stay in the body for a long time. Although you are a believer you cannot act on faith until you have cleansed your heart by repentance.

THE ADVANTAGE OF STRONG FAITH

"Thou wilt keep him in
perfect peace, whose mind is
stayed on thee" (Isaiah 26:3).

If only you knew the many advantages of strong faith over weak faith you would not rest a minute until it was yours. Strong faith conquers those temptations which take weak a prisoner. When David's faith prevailed, he looked death in the face fearlessly. "For the people spake of stoning him, but David encouraged himself in the Lord his God" (1 Samuel 30:6). Yet when his faith was weak, he was ready to run and hide in the nearest hole to save himself (1 Samuel 21:13).

Strong faith frees the Christian from those thoughts which oppressed weak faith. "Thou wilt keep him in perfect peace, whose mind is stayed on thee" (Isaiah 26:3). The more faith, the more inward peace and quietness; if little faith, then little peace and serenity through the storms that unbelieving fears will surely gather.

Weak faith will as surely take the Christian to heaven as strong faith; for it is impossible that the least ounce of true grace should perish, since it is all incorruptible seed. But the doubting Christian will not have as pleasant a voyage there as will the believer with strong faith. Although everyone aboard the ship will arrive safely at the shore, yet the seasick traveler will not have so comfortable a trip as the man who is healthy. The sick person misses pleasant surprises during the delightful parts of the journey. But the strong man views it all with abundance of expectation; and while he wishes with all his heart he were already home, yet the joy he has shortens and sweetens his way to him.

Thus, Christian, there are many delights which saints traveling to heaven meet on their way there, besides what God has for them at the journey's end. It is the Christian whose faith is strong enough to act upon the promise who finds and possesses these pleasures.

O C T O B E R   2 0

CONTENTMENT WITH CHANGES IN PROVIDENCE

*Weak faith that gropes for some footing
for reason to stand on tries desperately to
reconcile God's promises and human reasoning.*

Skillful swimmers are not afraid to get into water over their heads, whereas young learners feel for the ground and stay close to the bank. Strong faith does not fear when God carries the creature beyond the depth of reason: "Neither know we what to do," said Jehoshaphat, "but our eyes are upon thee" (2 Chronicles 20:12). It is as if he had said, "We are swallowed up in a sea that is bigger than we are. We have no idea how to get out of this trouble, but our eyes are upon You. We will not give up as long as there is strength in Your arm, tenderness in Your heart, and truth in Your promise."

Weak faith that gropes for some footing for reason to stand on tries desperately to reconcile God's promises and human reasoning. And weak faith asks many questions. When Christ says, "Give ye them to eat," His disciples ask in return, "Shall we go and buy two hundred pennyworth of bread?" (Mark 6:37). As if Christ's bare word could not spare them that cost and trouble! "Whereby shall I know this?" says Zacharias to the angel, "for I am an old man" (Luke 1:18). His faith was too feeble to stand up to such wonderful news.

The more contented the Christian's heart under the changes which providence brings on his state and condition in the world, the stronger is his faith. Weak bodies cannot tolerate changes of weather as well as healthy ones. Heat and cold, fair and foul weather cause no great change in the strong man's constitution. But the weak person complains of them. Thus strong faith can live in any climate, travel in all weather, and handle any unpredictable condition. "I have learned, in whatsoever state I am, therewith to be content," says Paul (Philippians 4:11). Unfortunately, however, not all Christ's followers are like Paul in this; and weak faith has not yet mastered this hard lesson.

RESISTING TEMPTATIONS TO SIN

*The Christian's faith is strong
or weak as he finds it easy or hard
to break from temptations to sin.*

A big fish easily breaks through the same net which holds a little fish captive. The Christian's faith is strong or weak as he finds it easy or hard to break from temptations to sin. When an ordinary temptation entangles you like a fly in a spider's web your faith is very frail. Peter's faith was weak when nothing more than a maid's voice drove him to deny Christ; but it became strong when he withstood and refuted the threats of a whole council (Acts 4:20). Even when faith does not have a hand to throw down an enemy, it still has a hand to lift up against it and a voice to cry out to heaven for help. True faith finds a way to combat sin.

Christian, compare yourself with yourself. Do lusts snare your heart and lure it away from God as forcefully as they did several months ago? Or can you honestly say your heart is overcoming them? Since you now know more about Christ and have glimpsed His spiritual glories, can you now pass by their door and not look in? And when temptation knocks, can you shut the door in its face? If the power of sin dies, you can be sure your faith is lively and vigorous. The harder the blow, the stronger the arm that gives it. A child cannot deliver such a wound as a man. And while weak faith cannot deliver a fatal blow to sin, strong faith is both willing and able to do this. The more obedience and love in the Christian's walk, the stronger is his faith.

Faith works by love, and therefore its strength or weakness can be gauged by the strength or weakness of the love which it activates in a Christian's behavior. The strength of a man's arm that draws a bow is proved by the force in the arrow's flight. And certainly the strength of our faith may be known by the force with which our love mounts to God. It is impossible that weak faith—which is unable to draw the promise as strong faith can—should as powerfully impress the heart to love God as stronger faith can.

DOUBT AND ASSURANCE

"O thou of little faith,
wherefore didst thou doubt?"
(Matthew 14:31).

Our blessed Savior tells His disciples what wonders they will do if they believe and "doubt not" (Matthew 21:21); and that which is "faith without doubting" in Matthew is faith as a "grain of mustard seed" in Luke (Luke 17:6). The doubt against which Christ warned His followers is the kind which tries to steal the assurance of their faith's genuineness.

For example, you may have inward peace but no joy; and this apparent paradox may cause you to doubt your faith. The day may be still and calm though not all glorious and bright with sunshine. And although the Comforter may not come with emotional consolations, He has already hushed the storm of your troubled spirit. And true peace, as well as joy, is evidence of "unfeigned faith" (2 Timothy 1:5).

Another way doubt tries to cheat the Christian and prod him to deny his faith is through the absence of peace itself. We have peace with God as soon as we believe on Christ but we do not always have peace with ourselves. The pardon may be past the prince's hand and seal, yet not placed in the prisoner's hand. Do you not think the islanders were rash who accused Paul of being a murderer because the snake fastened itself on him? Then why do you condemn yourself as an unbeliever when afflictions and inward agonies fasten themselves on the spirit of the most gracious child God has on earth?

Yet Scripture relates doubt to the strength of faith, not to the existence of it. "O thou of little faith, wherefore didst thou doubt?" (Matthew 14:31). These are Christ's words to the sinking Peter, in which He chides doubts and at the same time acknowledges the reality of faith, even though it is very weak. All doubting is evil by its nature; but some doubting, though evil in itself, evidences grace in the person who doubts.

CLINGING TO THE SAVIOR

In spite of his doubts the
true believer leans on and
desires still to cling to Christ.

When David's doubts clogged up his faith he did not give up and let the ship run, as we say, before the storm. Instead of doubting if God loved him he communed with his own heart and his spirit searched diligently: "In the day of my trouble I sought the Lord" (Psalm 77:2). A person should no more sit down and be content in his unresolved doubt than one who thinks he smells fire in his house would go to bed and sleep. He will look in every room and corner until he is satisfied that everything is safe.

The doubting soul is much more afraid of waking with hellfire about it; but a soul under the power of unbelief is falsely secure and careless. Because the old world did not believe in an impending flood, the men settled down into a lethargic refusal to consider God's warning. And water reached their windows before they had the means to escape.

In spite of his doubts the true believer leans on and desires still to cling to Christ. While Peter's feet were faltering beneath the water he was lifting up prayer to Christ; and this proved the truth of his faith. Although Jonah had many fears, yet even in these his faith had some little secret hold on God: "Then I said, I am cast out of thy sight; yet I will look again toward thy holy temple" (Jonah 2:4). "When my soul fainted within me I remembered the Lord" (v. 7). And David also, though he could not get rid of all the fears which came in through his weak faith, as water into a leaking ship, raised a firm hand and cut them off. "What time I am afraid, I will trust in thee" (Psalm 56:3).

The weak Christian's doubting is like the wavering of a ship at anchor—he is moved, yet not removed from his hold on Christ; but the unbeliever's doubting is like the wavering of a wave which has nothing to anchor it and is wholly at the mercy of the wind. "But let him ask in faith, nothing wavering. For he that wavereth is like a wave of the sea driven with the wind and tossed" (James 1:6).

THE WAR BETWEEN FAITH AND UNBELIEF

You may say, "I have wrestled
with Satan and with my own heart,
and at last I have prevailed."

The devil is a sworn enemy against true faith. He persecutes it in the cradle, as Herod did Christ in the manger; he pours a flood of wrath on it as soon as it announces its own birth by crying after the Lord. If your faith is legitimate, "Naphtali" may be its name, and you may say, "I have wrestled with Satan and with my own heart, and at last I have prevailed." You know the answer Rebekah received when she asked God about the scuffle and striving of the children in her womb. "Two nations," God told her, "are in thy womb" (Genesis 25:23). If you find strife in your soul, comfort yourself because of it, Christian. This dispute is from two contrary principles, faith and unbelief, which lust against each other; and your unbelief, which is the elder—no matter how hard it fights for mastery—shall serve faith, the younger. Presumptuous faith lacks balance. It has one lame hand. It has a hand to receive pardon from God but no hand to give itself up to Him. But true faith has the use of both hands. "My beloved is mine"—there the soul takes Christ—"and I am his"—there she surrenders herself to His purposes (Song of Solomon 2:16). Have you ever freely given yourself to Him? Everybody professes this, but the presumptuous soul, like Ananias, lies to the Holy Ghost by keeping back the most important part of what he promised to lay at Christ's feet. The enjoyment of lust is entwined about his heart and he cannot persuade himself to deliver it up to God's justice. His life is bound up in it, and if God will have it from him He must take it by force; there is no hope of gaining his consent. Is this the picture of your faith? If it is, you have blessed yourself in an idol; you have mistaken a bold face for a believing heart.

On the other hand, if you count it a privilege that Christ should have a throne in your heart, as you have a room in His mercy, you prove yourself a sound believer.

THE WEAKNESS OF WICKEDNESS

*He rebuked kings for touching His anointed ones. Will He
stand still now and let those wicked spirits threaten His
life in you without coming to your rescue? It is impossible.*

God calls Satan wicked to encourage believers in their
combat with him. It is as if God says, "Do not be afraid of
him; it is a wicked company you go against. And they
who defend it are wicked too." If the saints must have enemies,
the worse they are, the better! It would put courage into a coward to fight with such a crew.

Wickedness must be weak. The devil's guilt tells them their
cause is lost before the battle is ever fought. They fear you,
Christian, because you are holy; so you do not need to fear
them at all. When you see them as subtle, mighty, and many,
your heart beats fast. But look on all these spirits as ungodly
wretches who hate God more than they hate you. And the only
reason they detest you at all is your kinship to Him. Whose side
is God on? In the past He rebuked kings for touching His
anointed ones. Will He stand still now and let those wicked
spirits threaten His life in you without coming to your rescue? It
is impossible.

The unity of the enemy is a challenge to believers. All the
legions of devils and multitudes of wicked men and women
form a single mystical body of wickedness, as Christ and his
saints are one mystical body. One Spirit unites Christ and His
saints and one spirit unites the devils and ungodly men. Their
darts are all shot from the same bow and by the same hand. The
Christian's fight, then, is a single duel with one great enemy.
But this enemy unites all forces to arm themselves with darts of
the worst kind.

The devil's darts are temptations which he aims with remarkable accuracy at the souls of men and women. These temptations are called "darts."

QUENCHING THE FIERY DARTS

*This dragon spits fire full
of indignation against God
and every one of His saints.*

A part from Christ, Satan has successfully deceived every man who ever lived. It was Christ's prerogative to be tempted but not to be led into temptation. And Job, a chief in God's army of saints, whom the Father calls "perfect and upright" (Job 1:1), is himself seriously injured by Satan's arrows. Yet in His time God is faithful to pluck him out of the devil's grip and bring healing and restoration to His servant.

Satan's warlike provision includes not just arrows but "fiery darts." Some scholars believe the term "fiery" denotes a particular kind of temptation, such as blasphemy or despair; but since faith is a shield for all temptations, we see that every one of Satan's arrows is fiery. But why does Scripture call these darts "fiery"?

First, Satan shoots them in fiery wrath. This dragon spits fire full of indignation against God and every one of His saints. Saul breathes out "threatenings and slaughter against the disciples of the Lord" (Acts 9:1). As one who is inwardly inflamed, his breath is hot—a fiery stream of persecuting rage comes out of him like a burning furnace. Such temptation is the breath of the devil's fury.

Further, these darts are called fiery because they lead to hell-fire if they are not quenched. There is a spark of hell in every temptation; and all the sparks fly to their own element. So then all temptations are bound for hell and damnation, according to Satan's intent and purpose.

Finally and most important, the devil's darts are said to be fiery because of the malignant effect they have on men's spirits, kindling a fire in their hearts and consciences. The apostle alludes to the custom of cruel enemies who used to dip the heads of their arrows in poison, making them even more deadly. They not only wounded the part where they penetrated the victim, but infected the whole body, a condition which made healing almost impossible.

FAITH'S POWER TO QUENCH TEMPTATIONS

"For all that is in the world, the lust of the flesh,
and the lust of the eyes, and the pride of life,
is not of the Father, but is of the world" (1 John 2:15–16).

Faith empowers a soul to quench the pleasing temptations of the wicked one. This is called our "victory that overcometh the world, even of faith" (1 John 5:4). Faith plants its triumphant banner on the world's head. And John tells us what God means by "the world": "Love not the world. . . . For all that is in the world, the lust of the flesh, and the lust of the eyes, and the pride of life, is not of the Father, but is of the world" (1 John 2:15–16). All that is in the world is food and fuel for lust. Now faith enables the soul to quench those darts which Satan dips into the poison of worldly lusts—called by some the world's "trinity."

This is temptation which promises pleasure to the flesh. It carries such fire in it that when it finds a carnal heart, it quickly inflames with unruly passions and coarse affections. The adulterer burns in his lust and the drunkard is inflamed with his wine.

No temptations work more eagerly than those which promise delight to the flesh. Sinners are said to "work all uncleanness with greediness"—with a kind of covetousness; for the Word suggests they can never have enough (Ephesians 4:19). No drink will quench a poisoned man's thirst. Nothing but faith can help a soul in these flames. In hell Dives burns without a drop of water to cool the tip of his tongue. The unbelieving sinner is in a hell above ground; he burns in his lust without a drop of water, for lack of faith, to quench the fire.

By faith the martyrs "quenched the violence of fire" (Hebrews 11:34). "We ourselves also were sometimes foolish, disobedient, deceived, serving diverse lusts and pleasures. . . . But after that the kindness and love of God our Saviour toward man appeared . . . he saved us" (Titus 3:3–5). No one can ever shake off the old companions of lust until by faith he becomes intimate with the grace of God revealed in the Gospel. Faith strips away the veil from the Christian's eyes so he can so sin in its nakedness before Satan disguises it with flattering costumes.

THE PLEASURE OF SIN IS SHORT-LIVED

*Now is it not better to swim by faith through an ocean of
trouble and get safely to heaven than to sit in the lap
of sinful pleasures until we drown in hell's gulf?*

Faith enables the soul to recognize not only the nature of
sin void of all true pleasure, but also the temporal quality
of its frivolous elation. Faith persuades us not to give up
God's sure mercies for Satan's transient thrills. This persuasion
makes Moses run from the enchantments of the Egyptian court
into the fire of "affliction" because he knows them for what
they are—"pleasures . . . for a season" (Hebrews 11:25). If you
saw a man jump from a ship into the sea, at first you might
think him insane; but later if you saw him standing on the shore
and the ship swallowed up by the waves, you would know he
took the wise course.

Faith sees the world and all the stimulus of sin sinking;
there is a leak in them which the wisdom of man cannot repair.
Now is it not better to swim by faith through an ocean of trouble and get safely to heaven than to sit in the lap of sinful pleasures until we drown in hell's gulf?

Sin's enjoyment cannot last long because it is not natural.
Whatever is not natural soon decays. The nature of sugar, for
example, is to be sweet and therefore it holds its sweetness; but
artificially sweetened wine loses its good taste in just a few days.
The pleasure of sin is foreign to its nature and will corrupt the
life it touches. None of the sweetness which now satisfies sinners will be tasted in hell; only bitterness will spice the sinner's
cup there.

Another reason sin's exhilaration must be short-lived is that
life itself does not last long, and they both end together. Many
times the pleasure of sin dies before the man dies. Sinners live
to bury their worldly joy. The worm breeds in their conscience
before it breeds in their flesh by death. But be sure the advantages of sin never survive this world. The word has gone out of
God's mouth: He "distributeth sorrows in his anger" (Job
21:17). Hell's climate is too hot for evil delights to survive.

HOW FAITH QUENCHES "THE PRIDE OF LIFE"

"Behold, his soul which is lifted up
is not upright in him; but the just shall
live by his faith" (Habakkuk 2:4).

There are several distinctive ways in which faith quenches the pride of life: it takes away the fuel that feeds the temptation; it causes the Christian to expect all honor from Christ; it shows the dangers of bargaining with Satan for worldly glory; and it reveals precedents to believers.

Faith takes away the fuel that feeds this temptation. Pride is the fuel for temptation. Take away the oil and the lamp goes out. Where this lust is present in any strength, the creature's eyes are dazzled with the sight of something which suits the desires of the heart. By temptation the devil gives vent to what the heart itself is full of. Simon Magus had a haughty spirit; and when he first saw the chance to upstage the apostle, his desire was on fire to have a gift to work miracles himself. On the other hand, a man of humble spirit loves a low seat; he is not ambitious to tower above the thoughts of others; and while he stoops in his own opinion himself, the same bullet flies over his head which hits the proud man in the chest. Faith settles the heart down. Pride and faith are opposites; like a pair of balance scales, if one goes up, the other must go down. "Behold, his soul which is lifted up is not upright in him; but the just shall live by his faith" (Habakkuk 2:4).

Faith is Christ's favorite and makes the Christian expect all his honor from Him. When temptation comes, faith casts the soul on Christ as being all-sufficient to make it happy. And when temptation promises to bring you honor if you will allow a sin, faith chokes the bullet. Remember whose you are. Princes will not let their subjects become indebted to a foreign prince—least of all to one who is hostile to them. Faith declares that the honor or applause you get by sin makes you subject to the devil himself, who is God's greatest enemy. Faith shows the danger of bargaining with Satan to gain the glory of the world for one sin.

THE SECURITY OF FAITH'S VICTORY

*It is not the possession of a shield itself
that defends the Christian; we must hold it up
and use it in battle against Satan's fiery darts.*

M any men say they believe; they thank God they are not infidels. But what can your faith do? Can it defend you in battle and cover your soul when Satan's darts fly all around you? Or is it such a sorry shield that it lets every arrow of temptation through to wound your heart?

If Satan tells you to lie or cheat in your business and your passive faith makes no resistance, you are sinning not only against your fellow men but against faith itself. God forbid that you should think your faith is saving faith. Will faith which cannot bring you out of hell ever take you to heaven? Do not venture out in life with such a paper shield. To get faith that keeps you secure and strong, come to him who is the Faith Maker—God, I mean.

It is not the possession of a shield itself that defends the Christian; we must hold it up and use it in battle against Satan's fiery darts. Do not let him take you when your faith is not ready to hand, as David found Saul unarmed in the cave, with his spear on the ground when it should have been in his hand.

Let your faith ask God to come and defend you against Satan's fiery darts. There are three particular acts of faith which will require God to help—and we say this with reverence—because He binds Himself to do so.

Open your case to God in prayer and call in help from heaven, as the commander of a station under fire sends a secret messenger to let his general know the seriousness of his need. The apostle James says, "ye fight and war, yet ye have not, because ye ask not" (James 4:2). If we have any victory it must drop from heaven—but it will stay there until believing prayer comes for it. Although God purposed to deliver Israel out of Egypt, there was no sign of His coming until the groans of His people rang in His ears.

FAITH AND CONFIDENCE

*The same faith which caused you to work against
your sins as God's enemies will undoubtedly
move Him to work for you against them.*

G od broke my heart," says the Christian, "when it was like
flint, and brought me home when I was walking in the
pride of my heart against Him; but can He give bread to
nourish my weak grace? I have come out of Egypt; but can He
master those giants in iron chariots which stand between me
and Canaan? He helped me in one temptation; but what will I
do the next time?" Do not grieve a good God with such heart-
breaking questions. You have "the former rain." Why should
you question "the latter"? The grace which God has given you is
a sure pledge that more is on the way.

Faith's confidence in God is well demonstrated. After Jehoshaphat had prayed and anchored his faith on the word of
promise, he marched out under this victorious banner against
his enemies (2 Chronicles 20). Christian, do what he did; hasten
as he did. And I give you the same counsel which David gave
his son Solomon: "Arise therefore, and be doing, and the Lord
be with thee" (1 Chronicles 22:16). The same faith which
caused you to work against your sins as God's enemies will undoubtedly move Him to work for you against them.

The lepers in the Gospel were cured not as they sat but as
they walked. They met their healing in an act of obedience to
Christ's command. The promise says, "Sin shall not have dominion over you" (Romans 6:14). So go ahead and make a valiant
attempt against your lusts—and in doing your duty you will find
God's performance of the promise.

The reason so many Christians complain about the power of
their corruptions lies in one of two roots—either they try to
overcome sin without acting on the promises, or else they only
pretend to believe. They use faith as an eye but not as a hand;
they look for victory to drop from heaven upon their heads but
do not prayerfully fight to get it.

FAITH'S POWER OVER FEARFUL TEMPTATIONS

*It is true that the devil, who
cannot himself turn atheist, cannot
make God's children an atheist either.*

The devil must work even harder when Christ captures the castle and keeps it by the power of His grace. It is obvious that all the darts shot against Job were of this kind. When God let the devil practice his skill, why did he not tempt Job with some golden apple of profit or pleasure? Surely the high testimony God gave to His servant discouraged Satan from choosing this method; no doubt he had already tried Job's manhood and found him impenetrable. So he had no other way left but this. Now let us study three instances of this type of fiery dart and show how faith can quench them all—temptations to atheism, blasphemy, and despair.

The fiery dart of atheism tempts us to deny God. The first of Satan's fearful temptations is his dart of atheism, an arrow which he boldly aims at the being of God Himself. It is true that the devil, who cannot himself turn atheist, cannot make God's children an atheist either, for he has not only, in common with other men, an indelible stamp of deity in his conscience, but also such a sculpture of the divine nature in his heart as irresistibly demonstrates a holy God. It is impossible for a holy heart to be fully overcome with this temptation, because God's image within proves he has been created "after God . . . in righteousness and true holiness" (Ephesians 4:24).

The wicked are not cleared from atheism by their naked profession of God as long as their weak thoughts fail to produce obedience to Him. "The transgression of the wicked saith within my heart, that there is no fear of God before his eyes" (Psalm 36:1). Thus David traces the wickedness of the sinner's life to the atheism in his heart. On the contrary, the holy life of a person saved by grace says that the fear of God is before his eyes and his belief in God is plain to see. Although a Christian can never be slain by the temptation of atheism, he may be haunted by it.

ATHEISM AND THE FALLEN NATURE

Even if reason could demonstrate all that God is,
it would be dangerous to dispute it with Satan.
He has sharper reasoning than you.

Our human nature is so blind that we have deformed thoughts of God until with the eye of faith we see His face in the mirror of the Word. With the exception of Jesus, all men are atheist by nature because at the same time as they acknowledge a God they deny His power, presence, and justice. They allow Him to be only what pleases them: "Thou thoughtest that I was altogether such an one as thyself" (Psalm 50:21).

Even if reason could demonstrate all that God is, it would be dangerous to dispute it with Satan. He has sharper reasoning than you. There is more difference between you and Satan than between the weakest idiot and the greatest theologian in the world. But in the Word there is a strong divine authority that builds a throne even in the conscience of the devil himself.

Although Christ was able to baffle the devil by reason, He chose to overthrow him in the way that we ourselves must use in skirmishes with Satan. He repelled him simply by lifting up the shield of the Word: "It is written," said Christ (Matthew 4:4, 7, 10). It is undeniable that Christ's quoted word had power to stun Satan; the shrewd enemy had no reply to Scripture but was stilled at the very mention of the Word.

If only Eve had stood by her first answer—"God hath said" (Genesis 3:3)—she too could have silenced Satan. Thus the Christian must stand in the heat of temptation and place God's own Word between himself and Satan's blows: "I believe that God is, though I cannot understand His nature; I believe the Word." When this happens, Satan may trouble him but he cannot hurt him—and he probably cannot even bother him for very long. The devil hates the Word so much that he does not want to hear it. But if you throw down the shield of the Word and try to cut through the temptation by the force of reason, you may soon be surrounded by your subtle enemy.

FAITH HEARS FROM GOD

*Faith conceives all its ideas of God by
the Word, solves all cases of conscience,
and interprets mysteries by this Word.*

People who slander the names of others do it behind their
backs. And sin seldom blasphemes God to His face; that is
the language of hell. . . .

But faith sees God eyeing the soul to preserve it. . . . Faith
warns, "Do not blaspheme the God of heaven; you cannot even
whisper softly enough for Him not to hear. For he is closer to
you than you are to yourself," Thus faith breaks the devil's
snare. When God came to Job in His majesty, all Job's long
speeches suddenly vanished and he covered his face with humility before the Lord: "Now mine eye seeth thee. Wherefore I
abhor myself, and repent in dust and ashes" (Job 42:5–6).

Faith accepts no report of God except from God's own
mouth. . . . Faith conceives all its ideas of God by the Word,
solves all cases of conscience, and interprets mysteries by this
Word. . . . [Satan] drives the person who is in a hard situation to
entertain wrong thoughts of God. Thus he criticizes God's justice when blatant sinners have not been judged quickly; or he
says he will not serve a God who permits His servants to wear
ragged clothing. These are the broken glasses that Satan mirrors
God in, so that he may distort His goodness to the doubting
eye. And if we judge God to be what He appears in Satan's jagged pieces of deception, we might condemn the Holy One and
be caught in a dangerous tornado of temptation.

Faith praises God in sad conditions. Blessing and blasphemy
are contrasting tunes. They cannot be played on the same instrument without changing all the strings. It is beyond Satan's skill
to strike such a harsh stroke as blasphemy on a soul tuned for
praise. "My heart is fixed," says David—there was his faith. And
then he says, "I will sing and give praise" (Psalm 57:7). It was
faith that tuned his spirit and prepared his affections to praise.

Faith can praise God because it sees mercy even in the greatest affliction. Thus Job quenched this dart which Satan shot at
him from his wife's tongue. "Shall we receive good at the hand
of God, and shall we not receive evil?" (Job 2:10). Will we let a
few present troubles become a grave to bury the memory of all
His past mercies? What God takes from us is less than we owe
Him, but what He leaves us is more than He owes.

TEMPTATION TO EVIL THOUGHTS

*The violent entry of these blasphemous temptations
into the Christian's mind betrays their breeding
place—Satan, not the person's own heart.*

In a word, does it not seem strange that when the Christian was an enemy to God he dared not venture into this sin because of its monstrous nature, yet now that he begins to love God these blasphemies, which were too big and horrible before, would fill his mouth?

The violent entry of these blasphemous temptations into the Christian's mind betrays their breeding place—Satan, not the person's own heart. They flash like lightening into the person's thoughts before he has time to decide what he is doing. Lust which overflows from the heart is, on the other hand, ordinarily more gradual in its persuasion.

Not only their sudden violence, but their incoherence with the Christian's former thoughts, heightens the probability that these temptations are darts shot from the devil's bow. Peter was known to be a member of Christ's company by his voice: "Thy speech," they say, "agreeth thereto" (Mark 14:70). He talked like them and was judged to be one of them. On the contrary, we may say of these blasphemous thoughts, "They are not the Christian's. Their language shows them to be the belching of a devil, not the voice of a saint. If they were woven by the soul, they would be something like the whole piece from which they were cut." There is ordinarily a continuity in our thoughts, like a circle rising out of another circle in stirred water.

Sometimes as the Christian worships God, an intruding blasphemous thought barges in like a rude stranger. The tenant never ushers in a thief. If a holy thought surprises us when we are far from heavenly meditation, we may take it as a pure moving of Christ's Spirit. Who but He could appear so suddenly in the midst of the soul when the door is shut, even before the person can turn his thoughts to open it for Him?

FAITH AND DESPAIR

Despair, more than other sins,
puts a man into a kind of
possession of hell itself.

Satan begins with his more pleasant sins so that he may later entangle the victim more hopelessly. But the devil is too clever to lay his net of despair in the bird's sight. Other sins are only the top cover, and once he flatters his prey into it, he has trapped him for eternity.

Despair, more than other sins, puts a man into a kind of possession of hell itself. As faith gives substance to the word of promise, so the cruelty of despair gives existence to the torments of hell in the conscience. This drains the spirit and makes the creature become his own executioner.

Despair puts a soul beyond all relief; the offer of pardon comes too late. Faith and hope can open a window to let out the smoke that offends the Christian in any circumstances. But the soul will be choked when it is fastened up within despairing thoughts of its own sins, and no crevice of hope is left for an outlet to the dread which smothers him.

Faith quenches the fiery dart of despair. The chief of Satan's strengths is the greatness and the multitude of a person's sins, which he can use to bring a soul into such despair that he sees no way of escape from God's verdict against them. When the conscience is breached and waves of guilt pour in upon the soul they soon drown all the creature's efforts, as the great flood covered the tallest trees and highest mountains. And as nothing was visible then but sea and heaven, the despairing soul sees nothing except sin and hell. His sins stare him in the face as with the eyes of many devils, ready to drag him into the bottomless pit.

A mere fly dares to crawl over the sleeping lion, an animal whose awesome voice makes all beasts tremble when he is awake. Fools freely mock sin as soon as the eye of conscience is shut. But when God arms sin with guilt and lets this serpent sting the conscience, then the proudest sinner flees before it. Only faith handles sin in its fullest strength by giving the soul a glimpse of the great God.

FAITH SEES GOD'S HOLINESS AND FORGIVENESS

*"I will help thee, saith the Lord,
and thy redeemer, the Holy
One of Israel" (Isaiah 41:14).*

I t is God's holiness which makes Him faithful in all His promises. When the doubting man reads the precious promises given to returning sinners, why cannot he take comfort in them? Surely it is because he is still not sure God is faithful enough to perform them.

But the strongest argument which faith has to put this question out of doubt, and cause the sinner to accept the promise as a true word, rests in the holiness of God, the Promise Maker. He gently persuades the person to trust Him by prefixing His promises with the attribute of holiness: "I will help thee, saith the Lord, and thy redeemer, the Holy One of Israel" (Isaiah 41:14). The Hebrew word for "mercies" is often translated "holy things," and because God's mercies are founded in His holiness, they are therefore sure mercies (see Isaiah 55:3). How many times did Laban change Jacob's wages after his promise? Yet God's covenant with Jacob was always kept, although Jacob was not faithful on his part. Why? Because he was dealing with the holy God.

Another of God's attributes which kindles fear in the awakened sinner is His justice. The soul sees no way except hell for God to vindicate His justice. But faith empowers the soul to walk around in this fiery attribute with his comfort unsinged, even as the Hebrew children prospered in the flaming furnace (Daniel 3).

Faith relieves the soul which fears God's justice. One might wonder whether or not God can be both just and righteous in pardoning a sinner. Faith shows that God may pardon sins, no matter how great, with safety to His justice. This question was settled at the council board of heaven by God Himself and He has expressed His decision in the form of a precious promise: "I will betroth thee unto me forever; yea, I will betroth thee unto me in righteousness, and in judgment." (Hosea 2:19).

GOD SEALS CHRIST'S ATONEMENT FOR SIN

*When Satan lines up the believer's sins
against him and confronts him with their severity,
faith runs under the shelter of this Rock.*

Christ is the One "whom God hath set forth to be a propitiation through faith in his blood" (Romans 3:25). He is the
One the Father has sealed and singled out from all others
and set forth as the Person chosen to make atonement for sinners, as the lamb was taken out of the flock and set apart for the
Passover.

Therefore when Satan lines up the believer's sins against
him and confronts him with their severity, faith runs under the
shelter of this Rock. "Surely," says faith, "my Savior is infinitely
greater than my greatest sins. I would be rejecting the wisdom
of God's choice to doubt." God knew what a heavy burden He
had to lay upon Christ's shoulders but He was fully persuaded
of His Son's strength to carry it. A weak faith may save but a
weak Savior cannot. Faith has Christ to plead for it but Christ
had none to plead for Him. Faith leans on Christ's arm, but
Christ stood alone. If the burden of our sins had prevailed
against Him, no one in heaven or on earth could have helped
Him stand.

God's mercy declares his righteousness. Everyone believes
God is merciful to forgive; but it is harder to believe how He
can be righteous in forgiving sinners. "To declare, I say, at this
time his righteousness: that he might be just, and the justifier of
him which believeth in Jesus" (Romans 3:26). God was saying,
"I know why it seems so incredible that I should pardon all
your iniquities. You think because I am a righteous God that I
would rather damn a thousand worlds of sinners than bring My
name under the least suspicion of unrighteousness. I would indeed damn them over and over again, rather than stain the hon-
or of My justice—which is Myself. But I command you and the
greatest sinners on earth to believe it: I can be just and yet the
justifier of those sinners who believe in Jesus."

THE GREATNESS OF GOD'S PROMISES

Where there is faith to chase
the promise, there the promise will
give comfort and peace in abundance.

Believing souls now sing praises to the mercy and justice of Him who redeemed them, and will sing the same song forever. Now how much better are the voluntary sufferings of Christ than the forced torments of the damned? And the melodious praises of saints in heaven than the forced acknowledgments of souls in hell?

Only faith can see God in His greatness; and therefore nothing but faith can see the promises in their greatness because their value lies in the worth of Him who makes them. This is why promises have so little effect on an unbelieving heart, either to keep it from sinning or to comfort it because of sin's torment. Where there is faith to chase the promise, there the promise will give comfort and peace in abundance. It will be as sweet wine glowing with inward joy in the believer; but on an unbelieving heart the promise lies cold and ineffectual. It has no more effect on such a soul than medicine poured down a dead man's throat.

The promises do not comfort actually and formally, as fire has heat; if this were true we could be comforted merely by thinking about a promise. But the promises comfort virtually, as fire is in the flint, which requires labor and art to strike it out and draw it forth. Only faith can teach us this skill of drawing out the sweetness and virtue of the promise, and it does this in three ways.

Faith goes to the source of the promises. Here the Christian can take advantage of the best view of their precious qualities. We can understand very little about something unless we trace it to its source and see its beginnings. A soul knows his sins are great when he sees them flowing from an envenomed nature which teems with enmity against God. The sinner will tremble at the threatenings that roll like thunder over his head when he sees where they come from and the perfect hatred God has of sin.

NOVEMBER 9

GOD'S PARDONING MERCY

*"But God, who is rich in mercy, for his great
love wherewith he loved us . . . hath quickened
us together with Christ" (Ephesians 2:4–5).*

D o not sin just because the promises of mercy exceed
your sins as far as God in His greatness surpasses the
creature. It is as if your servant should find your cellar of
strong wines and become drunk, when you keep them only to
help those get well who are sick. Be careful not to misuse the
holy vessels of the sanctuary of God's mercy. It is the sorrowing
soul, not the sinning soul, which this wine of consolation belongs to.

Faith provides witness to whom God's promise has been fulfilled. God verifies His fulfilled promises by working through
the weaknesses of the faithful cloud of witnesses. He would
never have left the saints' great blots in the Scriptures open to
the inspection of all succeeding generations if He had not intended to help tempted souls overcome this fearful temptation
to doubt His promise of mercy.

Paul gives this very reason why such acts of pardoning mercy to great sinners are recorded. He shows first what filthy creatures he and other believers were before they were made
partakers of Gospel grace. "Among whom also we all had our
conversation in times past in the lusts of our flesh" (Ephesians
2:3). Then he magnifies the rich mercy of God which rescued
and took them out of that damned state. "But God, who is rich
in mercy, for his great love wherewith he loved us . . . hath
quickened us together with Christ" (Ephesians 2:4–5).

But God designed His plan of mercy to cover more generations than the contemporaries of Paul. "That in the ages to
come he might shew the exceeding riches of his grace in his
kindness toward us through Christ Jesus" (Ephesians 2:7).
Wherever the Gospel comes, even to the end of the world, the
records of God's mercy will stop the mouth of unbelief. And
this arrow on Satan's string will be made headless and harmless.

UNBELIEF IS THE MOST DANGEROUS SIN

*"To him that worketh not, but believeth
on him that justifieth the ungodly, his faith
is counted for righteousness" (Romans 4:5).*

Faith tells you that the whole virtue and power of Christ's blood, by which the world was redeemed, is offered to you. And He personally brings it to you. Christ does not ration out His blood, some to one and some to another; but He gives His whole self to the faith of every believer. You belong to the Redeemer. And He is yours. Faith opposes despair.

The greatest command in the whole Bible is to believe. When the Jews asked our Lord Jesus, "What shall we do, that we might work the works of God?" notice His reply: "This is the work of God, that ye believe on him whom he hath sent" (John 6:28–29). It is as if he had said, "Receive Me into your hearts by faith; do this, and you do it all." This is the all in all. Everything you do is futile until this work is done; but when you have believed, God appreciates it as much as if you had kept the whole law. In fact, it is accepted in lieu of it: "To him that worketh not, but believeth on him that justifieth the ungodly, his faith is counted for righteousness" (Romans 4:5).

This man's faith in Christ is accepted for righteousness; that is, at the judgment he will escape the sentence as if he had never strayed a step from the path of the law. If faith is the work of God above all other, then unbelief is the work of the devil. He works harder to make men unbelievers than drunkards or murderers. And despair is unbelief at its worst. Unbelief among sins is as the plague among diseases, the most dangerous; but when it settles into despair, then it is like the plague which brings certain death with it. Unbelief is despair in the bud, but despair is unbelief at its full growth.

Every sin wounds the law and the name of God. But this wound is healed when the penitent sinner by faith comes to Christ and unites with Him. And through Christ God receives the sinner in the fullness of righteousness and vindicates His own name.

THE CHRISTIAN'S HELMET

*As a Christian soldier you must always stand in
a defensive posture with your armor on, ready
to defend the treasure God has given you to keep.*

A nd take the helmet of salvation" (Ephesians 6:17). These words of Scripture present us with another piece in the Christian's armor—the helmet of salvation to cover his head in the day of battle. This helmet, together with most of the other pieces of armor, are defensive arms, to protect the Christian from sin but not to keep him from suffering.

Only one piece in the whole armor is for offense—the sword. Scripture hints that the Christian's war lies chiefly on the defense and therefore requires defensive arms to fight it. God has deposited a rich treasure of grace in every saint's heart, which the devil spitefully tries to rob the Christian of by waging a bloody war against him. And so the believer overcomes his enemy when he himself is not overcome. He wins the day when he does not lose his grace, his work being to keep what is his rather than to get what is the enemy's. Because the saint's war lies chiefly on the defense, we must instruct the Christian how to manage combat with both Satan and his weapons of war.

As a Christian soldier you must always stand in a defensive posture with your armor on, ready to defend the treasure God has given you to keep, and to repel Satan's assaults. But do not step outside the line of your calling which God has drawn about you. Let Satan be the assailant and come if he will to tempt you; but do not go out and tempt him to do it.

Even when the devil's instruments of war reproach the Christian, the Gospel does not allow him to use the devil's weapons to return them stroke for stroke. "Be pitiful, be courteous: not rendering evil for evil, or railing for railing: but contrariwise blessing" (1 Peter 3:8–9). You have a girdle and breastplate to defend you from their bullets—the comfort of your own sincerity and holy walk. With these you can repel the sordid arsenal thrown at you—but there is no weapon for self-revenge.

LOVE AND FAITH

"He that hath seen me hath seen the Father" (John 14:9).
So if you have seen your love for Christ,
you have also seen faith in the face of that love.

D o you have a sincere desire to please Jesus or a deep sad-
ness when you have done something that grieves Him?
These are two veins full of the lifeblood of love for
Christ. Your love can tell you news of your faith. As Christ says,
"He that hath seen me hath seen the Father" (John 14:9). So if
you have seen your love for Christ, you have also seen faith in
the face of that love.

But what if your love for Christ is hidden in a cloud? Then
see if you can find some repentance, despising yourself with the
sight of your sins and rousing you to hate these sins as the enemies which have lured you into rebellion against God. For they
are the bloody weapon which wounded God's name and mur-
dered His Son. The grace you look for stands before you. What
is love of God if not passion against sin as His enemy?

But sometimes you cannot see the love for the zeal or the
fire for the flame. As by taking hold of one link you may draw
up the rest of the chain which lies under water, so by discover-
ing one grace you may find them all. And while this sanctifying
grace relieves the sincere Christian's doubt, it shames the hypocrite who grasps for one particular grace but shuns another.

The Spirit of God does not come into a soul with half of His
sanctifying graces but with all of them. If your heart is set
against one grace it proves that you are a stranger to the others.
Love and hatred are of the whole kind; he who loves or hates
one saint loves or hates every other saint. And the person who
embraces one grace will find every grace dear; for they are as
kin to each other as one beam of the sun is to another. There is
a connection of the sanctifying graces in their growth and decay. Increase one grace and you strengthen then all; impair one
and you will be a loser in all.

HOPE AND FAITH

*Faith cleaves to the promise as a true and
faithful word, and then hope lifts up
the soul to wait for the performance of it.*

True hope is a precious gem which no one can wear but Christ's bride, for Christless and hopeless are joined together (Ephesians 2:12). Because hope and faith are inevitably kin, let us now look at their relationship. In regard to time, one does not come before the other; but in order of nature and operation, faith takes the precedence.

First, faith cleaves to the promise as a true and faithful word, and then hope lifts up the soul to wait for the performance of it. Who runs out to meet someone that he believes will not come? The promise is God's love letter to His bride in which He opens His very heart and tells everything He will do for her. Faith reads and embraces it with joy, while hope looks out of the window with a longing expectation to see her husband's chariot coming toward her.

We run away from an evil thing; but if it is good we wait for it. Both hope and faith draw their lines from the same center of the promise, but there is one important difference between them. Faith believes evil as well as good; hope will not talk about anything but good. Hope without a promise is like an anchor without ground to hold by; it carries the promise on its name. David shows where he moors his ship and casts his anchor—"I hope in thy word" (Psalm 119:81). And God's design fits the highest hope a Christian can have: "No good thing will he withhold from them that walk uprightly" (Psalm 84:11).

Just as God has encircled all good in the promise, so He promises nothing but good. The object of hope is everything that the promise holds. God Himself is the highest good and His fullness is promised as the believer's highest joy. Therefore true hope aims at God and lifts the soul nearer Him, "the hope of Israel" and "the fountain of living water" (Jeremiah 17:13).

THE HELMET DEFENDS THE SOUL

"When these things begin to come to pass,
then look up, and lift up your heads;
for your redemption draweth nigh" (Luke 21:28).

As the helmet defends the head, a principal part of the body, so this "hope of salvation" defends the soul, the principal part of man. The helmet protects the believer from dangerous or deadly impressions of sin or Satan. It defends the Christian because it is hard for temptations to snare a person who is satisfied with princely favor and who stands on the stairs of hope, expecting to be called at any time to the highest place a king can bestow.

On the other hand, weapons of rebellion are usually forged in discontent. When subjects think they are neglected by their prince, this feeling softens them to receive any impression of disloyalty that the king's enemy attempts to stamp upon them. Thus once the soul fears God has no inheritance for him he will commit any sin, great or small, at the sound of the tempter's trumpet.

The helmet makes the heart bold. As the helmet defends the soldier's head from wounds, so it also protects the Christian's heart from failing. Whoever wears this helmet need never be ashamed to boast in his holy God. For God Himself allows him to do this and confirms the rejoicing of his hope. "Thou shalt know that I am the Lord: for they shall not be ashamed that wait for me" (Isaiah 49:23). Confidence in God made David courageous in the midst of his enemies: "Though an host should encamp against me, my heart shall not fear" (Psalm 27:3). He had his helmet of salvation on and therefore could declare, "Now shall mine head be lifted up above mine enemies round about me" (v. 6).

A man cannot drown as long as his head is above water, and now it is the work of hope to do this for the Christian in dangerous places. "When these things begin to come to pass, then look up, and lift up your heads; for your redemption draweth nigh" (Luke 21:28). Only Christ can tell His disciples to lift up their heads when they see other "men's hearts failing them for fear, and for looking after those things which are coming on the earth" (v. 26).

HOPE AND WORTHY ACHIEVEMENTS

*What makes the daring soldier rush into the mouth of
death itself? Hope is the helmet and shield which
make him calm in the face of every danger.*

Hope of salvation moves the Christian to perform high and
worthy services. It is a grace conceived for great action.
As carnal hope stirs carnal men to achievements which
gain them a reputation in the world, so this heavenly hope influences the saint's undertakings.

What makes the daring soldier rush into the mouth of death
itself? He hopes to rescue honor from the jaws of death. Hope
is the helmet and shield which make him calm in the face of every danger. What makes a man tear his hands and crawl up
some craggy mountain which proves only a bleak, barren place
to stand in? There he is wrapped up in clouds and can look
over other men's heads and see a little farther than they. Now if
these hopes—which borrow motives from human ambition and
imagination—turn men toward accomplishments, how much
more does the believer's hope of eternal life provoke him to
noble exploits! Let us look at some examples.

Hope frees from lust. When Moses came to give Israel the
hope of God's approaching salvation, his people experienced a
mighty change. Whereas they had cowered under Egyptian burdens and had not tried to shake off the oppressor's yoke, now
they broke free and marched toward their promised rest. It did
not seem to make any difference that Pharaoh chased them with
a raging determination—they were fortified with hope.

How helpless is the person who does not have this heavenly
hope! Satan makes a slave of him and he becomes the footstool
for the every base lust to trample upon. He lets the devil ride
him anywhere, at any time. No mud puddle is too filthy for Satan to lead him through with a twine thread. And the poor man
follows because he does not know a better master, nor better
wages than the sensual pleasures of his lusts.

DILIGENCE IN THE SMALLEST SERVICE

To arm the Christian against discontent and
discouragement, God promises as great a reward
for faithfulness in the most menial service
as He gives in more honorable service.

God sets some men on the high places of the earth and appoints them to exciting challenges. But He orders others to pitch their tents on lower ground and not be ashamed of their assignment, no matter how inferior it seems. Now to encourage every Christian to be faithful in his particular place, God has made promises which apply to them all. And His promises are like the beams of the sun: they shine as freely through the window of the poor man's cottage as through the prince's palace.

God's promises strengthen our hands and hearts against the discouragement that is most likely to weaken us in His service. They support and guard us against the furious opposition of an angry world: "I will not fail thee, nor forsake thee. Be strong and of a good courage" (Joshua 1:5–6). This was a promise God gave to Israel's chief magistrate. And the minister's promise agrees with it, having generally the same trials, enemies, and discouragements: "Go ye therefore, and teach all nations; . . . and lo, I am with you always, even unto the end of the world" (Matthew 28:19–20).

The temptation which usually troubles those in lower callings is envy to see themselves on the floor and their brothers elevated to higher service. Sometimes these temptations produce dejection when the believers feel like eunuchs who bring no glory to God, dry trees which are unprofitable in His kingdom.

To arm the Christian against discontent and discouragement, God promises as great a reward for faithfulness in the most menial service as He gives in more honorable service. Is anything more degrading than the role of a slave? Yet nothing less than heaven itself is promised to the faithful servant: "Whatsoever ye do, do it heartily, as to the Lord, and not unto men; knowing that of the Lord ye shall receive the reward of the inheritance: for ye serve the Lord Christ" (Colossians 3:23–24).

REJOICE IN HOPE

*All the joy which sustains the suffering saint
is sent in by hope at the cost of Christ,
who has prepared unspeakable glory in heaven.*

Waiting on God for deliverance during affliction is closely linked with holy silence. "Truly my soul waiteth upon God: from him cometh my salvation" (Psalm 62:1). The Hebrew literally reads, "My soul is silent."

Hope fills the afflicted soul with joy. Hope brings such consolation that the afflicted soul can smile even when tears run down the face. This is called "the rejoicing of the hope" (Hebrews 3:6). And hope never produces more joy than in affliction. The sun paints the beautiful colors in the rainbow on a watery cloud. "Rejoice in hope of the glory of God. And not only so, but we glory in tribulations" (Romans 5:2–3). Glorying is a rejoicing which the Christian cannot contain within himself; it comes forth in some outward expression to let others know what a feast he has inside. The springs of comfort lie high indeed when joy flows from the believer's mouth. And all the joy which sustains the suffering saint is sent in by hope at the cost of Christ, who has prepared unspeakable glory in heaven. Should we pity ourselves for the tribulations we go through on the way to Christ's glory?

While troubles attack with oppression, the gracious promises anoint with blessings. Hope breaks the alabaster box of the promises over the Christian's head and sends consolations abroad in the soul. And like a precious ointment these comforts exhilarate and refresh the spirit, heal the wounds, and remove the pain. Paul says, "Hope maketh not ashamed; because the love of God is shed abroad in our hearts by the Holy Ghost which is given unto us" (Romans 5:5).

Faith and hope are two graces which Christ uses above all others to fill the soul with joy, because these fetch all their wine of joy out of doors. Faith tells the soul what Christ has done and hope revives the soul with the news of what He will do. But both draw sweet wine from the same source—Christ and His promise.

DELAYING THE PROMISES

*Patience has two shoulders, one to bear
the present evil and another to wait for
the future good promised but not yet paid.*

God does not take up the ax of His sovereignty into His hand to make chips. When He has pruned severely and driven His ax the deepest, His people may expect some beautiful piece of work when all is finished.

It is sweet to meditate on Romans 8:28. "We know that all things work together for good to them that love God." If you should get up some morning and hear men on your house tearing off the tiles and taking down the roof with hammers and axes, you might think a gang of vicious enemies had come to destroy your home. But as soon as you understand that these workmen have been sent by your father to mend your house, you gladly endure the noise and trouble. Indeed, you thank your father for his care and expense. The very hope of the advantage that will come from the repairs makes you willing to dwell awhile in the inconvenient rubble of the old house.

The promise assures the believer that the heavenly Father intends no harm, only good, as He rebuilds the ruined frame of your soul into a glorious temple. And afflictions have a hand in the work. This insight frees you to pray, "Lord, cut and shape me however You will, that at last I may be framed according to the pattern which Your love has drawn for me!" Some ignorant men fear the fuller's soap might spoil their clothing, but one who understands what refining means will not be afraid.

Hope quiets the Christian's spirit when God waits a long time before He comes to perform promises. I have already told you that patience is the back where the Christian carries his burdens, and hope the pillow between the back and the burden. Now patience has two shoulders, one to bear the present evil and another to wait for the future good promised but not yet paid. And as hope makes the burden of the present cross light, it makes the longest delay of promised good seem short.

NOVEMBER 19

HOPE PROVIDES STRENGTH

*Today many souls throw themselves into the
embraces of the adulterous world because the comfort
and joy of the promise is temporarily withheld.*

Where there is no hope there is no strength. "And I said,
My strength and my hope is perished from the Lord"
(Lamentations 3:18). God protected and provided for Israel in the wilderness, but as soon as they used up their Egyptian supplies they resented both Moses and God. Why? Their hope was grounded in human help.

Moses climbed the mountain and was out of the Israelite's sight for only a few days; yet they had to have a golden calf. They thought they would never see him again and gave him up for lost. God wants His servants to wait for what He means to give them, but few stay with Him because most are short-spirited.

You know what Naomi said to her daughter: "If I should have an husband also tonight, and should also bear sons; would ye tarry for them till they were grown? Would ye stay for them from having husbands?" (Ruth 1:12–13). The promise has salvation in its womb; but will the unbeliever wait until the promise ripens and this happiness has grown up? No, he would rather mate with any base lust which pays him in some present pleasure than wait a long time, even if it is for heaven itself.

Tamar played the harlot because her promised husband was not given as soon as she wanted him (Genesis 38). Today many souls throw themselves into the embraces of the adulterous world because the comfort and joy of the promise is temporarily withheld, and God wants them to wait for their reward. "Demas hath forsaken me, having loved this present world" (2 Timothy 4:10). Only the soul which has this divine hope will patiently wait for the good of the promise. Now, in handling this service of hope God often waits a long time before fulfilling a promise; secondly, it is our duty to wait; and thirdly, hope enables us to wait.

ASSURANCE FOR THE APPOINTED TIME

*"Though God seldom comes at our day,
because we seldom reckon right,
yet he never fails His own day."*

Though the promise tarries until the appointed time, yet it will not tarry beyond it! "When the time of the promise drew nigh, which God had sworn to Abraham, the people grew and multiplied in Egypt" (Acts 7:17). Herbs and flowers sleep underground all winter in their roots but come up out of their beds, where they have lain unseen for so long, when spring approaches. And the promise will do this in its season.

Every promise is dated, but with a mysterious character; and because we cannot understand God's chronology, we think He must have forgotten us. It is as if a man should set his watch by his own hungry stomach rather than by the sun, and then say it is noon and complain because his lunch is not quite ready. We covet comfort and expect the promise to keep time with our impatient desires. But the sun will not move any faster if we set our watch forward, nor the promise come sooner if we antedate it.

It is most true, as someone has said, that "though God seldom comes at our day, because we seldom reckon right, yet he never fails His own day." The apostle exhorts the Thessalonian church not to "be soon shaken in mind, or be troubled . . . as that the day of Christ is at hand" (2 Thessalonians 2:2). But why did these saints need such an exhortation when they were looking for their greatest joy to come with that day? It was not the coming of that day which was so alarming, but the time in which some seducers would have persuaded them to expect it—before many prophecies had been fulfilled. "For that day shall not come, except there come a falling away first, and that man of sin be revealed, the son of perdition" (v. 3). The promise waits only until those intermediate truths—which span a much shorter period—are fulfilled, and then nothing can possibly hold back the promise after that.

HIS COMING ACCORDING TO PROMISE

*"Behold, the husbandman waiteth for the precious fruit
of the earth, and hath long patience for it, until he
receive the early and latter rain. Be ye also patient."*

Wait on God as long as you have to, until He comes according to His promise and takes you out of your suffering. Do not be hasty to take yourself out of trouble. "Behold, the husbandman waiteth for the precious fruit of the earth, and hath long patience for it, until he receive the early and latter rain. Be ye also patient; stablish your hearts: for the coming of the Lord draweth nigh" (James 5:7–8). Although the farmer wishes his corn were already in the barn, he waits for it to ripen in the ordinary course of God's providence. He is glad when the former rain comes, but he wants the latter rain too, and waits for it, though it is long in coming. And have we not all seen that a shower falling close to harvest time brings the ear to its completeness? The fullest mercies are the ones we wait for the longest. Jesus did not immediately supply wine at the marriage of Cana, as His mother had asked, but they had the more for waiting awhile.

Hope assures the soul that while God waits to perform one promise, he supplies another. This comfort is enough to quiet the heart of anyone who understands the sweetness of God's methods. There is not one minute when a believer's soul is left without comfort. There is always some promise standing ready to minister to the Christian until another one comes. A sick man does not complain if all his friends do not stay with him together, as long as they take turns and never leave him without someone to care for him.

We read of a tree of life which bears "twelve manner of fruits, and yielded her fruit every month" (Revelation 22:2). What is this tree but Christ, who brings all manner of fruit in His promises and comfort for all times and all conditions? The believer can never come to Him without finding some promise to supply strength until another is ripe enough to be gathered.

IGNORANCE AND SALVATION

"Be ready always to give an answer
to every man that asketh you a reason
of the hope that is in you" (1 Peter 3:15).

The most notorious false prophet in the world, and the one who deceives the most, is the vain hope which men take up for their salvation. It prophesies peace, pardon, and heaven as the portion of one who was never God's heir. But the day is coming, and soon, when this false prophet will be confounded. Then the hypocrite will confess he never had any real hope for salvation except an idol of his own imagination; and the religious man will throw off his profession, by which he deceived himself, and appear naked in his sinfulness. It is enough to make us carefully search our own hearts and find out what our hope is built upon.

Now hope of the right kind is well grounded. "Be ready always to give an answer to every man that asketh you a reason of the hope that is in you" (1 Peter 3:15). All Christians, no matter how weak, have grounded their hearts in Scripture for the hope they profess. What entitles you to inherit God's kingdom without a promise from Him? If someone should say that your house and land were his, would you give him your property just because he demanded it? Yet many hope to be saved who can give no better reason than this.

Just as a saint conquers fear by asking his soul why it is disquieted, a similar question can throw the bold sinner from his prancing hopes. "What reason do you find in the whole Bible for you to hope for salvation, when you live in the ignorance of God?" Certainly his soul would be as speechless as the man without the wedding garment was at Christ's question. This is why some dare not let themselves think about salvation—they know this thought would make a disturbance in their conscience that will not be stilled quickly. Or if they do ask, it would be like Pilate, who asked Christ what was truth but had no intention of waiting for His answer.

BE THANKFUL FOR THIS UNSPEAKABLE GIFT

Earth's greatest king would
be glad to change his crown for
your helmet at his dying hour.

I do not believe you have it if your heart is not thankful for it. "Blessed be the God and Father of our Lord Jesus Christ, which according to his abundant mercy hath begotten us again unto a lively hope . . . to an inheritance incorruptible, and undefiled, and that fadeth not away" (1 Peter 1:3–4). Do you have heaven in hope? It is more than if the whole world were in your hand. Earth's greatest king would be glad to change his crown for your helmet at his dying hour. His crown will not get him this helmet, but your helmet will bring you a crown, a crown not of gold, but of glory, which once on will never be taken off.

Remember, Christian, it has not been long since you had only a fearful expectation of hell instead of a hope of salvation. But God took away the chains of guilt which weighed your soul down in despair and gave you favor in His celestial court. Of all men in the world, you are the most indebted to God's mercy. If you thank Him for crust and rags—food and clothing—how much more should you thank Him for your crown?

After you have praised Him with your spirit, you should collect the praises to God of your friends too—and then, in heaven, continue thanking Him throughout eternity for your helmet of salvation. It will be a debt you will never be able fully to pay.

Live up to your hopes. Let there be a suitable agreement between your principles and your practices—your hope of heaven and your walk on earth. As you look for salvation, walk the way your eye is looking. If the Christian fails to walk in the worthiness of his calling, he betrays God's hope for him. And the Word emphasizes the necessity of this walk. It stirs us up to act "as becometh saints" (Romans 16:2) and as "it becometh the gospel of Christ" (Philippians 1:27).

YOUR MANNER OF LIVING

*Why has this wedding day been put off
for so many years? It has taken a long time
for the bride's garment to be completed.*

"What manner of persons ought ye to be in all holy conversation and godliness, looking for and hastening unto the
coming of the day of God?" (2 Peter 3:11–12). Every believing soul is Christ's spouse. The day of conversion is the day
when she is betrothed by faith to Christ; and therefore she lives
in hope for their marriage day when He will come and take her
home to His Father's house—as Isaac took Rebekah into his
mother's tent. And there they will live in His sweet embraces of
love, world without end. When the bridegroom comes, does the
bride want him to find her in dirty garments? "Can a maid forget her ornaments, or a bride her attire?" (Jeremiah 2:32). Has a
bride ever forgotten to have her wedding dress ready on her
marriage day? Or does she forget to put it on when she expects
her bridegroom's coming?

Holiness is the "raiment of needlework" in which you will
be "brought unto the king," your husband (Psalm 45:14). Why
has this wedding day been put off for so many years? It has tak-
en a long time for the bride's garment to be completed. But
when its preparation is finished and you are dressed in it, then
that joyful day will come: "The marriage of the Lamb is come,
and his wife hath made herself ready" (Revelation 19:7).

Christian, you have no more effective argument to defeat
temptation than your hope. Of course it is good when temptation is defeated, no matter what the weapon is. Yet the Israelites
used poor judgment when they borrowed the Philistines' grind-
stone to "sharpen every man . . . his axe, and his mattock" (1 Samuel 13:20). So the Christian's choice is inferior when he must
use the wicked man's argument to cut through temptation. The
saint has more purity of spirit than this. Hope's innocent argument will put you into a stronger tower against sin than all the
sophisticated weapons of the uncircumcised world.

FEAR OF GOD IS A GREAT GIFT

*After Satan has thrown the Christian into some filthy sin
he asks God, "Is this the assurance You gave of heaven
—and this the garment of salvation You put on him?*

T he Lord taketh pleasure in them that fear him, in those
that hope in his mercy" (Psalm 147:11). Too often children
forget to respect their parents once their inheritance is
settled. And though the doctrine of assurance cannot rightly be
accused of producing such bitter fruit, we are too prone to
abuse it. Even the best of saints may be led far into temptation
after the love of God with eternal life has been passed over to
them under the seal of hope's assurance, and may fall into great
sin.

God opened the depths of His heart and demonstrated His
love to David and Solomon in great measure before both of
them gave into sin. A blot left on their history shows the som-
ber shadows of their sin in the light of such divine love. And
while their story leaves us examples of human frailty, it also
portrays indelible assurance. Because this assurance spreads itself into highest rejoicing from the certainty of our expected
glory, we must nourish a holy fear of God in our hearts.

The devil is delighted if he can cause saints to sin, but he
glories most when he can lay them in the dirt in their Sunday
clothes and make them defile their garments of salvation. If he
succeeds, he tries to insult God by showing Him what a predicament His child is in and holds up the Christian's assurance for
the world to laugh at. After Satan has thrown the Christian into
some filthy sin he asks God, "Is this the assurance You gave him
of heaven—and this the garment of salvation You put on him?
Look where he has laid it—and what a mess he has made of
your grace." We tremble at the thought of putting such blasphemy of our living God into the devil's mouth!

God's beloved children must not loiter in the sunshine of
divine love but keep moving their feet in the path of duty because God has been so kind as to make our walk most full of
cheer. But we must not lose our reverential fear of God in His
familiarity with us.

HOPE IN THE KING

*If you have some hope of heaven, and you believe that
your eternal happiness or misery depends on it,
you must search your heart by the light of God's Word.*

The more we prize something good the harder we work to have it. If a prince should lose a penny and one should bring him news that it has been found, it is such a petty thing that he would not care whether it were true or not. But if his kingdom lay at stake in battle and a report comes that his army has defeated the enemy, he would long to have this message confirmed.

Is heaven worth so little that you can be satisfied with a few probabilities and uncertain maybes that you will ever get there? You must despise the blessed peace if you are no more interested in your right to it than that. When Ahab advanced his army against Ramoth-gilead, Micaiah prophesied victory—"Go, and prosper" (1 Kings 22:15). But the king had good reason to suspect that Micaiah's words were empty of truth and rebuked him: "And the king said unto him, How many times shall I adjure thee that thou tell me nothing but that which is true in the name of the Lord?" (1 Kings 22:16).

If you have some hope of heaven, and you believe that your eternal happiness or misery depends on it, you must search your heart by the light of God's Word. And after an impartial review of what you read there, command your conscience to tell you the naked truth—what your spiritual standing is and whether or not you may hope that salvation is yours.

When Peter heard about Christ's resurrection he did not fully believe; but he ran as fast as he could and looked into the sepulcher, proving how dearly he loved his Lord. Thus, Christian, even if the promise of eternal life has not yet produced such an assurance of hope that you can enjoy it without doubting, you can show your appreciation of it by trying to strengthen your hope and put away all doubt of it.

FOOD IN HIS WORD

*The devil deprives some people of this scriptural relief by
mere laziness. They complain about doubts and fears like
sluggards crying out of their poverty as they lie in bed.*

Strengthen hope by studying God's Word diligently. The
Christian is bred by the Word and he must be fed by it or
his grace will shrivel up and die. The growing baby feeds
often at the breast. As God has provided food in His Word to
nourish every grace, so the Scriptures provide nutrients for the
saint's strong and solid hope. "That we through patience and
comfort of the scriptures might have hope" (Romans 15:4). The
devil knows this so well that he works hard to deprive the
Christian of the help stored in the Word. And he is right, for as
long as this river remains unblocked which makes glad the City
of God, with comfort brought in on the stream of its precious
promises, he can never besiege the City.

The devil deprives some people of this scriptural relief by
mere laziness. They complain about doubts and fears like sluggards crying out of their poverty as they lie in bed. But they will
not get up and search for the Word for the satisfaction of their
need. Of all others, these sell their comfort most cheaply. Who
pities the starving man who has bread before him but refuses to
move his hand to take it?

To some Christians, Satan presents false applications of the
Word and thereby troubles their spirits. The devil is an excep-
tionally bright student in theology and makes no other use of
his Scripture knowledge than to lure the saint into sin—or into
despair for having sinned. He is like a dishonest lawyer who at-
tains legal skill merely to force an honest man into serious
problems by the tangled suit he brings against him.

Now if Satan so proficiently manipulates the Word to weak-
en your hope and deprive you of your inheritance, you should
develop a holy skill to maintain the right and defend your hope.
In your study of the Word, then, you must closely pursue two
goals—and pursue them until they are yours.

KEEP A PURE CONSCIENCE

Living godly in this present world and
"looking for that blessed hope"
are joined together (Titus 2:12–13).

T he Christian can say, "I know from the Word that the repentant, believing sinner will be saved; my conscience
shows me that I repent and believe. And although I am un-
worthy, I can firmly hope that I shall be saved." And as forcefully as the Christian agrees with God's truth and repents, so his
hope will be—strong or weak. If his assent to the truth of the
promise is weak, or his evidence of faith and repentance is uncertain, his hope that is born of these will inherit its parents'
infirmities.

Living godly in this present world and "looking for that
blessed hope" are joined together (Titus 2:12–13). Thus a soul
void of godliness must be destitute of all true hope, and the
godly person who is careless in his holy walk will soon find his
hope faltering.

All sin brings trembling fears and shakings of heart to the
person who tampers with it. But sins which are deliberately
committed are to the Christian's hope as poison is to his body,
which eventually drinks it up. Sins produce a lifeless Christian
and make thoughts of God dreadful to him: "I remembered
God, and was troubled" (Psalm 77:3). They make the man afraid
to look on the God of judgment. After all, does the servant want
his master to come home and find him drunk?

When Calvin's friends tried to persuade him to give up his
night studies, he asked if they wanted his Lord to come and find
him idle. God forbid that death should find you lying in the
puddle of some sin unconfessed and unrepented of! Can your
hope then carry you to eternity with joy? Can a bird fly with a
broken wing? Faith and a good conscience are the two wings of
hope. If you have wounded your conscience by sin, renew your
repentance so that you may act in faith for the forgiveness of it
and redeem your hope.

NOVEMBER 29

ASK GOD FOR A STRONGER HOPE

*Be sure you humbly acknowledge God by
constantly waiting on Him for your spiritual
growth. "The young lions" are said to
"seek their meat from God" (Psalm 104:21).*

N ow the God of hope fill you with all joy and peace in believing, that ye may abound in hope, through the power
of the Holy Ghost" (Romans 15:13). God is the God of
hope; not only of the first seed but also of the whole growth
and harvest of it in us. He does not give a saint the first grace of
conversion and then leave the completion of it wholly to his human skill.

Be sure you humbly acknowledge God by constantly waiting
on Him for your spiritual growth. "The young lions" are said to
"seek their meat from God" (Psalm 104:21). God has taught
them to express their wants when they are hungry; and by this
they have learned that their Maker is also their Supplier. At first
a baby expresses his needs only by crying; but as soon as he
knows who his mother is, he directs his cries to her.

The Father can always find you, Christian. He knows what
you want but He waits to supply you until you cry to Him. Does
God care for the beasts in the field? Then surely He will care
for you, His child in His house. You might pray for more riches
and be denied; but a prayer for more grace is sure to be answered quickly.

Love has a secret yet powerful influence on hope. Moses be-
friended the Israelite when he killed the Egyptian who had
fought with him. And love kills slavish fear—one of the worst
enemies hope has—and thereby strengthens hope's hand. Whoever pulls up the weeds helps the corn to grow. It is fear that
oppresses the Christian's spirit so that he cannot act or hope
strongly. "Perfect love casteth out fear" (1 John 4:18). The
freewoman will cast out the bondwoman. Fear is one of Hagar's
breed—an affection that keeps everyone in bondage who par-
takes of it.

Love cannot tolerate fear. The loving soul asks, "Can I fear
that the One who loves me most will ever hurt me? Fear and
doubt, away with you! There is no room for you in my heart."
Charity "thinketh no evil" (1 Corinthians 13:5).

CHOSEN FOR HEAVEN

*When your hope is at a loss and you question
your salvation in another world, look backward
to see what God has done for you in this one.*

I f we spend all our thoughts on our unworthiness of heaven we shall never realize we are among the chosen ones who will enjoy it. But when we believe the pleasure God takes in demonstrating His greatness—making miserable creatures happy instead of allowing their misery to continue in eternal damnation—and the cost He paid for His mercy to reach us, we see Him as the Most High God! When we weigh and meditate on these truths they open our hearts, though fastened with a thousand bolts, to believe without question all that He has said.

Recall past mercies from God's hand. When the strong Christian's spiritual rest is broken by very great fears for the future, he can read the history of God's gracious dealings with him. Thus he endures his night of affliction with comfort and hope. But those who have not penned in their memories the remarkable instances of God's loving favor to them miss comfort's sweet companionship.

Sometimes little scraps of writing found on a man's desk help save his estate, for without these records he would have spent the rest of his life in prison. And often it is one experience remembered which frees the soul from despair—a prison where the devil longs to trap the Christian. God's dealings with David were often the subject of his meditation and of his songs; and when his hope faltered, he regained it by recalling God's goodness to him: "I said, This is my infirmity: but I will remember the years of the right hand of the most High" (Psalm 77:10).

When a hound has lost the scent, he hunts backward to recover it and pursues his game with a louder cry of confidence than before. Thus Christian, when your hope is at a loss and you question your salvation in another world, look backward to see what God has done for you in this one.

HOLD ON TO THE POWER OF GOD

*Another way to let God rescue you
from despair is to remember how often He
has proved your unbelief to be a false prophet.*

Y ou have seen God bare His arm to help you. So unless you think He has lost the strength or use of it, hope still has an object to act upon, to lift your head above the water. No person ever drowns in despair unless he loses his hold on the power of God.

Another way to let God rescue you from despair is to remember how often He has proved your unbelief to be a false prophet. Has He not knocked at your door with inward comfort and outward deliverance after you had already put out the candle of hope and given up looking for Him? He came to Hezekiah after he had concluded that his case was beyond hope and help (Isaiah 38:10–11). Have you ever been left alone with fear as if an everlasting night had come and there would never be another morning? Yet even then God proved those despairing thoughts all liars by an unlooked-for surprise of sweet mercy which He crept in and gently brought to you. Why then are you frightened again and again by your distrustful thoughts, which God has so often proved liars? Stop feeding your hopes on the corpses of slain fears!

Remember too how even when you have been impatient and despairing in your afflictions, nevertheless God's mercy has been at work all the while to deliver you from them. David is an instance of this: "I said in my haste, All men are liars. What shall I render unto the Lord for all his benefits toward me?" (Psalm 116:11–12); "I said in my haste, I am cut off from before thine eyes: nevertheless thou heardest the voice of my supplications when I cried unto thee" (Psalm 31:22). He was saying, "I prayed with so little faith that I unprayed my own prayer! I assumed my dilemma was hopeless but God forgave my hasty spirit and gave me the mercy which I had hardly any faith to expect." And with his experience, David raises every saint's troubled hope: "Be of good courage, and he shall strengthen your heart, all ye that hope in the Lord" (v. 24).

HOPELESSNESS IS A SAD CONDITION

Are you cutting your short life into
chips by wasting time on trivia when our
salvation still has not been worked out?

I f God is not in your conscience to comfort it, you must be a raging devil or a stupid atheist. If God is not in you, the devil is; for a man's heart is a house that will not stand empty.

You cannot afford to be without hope in life or in death. It is a sad legacy that shuts out the rebellious child from all claim to his inheritance. But even if you do have wealth, it is all you have. Does it not make your heart ache to think that your reward is all paid here, and will be spent by the time the saints start receiving theirs?

Yet it is far worse to be without this hope when death comes. The condemned prisoner had rather stay in his cell than accept deliverance at the executioner's hand. The hopeless soul has more reason to prefer to spend his eternity in earth's worst dungeon than to be eased of his pain with hell's torment. Here is the sad confusion in the thoughts of guilty men when their souls leave their bodies. If the sobs of mourning friends in the room of a dying man make his passage harder, how much more will the horror of the sinner's own conscience frighten him when he sees the flaming inevitability of his approaching destination?

Are you cutting your short life into chips by wasting time on trivia when our salvation still has not been worked out? Are you pampering and decorating your body while your soul is slipping into hell? This is like painting your door when the house is on fire. It would be far more becoming for you to call upon God and lie in repentant tears for your sins at His feet than to wallow in your sensual pleasures and let your sleeping conscience temporarily ease the dread thought of your approaching punishment.

It is possible to obtain a hope of salvation. I do not mean the way you are now, for it is as impossible for you to get to heaven without salvation as it is for God to lie. If any devil in hell had a thousand worlds at his disposal, he would give them all for this hope and count it a bargain.

DECEMBER 3

THE CHRISTIAN'S SWORD

"And the sword of the Spirit,
which is the word of God"
(Ephesians 6:17).

Here we have the sixth and last piece in the Christian's armor brought to our hand—the sword of the Spirit. Throughout the ages the sword has been a most necessary part of the soldier's equipment and has been used more than any other weapon. A pilot without his chart, a student without his book, a soldier without his sword—all are ridiculous. But above these, it is absurd to think of being a Christian without knowledge of God's Word and some skill to use this weapon.

The usual name in Scripture for war is "the sword." "I will call for a sword upon all the inhabitants of the earth" (Jeremiah 25:29); that is, "I will send war." Now such a weapon is the Word of God in the Christian's hand. By the edge of this sword his enemies fall and all his great exploits are done: "They overcame him by the blood of the Lamb, and by the word of their testimony" (Revelation 12:11). But before we enter into a detailed discussion of the sword of the Spirit, let us notice the kind of arms here presented for the Christian's use and the place and order in which it stands.

This weapon is both defensive and offensive. The rest of the apostles' armor are defensive arms—girdle, breastplate, shield, and helmet. But the sword both defends the Christian and wounds his enemy.

No matter how glorious the Christian's other pieces of armor, he would easily be disarmed without a sword in his hand. And surely the believer would be stripped of all his graces if he did not have this sword to defend them and himself too against Satan's fury. "Unless thy law had been my delight, I should then have perished in mine affliction" (Psalm 119:92).

This is like God's flaming sword which kept Adam out of paradise. The saint is often compared to Christ's garden and orchard; and with the sword of the Word he keeps his orchard from being robbed of God's sweet comforts and graces by Satan's constant invasions.

THE ETERNAL SON OF GOD

*"Out of his mouth goeth a
sharp sword, that with it he should
smite the nations" (Revelation 19:15).*

H is name is called "The Word of God" (Revelation 19:13).
This speaks of a person, and He is no other than Jesus
Christ the Son of God. But Christ is not the Word of God
referred to in this text. The Spirit is Christ's sword, rather than
Christ the sword of the Spirit: "Out of his mouth goeth a sharp
sword, that with it he should smite the nations" (Revelation
19:15).

When the earth had only a few people, and they lived a long
time, God declared His mind by dreams and visions and by immediate revelations to faithful witnesses, who in turn instructed
others. They lived so long that three holy men were able to preserve the purity of religion by tradition from Adam's death until
the time just prior to the Israelites' going down to Egypt. Thus
God delayed committing His will to writing because it was safely kept by a few trustworthy men.

But after the age of man's life was shortened and the population multiplied, God wrote the Ten Commandments with His
own finger on tables of stone to keep His people from idolatry
and corrupt worship. Later He commanded Moses to write the
other words he had heard from Him on the mount; and all the
while God continued to demonstrate His will by supernatural
revelations.

Finally, it pleased God for His sacred Word to be finished by
Christ the great Teacher of the church, and by the apostles, His
public notaries, for saints to use until the end of time. A curse
from Christ's own mouth belongs to anyone who adds to or
takes away from God's written Word: "If any man shall add unto
these things, God shall add unto him the plagues that are written in this book: and if any man shall take away from the words
of the book of this prophecy, God shall take away his part out of
the book of life, and out of the holy city, and from the things
which are written in this book" (Revelation 22:18–19).

CREATION IN SCRIPTURE

*Heathens, by inquiry of natural reason, have
discovered that the world had a beginning and that
it could be the workmanship of no one but God.*

What resource could man possibly have in his reading and learning to enable him to write the history of the creation? Heathens, by inquiry of natural reason, have discovered that the world had a beginning and that it could be the workmanship of no one but God. But how does their discovery compare to the compiling of a distinct history of how God worked to produce the world, the order in which every creature was made, and the time involved? To be qualified for such a task a man would have to be preexistent to the whole world and an eyewitness to each day's work. And man, who was himself created on the last day, cannot do this.

Yet there is history even more ancient than the creation in Scripture, where we find what was done in heaven before the world began. Who could bring up reports of the everlasting decrees then resolved on, and the Father's promises to the Son of eternal life for His elect at the given time?

Some human authors accurately preserve the history of others, reflecting their faults and weaknesses as well as their accomplishments. But where are the men who objectively record the blemishes of their own house? At this point the pens often refuse to ink the whole truth. They can make a blot in their history but not on their own names; and even if they should mention any scars these will be found in extremely fine print.

But none of this self-love appears in the history of Scripture. The writers are free to expose their own shame and nakedness to the world. Thus Moses impartially branded his own tribe for their bloody murder on Shechem. Nothing escaped his pen—he chronicled the proud behavior of his sister and God's severe chastisement of her, and even the incest of his own parents (Exodus 6:20).

SATAN AND THE FUTURE

*What the devil told Saul would happen to his army
and kingdom was nothing but what he rationally
concluded from the premises which lay before him.*

When we consider Satan's many years of experience in studying natural knowledge, we will not accept his predictions as prophecies but see him as a learned naturalist with a short and dark text of natural causes.

What the devil told Saul would happen to his army and kingdom was nothing but what he rationally concluded from the premises which lay before him; in that God had rejected Saul and anointed another man to be king, together with the full measure of Saul's sins—culminating in his going to a witch for counsel—and a great Philistine army gathered against him. Coupled with his burning conscience, all these made it appear that the devil, without a gift of prophecy, had accurately envisioned Saul's doom.

God may reveal future events to Satan as His instrument. The hangman is not a prophet. He cannot tell a man when he will be executed until he gets a warrant from the king appointing him to carry out his orders. Satan could have told Job beforehand what afflictions would come to his estate, servants, children, and his own body because God had allowed him to be the instrument to bring all these trials upon Job. But neither Satan nor any other creature is able to foretell events which do not arise from natural causes nor follow moral and political probabilities.

Prophecies in Scripture are locked up in the cabinet of the divine will to prove their heavenly extraction. They must come from God, who can tell us what only He knows. Who else but God, for example, could have told Abraham where his heirs would be and what would happen to them four hundred years after his death?

Finally, how wonderful are the prophecies of Christ the Messiah! His person, birth, life, and death are as specifically set down many ages before His coming as if recorded by those who were with Him and saw with their own eyes all that happened.

SCRIPTURE'S PURE COMMANDS

God is "the Holy One" (Isaiah 43:3).
He alone is perfectly holy: "The heavens
are not clean in his sight" (Job 15:15).

Who could form laws to guide men's hearts or prepare rewards to reach their souls and consciences? An earthly king would be ridiculed if he made a law that his subjects love him or confess their unfaithful thoughts. And further, what mortal ruler could ever assume that he could keep the hearts and thoughts of men within his jurisdiction?

Throughout the years men have schemed to plan acts of murder but were attacked by their own consciences before anyone could accuse them. Their surrender came about not because of a law but because they dreaded the arrest of their conscience for violating God's law. For this law not only restrains hands from killing but also binds hearts from cursing. It rules in the consciences of vile men like a bit that God rides the most stubborn sinners with, and curbs them so they can never completely shake it out of their mouths.

God is "the Holy One" (Isaiah 43:3). He alone is perfectly holy: "The heavens are not clean in his sight" (Job 15:15). And as God is the only holy Person, so the Scripture is the only holy book. Dregs appear in even the holiest writings of the sincerest men when they have stood awhile under the observation of a critical eye. Scripture too has been exposed to the view of all sorts of men yet can never have the least impurity. It is so pure that it makes filthy souls clean: "Sanctify them through thy truth: thy word is truth" (John 17:17). There is nothing in Scripture to feed the flesh or afford fuel to any lust. It puts every sin to the sword and strikes through the loins of all sinners, affluent or penniless: "To be carnally minded is death; but to be spiritually minded is life and peace" (Romans 8:6).

Athenagoras well said, "No man can be wicked that is a Christian, unless he be a hypocrite.'

DECEMBER 8

THE POWER OF CONVICTION

Conscience is a castle safe from attack unless God carries on the fight. No power can direct it to stoop but that which heaven and earth must obey.

If the Word finds out something which escapes the examination of a man's own conscience, does this not prove a Deity is in it? The apostle persuades us to know the power of the preached Word to lay open the heart: "And thus are the secrets of his heart made manifest; and so falling down on his face, he will worship God, and report that God is in you of a truth" (1 Corinthians 14:25).

Conscience is a castle safe from attack unless God carries on the fight. No power can direct it to stop but that which heaven and earth must obey. He who disarms the strong man must be stronger than he is. And He who masters the conscience must be greater than it is. Now the Word is able to shatter this power of the soul which refuses to bow to anyone except God.

As long as Job was untouched by God's hand he enjoyed his prosperity and assumed that his spiritual wealth matched his material worth. But when the law charged him with sin, it stripped his conscience as naked as his outward condition would later become. For the first time he saw how empty of all holiness he really was. The Word had such power upon him that it laid him, with his fair skin of pharisaical strictness, trembling over the bottomless pit of his own unrighteousness.

What can move like the arm of the Word? When a prisoner preached to Felix the judge he shuddered under its convicting power. Who but God could make those men who were guilty of shedding the innocent blood of Christ and scorned His doctrine so terrified that they cried out in the middle of Peter's sermon, "Men and brethren, what shall we do?" (Acts 2:37). Does not this evidence carry as visible a print of a Deity as the moment when Moses split the rock with a small rod in his hand?

Conscience is God's prison in the persons' own heart, and no one can release him except the one who put him there.

DECEMBER 9
YOU ARE THE LETTER OF CHRIST

*"But after that the kindness and love
of God our Savior toward man appeared...
he saved us, by the washing of regeneration,
and renewing of the Holy Ghost" (Titus 3:3–5).*

We ourselves also were sometimes foolish, disobedient, deceived, serving diverse lusts and pleasures . . . But after that the kindness and love of God our Savior toward man appeared . . . he saved us, by the washing of regeneration, and renewing of the Holy Ghost" (Titus 3:3–5).

You who are the letter of Christ, written not with ink but with the Spirit of the living God, can you doubt that the Word which is able to bring you home to God has come from Him? Long may a man sit at the feet of a philosopher without giving up his old lustful heart and finding it replaced with a new and holy one!

But even the best philosopher of them all has sins—such as wrong attitudes—which are acted out behind the closed doors of the most private room of the inner man. Men could never find out about these sins; but the Word treads on the high places of spiritual wickedness and does not leave any stronghold untaken. It chases sin and Satan to their hiding places and digs lusts out of their holes where they have earthed themselves. The heart itself is no safe sanctuary for sin. The Word will take it—as it took Joab from the horns of the altar—in order to slay it.

I cannot give a better example of the Word's converting power than its miraculous conquests when the apostles were first sent out to preach the grace of Christ. Wherever they went the world was up in arms against them and the devil at the head of their troops to resist this ministry of the Word. Yet they turned the world upside down without drawing any other sword but the "everlasting Gospel." Nothing less than the arm of the Almighty could have achieved such triumphs—sinners renounced idolatries which had deceived them all their lives; and most important of all, sinners received a new Lord, the crucified Jesus.

FOOLS FOR CHRIST

*The doctrine of Christianity in its own native
excellency lays the axe to the root of every sin
and defies all who participate in wickedness.*

Christ's followers were as simple in their intellect as they
were in worldly sophistication. But this was what confounded their enemies, who recognized that these poor
men could personally contribute no more to the success that
followed them than the blowing of rams' horns did to the flat-
tening of Jericho's walls or the sounding of Jehoshaphat's musical instruments to the routing of formidable enemies. There is
only one explanation—the breath of God caused them to sound
the trumpet of the gospel; and His sweet Spirit humbled the
hearts of their hearers.

Their message was not only strange and new, but contrary
to man's corrupt nature. It contained nothing to please the sinner's lust. Christianity is easily embraced if it is presented in a
whore's dress, with its purity adulterated. But the doctrine of
Christianity in its own native excellency lays the axe to the root
of every sin and defies all who participate in wickedness.

This may make us step aside—as Moses did at the burning
bush—to see a doctrine believed and embraced that is pure
nonsense to carnal reason, teaching us to be saved by another's
righteousness. Indeed reason brings a wide gulf of objection
against the doctrine of trusting Christ to deliver from sin and
Satan; yet multitudes of believers through the ages have come
and offered themselves to it under baptism, even as soldiers
seal their enlistment with an oath.

If the Word had promised favor of kings or places of honor
we would not be surprised to see so many turn to Christianity.
But the gospel which the disciples preached did not come with
a single bribe in its hand; no golden apples were thrown along
the path to entice sinners. Christ tells His disciples not to stoop
or take up crowns for their heads but a cross for their backs: "If
any man will come after me, let him deny himself, and take up
his cross, and follow Me" (Matthew 16:24).

DESTRUCTION OF GOD'S ENEMIES

*Too often we look upon government as the forces that
control the earth's affairs, yet these are no more
than a fly on the wheel. It is the Word of God
which decides all that is done on the world's stage.*

I f God's enemies continue to harden themselves against the
truth by refusing to repent, destruction is all they can look
forward to. They are like animals "made to be taken and destroyed" (2 Peter 2:12). And they may know beforehand what
will destroy them—the Word of God: "If any man will hurt
them, fire proceedeth out of their mouth, and devoureth their
enemies: and if any man will hurt them, he must in this manner
be killed" (Revelation 11:5). These men freely butchered and
burned the saints, yet the Word the saints preached will destroy
their enemies. It lives on to avenge the saints on their enemies.
God's Word will give them the fatal stroke.

The sword of the Word has a long reach; it is at the breast of
every enemy God has. And although they feel secure and powerful, sooner or later God will open one door or another to let
destruction come upon them. The prophet expressed the impending ruin of the Philistines by announcing: "Woe unto the
inhabitants of the sea coast . . . the word of the Lord is against
you" (Zephaniah 2:5); as if he was saying, "You are a lost people and the whole world cannot save you now, because the
Word of the Lord is against you." Like lightning, the curse of the
Word burns to the very root of sin. All seven nations of Canaan
fell into the mouth of Israel as ripe fruit falls into the mouth of
the one who shakes the tree. The Word of the Lord had gone
before them and the fate of their foes was certain.

Too often we look upon government as the forces that control the earth's affairs, yet these are no more than a fly on the
wheel. It is the Word of God which decides all that is done on
the world's stage. "I have this day set thee over the nations and
over the kingdoms, to root out, and to pull down, and to destroy . . . to build, and to plant" (Jeremiah 1:10). The whole
earth is God's; and who has power to build on His ground, or
pull down, but Himself?

DECEMBER 12

THE WORD HELPS WITH TEMPTATIONS

Can we go against sin and Satan
with a better weapon than the one
Christ used to fight the tempter?

Augustine could never get free from his lusts until he heard a voice saying, "Take, read!" He opened his Bible at Romans chapter 13 and what he read caused a mighty earthquake in his soul. The prison doors of his heart immediately flew open and the chains of lusts which his own efforts could never file off now dropped away. He confessed that he had been a slave to these lusts and tied to them with unbreakable chains of pleasure linked with guilt. He had rolled around in his filthy lusts with as much amusement as if he had been resting on a bed of spices, anointing himself with precious ointments. Yet this one word came with such a commanding power that it tore every one of them out of his heart and turned his love into a defiant hatred of them.

As the Word is the weapon by which God brings sinners out of the devil's power into freedom, He also uses it to defend His saints from temptations which would draw them back into sin. Satan, now thrown out of his kingdom, tries diligently to reclaim the forgiven sinner.

But those kingdoms that we win by the sword we must keep by the sword. David tells you he stood his ground and guarded it against the enemy: "Concerning the works of men, by the word of thy lips I have kept me from the paths of the destroyer" (Psalm 17:4). It is as if he had said, "Would you like to know how I escape the ungodly things that most men like to do? The answer is God's Word, which keeps me safe from the temptations which carry men off to be slowly destroyed."

Can we go against sin and Satan with a better weapon than the one Christ used to fight the tempter? Of course He could easily have laid the devil at His feet with one beam shot from His deity if He had wanted to fight that way. Yet He chose to conceal the majesty of His divinity and let Satan come close to Him so that He could conquer him with the Word and demonstrate the value of that sword which He would leave with His followers to fight the same enemy.

KNOWLEDGE OF CHRIST IN THE WORD

*How did Peter expect people to grow in the
knowledge of Christ unless they read Scripture,
the only book where it can be found?*

D o not be led away with the error of the wicked but "grow
in grace, and in the knowledge of our Lord and Savior Jesus Christ" (2 Peter 3:18).

Light is the chariot which carries the influence of the sun.
So the knowledge of Christ brings with it the influences of His
grace into the heart. And how did Peter expect people to grow
in the knowledge of Christ unless they read Scripture, the only
book where it can be found? How wrong for teachers to want
the people to learn this knowledge solely from their preaching,
and not from the Bible! How can a congregation be sure they
are hearing truth unless they have Scripture, the only touch-
stone to try the purity of the doctrine? God Himself directs His
Word not to any one honored group—not to a select few—but
to every man (Romans 1:7; 2 Corinthians 1:1). Why are laws
made if they cannot be declared? And why was Scripture ever
written if not to be read and known of all men? By the same authority with which the apostle wrote his epistles, he commanded them to be read in the church. Did ministers of the early
church hide God's Word from the people instead of encourag-
ing them to hide it in their heart?

It is true that some men do wrest Scripture to their own destruction, just as occasionally somebody chokes on a piece of
bread if he is not careful when he eats. But must everyone
starve for fear of getting choked? Some hurt themselves with
sharp weapons; must the whole army then be disarmed, and
only a few officers be allowed to wear the sword? If this argument were enough to seal up the Bible, we must deny it to in-
tellectuals as well as to common men; for it is a known fact that
the grossest heresies have bred in the finest minds. Whenever
proud men insist on being wiser than God, their foolish minds
get darker and darker until they become so accustomed to the
blackness that they can no longer see His sovereignty.

DECEMBER 14

THANKSGIVING FOR THE WORD

There is no other way for us to
reach heaven without traveling
through the enemies' territory.

The devil cannot think of anything he had rather glory in than to wound God's name with His own sword. He coaxes man to sin and then brags that God made him do it. If God ever singles out a man on the face of the earth for His utmost wrath, it will surely be the person who shelters his sin under the wing of holy Scripture.

Instead of letting Satan wrest Scripture from us by his wily stratagems, let us be excited to bless God for the sword He has furnished us with out of His grace. If a man possesses a kingdom but has no sword to keep his crown he cannot expect to enjoy it very long. We live in a world where our lives are not safe unless we are fully armed. There is no other way for us to reach heaven without traveling through the enemies' territory. What are the hopes, then, of an unarmed soul ever reaching heaven at last?

When Israel marched out of Egypt toward the promised land, few or none would trust them to travel through their country without rising up in arms against them. And the Christian will find his march to heaven even more dangerous, for Satan has not become more meek than he used to be, nor the wicked world kinder to the people of God. What mercy God showed when he gave us a sword to take us out of danger of them all! This weapon is in your hand right now, Christian, as the rod was in Moses'. Even if an army of devils is behind you and a sea of sins before you, with this sword, wielded by your faith, you can cut your way through them. Truly Scripture is a mercy incomparably greater than the sun in the heavens. In fact, we can more easily spare the sun's warm beams of light than give up God's Word for the church. If the sun were gone we would lose our physical life; but if Scripture were eclipsed our souls would stumble into hell.

THE TRANSLATION OF SCRIPTURE

When you must stay at home because of
afflictions, you have God's Word to
keep you company in your loneliness.

The translated Word is our sword taken out of its scabbard.
How much good would it do a Christian who understood
only his mother tongue if this sword were sheathed in Hebrew or Greek? Like John, he might weep at the sight of the
sealed book which he could not read. So let us bless God who
sent not angels but men, equipped by God's anointing on their
work, with the ability to roll away the stone from the mouth of
the fountain!

Now Christian, when you must stay at home because of afflictions, you have God's Word to keep you company in your
loneliness. And though you cannot sit with your brothers and
sisters at the Father's communion table, you do not have to miss
a nourishing meal. Even if you cannot carve the main servings
as well as your minister can, still you are able to pick up comfort as the Holy Spirit helps you reach for it. God has made the
most necessary truths hang on the lower limbs of this tree of
life, well within the grasp of afflicted Christians who are of an
ordinary stature in knowledge.

Bless God for the ministry of the Word. Think about the
times when persecutors drew bloody swords to keep God's
people from coming close to this tree and you will have a clear
channel for thanksgiving to flow. And look back to all the years
of spiritual ignorance when this cellar of living water was
locked up in the original tongues and there was not a key anywhere in the city. Surely we can bless God for bringing His
Word all the way to our understanding.

God has opened a public school for His children to learn to
use their weapon. If a man thinks he no longer needs to attend
the Spirit's school, he takes the surest path to depriving himself
of the Spirit's teaching at home. "Quench not the Spirit. Despise not prophesyings" (1 Thessalonians 5:19–20). The two are
joined; if you despise one you lose both.

THE COMMAND TO STUDY SCRIPTURES

*If ignorance of the Word is condemned where
light shines, surely God commands us to open our
eyes to take in the knowledge it sheds forth.*

S earch the Scriptures" (John 5:39)—the command could not be any plainer. But even if God had not expressed this duty so explicitly, the very penning of His Word would unmistakably convey His purpose. The passage of a law is enough to make subjects obey it. And it does not do any good for us to plead ignorance; the publication of law carries with it an obligation for us to find out exactly what it means and how it applies to us.

Christ fastens condemnation on the ignorance of men when He himself has provided knowledge: "This is the condemnation, that light is come into the world, and men loved darkness" (John 3:19). Many people avoid the light because they do not intend to walk in it. Now if ignorance of the Word is condemned where light shines, surely God commands us to open our eyes to take in the knowledge it sheds forth; for a law must be broken before a condemning sentence is pronounced. Because you live within the sound of this gospel, you will be judged by it whether you know it or not.

The Jews once had the word deposited right into their hands: "Unto them were committed the oracles of God" (Romans 3:2). These Scriptures were given to them, and now to us, as a dying father leaves his will to his son, not for him to throw it aside among waste papers, but for him to study it so as to perform everything written in it.

God's Word is called "the faith which was once delivered unto the saints" (Jude 3)—delivered to their study and care. If we had lived when Christ was here in the flesh, and He left us one last special thing to take care of, would we not have abandoned everything else to perform the will of our dying Savior? It is for His sake that we keep and transmit this faith from one generation to the next as long as this world lasts.

RECEIVING HIS LIGHT

*"Strengthen ye the weak
hands, and confirm the
feeble knees" (Isaiah 35:3).*

Hell moves from below to meet you when you are headed toward it. It will stir up the dead for you and its prisoners will close in with taunting reproaches: "We are heathens but we do not have any reason to blame God for this punishment, though we never heard of such a thing as the gospel. We damned our own souls by rebelling against every tiny ray of light God sent. But you—you rejected God's Word and had to break through every one of His promises to get to this place!'

No one can enter into the knowledge of God's Word unless His Spirit unlocks the door. Even if you were a confirmed genius you would still be like the blind Sodomites around Lot's house, groping but not able to find the way into true saving knowledge. The person with the wrong key is as far from entering the house as the man with no key at all, if not further. At least the one without a key might call out to the person inside, while the other keeps trusting his false key. The Pharisees, for instance, were full of head knowledge of the Word but stumbled fatally over the whole truth of Christ which both Moses and the prophets taught.

At the same time, many people who these Pharisees considered ignorant began to see the Messiah. Make no mistake—no one is too smart for God to blind; but on the other hand, no one is too blind and ignorant for His Spirit to open his eyes. God moved on the waters at creation and changed a rude mass into the beauty we now enjoy; and His same power can move on your dark soul and enlighten it to look at Him. "The entrance of thy words giveth light; it giveth understanding unto the simple" (Psalm 119:130).

As soon as you enter the Spirit's school you begin to show progress. Then He commands us to encourage those who are in the habit of discouraging themselves: "Strengthen ye the weak hands, and confirm the feeble knees" (Isaiah 35:3).

LEARN MORE FEAR OF GOD

*"Princes have persecuted me without
a cause; but my heart standeth in
awe of thy word" (Psalm 119:161).*

Every man dreads falling into the hands which he fears most. So if God has gained the supremacy over your fear, you will rather run into the hottest flames the persecutor kindles than make Him your enemy.

"Princes have persecuted me without a cause; but my heart standeth in awe of thy word" (Psalm 119:161). David weighed man's anger and found God's hand to be heavier. Thus Scripture so clearly reveals the frailty of man's threatening rage compared with God's power that he no longer fears the worst which man can do to him. "Cease ye from man, whose breath is in his nostrils: for wherein is he to be accounted of?" (Isaiah 2:22). "Fear not them which kill the body, but are not able to kill the soul: but rather fear him which is able to destroy both the soul and body in hell" (Matthew 10:28).

Children are afraid of imaginary monsters that cannot possibly hurt them, but play with fire that will burn them. It is no less childish to be frightened by the threats of an enemy who has no more power than we give him, but to play with a very real hellfire, into which God can cast a person forever. What did John Huss lose when his enemies put a fool's cap on his head? They could not take off the helmet of hope he wore underneath it. Or how much nearer did this martyr come to hell because his persecutors committed his soul to the devil? No closer than some of their own cruel crew are to heaven for being sainted in the Pope's calendar.

Melancthon said Luther and the faithful servants were doubly cursed because the Pope had cursed them. But what does the psalmist say? "Let them curse, but bless thou" (Psalm 109:28). If you have God's good Word, you do not have to fear the world's bad words. A dog can bark all night long but the moon will never change color because of the noise he makes. And the saint need not change his countenance because of his persecutors' abuse.

DECEMBER 19

GOD'S PRESENCE AMONG YOUR ENEMIES

He has promised to go with you wherever
your enemies might force you to go; neither
fire nor flood can take you away from the Father.

If God does call you into fiery trials, His promise will take all responsibility out of our hands: "When they deliver you up, take no thought"—that is, do not worry—"how or what ye shall speak: for it shall be given you in that same hour what ye shall speak" (Matthew 10:19). It is "the Spirit of your Father which speaketh in you" (v. 20).

There is no mouth which God cannot make eloquent, no back so weak that He cannot strengthen it. And He has promised to go with you wherever your enemies might force you to go; neither fire nor flood can take you away from the Father. These promises make such a soft pillow for the saints' heads that many have experienced marvelous rest when roughly handled by cruel enemies. One persecuted Christian, for example, dated his letter "from the delectable orchard his prison"; another signed herself "Your loving friend, as merry as one bound for heaven." People like these have been far from pitying themselves in their sufferings; in fact, their main sorrow has been that they could not express more thankfulness for them. And where did their supernatural strength and joy come from? The Holy Spirit applied God's promises to them in the time of distress!

Believers' troubles are for Christ's cause. The ark may shake but it cannot fall; the ship of the church may be tossed but it cannot sink, for Christ is in it and will awaken in plenty of time to keep it safe. Therefore we have no reason to disturb Him with screams of unbelief when storms beat angrily against the church. In times like these our faith is in more danger of sinking than Christ and His church. God's promises hold them securely out of the reach of both men and devils.

Our source of security is an "everlasting gospel" (Revelation 14:6). Heaven and earth will pass away, but not one word of this Gospel will perish. "The word of the Lord endureth forever" (1 Peter 1:25).

USING THE SWORD AGAINST HERETICS

*If you are to lift it up in victory against this
dangerous enemy you must first give yourself
completely to the leading of the Spirit in God's Word.*

Since it is much more dangerous to part with God's truth than with our lives, heretics or seducers are more to be feared than persecutors. It is far worse to have our souls damned by God than to have our bodies killed by man. If the martyrs had dreaded death more than heresy they could never have walked willingly into persecutors' flames.

The sword of the Spirit in another person's hand will not defend you. If you are to lift it up in victory against this dangerous enemy you must first give yourself completely to the leading of the Spirit in God's Word. The outward expression of Scripture is only the shell, and the meaning is the pearl which you must search for until you find it. "He that hath an ear, let him hear what the Spirit saith unto the churches" (Revelation 2:7). God spoke an imperative here, not a suggestion—we must listen to what the Spirit says in the Word as we hear or read it, for the one who has an ear for the Spirit will not have an ear for the seducer.

To help you seek and find meaning in the Word, look through these windows that follow.

The only way you will ever know the mind of God in His Word is for the Spirit to reveal it to you. But the holy God will not take a filthy hand and lead you into understanding: "None of the wicked shall understand" (Daniel 12:10). The angel who took Lot's daughters into the house struck the Sodomites with blindness so that they would grope for the door but not find it—and so are those who come to Scripture with unclean hearts. The wicked have the Word of God but only the holy have "the mind of Christ" (1 Corinthians 2:16).

Paul persuades Christians with these words: "Be not conformed to this world: but be ye transformed by the renewing of your mind, that ye may prove what is that good, and acceptable, and perfect will of God" (Romans 12:2).

A HEDGE FROM OUR ENEMIES

*His greatest ambition is to
defile the children whom God
has washed in the blood of Christ.*

I t would not help if He kept us safe from one enemy but left us open to another. But Christ has made sure that His hedge comes all the way around His beloved ones.

Solomon says, "The mouth of strange women is a deep pit: he that is abhorred of the Lord shall fall therein" (Proverbs 22:14). And so is the mouth of a seducer who comes with strange doctrines and whorish opinions. If we look closely we see this pit as Satan's design to trap the saint, for if possible he would "deceive the very elect" (Matthew 24:24). His greatest ambition is to defile the children whom God has washed in the blood of Christ.

But God's intention is to punish the hypocrites and false teachers who would never embrace Christ and His truth. He leaves these people in the pit as prey to corrupt doctrines. "They received not the love of the truth, that they might be saved. And for this cause God shall send them strong delusion, that they should believe a lie: that they all might be damned who believed not the truth, but had pleasure in unrighteousness" (2 Thessalonians 2:10–12).

These men, like deer running across an open field, are shot down; but the ones inside the pasture fence are safe. It is the outer court that is left to be trampled underfoot. And although God gives up hypocrites to be deceived by false teachers, He speaks comfort to the elect. The same decree which appointed them to salvation provided also for them to embrace truth. And it still serves to show them how to find it. "But we are bound to give thanks always to God for you, brethren beloved of the Lord, because God hath from the beginning chosen you to salvation through sanctification of the Spirit and belief of the truth" (2 Thessalonians 2:13). And God has determined to posses our mind by the power of His truth.

COMPARE SCRIPTURE WITH SCRIPTURE

*This means Satan cannot transfuse his nature
into the Christian, as fire touching wood or
iron changes and absorbs it into its own nature.*

False doctrines, like false witnesses, do not agree among themselves. We might well name them "Legion," for they are many. But truth is whole, and one Scripture harmonizes sweetly with another. Thus, although God used many different men to pen His sacred Word, He made sure they all had but one mouth: "As he spake by the mouth of his holy prophets, which have been since the world began" (Luke 1:70). The best way, therefore, to know the mind of God in a particular text is to compare it to another text. The stonecutter uses a diamond to cut another diamond. Like crystal glass set next to each other, each Scripture casts a peculiar light on the others.

Now in comparing Scripture with Scripture, be careful to interpret the obscure by the more plain, not the clear by the dark. Error creeps into the most shaded places and takes sanctuary there: "Some things hard to be understood, which they that are ... unstable wrest" (2 Peter 3:16). But no wonder people stumble in these dark places, when they have turned their backs on the light of plainer passages offering to lead them safely through.

"Whosoever is born of God sinneth not; but he that is begotten of God keepeth himself, and that wicked one toucheth him not" (1 John 5:18). Some people run away with this text and rationalize that they can claim perfection and freedom from all sin in this life; but a multitude of plain Scripture like 1 John 1:8 testify against such a conclusion: "If we say that we have no sin, we deceive ourselves, and the truth is not in us." So we must understand, then, that it is in a limited sense that one "born of God sinneth not." In other words, he does not sin finally, as the carnal man does. And notice a similar example: "... that wicked one toucheth him not" (1 John 5:18)—this means Satan cannot transfuse his nature into the Christian, as fire touching wood or iron changes and absorbs it into its own nature.

DECEMBER 23

SPIRITUAL WARFARE FOR A LIFETIME

Remember, it is only the unbelieving world—
without spiritual arms and abandoned by God—
that is left to become the prey of Satan.

Spiritual warfare is noble because it is just. It is all too true that most people join in political and military battles without ever knowing why. But there is no doubt about the cause of holy war—it is against the only enemy God has who claims the right to rule His world. For this reason God calls all mankind—some by the voice of natural conscience and others by the loud shout of His Word—to join with Him "against the mighty" (Judges 5:23). he does this not because He needs our help but because He prefers to reward obedience rather than to punish rebellion.

This noble warfare is not only just, but it is also hard. Our stubborn enemy is strong and will do everything he can to try our skill to the limit. Cowards can never hope to overcome him. When sin loses ground it is only an inch at a time, and what it holds it will not easily let go.

Spiritual warfare against lust is enlistment for a lifetime career. If you have a daring, adventurous spirit, here is what you have been looking for. Fighting with men is child's play compared to repelling demons and lusts: "He that is slow to anger is better than the mighty; and he that ruleth his spirit than he that taketh a city" (Proverbs 16:32).

It is sad that many of world's finest swordsmen who courageously risked their lives for freedom have died slaves to sin. Hannibal, for example, enjoyed victory in foreign expeditions but was defeated in his own country. So too many of the bravest heroes, who have had great victories abroad, have been miserably beaten and trampled upon by their own personal corruptions.

But do not be afraid because your enemies are mighty and many; your victory will be so much greater. And do not worry, either, when you see Caesars stripped of their insignias and forced to die in chains of lust. Remember, it is only the unbelieving world—without spiritual arms and abandoned by God—that is left to become the prey of Satan.

THE NAMES OF SIN

*Satan trains sinners to cover sin with approved nick-
names—superstition may become devotion; covetousness,
thrift; pride, self-respect; carelessness, freedom.*

G od has never made a mistake. If something is sweet he
will not say it is bitter; if it is good, He will not call it
evil. Do not ever expect to find honey in the pot if God
has written "poison" on its lid. Instead, let us say of sin what
Abigail said about her husband—whatever Scripture names it,
so it is.

But Satan trains sinners to cover sin with approved nick-
names—superstitions may become devotion; covetousness,
thrift; pride, self-respect; carelessness, freedom; and idle word,
cleverness. Sinners have to do this of course; a horsemeat sand-
wich would make them sick immediately if they knew what it
was. Persecutors used to wrap Christians in animal skins so that
the wild beasts would devour them quickly; and Satan sharpens
our appetites by sins garnished with appealing temptations
which conscience cannot easily recognize and reject.

Are you willing to be cheated like that? Your hand will be
just as much charred if you reach out and take a log out of fire
after a hateful fool promises the fire will not burn you. Hear
what the God of truth names sin—vomit of dogs; venom of serpents; stench of rotten tombs and sewers; sores, gangrene, and
plague. Because even the horrors of hell struggle to find a
name repulsive enough for it, the worst expression of its putrid
nature is to call it by its own name—"sinful sin" (cf. Romans
7:13). Now what should we do to the thing that the great God
loathes so much; and loads with names of dishonor? We must
pursue it with the sword He left us until we have executed the
judgment written upon it—utter destruction!

The nature of sin is clearly laid out in the Word. God's Word
defines it: "Sin is the transgression of the law" (1 John 3:4). In
these few words is enough weight to press the sinning soul into
hell for eternity, or to press sin itself to death in the saint's
heart, if he seriously considers truths concerning the nature of
sin.

DECEMBER 25

THE SUFFERING SIN CAUSES

*"There is no soundness in my flesh
because of thine anger; neither is there any
rest in my bones because of my sin" (Psalm 38:3).*

Who can describe the convulsions that disturb the rest of the sinning soul? "There is no peace, saith my God to the wicked" (Isaiah 57:21). The cries of condemned sinners evidence the disturbing quality inherent in sins of their own choosing: "There is no soundness in my flesh because of thine anger; neither is there any rest in my bones because of my sin" (Psalm 38:3). "My punishment is greater than I can bear" (Genesis 4:13). Perhaps the prime example, though, is Judas. When he was not able to stand up under his guilt he ran from it, and hanged himself, throwing himself into hell to erase the torment of his sin.

Just as sin disturbs the inward peace of a soul, it also interrupts outward peace in the world. What else but sin has caused such confusion? "From whence come wars and fightings among you? Come they not hence, even of your lusts that war in your members?" (James 4:1). Delilah betrayed her own husband into the enemies' hands. And Absalom tried to take the life of his dear father. Sin is the subtle whisperer which separates friends and families and even the sweet communion of saints.

Sin has such a kindle-fire nature that as deadly sparks fly not only from one neighbor's house to another but from nation to nation. All the water in the seas cannot quench the wars it ignites between kingdoms; instead, it makes men who live at one end of the world thirst for the blood and possessions of those who live at the other end. The earth has become an arena where there is little else but fighting and killing. Is this the guest you welcome within your heart?

Sin has a damning property. If sin's damage could be confined to this world, it would be bad enough. Considering our short stay here, we might take a measure of comfort in the fact that it would soon be over. But to be bothered by it here and then damned to eternal torment in the next world—it is unbearable!

SECRET SINS' EFFECTS

*"Thou hast set our iniquities
before thee, our secret sins in the
light of thy countenance" (Psalm 90:8).*

D o not be deceived—one sin will send you to hell as fast
as a thousand. "Neither fornicators, nor idolaters, nor
adulterers, nor effeminate, nor abusers of themselves
with mankind, nor thieves, nor covetous, nor drunkards, nor re-
vilers, nor extortioners, shall inherit the kingdom of God" (1
Corinthians 6:9–10). Scripture excludes not only the man who
is all of these, but he who is any of them. All men must die, but
they do not die of the same disease. And it is just as certain that
all unrepentant sinners will be damned—one for a particular
sin and another for something else. But they will all meet in the
same flaming hell.

Satan tempts us with secret sins. Saul was ashamed to
approach Endor in his princely robe because he had told the
world of his hatred of witchcraft, making it punishable by death.
But he was not afraid to go to a witch in disguise. What weight
it added, then, to the devil's sinister motive when he tempted
Christ in the wilderness, soliciting Him to a secret acknowledging of him, just between the two of them. But how much greater
was Christ's glory in His victory that day! He won the battle over
Satan's assaults with the sword of the Word—and it is time for
us to take up His weapon to fight the same enemy. This defense
takes on several specific expressions.

Scripture says God knows every secret sin. "Thou hast set
our iniquities before thee, our secret sins in the light of thy
countenance" (Psalm 90:8). God sees secret sins as plainly as
we see things at high noon. And He not only knows them but
sets them up as targets for His arrows of vengeance.

"The eyes of the Lord are in every place, beholding the evil
and the good" (Proverbs 15:3). He sees when you close your
closet door to pray in secret and rewards your sincerity; but He
also sees when the door is closed for you to sin in secret—and
He will not fail to reward your hypocrisy.

EXAMPLES TO KEEP YOU FROM SIN

*"Thy word have I hid in
mine heart, that I might not sin
against thee" (Psalm 119:11).*

Scripture commands us to bring examples to the Word for testing. Are people constantly quoting opinions? "To the law and to the testimony: if they speak not according to this word, it is because there is no light in them" (Isaiah 8:20). We follow a man for the light in his lamp; but if that goes out we leave him. And this Scripture certifies that the person cannot have any light at all unless his opinion has been established in the Word. If he does not know where he is going, how can we know where he might lead us?

Examples are precepts, not warrants. "Thou shalt not follow a multitude to do evil" (Exodus 23:2). An example will not bring acquittal just because you have a precedent to sin. Adam tried that when he said the woman gave him the fruit; yet it did not excuse him from paying the price with her. She was the leader in sin but punishment followed them both. Would you be willing to eat poison if another person offered to taste it first? Does his example make it any less deadly?

The Word warns that dedicated saints can sin. When Paul called others after him, he counseled them to keep their eyes open to see whether he followed Christ: "Be ye followers of me, even as I also am of Christ" (1 Corinthians 11:1). The holy life of the best saint on earth is only an imperfect translation of the perfect standard in God's holy Word and therefore must be tried by it. It is the character of sincerity to look to the way rather than to the crowd. "The highway of the upright is to depart from evil" (Proverbs 16:17).

I am showing you how this sword of the Word—like the one in the cherubim's hand—may be turned every way to protect the Christian from venturing into sin, no matter how right it seems.

This was David's refuge: "Thy word have I hid in mine heart, that I might not sin against thee" (Psalm 119:11). It was not the Bible in his hand, the word on his tongue or in his mind, but the hidden Word in his heart, which kept him from sin.

THE WELLS OF SALVATION

"A new heart also will I give you"
(Ezekiel 36:26).

There is forgiveness with the Lord Jesus. No matter what the trouble, this truth brings comfort to saints. You know how a cool spring is welcomed in a parched desert. And when you recall what sweet refreshment you have had from God's wells of salvation you will cry out with David: "I will never forget thy precepts: for with them thou hast quickened me" (Psalm 119:93). It is no surprise that Satan tries to stop your well of comfort; but it is more than tragic if he can persuade you to do it yourself.

As the veins in the body have arteries to bring them life, so precepts in the Word have promises to encourage and empower Christians to perform their vows to God. Is there a command to play? There is also a promise: "Likewise the Spirit also helpeth our infirmities: for we know not what we should pray for as we ought: but the Spirit itself maketh intercession for us with groanings which cannot be uttered" (Romans 8:26). Does God ask for your heart? The promise says, "A new heart also will I give you" (Ezekiel 36:26). Does He require us to crucify the flesh? Not without His promise: "Sin shall not have dominion over you" (Romans 6:14). But to make this promise serve your need, you must humbly and boldly press it believingly at the throne of grace. What the precept commands, the prayer of faith begs and receives. In other words, first conquer heaven and then you do not need to fear overcoming hell.

Do not forget—you are warring at God's expense, not your own. David was a military man who could handle one enemy as well as another, but he dared not promise himself success until he had heard from God: "Order my steps in they word: and let not any iniquity have dominion over me" (Psalm 119:133). But if you have decided to steal victory in your own strength, expect an overthrow. It will be a mercy, for defeat will bring humility with it but victory will only increase your pride in your own strength.

INTO THE FATHER'S ARMS

*When a believer holds the title to a promise proved
true to his conscience from Scripture, he will not
easily be wrangled out of his comfort.*

K now your right to God's promises. This is the hinge on
which the dispute between you and Satan will move in the
day of trouble. How pathetic for a Christian to stand at the
door of promise in the darkest night of affliction and be afraid
to turn the knob! That is the very time when we should go right
in and find shelter as a child runs into his father's arms. "Come,
my people, enter thou into thy chambers, and shut thy doors
about thee: hide thyself as it were for a little moment, until the
indignation be overpast" (Isaiah 26:20).

When a believer holds the title to a promise proved true to
his conscience from Scripture, he will not easily be wrangled
out of his comfort. Job produced his evidence from heaven:
"Till I die I will not remove mine integrity from me" (Job 27:5).
Satan did his best to make Job tear it up, but his title was clear
and Job knew it. Even when God seemed to disown him he testified before heaven and hell that he refused to let Satan dispute him out of his right: "Thou knowest that I am not wicked"
(Job 10:7). This assurance was what kept the chariot of his hope
on its wheels along the rough road of suffering; it shook and
rattled but nothing could overturn it.

The promises are not a pigpen for swine to root in; they are
Christ's sheep walk for His flock to feed in. "If ye be Christ's,
then ye are Abraham's seed, and heirs according to the promise" (Galatians 3:29). The promise is the joining which takes
place only when the Person of Christ is taken in marriage. And
faith is the grace by which the soul gives consent to accept
Christ as the Gospel offers Him, a union called the receiving of
Christ.

A HEART RESPONDS TO GOD'S COMMAND

*Scripture is a garden which
grows a comforting promise
for every sorrow.*

I t is not hard to smile at the promise, but does your countenance change to a frown when you remember that you need
to obey God's command? As if He were some stern master
who breaks the backs of His servants with heavy burdens! If
only you could ignore a command now and then without giving
up your claim to His promise! If the shoe fits, you have wandered away from the comforting lap of God's promises.

On the other hand, you may not be offended by the command at all, but by your own failure to obey perfectly. Although
your foot may slip often, yet your heart cleaves to God's commands and will not let you lie where you fell, but you get up
again, resolved to watch your step better. Know this, then, that
your sincere respect for the commandment is ample evidence
of your title to the promise.

When David confessed to his love for God's law he did not
question his title to the promise: "I hate vain thoughts; but thy
law do I love" (Psalm 119:113). He did not say that he was free
from vain thought but that he hated them. And he did not say
that he fully kept the law but he loved it, even though he sometimes failed in total obedience. Because of the testimony which
conscience gave concerning David's love for the law, his faith
settled the question once for all: "Thou art my hiding place and
my shield: I hope in thy word" (Psalm 119:114).

Gather and sort the promises into their different applica-
tion. God does allow his children to walk through many different trials and temptations: "Many are the afflictions of the
righteous" (Psalm 34:19). But Scripture is a garden which grows
a comforting promise for every sorrow. And a wise Christian
gathers one of every kind and writes them down as a doctor
keeps records of tried and proven prescriptions for diseases.

MEDITATE ON GOD'S FAITHFULNESS

*"To them that have their mind
fettered to the body as a thief's foot
is to a pair of stocks, it is hard to die."*

B e careful, Christian, to practice this duty of meditation. Do not just chat with the promise in passing; but like Abraham with the angels, invite it to stay in your tent door so you can enjoy it fully. This is how saints through the centuries have caused their faith to triumph over the most tragic troubles. "My beloved," said the woman, "shall lie all night betwixt my breasts" (Song of Solomon 1:13). In other words, when sorrows press in to cause fear she will spend the night meditating on the love and loneliness of Jesus, on His beauty and tenderness toward her. When you have learned to do this you will not feel the severity of affliction any more than you feel the bitter cold of a north wind as you wait by a glowing fireplace.

Julius Palmer, an English martyr, shared how he lifted his thoughts above suffering by heavenly meditation on God's "great and precious promises": "To them that have their mind fettered to the body as a thief's foot is to the a pair of stocks, it is hard to die. But if any be able to separate his soul from his body, then by the help of God's Spirit, it is no more mastery for such a one than to drink this cup." A soul in heaven feels none of the struggles we have here on earth. Here, Christian, is the most glorious picture to be seen this side of heaven!

When a Christian can stand upon this Pisgah of meditation and look with the eye of faith across the panorama of the great and precious things which the faithful God has prepared for him, it is easy to turn from the world's love and rejection alike. But it is hard for some of us to get up there because we get tired after only a few steps of climbing toward God's mount. That is when we must call out, "Lead me to the rock that is higher than I." Who will lift us up to this holy hill of meditation, higher than the surging waves that dash upon us from beneath? God's Spirit will pick us up in His everlasting arms and take us there.